● Eighth Edition

What is your neighborhood?

Qualitative Research Methods for the Social Sciences

Bruce L. Berg

California State University, Long Beach

Howard Lune

Hunter College, CUNY

PEARSON

Boston   Columbus   Indianapolis   New York   San Francisco   Upper Saddle River
Amsterdam   Cape Town   Dubai   London   Madrid   Milan   Munich   Paris
Montreal   Toronto   Delhi   Mexico City   Sao Paulo   Sydney
Hong Kong   Seoul   Singapore   Taipei   Tokyo

Editorial Director: Craig Campanella
Editor in Chief: Dickson Musslewhite
Publisher: Karen Hanson
Editorial Assistant: Joseph Jantas
Director of Marketing: Brandy Dawson
Executive Marketing Manager: Kelly May
Marketing Assistant: Janeli Bitor
Media Director: Brian Hyland
Media Editor: Tom Scalzo
Production Manager: Meghan DeMaio
Creative Director: Jayne Conte
Cover Designer: Suzanne Behnke
Cover Image: (c) Gary Blakeley/Fotolia
Editorial Production and Composition Service: George Jacob/Integra Software Services
Printer/Binder/Cover Printer: R. R. Donnelley & Sons

Credits and acknowledgments borrowed from other sources and reproduced, with permission, in this textbook appear on appropriate page within text.

Many of the designations by manufacturers and seller to distinguish their products are claimed as trademarks. Where those designations appear in this book, and the publisher was aware of a trademark claim, the designations have been printed in initial caps or all caps.

Library of Congress Cataloging-in-Publication Data
Berg, Bruce L. (Bruce Lawrence)
  Qualitative research methods for the social sciences / Bruce L. Berg, Howard Lune. —8th ed.
    p. cm.
  Includes bibliographical references and index.
  ISBN-13: 978-0-205-80938-7 (alk. paper)
  ISBN-10: 0-205-80938-3 (alk. paper)
  1. Social sciences—Research—Methodology.   I. Lune, Howard   II. Title.
  H61.B4715 2012
  300.72—dc23

                                                                    2011025015

10 9 8 7 6 5 4 3 2 1   13 12 11

ISBN-10: 0-205-80938-3
ISBN-13: 978-0-205-80938-7

Contents

iii

Chapter 3

Ethical Issues   61

Chapter 4

A Dramaturgical Look
at Interviewing   105

Chapter 5

Focus Group Interviewing   164

Chapter 6

Ethnographic Field Strategies   196

Chapter 7

Action Research   258

Chapter 8

Unobtrusive Measures in Research   280

Chapter 9

Social Historical Research and Oral Traditions   304

Chapter 10

Case Studies   325

Chapter 11

An Introduction to Content Analysis   349

Chapter 12

Writing Research Papers: Sorting the Noodles from the Soup   386

Preface

WHEN BRUCE BERG BEGAN to outline the first edition of *Qualitative Research Methods for the Social Sciences* 25 years ago, qualitative methods were widely perceived as a narrow area of specialization favored by anthropologists and people from Chicago. Hard-core methodologists studied statistics and quantitative analysis first, with some qualitative training added on after. The landscape for teaching qualitative methods was not barren; but there was nothing like this book to introduce new scholars in the social sciences to the range of qualitative techniques available to them. Bruce knew that he was a trailblazer, and his text was quickly adopted as a standard part of the new methodological repertoire.

From that point on, one can trace the growth of qualitative methods by reading the prefaces of each subsequent edition of Berg's *Qualitative Research Methods* book. As research ethics and IRBs grew in importance to one's research training, Berg's ethics chapter grew. While other sociologists discussed the open questions of the field concerning researcher subjectivity, the voice of the author, and the "production" of knowledge, Bruce wrote in the first person, identified and discussed his own perspective and experiences, and included examples from research that disagreed with his own work. Most recently, as with this present edition, a considerable portion of the new material followed advances in technologies and the integration of software and hardware into the daily routines of researchers. If one thinks of the expansion and integration of qualitative methods in the social sciences as a quiet revolution, then Berg was a quiet revolutionary leader.

In this eighth edition, I seek to build on the strengths of this foundation. Having taught from this book for over 10 years, I have worked in discussions and elaborations of points with which my students have struggled. I have added discussions of recently published research, and I have included some suggested exercises that I have found useful in my own classes. Other changes in content and organization are intended to assist those instructors who use this book as their primary text, and to better reflect the nature of our work in the twenty-first century.

This edition of *Qualitative Research Methods for the Social Sciences* may be read straight through, at approximately one chapter per week, for 12–15 weeks. Or, one can read selectively and in any order. For those whose classes meet twice a week, I have altered the pacing and content of the longer chapters to create logical blocks of materials that can be discussed on their own. For those who pair the book with a reader, the smaller subsections can serve as an introduction to the methods demonstrated in the published research examples. And for those who pair this book with a quantitative text for a general methods class, one can delve into essential topics such as interviews (Chapter 4) and content analysis (Chapter 11), while skimming more specialized subjects such as case studies (Chapter 10) and action research (Chapter 7). But everyone should read Chapter 12.

As with the last couple of revisions, this edition seeks to keep the reader up to date with research technology and the integration of Web-based tools and services. This, of course, is an impossible goal. Most likely, before this edition is even printed and distributed there will be a new set of phone apps that render digital recorders obsolete or which perform sociogram mappings for the user. Nonetheless, as one who has adopted numerous technologies for my own use long before it became safe or cost-effective to do so, I have altered or expanded upon most of the useful advice found in this book to incorporate available electronic media that I have found to be so useful, and which younger readers have known since birth. I hope I can even introduce readers to some tools that they have not already seen.

Of far greater importance than the changes that I have introduced are the elements that I have left unchanged. All editions of *Qualitative Research Methods for the Social Sciences* have shared the same easy style that Bruce Berg brought to his teaching. He and I have shared an understanding of the qualities that good pedagogical materials must have. For that reason, this book gives more attention to the depth of explanations than to the breadth of topics. Our measure of success is understanding, not recitation. As Berg wrote, "I continue to believe that researchers learn their craft through a combination of trial and error and 'getting their hands dirty' with data. I also believe this process works best when guided by a more experienced researcher—a mentor. Yet even this approach works more effectively when the apprentice has a firm understanding of the basic elements of the research process. This book is designed especially for accomplishing this purpose."

As with past editions, this one uses the language of sociology, but with examples and discussions that apply to all of the social sciences and related fields such as nursing research, criminology, education, social work, and business. The underlying purpose is to get the reader from a research question to an answer. You can provide your own questions according to your own needs.

Bruce Berg adopted the theoretical framework of symbolic interactionism to guide his priorities, to select his examples, and to give form to his explanations. He called this a "personal bias." I heartily embrace this focus on the symbolic forms of communication, the everyday encounter, and the simultaneous creation and discovery of meaning. It is as "social" an approach as one can bring to research. Yet one does not have to subscribe to any given perspective to practice the methods of qualitative social research, and this book makes no assumptions about the intentions or goals of research. As to my own biases, I direct an applied social research program and I find that I have a preference for practical applications, problem solving, and the heavy-handed presence of empirical data in all discussions of what we are to do and how we are to do it.

I make one assumption in writing this text. I imagine that the reader will actually get to do some or all of the things that are presented here. The practice of research is driven by social theory, but it is not a theoretical exercise. Gathering data is an act, or an adventure. Anyone can learn to discuss coding, but it is only through the process of turning masses of disorganized information into data, and data into findings, that one can really understand what coding is. Likewise, even when studying one's own neighbourhood, the act of "gaining entry" into the field is a transformative process that turns a resident into a researcher. And as Chapter 3 indicates, there is nothing quite like failing to account for some potential harm to yourself or your subjects to teach you about the importance of ethical research design. Learning to practice research is best accomplished by trying, much as swimming is learned by diving in, except that in our case you don't have to worry about drowning.

Instructor's Manual and Test Bank (ISBN 0205225284): The Instructor's Manual and Test Bank has been prepared to assist teachers in their efforts to prepare lectures and evaluate student learning. For each chapter of the text, the Instructor's Manual offers different types of resources, including detailed chapter summaries and outlines, learning objectives, discussion questions, classroom activities and much more.

Also included in this manual is a test bank offering multiple-choice, true/false, fill-in-the-blank, and/or essay questions for each chapter. The Instructor's Manual and Test Bank is available to adopters at www.pearsonhighered.com.

MyTest (ISBN 0205225276): The Test Bank is also available online through Pearson's computerized testing system, MyTest. MyTest allows instructors to create their own personalized exams, to edit any of the existing test questions, and to add new questions. Other special features of this program include random generation of test questions, creation of alternative versions of the same test, scrambling question sequence, and test preview before printing. Search and sort features allow you to locate questions quickly and to arrange them in whatever order you prefer. The test bank can be accessed from anywhere with a free MyTest user account. There is no need to download a program or file to your computer.

PowerPoint Presentations (ISBN 0205809405): Lecture Power-Points are available for this text. The Lecture PowerPoint slides outline each chapter to help you convey sociological principles in a visual and exciting way. They are available to adopters at www.pearsonhighered.com.

MySearchLab: My SearchLab provides a host of tools for students to master a writing or research project, It provides online access to reliable content for internet research projects, including thousands of full articles from the EBSCO ContentSelect database a complete online handbook for grammar and usage support. A tutorial on understanding and avoiding plagiarism, and AutoCite, which helps students correctly cite sources.

Acknowledgments

All researchers stand on the shoulders of giants. In this case, I am particularly grateful to Bruce Berg, who created this book. I also owe a debt to Jeff Lasser and Lauren Macey at Pearson, who have entrusted me not to mess it up and have helped to see this edition through. I have also benefitted from the insightful comments and suggestions of seven anonymous reviewers.

I have also benefitted from the insightful comments and suggestions of the following reviewers:

Susan Wortmann, Nebraska Wesleyan University;
Meredith Kneavel Boyd, Chestnut Hill College;
Chris Podeschi, Bloomsburg University of Pennsylvania;
Paula Fernandez, William Paterson University;
Kimberly Mahaffy, Millersville University;
Janelle Wilson, University of Minnesota Duluth.

My colleagues and past coauthors Enrique Pumar and Ross Koppel have distinctly honed my skills at explaining research. My wife, Maureen, provided support and assistance in innumerable ways while I was preparing the manuscript. Our son, Quinn, provides inspiration in his own ways.

Above all, I remain grateful to my students in the Graduate Social Research program at Hunter College, who keep me on my toes concerning all matters related to the research endeavor.

Chapter 1

Introduction

I
N 1989, WHEN BRUCE BERG FIRST PUBLISHED *Qualitative
Research Methods for the Social Sciences*, there were few books
that concentrated on how to do qualitative research and how
to conduct relevant qualitative analysis. In earlier editions of this book he
had noted that by the 1980s many of the classic works in qualitative research
had gone out of print. Books such as Becker's *Sociological Work: Methods and
Substance* (1970), Denzin's *The Research Act* (1978), Filstead's *Qualitative
Methodology* (1970), Glaser and Strauss's *The Discovery of Grounded Theory*
(1967), and Webb and his associates' *Unobtrusive Measures: Nonreactive
Research in the Social Sciences* (1966, 1981) ceased in large part to be on the
required reading lists of most students of the social sciences. Today, student
researchers in the social sciences may not have heard of most of these and other
classic works, let alone read them. One of the pleasures, for me, in using the
various editions of this book is that they preserve both the language and the
wisdom of the *early risers* of the field.

Qualitative materials experienced a revival of sorts throughout the late
1980s and 1990s, with Sage's development of a string of short works called Sage
University Papers Series on Qualitative Research Methods. In addition, in 1989,
Sage began publishing a series of lengthier works on qualitative methods in its
Applied Social Research Methods Series. This series may have gotten the ball
rolling, but it is no longer unique.

Today a growing number of texts examine various aspects of qualitative
research—even books once nearly exclusively associated with quantitative research,
such as Earl Babbie's *The Practice of Social Research* (2007), which began in 1998
to contain whole chapters on qualitative interviewing, field research, and unobtrusive measures. Others such as W. Lawrence Neuman's *Social Research Methods*
(2005) and Frank Hagan's *Research Methods in Criminal Justice and Criminology* (2006) offer a taste of both quantitative and qualitative research strategies. As

1

for books that are entirely devoted to qualitative research and analysis, Berg was correct to see them as "imitating" his lead. This book, *Qualitative Research in the Social Sciences*, was a daring standout when it first emerged and has remained my favorite teaching resource through each subsequent update.

Bruce Berg died in 2009, relatively young and at the height of his professional powers. A popular instructor, dedicated mentor, energetic researcher and writer, and always a deep thinker with an interest in virtually everything, he had seemingly mastered the art of conveying complicated ideas with a few simple words.

We, Bruce and I, now offer the eighth edition of this book, once again focusing on innovative ways of collecting and analyzing qualitative data collected in natural settings. Closely following Berg's format, I continue to address those data-collection strategies that may be characterized as mainstream strategies, the basic building blocks for emerging researchers. As in past editions, this text concentrates on basic procedures. Adhering to the teaching style that Berg emphasized and which I have adopted over the years, this text avoids the cookbook approach to research; there are very few instruction lists or absolute statements of what you must do for your research to count as an example of one technique or other. Instead, my goal is to offer a handle on what these techniques are; why, when, and how we use them; and what we can get out of them. Of course, this also includes cautionary notes about their limitations. Throughout, I make a few simple assumptions. First, if you are reading this book, then you are training to do research, and therefore probably want to know how to take charge of your own projects and get the good results that will answer your questions. Second, that if you want to apply some specific technique or creative combination of techniques, but want more of a checklist to go with it, you know how to find one. I'm not saying that such things aren't useful, only that our priorities lean more toward depth of understanding and away from vocabulary tests and recipes. Finally, I assume that the first draft of anything any of us comes up with will not be sufficient. For that reason, I imagine that you, students, will be reading parts of the chapters for instructions on how to get started, and then returning for ideas about how to fix whatever design or plan you have started on. The organization of most chapters is intended to support such an approach.

Inevitably, many of the updates that you will find in this edition are technological in nature. The tools that accompany our techniques change much more quickly than the concepts behind them. I have no doubt that some of what I have written this month will be out of date before you read it, but not unrecognizably so. In addition, I have included more discussion of some of the best examples of recent research throughout the book. And I have added my thoughts and experiences on researcher safety in fieldwork. Other changes to the content include some expansion and elaboration on the topic of protecting human subjects and working with informants in the field. As for structural changes, I have altered the pacing of some of the chapters to better suit the experiences of my students using the earlier editions over the years. Also drawing on my experiences teaching from this book, I have included some of the questions and answers that my students and I discussed when reading it. Hopefully, I have not interfered in any way with Berg's subtle humor, which enlivens the text throughout.

Quantitative versus Qualitative Schools of Thought

In his attempt to differentiate between quantitative and qualitative approaches, Dabbs (1982, p. 32) indicated that the notion of *quality* is essential to the nature of things. On the other hand, *quantity* is elementally an amount of something. Quality refers to the what, how, when, where, and why of a thing—its essence and ambience. Qualitative research, thus, refers to the meanings, concepts, definitions, characteristics, metaphors, symbols, and descriptions of things. In contrast, quantitative research refers to counts and measures of things, the extents and distributions of our subject matter. This distinction is illustrated in Jackson's (1968) description of classroom odors in an elementary school:

> [The] odors of the classroom are fairly standardized. Schools may use different brands of wax and cleaning fluid, but they all seem to contain similar ingredients, a sort of universal smell which creates an aromatic background that permeates the entire building. Added to this, in each classroom, is the slightly acrid scent of chalk dust and the faint hint of fresh wood pencil shavings. In some rooms, especially at lunch time, there is the familiar odor of orange peels and peanut butter sandwiches, a blend that mingles in the late afternoon (following recess) with the delicate pungency of children's perspiration.

It would be impossible to capture the odors that Jackson alludes to with any type of count or measure. Clearly, certain experiences cannot be meaningfully expressed by numbers. Furthermore, such things as smells can trigger memories long obscured by the continuing demands of life. Qualitative research strategies provide perspectives that can prompt recall of these common or half-forgotten sights, sounds, and smells.

The meanings that we give to events and things come from their qualities. To understand our lives, we need qualitative research. But can we really measure the unquantifiable essences of the phenomena that imbue our lives? Can we ever, in a word, *know*? The answer is yes, though it is a qualified yes. We can study and measure qualities as collections of meanings, as a spectrum of states of being, but not as precise and solid objects. Qualities are like smoke; they are real and we can see them, but they won't stand still for us or form straight lines for our rulers to capture. Clearly, qualitative research requires some specialized tools and techniques.

Some writers perceive the different types of data as opposing camps, as though researchers had to take sides. For example, Miles and Huberman (1994, p. 40) quoted quantitative researcher Fred Kerlinger as saying, "There is no such thing as qualitative data. Everything is either 1 or 0." Countering this argument, D. T. Campbell has stated, "All research ultimately has a qualitative grounding" (Miles & Huberman, 1994, p. 40). Yet this sort of back-and-forth arguing would seem rather unproductive, and it seems more useful to consider the merits of both quantitative and qualitative research strategies.

As Dabbs (1982) remarked, "Qualitative and quantitative are not distinct." Unfortunately, because qualitative research tends to assess the quality of things using words, images, and descriptions whereas most of quantitative research relies chiefly on numbers, many people erroneously regard quantitative strategies as more scientific than those employed in qualitative research. The error of think-ing underlying this particular critique is that of confusing the study of imprecise subject matter with the imprecise study of subjects. For this reason alone, quali-tative researchers need to be more precise, more careful in their definitions and procedures, and clearer in their writing than most other scientists. From my per-spective, this means conducting and describing research that can stand the test of subsequent researchers examining the same phenomenon through similar or different methods. Qualitative research is a long hard road, with elusive data on one side and stringent requirements for analysis on the other. Admittedly, this means that students have a lot to learn and not a lot of room for errors.

Colleges require students to study research methods to both learn the major work of our fields of study and acquire pragmatic skills. Thus, students must confront the myriad problems associated with understanding empirical results as well as the process of research itself. This book provides much needed assistance for all researchers, including the inexperienced, through a discussion of various qualitative research strategies, design development, data organiza-tion and presentation, and analysis procedures.

Like other texts on qualitative methods, this one emphasizes methodologi-cal strategies. However, methodology cannot be examined in a vacuum. Instead, the core substance of qualitative sociological practice, including methods, theory, and substantive interests, has to be explored (Creswell, 2007; Denzin, 1978; Denzin & Lincoln, 2005, 2008; Leninger, 1998; Lofland & Lofland, 1995; Lofland, Snow, Anderson, & Lofland, 2006; Lune, Pumar, & Koppel, 2009; Miles & Huberman, 1994). In this text, data-gathering techniques are intentionally coupled with theoretical perspectives, linking method to theory.

Data gathering, therefore, is not distinct from theoretical orientations. Rather, data are intricately associated with the motivation for choosing a given subject, the conduct of the study, and ultimately the analysis.

This book describes in detail seven primary ways to collect qualitative data: interviewing, focus groups, ethnography, sociometry, unobtrusive measures, historiography, and case studies. In addition, this book examines a framework for undertaking participatory research studies, sometimes called action research. These methods include an examination of the basic theoretical assumptions of each technique and advice on how to start each procedure and how to resolve problems that may arise. Furthermore, we present the technique of content analysis as the model for the analysis of most qualitative data, particularly those that we call "social artifacts." Also as an essential element or consideration in any research study, this book explores the ethical dimensions of conducting research on humans; it is within the context of this ethical dimension to research that the section on *critical ethnography* has been included. This eighth edition of *Qualitative Research Methods for the Social Sciences* begins with the assumption that the reader knows little or nothing about the research process. Chapter 2, therefore, offers a basic description of how to design a research project. Most of the rest of the book can be read in almost any order.

Use of Triangulation in Research Methodology

Most researchers have at least one methodological technique they feel most comfortable using, which often becomes their favorite or only approach to research. Furthermore, many researchers perceive their research method as an atheoretical tool, distinct from the conceptual frameworks that shape their research questions (Denzin, 1978). Because of this, they fail to recognize that methods impose certain perspectives on reality. For example, when researchers canvass a neighborhood and arrange interviews with residents to discuss some social problem, a theoretical assumption has already been made—specifically, that reality is fairly constant and stable and that people can reliably observe and describe it. Similarly, when they make direct observations of events, researchers assume these events are deeply affected by the actions of all participants, including themselves. (I'm not saying that this is not a fair assumption, only that it is a more or less hidden assumption that precedes the application of "theory.") Content analysis of important speeches generally relies on the assumption that the people who give these speeches write, or at least endorse, their own words. Analysis of news articles in the study of key social events relies on the assumption that key events are represented with descriptive accuracy in the news. Each method, thus, reveals slightly different facets of the same symbolic reality. Every method is a different line of sight directed toward the same point, observing particular aspects of the social and symbolic reality. By combining several lines of sight, researchers obtain a better, more substantive picture of reality; a richer, more complete array of symbols and theoretical concepts; and a means of verifying many of these elements. The use of multiple lines of sight is frequently called *triangulation*.

Triangulation is a term originally more common in surveying activities, map making, navigation, and military practices. In each case, three known points or objects are used to draw sighting lines toward an unknown point or object. Usually, these three sighting lines will intersect, forming a small triangle called the *triangle of error*. The best estimate of the true location of the new point or object is the center of the triangle, assuming that the three lines are about equal in error. Although sightings could be done with two sighting lines intersecting at one point, the third line permits a more accurate estimate of the unknown point or object (Berg & Berg, 1993).

Triangulation was first used in the social sciences as a metaphor describing a form of *multiple operationalism* or *convergent validation* (Campbell, 1956; Campbell & Fiske, 1959). In those cases, triangulation was used largely to describe multiple data-collection technologies designed to measure a single concept or construct (data triangulation). However, Denzin (1978, p. 292) introduced an additional metaphor, *lines of action*, which characterizes the use of multiple data-collection technologies, multiple theories, multiple researchers, multiple methodologies, or combinations of these four categories of research activities (see Figure 1.1).

For many researchers, triangulation is restricted to the use of multiple data-gathering techniques (usually three) to investigate the same phenomenon. This is interpreted as a means of mutual confirmation of measures and validation of findings (Casey & Murphy, 2009; Leedy, 2001; Leedy & Ormrod, 2004). Fielding and Fielding (1986, p. 31) specifically addressed this aspect of triangulation. They suggested that the important feature of triangulation is not the simple combination of different kinds of data but the attempt to relate them so as to counteract the threats to validity identified in each.

Denzin insists that the multiple-methods approach is the generic form of this approach. But triangulation actually represents varieties of data, investigators, theories, and methods. Denzin (1978, p. 295) outlined these four categories as follows:

(1) Data triangulation has three subtypes: (a) time, (b) space, and (c) person. Person analysis, in turn, has three levels: (a) aggregate, (b) interactive, and (c) collectivity. (2) Investigator triangulation consists of using multiple rather than single observers of the same object. (3) Theory triangulation consists of using multiple rather than simple perspectives in relation to the same set of objects. (4) Methodological triangulation can entail within-method triangulation and between-method triangulation.

Figure 1.1 Multiple Lines of Action in Triangulation

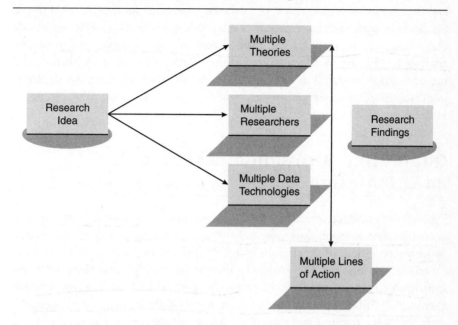

It is difficult for a single text or course to prepare students to accomplish all that. Triangulation, as a model for research, requires researchers to be fluent in multiple methods. Yet it is useful to study qualitative and quantitative techniques somewhat independently, if only to give each its due credit. Some authors of general purpose research texts associate qualitative research with the single technique of participant observation. Other writers extend their understanding of qualitative research to include interviewing as well. However, qualitative research also includes such methods as observation of experimental natural settings, photographic techniques (including videotaping), historical analysis (historiography), document and textual analysis, sociometry, sociodrama, and similar ethnomethodological experimentation, ethnographic research, and a number of unobtrusive techniques. In the interests of triangulation, primarily qualitative studies need not exclude quantitative data-gathering techniques as well, though we won't be discussing them here.

This book stresses several discrete yet intertwined strategies and techniques involved in each of the seven primary research schemes. In fact, the decision to discuss field research strategies under the broad umbrella of *ethnography* ensures the inclusion of a wide combination of elements, such as direct observation, various types of interviewing (informal, formal, semiformal), listening, document analysis (e.g., letters or newspaper clippings), and ethnomethodological experimentation. Novice researchers are thus instructed in the use of research strategies composed of multiple methods in a single investigation. I also follow Denzin's (2010) approach that triangulation includes multiple theoretical perspectives and multiple analysis techniques in addition to multiple data-collection procedures. The use of multiple research design strategies and theories increases the depth of understanding an investigation can yield (see also Dittmann, 2005; Miles & Huberman, 2002).

Qualitative Strategies: Defining an Orientation

We do not conduct research only to amass data. The purpose of research is to discover answers to questions through the application of systematic procedures. Qualitative research properly seeks answers by examining various social settings and the groups or individuals who inhabit these settings. Qualitative researchers, then, are most interested in how humans arrange themselves and their settings and how inhabitants of these settings make sense of their surroundings through symbols, rituals, social structures, social roles, and so forth.

Research on human beings affects how these persons will be viewed (Bogdan & Taylor, 1998). When humans are studied in a symbolically reduced, statistically aggregated fashion, there is a danger that conclusions—although arithmetically precise—may misrepresent the people or circumstances studied (Mills, 1959). Qualitative procedures seek patterns among cases, but do not reduce these cases to their averages. They provide a means of accessing unquantifiable knowledge about the actual people researchers observe and talk to or about people represented by their personal traces (such as letters, photographs, newspaper accounts, and diaries). As a result, qualitative techniques allow researchers to share in the understandings and perceptions of others and to explore how people structure and give meaning to their daily lives. Researchers using qualitative techniques examine how people learn about and make sense of themselves and others.

This explanation of the general purpose of qualitative research derives from a symbolic interactionist perspective that is central to the concept of qualitative methodology presented here. *Symbolic interaction* is an umbrella concept under which a variety of related theoretical orientations may be placed. The theme that unites the diverse elements of symbolic interaction is the focus on subjective understandings and the perceptions of and about people, symbols, and objects.

From a Symbolic Interactionist Perspective

Symbolic interactionism is one of several theoretical schools of thought in the social sciences. It involves a set of related propositions that describes and explains certain aspects of human behavior. Human beings are unique animals. What humans say and do are the results of how they interpret their social world. In other words, human behavior depends on learning rather than biological instinct. Human beings communicate what they learn through symbols, the most common system of symbols being language. Linguistic symbols amount to arbitrary sounds or physical gestures to which people, by mutual agreement over time, have attached significance or meaning. The core task of symbolic interactionists as researchers, then, is to capture the essence of this process for interpreting or attaching meaning to various symbols. In other words, people encode their meanings and intentions through language and other symbol systems. Much of research is about decoding these systems.

The substantive basis for symbolic interaction as a theory is frequently attributed to the social behavioral work of Dewey (1930), Cooley (1902), Parks (1915), Mead (1934, 1938), and several other early theorists, but Blumer is considered the founder of *symbolic interactionism*. In fact, he coined the term *symbolic interaction*. In articulating his view of what symbolic interaction is, Blumer (1969) first established that human beings account for *meaning* in two basic ways. First, meaning may be seen as intrinsically attached to an object, event, phenomenon, and so on. Second, meaning may be understood as a "psychical accretion" imposed on objects, events, and the like by people. As Blumer (1969, p. 5) explained:

> Symbolic interactionism...does not regard meaning as emanating from the intrinsic makeup of the thing, nor does it see meaning as arising through psychological elements between people. The meaning of a thing for a person grows out of the ways in which other persons act toward the person with regard to the thing. Their actions operate to define the thing for the person; thus, symbolic interactionism sees meanings as social products formed through activities of people interacting.

Blumer thereby suggests that meanings derive from the social process of people or groups of people *interacting*. Meanings allow people to produce various realities that constitute the sensory world (the so-called real world), but because these realities are related to how people create meanings, reality becomes an interpretation of various definitional options. Consequently, as

Thomas famously stated, "It is not important whether or not the interpretation is correct—if men define situations as real, they are real in their consequences" (Thomas & Swaine, 1928, p. 572).

For instance, the first day of each semester, students walk into their classroom and see someone who appears to be the professor. This supposed professor begins to lecture, distribute syllabi, discuss course requirements, and conduct various other traditional first-day activities. Few, if any, students ask to see their professor's credentials. Yet the students, within certain limits, perform their roles as students so long as this professor continues to perform the role of instructor. Suppose that several weeks into the semester, however, the class is notified that the person they assumed to be a professor is really a local dog-catcher who has no academic credentials. The question then becomes whether the reality of the classroom experience during the previous weeks is void merely because the dogcatcher was incorrectly interpreted as a professor. It would, of course, remain to be seen whether any information conveyed by the dogcatcher was accurate, and certainly, the classroom remained a classroom and students continued to perform their expected roles. From Thomas's perspective, these youths had defined the reality as a class, and it became one for them.

Symbolic interactionists tend to differ slightly among themselves regard-ing the relative significance of various aspects of an interactionist perspective. Several basic elements, however, tend to bind together even the most diverse symbolic interactionists. First, all interactionists agree that human interac-tions form the central source of data. Second, there is a general consensus that participants' perspectives and their ability to take the roles of others (empathy) are key issues in any formulation of a theory of symbolic interaction. Third, interactionists agree with Thomas concerning "definitions of a situation"; that is, the view that how inhabitants of a setting define their situation determines the nature and meaning of their actions as well as the setting itself.

Historically, the symbolic interactionist orientation that originated with Dewey, Cooley, Parks, and Mead, and later Blumer, among others, is called the Chicago School orientation because it arose in the Department of Sociol-ogy at the University of Chicago and evolved during the development of the city of Chicago, which served as a kind of natural research laboratory for these researchers. The basic orientation that evolved, sometimes referred to as the social-ecological perspective, examined social conditions in the emerging and developing city and neighborhoods of Chicago. After World War II, another segment of the symbolic interaction paradigm began to arise in the Depart-ment of Sociology at the University of Iowa, under the leadership of Manford Kuhn (Holstein & Gubrium, 2000) and later under Carl Couch (1988).

The Iowa School became distinctive for operationalizing concepts in symbolic interaction, including concepts such as the self and reference group in standardized ways so that hypothesis testing could be accomplished. Among the more prominent contributions to symbolic interaction from the Iowa School is the development of a research instrument called the *twenty-statement test* (TST). The TST can be used to identify self-designations that result from social roles an individual plays rather than from his or her personal self-concepts. The TST is a rather simple tool that asks the subject the question, "Who am I?" The subject then fills out 20 blank spaces in answer to this question. The responses are scored as representing either an external or internal self-concept. Figure 1.2 offers an example of the TST.

Figure 1.2 The Twenty Statements Test

Please write twenty answers to the question "Who am I?"
I am…

1. _____ 11. _____
2. _____ 12. _____
3. _____ 13. _____
4. _____ 14. _____
5. _____ 15. _____
6. _____ 16. _____
7. _____ 17. _____
8. _____ 18. _____
9. _____ 19. _____
10. _____ 20. _____

Scoring Instructions: Categorize each of the twenty statements in terms of each giving a description of the subject as **external** or **internal**.

External: This phrase locates the individual in society by describing some social role he or she plays or enacts. For example, the names of social roles one holds are all *external*: mother, father, son, daughter, student, salesman, police officer, store clerk, baseball fan, etc.

Internal: This phrase locates the individual inside his or her self by describing an internal or interior quality or trait one possesses. For example, names of

(continued)

(*continued*)

personal intrinsic qualities or characteristics one possesses are all *internal*: shy, ambitious, insecure, happy, sad, ambiguous, curious, depressed, hard working, industrious, etc.

Place an E for external or an I for internal beside each of the twenty statements; then, total up the number of statements representing each category.

Total Number of External Descriptors: _____

Total Number of Internal Descriptors: _____

The twenty-statement test can be used for a rough assessment of an individual's sense of self or identity. The test has the virtues of being straightforward and simple and providing a relatively direct measure of the subject's self-concepts. In contrast to this systematic orientation, the Chicago School's orientation relied more heavily on participant observational research. Thus, the Chicago School was somewhat more anthropological and sought to understand the meanings of individuals and groups without an emphasis on revealing generalizable patterns of human behavior.

In terms of similarities, followers of both the Chicago and Iowa Schools agree that humans have certain creative capacities that allow them to develop and employ symbols to identify and define various aspects of the world around them. What makes humans unique, according to these perspectives, is their ability to use symbols. Humans are able to symbolically designate specific words and understandings for these words to social objects; in turn, these can be used to shape their interactions with others. Further, humans are able to engage in self-reflection during which they are capable of objectifying themselves (Herman, 1995). In terms of sociological methods, the Chicago and Iowa Schools also agree that methods must focus on the social process used by humans to define situations and to select particular courses of action in given situations. From this initial point, however, Blumer and Kuhn, along with their respective followers, diverge in terms of what each considers the most appropriate method to use in the study of humans and society. Each group's methodological preferences follow from the ontological assumptions about what people are capable of discovering in research. Of course, most people's methodological preferences follow from their ontological assumptions, though those assumptions are rarely examined.

The differences between Blumer's and Kuhn's methodological approaches center on their assumptions concerning the operation of symbolic processes. To a considerable measure, this involves the issue of *causality*. In other words, when one considers deterministically what *causes* certain events, this understanding bears on the methodology used. From Blumer's (1969) indeterministic orientation, social structures are to be understood as emergent phenomenon, and, in effect, as the product of shared interpretations held by people. Consequently, these understandings are the result of internal symbolic processes that allow an individual to group together various behaviors into an organized coherent pattern, such that it offers meaning. These understandings, however, are not the result of system forces, societal needs, or structural mechanisms. Social organization from this point of view is the result of mutual interpretations, evaluations, definitions, and social mappings created by individuals (Herman, 1995). For Blumer and his followers, the symbolic processes of humans cannot be conceived as a mechanism through which social forces operate; rather, they must be viewed as shaping the way structures are created, maintained, and transformed. In this sort of orientation, it is difficult to establish causality. Social structures or organizations do *not* cause human behaviors; instead, these are merely types of objects in the individual's environment and symbolic thought processes. Research, therefore, must focus on subjects' meanings, expectations, and perceptions first, with actions and decisions following.

In contrast, Kuhn argued for a deterministic model of social organization. From this perspective, social institutions are viewed as representing relatively stable networks of social positions accompanied by associated norms and expectations. Symbolic interactions between individuals, then, are adept at creating and altering situations and structures. Once these structures are created, they are capable of constraining individuals. From this perspective, social structures are understood as fairly stable, especially when the individual's core self is invested in these social structures and networks of positions. If one can learn about the nature of one's core self, of the expectations one has internalized, as well as one's expectations in a given situation, it is possible, according to Kuhn, to *predict* people's definitions of a situation as well as their behaviors. The social setting constrains much of the meaning systems that the people in the setting use, and this setting can be studied independently of the people in it.

These divergent assumptions about human behavior and issues of causality resulted in followers of the Chicago School and the Iowa School adopting different methodological approaches. Blumer and his followers borrowed from the phenomenologists and oriented their methodological strategies toward non-generalizing and idiographic methods. The primary goal of this approach was to make social life intelligible. From this perspective, the act of research must be viewed as a process of symbolic interaction wherein the researcher takes the role of the subjects who are being studied. Blumer and his followers, then, saw research as possessing a two-fold agenda: (1) exploration, where the researcher examines and observes specific situations and events, followed by (2) inspection

2 different
methodologies

wherein the researcher uses data (systematically collected) to refine concepts, and then to use these in general statements describing human life and behavior.

In contrast to this, Kuhn and his followers maintained a deterministic emphasis, stressed the commonality of methods across all the sciences, and tended to follow the basic principles of logical positivism. From this perspective, the goal of methodology is to specify operational definitions of concepts that can be tested (Herman, 1995; Maines, Sugrue, & Katovich, 1983). Objects, people, situations, and events do not in themselves possess meaning. Meaning is conferred on these elements by and through human interaction. For example, a DVD player in a college classroom may be defined by the professor as a teaching device to be used for showing educational videos. For the student using a DVD player in his or her dormitory to view rented movies, this instrument may be seen as a source of entertainment and pleasure, while for the inmate held in a maximum security prison who watches home movies sent from his or her family, it may be considered a window to the outside world. The meanings that people attach to their experiences and the objects and events that make up these experiences are not accidental or unconnected. Both the experiences and the events surrounding them are essential to the construction of meanings. To understand behavior, one must first understand the definitions and meanings and the processes by which they have been created. Human behavior does not occur on the basis of predetermined lockstep responses to preset events or situations. Rather, human behavior is an ongoing and negotiated interpretation of objects, events, and situations (Bogdan & Biklen, 2003). For researchers to understand the meanings that emerge from these interactions, they must either enter into the defining process or develop a sufficient appreciation for the process so that understandings can become clear.

Although social roles, institutional structures, rules, norms, goals, and the like may provide the raw material with which individuals create their definitions, these elements do not by themselves determine what the definitions will be or how individuals will act. In essence, symbolic interactionism emphasizes social interactions (action with symbolic meaning), negotiation of definitions, and emphatic role-taking between humans (Gecas, 1981; Turner, 1978). Measuring these interactions forms the core of the data-collection strategies that we will be studying in this book.

Why Use Qualitative Methods?

Many researchers believe that the social sciences have depended too much on sterile survey techniques, regardless of whether the technology is appropriate for the problem. For instance, nurses, when encouraged to do research at all, are strongly urged to use *scientific* strategies of quantification over more sociologically or anthropologically oriented ones considered less scientific. Unfortunately, clinical settings in which nurses are likely to conduct their research fail to meet most quantitative requirements for representativeness and sufficiency of sample size to allow statistically meaningful results.

For instance, let us say the average number of beds in a critical care unit varies between 8 and 12. Even when there are multiple units (e.g., in a medical intensive care unit or a cardiac intensive care unit), typically, fewer than 40 cases are available at any given time. With regard to research strategy, such a situation should preclude most quantitative investigations. On the other hand, 40 cases would prove ample for a number of qualitative strategies. In fact, as Chapter 8 describes, a setting such as a hospital would provide researchers with numerous opportunities to implement unobtrusive measures.

Scientific researchers may emphasize a more positivist view or may be primarily interested in individuals and their so-called life-worlds. In the case of the former, positivists utilize empirical methodologies borrowed from the natural sciences to investigate phenomena. Quantitative strategies serve this positive-science ideal by providing rigorous, reliable, and verifiably large aggregates of data and the statistical testing of empirical hypotheses.

In the case of life-worlds, researchers focus on naturally emerging languages and the meanings individuals assign to experience. Life-worlds include emotions, motivations, symbols and their meanings, empathy, and other subjective aspects associated with naturally evolving lives of individuals and groups. These elements may also represent their behavioral routines, experiences, and various conditions affecting these usual routines or natural settings. Many of these elements are directly observable and as such may be viewed as objectively measurable data. Nonetheless, certain elements of symbolism, meaning, or understanding usually require consideration of the individual's own perceptions and subjective apprehensions. This is qualitative data.

A Plan of Presentation

Having briefly outlined the basic assumptions and qualitative orientations of symbolic interaction, it is now possible to weave in various methodological strategies. Chapter 2 provides the basic information necessary for understanding the research enterprise. This chapter discusses the research process and proposes a spiraling model to follow when developing a research agenda. Chapter 2 also offers advice to the novice researcher about how to organize and conduct a literature review.

Chapter 3 considers a number of ethical concerns that are important for new investigators to understand before actually conducting research. Among the salient issues considered are covert versus overt research concerns, privacy rights, human subject institutional review boards, and informed consent in human subject research.

In addition to providing a general discussion of various forms and styles of traditional interviewing techniques, Chapter 4 uses a kind of symbolic interaction known as *dramaturgy* and suggests an effective research strategy for conducting in-depth interviews.

Chapter 5 also addresses the area of interviewing but moves toward a specialized style, namely, focus groups. This chapter examines the early origins of focus group interviews, their development during the past several decades, and their growing use in the social sciences.

Chapter 6 builds on the foundation constructed in Chapters 1 through 4 and extends the research process into the natural setting by examining ethnography. Along with interviewing, Chapter 6 discusses watching and listening, field notes, and a number of other field research concerns. This chapter examines ethnography both as a means of collecting data (what some call the *new ethnography*) and as an end in itself (narrative ethnographic accounts). This edition further explores critical ethnography, and the role it may play in the ethical conduct of naturalistic research.

Chapter 7 considers a dynamic mode of research, namely, action research. Action research has a substantial history in educational and nursing research and is moving rapidly into broader scientific endeavors as well.

While Chapters 4, 5, and 6 separately address the concept of interviewer reactivity, Chapter 8 offers several strategies that avoid reactivity entirely: It explores the use of unobtrusive measures.

As foreshadowed slightly in Chapter 8, the use of certain unobtrusive data has grown quite specialized. Chapter 9 examines a specialized and systematic use of certain kinds of running records, namely, historiography. In addition to the use of records, Chapter 9 considers oral histories and life histories as variations in historiography.

Chapter 10 examines a technique used to study individuals in their unique settings or situations. This technique is commonly called the *case study method*. This chapter also discusses how case studies may be undertaken on communities and organizations.

Chapter 11 dovetails with each of the preceding chapters on research techniques. Included in this chapter are recommendations for how novice researchers may organize their data and begin to make sense of what may be volumes of notes, transcripts, and trace documents and artifacts. Chapter 11 also briefly discusses the use of computers to assist in this data management scheme.

Chapter 12, the final chapter, offers recommendations for how novice qualitative researchers can disseminate their research findings.

"Trying It Out," a section at the conclusion of each of the data-collection technique chapters, offers suggestions for practicing each of the seven strategies.

REFERENCES

Babbie, E. (2007). *The Practice of Social Research* (11th ed.). Belmont, CA: Wadsworth Publishing.

Becker, H. S. (1970). *Sociological Work: Method and Substance.* Chicago, IL: Aldine.

Berg, B. L., & Berg, J. (1993). A reexamination of triangulation and objectivity in qualitative nursing research. *Free Inquiry in Creative Sociology 21*(1), 65–72.

Blumer, H. (1969). *Symbolic Interactionism: Perspective and Method.* Englewood Cliffs, NJ: Prentice Hall.

Bogdan, R., & Biklen, S. K. (2003). *Qualitative Research for Education* (4th ed.). Boston, MA: Allyn and Bacon.

Bogdan, R., & Taylor, S. J. (1998). *Introduction to Qualitative Research Methods* (3rd ed.). New York: John Wiley and Sons.

Campbell, D. T. (1956). *Leadership and Its Effects Upon the Group.* Columbus, OH: Ohio State University Press.

Campbell, T. T., & Fiske, D. W. (1959). Convergent and discriminant validation by the multivariate-multimethod matrix. *Psychological Bulletin 56*, 81–105.

Casey, D., & Murphy, K. (2009). Issues in using methodological triangulation in research. *Nurse Researcher 16*(4), 40–55.

Cooley, C. H. (1902). *Human Nature and the Social Order.* New York: Scribner.

Couch, C. (1988). *Social Process and Relationships.* New York: Rowman & Littlefield.

Creswell, J. W. (2007). *Qualitative Inquiry and Research Design.* Thousand Oaks, CA: Sage.

Dabbs, J. M., Jr. (1982). Making things visible. In J. Van Maanen (Ed.), *Varieties of Qualitative Research.* Beverly Hills, CA: Sage.

Denzin, N. K. (1978). *The Research Act.* New York: McGraw-Hill.

Denzin, N. K. (2010). Moments, mixed methods, and paradigm dialogs. *Qualitative Inquiry 16*(6), 419–427.

Denzin, N. K., & Lincoln, Y. S. (2005). *The Sage Handbook of Qualitative Research* (3rd ed.). Thousand Oaks, CA: Sage.

Denzin, N. K., & Lincoln, Y. S. (2008). *The Landscape of Qualitative Research* (3rd ed.). Thousand Oaks, CA: Sage.

Dewey, J. (1930). *Human Nature and Conduct.* New York: Modern Library.

Dittmann, M. (2005). Psychologists tout multiple methodologies in educational research. *Monitor on Psychology 36*(2), 20.

Fielding, N. G., & Fielding, J. L. (1986). *Linking Data.* Newbury Park, CA: Sage.

Filstead, W. (1970). *Qualitative Methodology: Firsthand Involvement and the Social World.* Chicago, IL: Markham.

Gecas, V. (1981). Contexts of socialization. In M. Rosenberg & R. H. Turner (Eds.), *Social Psychology: Sociological Perspectives* (pp. 165–199). New York: Basic Books.

Glaser, B., & Strauss, A. L. (1967). *The Discovery of Grounded Theory: Strategies for Qualitative Research.* Chicago, IL: Aldine.

Hagan, F. E. (2006). *Research Methods in Criminal Justice and Criminology* (7th ed.). Boston, MA: Allyn and Bacon.

Herman, N. J. (1995). Interactionist research methods: An overview. In N. J. Herman & L. T. Reynolds (Eds.), *Symbolic Interaction: An Introduction to Social Psychology*. Dix Hills, NY: General Hall Publishing.

Holstein, J., & Gubrium, J. (2000). *The Self We Live By: Narrative Identity in a Postmodern World*. New York: Oxford University Press.

Jackson, P. W. (1968). *Life in Classrooms*. New York: Holt, Rinehart, & Winston.

Leedy, P. D. (2001). *Practical Research: Planning and Design* (7th ed.). Upper Saddle River, NJ: Prentice Hall.

Leedy, P. D., & Ormrod, J. E. (2004). *Practical Research: Planning and Design* (8th ed.). Upper Saddle River, NJ: Prentice Hall.

Leninger, M. M. (1998). *Qualitative Research Methods in Nursing* (2nd ed.). Columbus, OH: Greyden Press.

Lofland, J., & Lofland, L. H. (1995). *Analyzing Social Settings* (3rd ed.). Belmont, CA: Wadsworth Publishers.

Lofland, J., Snow, D., Anderson, L., & Lofland, L. H. (2006). *Analyzing Social Settings* (4th ed.). Belmont, CA: Wadsworth Publishers.

Lune, H., Pumar, E., & Koppel, R. (2009). *Perspectives in Social Research Methods and Analysis. A Reader for Sociology*. Thousand Oaks, CA: Sage Publications.

Maines, D. R., Sugrue, N. M., & Katovich, M. A. (1983). The sociological import of G.H. Mead's theory of the past. *American Sociological Review 48*(2), 161–173.

Mead, G. H. (1934). *Mind, Self, and Society*. Chicago, IL: University of Chicago Press.

Mead, G. H. (1938). *The Philosophy of the Act*. Chicago, IL: University of Chicago Press.

Miles, M. B., & Huberman, M. A. (1994). *Qualitative Analysis: An Expanded Sourcebook* (2nd ed.). Thousand Oaks, CA: Sage.

Miles, M. B., & Huberman, M. A. (2002). *The Qualitative Researcher's Companion*. Thousand Oaks, CA: Sage.

Mills, C. W. (1959). *The Sociological Imagination*. New York: Oxford University Press.

Neuman, W. L. (2005). *Social Research Methods. Qualitative and Quantitative Approaches* (6th ed.). Boston, MA: Allyn and Bacon.

Parks, R. (1915). *Principles of Human Behavior*. Chicago, IL: Zalaz.

Thomas, W. I., & Swaine, D. (1928). *The Child in America*. New York: Knopf.

Turner, V. (1978). Foreword. In B. Myerhoff (Ed.), *Number Our Days*. New York: Simon and Schuster.

Webb, E. J., Campbell, D. T., Schwartz, R. D., & Sechrest, L. (1966). *Unobtrusive Measures: Nonreactive Research in the Social Sciences*. Chicago, IL: Rand McNally.

Webb, E. J., Campbell, D. T., Schwartz, R. D., Sechrest, L., & Grove, J. B. (1981). *Nonreactive Measures in the Social Sciences*. Boston, MA: Houghton Mifflin.

Chapter 2

Designing Qualitative Research

THIS CHAPTER CONSIDERS VARIOUS ways of thinking about and designing research. It includes discussion of the relationships among ideas, theory, and concepts, and of what I have long believed is the most difficult facet of research: operationalization. This chapter further offers a strategy for conducting literature reviews and explains the importance of carefully designing and planning research in advance. Let's begin with some thoughts about ideas, concepts, and theory.

Theory and Concepts

In the natural sciences, certain patterns of relationships occur with such regularity that they are deemed laws: occurrences of universal certainty. No such laws are found in the social sciences. This does not, however, mean that social life operates in a totally chaotic or completely irrational manner. Rather, social life operates within fairly regular patterns, and when carefully examined, these patterns make considerable sense. Unlike laws, patterns are tendencies, representing typical and expected forms of action around which innumerable individual variations may be found. As well, patterns of expected action often include smaller patterns of reaction against the expected actions. It is as though for every large group of balls that fall down, a few fall up or to the side. Gravity defines the general pattern, while other actions unrelated to gravity form a smaller pattern within the whole.

One purpose of social scientific research is to find the meaning underlying these various patterns. This is accomplished by creating, examining, testing, and refining theory. What then is theory? Theory can be defined as a general

2 Types of theories

and more or less comprehensive set of statements or propositions that describe different aspects of some phenomenon (Hagan, 2006; Silverman, 2006). In an applied context, theories can be understood as interrelated ideas about various patterns, concepts, processes, relationships, or events. In a formal sense, social scientists usually define theory as a system of logical statements or propositions that explain the relationship between two or more objects, concepts, phenomena, or characteristics of humans—what are sometimes called variables (Babbie, 2007; Denzin, 1978; Polit, Beck, & Hungler, 2003). Theory might also represent attempts to develop coherent narratives about reality or ways to classify and organize events, describe events, or even predict future events (Hagan, 2006). Theories are explanations. The theory of gravity explains why things fall, as well as predicting and explaining orbits and the physical stability of the universe. Theories of inequality contribute to our explanations for all kinds of economic behavior, from consumption to crime to wedding receptions.

concepts

In order to construct theories, one needs some smaller components or what Jonathan Turner (1989, p. 5) calls the "basic building blocks of theory," namely, concepts. Concepts, then, are symbolic or abstract elements representing objects, properties, or features of objects, processes, or phenomenon. Concepts may communicate ideas or introduce particular perspectives, or they may be a means for explaining a broad generalization. In terms of ideas, concepts are important because they are the foundation of communication and thought. Concepts provide a means for people to let others know what they are thinking and allow information to be shared. Thus, instead of describing a youth who is involved with drugs, crime, or truancy, or has problems with parents and other adults, I might simply use the concept of *delinquent* to communicate these same elements (ideas). By *conceptualizing* a set of behaviors or ideas as part of a coherent package, we can describe a range of possible ideas, relations, and outcomes with a single term. Since concepts are abstract representations, of course, they contain a much broader range of possibilities than what any individual case is likely to contain. Most delinquent youths, for example, are not all that delinquent, while others are so far out there that we might prefer the term "criminal."

Concepts can be found everywhere, and people use them all of the time without actually thinking about them as concepts (Silverman, 2006). For example, age is a concept that is so commonly used that few people stop to think about what it means. Even though people often think they understand the meaning of the concept, they may hesitate when asked to offer a specific definition. We often use precise numbers to describe ages when we are really seeking to communicate abstract concepts, such as "young" or "elderly." Or we mentally translate such terms from the abstract "middle-aged" to some approximate age. As data, age actually represents an abstract idea about the *age =*

number of cumulative years that an individual has been alive. Other related ideas, such as health or infirmity, stage in the life course, or work experience, must be specified separately rather than assumed as attributes of one's age. Although this may seem to make the term stiff, it also ensures that there is a common understanding for the meaning of this concept. Concepts used in social scientific research similarly may seem obvious at first, but they must always be clearly defined.

Typically concepts have two distinct parts: a *symbolic* element (a word, symbol, term, etc.) and an associated *definitional* element. People learn definitions for certain concepts in a variety of ways. For example, children may learn the concept of *honesty* explicitly when a parent or teacher specifically instructs them on its meaning. Or it may be learned implicitly through a more diffuse, nonverbal process of observed instances in which either dishonest behavior is corrected or honest behavior is rewarded (either through comments or actions). In either case, eventually each of us comes to apprehend the meaning of honesty. Yet, if asked to define it, people may offer slightly different shades of understanding. One person might say, "Honesty is not lying to people." Another might offer, "Honesty is not taking property that belongs to other people," and a third individual might claim that "honesty is being able to be trusted to do what you promise to do." Obviously, these responses suggest that even a fairly common concept may have multiple meanings. Each of these definitions is valid on its own merits (some would say "true"). Yet, they are different from one another and therefore each definition addresses only some small portion of the larger concept. In the social sciences, vague or unclear definitions create enormous problems. Specificity is critical when conducting research. Therefore, an important part of developing social scientific theory is first to define relevant concepts that will be used in a given research process or project. Indistinct, unclear, or vague definitions of concepts create obstacles to the advancement of knowledge and science. After noting that there were many different definitions in the literature for the concept *gang*, Richard Ball and G. David Curry (1995, p. 239) explained the problem:

> Few if any gang researchers and theorists have been sufficiently conscious of their own definition strategies, with the result that their definitions carry too many latent connotations, treated correlations or consequences as properties or causes, or contributed to similar errors of logic.

By "latent connotations" the authors refer to the vast world of conceptual associations that the term "gang" carries. While one researcher might describe a new pattern of urban school kids grouping together for status and mutual protection as "increasing gang presence in the schools," readers might well assume that gang presence means weapons, drugs, fights, or the allegiance of school groups to well-known regional gangs such as the Crips or the Latin Kings. Presumably, fewer people will assume that the term refers to biker gangs or chain gangs. But any vagueness in the use of key concepts invites speculation. The need for this sort of specific definition of concepts will be made clearer later in the discussion on operationalization.

Concepts rarely occur in isolation. Rather, they occur in what Neuman (2000, p. 43) refers to as *concept clusters* or what others may call *propositions*. One can connect different concepts or conceptual thoughts to each other through propositions. Propositions, then, are statements about relationships between concepts (Maxfield & Babbie, 2007). Taylor and Bogdan (1998) suggest that although a concept may not fit (may not convey the intended meaning), propositions may be either right or wrong statements of fact, although the research may not be able to prove them. Testable propositions about the relations among our research concepts form a special class of propositions called *hypotheses*. Propositions, as discussed later, are the statements that make up theories.

Hypotheses are testable

Ideas and Theory

Every research project has to start somewhere; typically, the starting point is an idea. The big question, however, is how to go about finding an idea that will serve as a good launching point to a research project. For some students, this genuinely is the most difficult part of the research process. Actually, many people arrive at their research ideas simply by taking stock of themselves and looking around. For example, a nurse might observe a coworker coming to work under the influence of alcohol and begin to think about how alcohol would influence nursing care. From this initial thought, the idea for researching impaired nurses might arise. A counselor at a delinquency detention center might notice that many of her clients have been battered or abused prior to their run-in with the law. From her observation, she might wonder how abuse might be linked with delinquency and how she could investigate this linkage.

Consider Phil Brown (1998, 2002), who grew up in the Catskill Mountains and watched as this once thriving, largely Jewish resort area in upstate New York lost its luster and faded into near oblivion. As an adult, Brown has written extensively—and largely autobiographically—about this once culturally rich and influential area.

In some situations, ideas move from information you hear but may not actually experience yourself. For instance, you're sitting at home listening to the news, and you hear a report about three youths from wealthy families who have been caught burglarizing houses. You wonder: Why on earth did they do something like that? What motivates people who don't need money to steal from others? Or, you read in the newspaper that a man living around the corner from you has been arrested for growing marijuana in his garage. You think back to the times you passed this man's house and smiled a greeting at him. And you wonder: Why didn't I realize what he was up to? Who was he going to sell the marijuana to anyhow? From these broad curiosities, you might begin to think about how these questions could be explored or answered, and how you might research these phenomena. Or you might think more generally about how we define particular forms of crime as "urban" as though they couldn't occur in the suburbs, from which you might define research questions about why some people receive long prison sentences and others short ones for the same crimes.

The preceding examples serve two important purposes. First, they point out how ideas promote potential research endeavors. Second, and perhaps more important, they suggest a central research orientation that permeates this book. This orientation is the attitude that the world is a research laboratory and that you merely need to open your eyes and ears to the sensory reality that surrounds all of us to find numerous ideas for research. In fact, once you become familiar with this orientation, the biggest problem will be to filter out all the many possible researchable ideas and actually investigate one!

Most experienced qualitative researchers will agree that if you drop an investigator into any neighborhood, he or she will manage to identify a research idea, develop a research plan, and project potential research findings before lunch. I sit on a morning commuter train and look around me. The difference between the crowded rush hour trains and the sparsely populated later trains is extreme. How did we come to define "work hours" in such a regimented fashion? How is this changing as more people are able to "telecommute"? If the manufacturing sector is shrinking in the United States, while service work is growing, and service work is increasingly done around the clock, why is rush hour still so crowded? And what about other parts of the world where manufacturing is increasing? Are these places experiencing greater rush hour traffic than before? How will they chose whether to build more roads for private cars or more train lines for mass transit? And finally, why do people making private phone calls in public places, like trains, talk so much more loudly than everyone else? I could spend the rest of my career trying to understand this train.

This notion is likely to contrast dramatically with the inexperienced researcher's fear that he or she cannot even think of anything worthwhile to research. There may be considerable truth to the optimistic view of experienced researchers. This does not mean, however, that all research ideas will be equally easy or interesting to research.

Some ideas will be more difficult to investigate than others. This is because those who control access to a given location—what the literature calls gatekeepers—or the subjects themselves may be reluctant to cooperate. Gatekeepers are discussed in greater detail in Chapter 6. Also, some ideas may initially seem extremely interesting but become rather plain or uninspiring on further investigation. Some ideas are interesting to think about but impractical, unethical, or even impossible to study in a rigorous fashion. The impacts of emotional trauma, for example, can be inferred through many case studies of trauma victims, but you cannot test these inferences in an isolated experimental setting without deliberately inflicting trauma on your research subjects. Some students understand research in relation to findings that they have been taught in other sociology classes. For example, the research question, "Do advertisements represent women in a sexually exploitive fashion?" was once an important question to look into. Now, after years of study, we know the answer is yes, and until something changes in the advertising field to call that into question, it is much less useful or interesting to conduct new research just to show that it's still the same.

So, you begin with an idea. But how is this related to theory? There are some who argue that ideas and theory must come before empirical research. This has been called the *theory-before-research model* (Frankfort-Nachmias & Nachmias, 2007). This orientation has been nicely described by Karl Popper (1968), who suggested that one begins with ideas (conjectures) and then attempts to disprove or refute them through tests of empirical research (refutation).

In contrast to the theory-before-research proponents, there are some who argue that research must occur before theory can be developed. This *research-before-theory* orientation can be illustrated by a statement from Robert Merton (1968, p. 103):

> It is my central thesis that empirical research goes far beyond the passive role of verifying and testing theory; it does more than confirm or refute hypotheses. Research plays an active role: it performs at least four major functions, which help shape the development of theory. It initiates, it reformulates, it deflects, and it clarifies theory.

In other words, research may suggest new problems for theory, require theoretical innovation, refine existing theories, or serve to vary past theoretical assumptions.

Both Popper's and Merton's perspectives have served researchers well, and proven their usefulness for over 40 years. The approach offered in this book views theory-before-research and research-before-theory perspectives as highly compatible. Often methods texts and courses describe the research enterprise as a linear progression. In this progression, you begin with an idea, gather theoretical information, design a research plan, identify a means for data collection, analyze the data, and report findings (see, e.g., Punch, 2006). This may be diagrammed as follows:

Idea → Theory → Design → Data Collection → Analysis → Findings

For the most part, this orientation resembles the theory-before-research model. But it could also be drawn as the research-before-theory model.

In either case, you have the feeling that each of these components is a distinct and separate successive stage, that you first derive an idea and then move on to either theory or design and so forth. In essence, it seems that you complete various necessary tasks of each stage and then move forward, leaving the completed state behind.

In this chapter, I argue for a different model for the research enterprise, a model that encompasses both the research-before-theory and theory-before-research models. This is possible because the proposed approach is conceived as spiraling rather than linear in its progression. In the proposed approach, you begin with an idea, gather theoretical information, reconsider and refine your idea, begin to examine possible designs, reexamine theoretical assumptions, and refine these theoretical assumptions and perhaps even your original or refined idea. Thus, with every two steps forward, you take a step or two backward before proceeding any further. What results is no longer a linear progression in a single, forward direction. Rather, you are spiraling forward, never actually leaving any stage behind completely. This spiraling approach is drawn in Figure 2.1.

To simplify understanding of the individual elements of this model as I discuss them, let's redefine the stages slightly, as follows:

Ideas → Literature Review → Design → Data Collection and Organization → Analysis and Findings → Dissemination

Figure 2.1 The Spiraling Research Approach

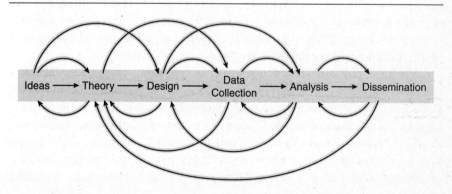

As illustrated, you begin with some sort of rough *idea* for a research study. The next stage in the process is to begin thinking and reading about the topical idea. As you begin reading related and relevant literature on the topic, you should also start turning this idea into a *research question* or even a set of researchable foci. As suggested by the fluidity of the spiraling approach offered in this chapter, your research idea should flow into a potential research question that may continue to shift, change, and take form as the research process unfolds. Even though your research question(s) may change as you proceed through the research process, it is important to establish a focus for your research question or a series of research aims.

Reviewing the Literature

After developing a rough idea for the study, you will need to begin examining how others have already thought about and researched the topic. Let's say an idea for some research begins with an interest in alcohol use by male college students. You might formulate a rough question for research such as: What is the relationship between college and drinking among American males? This rough idea already shows elements of refinement. It has been limited to consideration of only American males. The next step is to visit the library or its Web site to get started on a literature review. Because every library is different, you will need to familiarize yourself with the sorts of databases, periodicals, and books that are readily available to you. Most periodicals are available to browse online through databases such as Infotrac or Research Navigator's ContentSelect, but for books you have to actually go to a building. Some libraries have subscriptions to many journals, but not all of these may be useful for social science research, let alone a specific topic such as alcohol drinking by American male college students. Different libraries also provide different methods for accessing materials, including large selections of in-print periodicals maintained both in current stacks and in bound versions in back stacks or in the open library. As convenient as PDFs are, the fastest way to immerse yourself in a new topic is still to spend a few hours pulling bound volumes off of shelves and browsing the most promising articles in them.

The next task is to begin thinking creatively about cryptic subject topics related to your rough research idea or question and to search for these topics in the indexes. For the preceding example, you might make a list that includes "alcohol use," "collegiate alcohol use," "alcohol on campus," "drinking," "males and alcohol," "Americans and alcohol," "social drinking," "substance abuse in college," "campus problems," and so forth. It is important to develop a number of different subject areas to search. Some will be more fruitful than others, and perhaps some will yield little information. This is because both the print versions and computer-based versions of indexes are created by humans. Because of this, indexes unavoidably suffer from the problem of terminological classification bias. In other words, even though these indexes are cross-referenced, if you do not use the same term or phrase used by the original indexer, you may not locate the entries he or she has referenced.

For instance, some years ago, Bruce Berg became interested in the idea of doing research about women in policing. More directly, he was interested in the effect of policing on female officers. He asked his graduate student to see if she could locate some material about female police officers. (Getting your graduate students to do an initial search is one of the most effective ways to begin a project.) When she returned the next day, she reported that there was virtually nothing in any of the index databases on the topic "female police officers." Berg asked if she had tried "women in policing," or "women police officers," or even "minorities in policing." Sheepishly, she explained she had not thought to do that and returned to the library. When she returned, she was carrying a list of literally dozens of references. I have seen many instances of similar thinking among students who are first learning to conduct research. Returning to the preceding example, many of my past students have proposed research on male college drinking only to declare that there is virtually no literature on "campus drinking by men" or "why men in college drink." Yet, using the separate searches mentioned earlier would yield thousands of relevant articles. The lesson to be learned from this is that you must not be too restrictive in your topics when searching for reference materials in indexes. In fact, most online indexes provide users with a thesaurus to assist them in locating subject terms used to index material in the database.

One important recommendation is that you avoid becoming too computer dependent during your literature search. Again, because computer listings are sometimes limited by the way they are indexed, not all the relevant information for a study may be recognized in a computer-based search. During one revision of this book, Berg asked one of his graduate students to locate some recent materials on "active informed consent." This ethical concern is discussed in Chapter 3. Naturally, he sought an answer to the request by diving right into the Internet.

Several days later the student reported that there were no such materials. As Berg described, in the last edition of this book, "I asked if he had gone to the library and looked up 'informed consent,' 'passive consent,' 'active consent,' or any similar topics. With a note of anger in his tone, he informed me that he had done better: He had checked with various Internet information sources and search engines. I then asked if he had gone to the library and physically looked through the last several years of such journals as *Journal of Ethics* or *Social*

Problems, or through any educational, nursing, or medical journals. With even more anger, because I was questioning his work, he admitted he had not. He also naively insisted that if he couldn't find it through the Internet, it didn't exist."

You know how this story ends. Berg walked with the student into the library and began pulling relevant works off the shelves within 15 minutes.

The moral of this story is simple. Search engines and the vast information available via the Internet are wonderful tools and places to begin searching for literature. They can provide enormous amounts of information. But they only give you access to the information that someone else has already added to the pertinent databases. Frequently, however, there is no substitute for physically thumbing through journal indexes. It is also important when using the Internet to be careful about the legitimacy of materials taken from the Web, which we will now consider in detail.

Evaluating Web Sites

In the years since the first edition of *Qualitative Research Methods for the Social Sciences* was published, Internet searches have become the first, and often the only, information source for many millions of users, including professional researchers. Google even provides separate search levels called *Scholars* and *Books*. We strongly endorse, and rely on, these different tools, but they are not the sole source of literary materials a good researcher should employ. Google Scholar, for example, is full of papers and articles that can be downloaded in their entirety; unfortunately many of these require a fee or membership in some sort of literary subscription. Google Books allows one to explore thousands of books—but not in their entirety. Sometimes, the topic one is seeking does yield enough information to be used, and the full citation information is provided in the search. However, at other times, only segments of the information are reproduced, and one must still acquire the actual text from the library or through a purchase. And unlike scientific research tools, Internet search engines retrieve far more information that is of possible general interest but mostly useless in formal research. For example, access the Internet and try running a search for the term *concept*. The initial results may be less than useful if you are writing a scholarly term paper, article, research report, or proposal.

We need to make an important distinction here between the Internet as a document delivery service and the Internet as a document repository. In the first case, the traditional materials of basic research—peer-reviewed scientific articles—may be downloaded via the Internet right to your computer. The *source* of the materials is the journal in which it was first published, whether you got your copy by photocopying, downloading, or from a reader (e.g., Lune, Pumar, and Koppel, 2009). The Internet just gets you the article faster.

In the second case, however, the materials were actually published on the Web and can only be accessed through an Internet search. As a very general rule of thumb, the first set of materials is valid and useful while the second is suspect and unreliable. Reviewing the literature in a field of study means reading valid research, not abstracts, blogs, magazine articles, rants, or encyclopedias.

Many people today, especially inexperienced researchers, take the Internet for granted; and such complacency with this technology can be dangerous for a researcher. Yes, the Internet is enormously fast, and yes, it has evolved in less than three decades to provide access to many millions of documents. However, the quality and integrity of all the available documents are not equal. The Internet epitomizes the concept of *caveat lector—Let the reader beware.*

The Internet allows you to access information from a variety of governmental and private sources as well as from online electronic journals, books, commentaries, archives, and even newspapers. Most governmental agencies have Web sites that offer the public copies of recent (and often backlogged) reports, pamphlets, news releases, and other forms of information. There are also Web sites, however, that offer inaccurate, erroneous, or fabricated information. I once had the unpleasant experience of reading a student "research" paper on homosexuality in America that was entirely based on information he had downloaded from a couple of hate-group sites. Amazingly, the student had (apparently) skimmed the materials so carelessly that he accepted their claims as established facts without even noticing the death threats, support for Nazi extermination programs, or frequent use of curses and other invectives. Granted, this is an extreme example; sort of the Internet-age version of writing your term paper on the bus ride to school on the morning that it's due.

Whether you surf the Web simply as a casual consumer of information or in order to research some topic, it is critical that you carefully evaluate documents before quoting them. Here are a few questions you might want to consider before accepting information from a Web site as valid:

1. *Whose Web site is it, and what's in the URL (Uniform Resource Locator)?* Before you even start to consider the veracity of the text on a particular Web site, look at the URL to get a sense of the authenticity of the material on that site. Some of the things to look for are as follows: Is this somebody's personal Web page? Check to see if the site is listed under a personal name (e.g., bberg or berg) preceded or followed by a tilde (~), a percent sign (%), or even the words *users, members,* or *people.* Personal pages are not necessarily inaccurate, but you should nonetheless consider the authority and expertise of the author very carefully. Today, just about anyone with a computer can launch and maintain his or her own Web site. Some people have sites to allow them to show off their vacations, poetry, or special mementos. Other

sites are intended as commercial ventures, selling everything from sex to Bible lessons. Many professors and professional researchers disseminate their research by simply making their reports and published articles (sometimes even entire books) available on their Web sites. When you consider using information taken from an individual's personal Web site, you still should be cautious and consider the credibility of the individual or group that is operating and maintaining the site.

2. *What is the nature of the domain?* The *domain* represents a kind of hierarchical scheme for indicating the logical and sometimes geographical venue of a Web page. In the United States, common domains are .edu (education), .gov (government agency), .net (network related), .com (commercial), and .org (nonprofit and research organizations). Outside the United States, domains indicate country: ca (Canada), cn (China), uk (United Kingdom), au (Australia), jp (Japan), fr (France), and so forth. Is this an official government Web site or that of a well-known and reputable organization? Is it operated and maintained by a private group that has a special purpose or motive for having the site and offering the materials you are considering? As I mentioned earlier, there are a number of Web sites sponsored by hate groups. The information offered on such sites may sound like the reports of scientific studies, and the reports and documents may even look official. Yet, much of the information on these sites is likely biased and designed to be self-effacing and positive in order to sway readers to think favorably about the group's viewpoints.

As an example of the importance of a domain name, suppose you were looking for information on the President of the United States. One source would be the official Web site of the White House in Washington, DC. You type in http://www.whitehouse.org, thinking this will bring you to the site, but the actual domain is .gov, not .org. If you compare the two, you will find extreme differences. Or have a look at the two sites www.gatt.org and www.gatt.org/gatt.html.

3. *Is the material current or dated?* You should check to see how frequently the Web site is updated. If the materials have not been updated recently, you may want to question how reliable a source it is. Consider also whether links are active or have expired or moved. You might also consider how current even the working links are (do these sites seem to be updated on a regular basis?). Naturally, just because a site is well maintained and information is regularly updated doesn't mean it is necessarily a good site in itself, and some material may not require constant updates. However, issues of currency are important when conducting research and should be considered when evaluating information taken from a Web site.

4. *Can the information be corroborated?* Sometimes the material you find on a Web site seems odd or unusual, and further investigation suggests that it may not be truthful. When this happens, do not use it! Often when you undertake a search using an Internet search engine, you get many hits. Do not use only the first one you find. Carefully check a number of comparable sites to ensure the information is comparable. If you find that there are glaring contradictions or discrepancies, you should be very cautious about using this information.

Although there are no absolutely certain ways to guard against inaccurate information on the Web getting into your research (unless you exclude any Web-based information), these suggestions will at least help in filtering out most of the false documentation from too easily sifting in. The safest approach, of course, is to limit your searches to research databases and journals, bypassing the universe of random Web sites entirely.

By now, you should have begun to amass a large quantity of documents to include in your review of the literature. Naturally, you will need to begin taking some form of notes on the various pieces of literature you have obtained. There are a number of ways you can keep such records and notes. What follows are a few general suggestions for organizing your work. There are no rules, however, and you will do best to discover the style that works best for your own ways of thinking.

Content versus Use

It is difficult to educate yourself on a new area of study while also learning who the key authors are in this area while also becoming familiar with the specialized vocabulary of research on the topic while thinking about the meaning of the findings presented while planning the paper that you will write. It helps if you can break the work down into different parts. I prefer to maintain a strict distinction between two questions: What does the material say? And how does this relate to me? In other words, taking notes on the content of the literature you study is distinct from taking notes on how to use that literature in your own work.

Writing notes on the content of research articles and books is a lot like preparing a junior high school book report. First, record the full citation information for the article or other source. Next, identify the major claim(s), methods, and subject matter of the work. Under that, begin to write out all of the best parts—the quotable explanations, definitions, and findings that make this work unique. Quote each exactly, with quotation marks, and note the page numbers.

How to do a lit review

When you are done, you should have a brief file that encapsulates the key parts of your source, making it much easier to draw on when you write. Chapter 12 discusses the problems with paraphrasing and with careless use of quotes in the section about plagiarism. There are other benefits to careful quoting.

Copying over exact quotes often seems tiresome and unnecessary. Since we are primarily interested in ideas, not phrases, one might think that a paraphrase is better. I recommend otherwise. If you, as an investigator, paraphrase material in your content notes, it is possible that you might slant or alter meanings. Without intending to, you might have misread, misinterpreted, or poorly paraphrased material. When you go through the notes looking for agreement among authors, you might find paraphrased statements that seem to represent similar ideas, but that actually do not accurately represent the sentiments of the original authors. Using verbatim excerpts ensures that this will not occur. Either the authors did say similar things or they did not.

I also recommend saving keywords with each file to describe the content. It may seem like extra work at the time, but it can be invaluable later when you need to find all of your sources on antidrug laws, or to locate that one piece you vaguely remember containing the story about the homeless dog. If it's possible, it also sometimes helps to make liberal use of subfolders to store your notes. Under the "social movements" folder I might have folders for "American" and "European" cases, or "cultural" movements in one and "material" goals in another. Of course the problem there is that you could have a European cultural movement that is pursuing the expansion of access to things of material value, in which case you could file that almost anywhere. This is why keywords are often more useful ways to identify source files.

With keywords, you can very quickly sort the summaries into different categories as you need them (e.g., placing all the notes about police detectives together, or all the theory pieces in one place). In this manner, you can assemble the material into an organized sequence that will reflect how you plan to write the report or paper. This allows you to read through the relevant materials for each section rather than repeatedly read through all of the material in order to write a single section.

Keyword searches also allow you to assess whether multiple authors actually have made similar statements about issues or situations. In turn, you are able to make strong synthesized statements regarding the work or arguments of others. For example, you might write, "According to Babbie (2007), Frankfort-Nachmias and Nachmias (2007), and Leedy and Ormrod (2004), the design stage is a critically important element in the development of a research project." Making such a synthesized statement, which collapses the arguments of three individuals into one, can be easily accomplished because you would have notes for each author conveying this sort of general sentiment.

I have violated all of this advice at times, and so I have learned the hard way about the importance of good record keeping. Before we all had laptops, I had actual folders with pieces of paper in them to store my notes. To save time, I would write the author's name on the top of a note sheet without writing down the title. Weeks later, after I had inserted a great quote from "Smith" into my paper, I would have to take it out again because I was unable to figure out if this was Dorothy Smith (1988) or Michael Peter Smith (1998). I still have a folder containing an entire conference presentation without a single citation in it. I would love to rewrite the material for publication, but I have no usable sources for any of my claims.

Fortunately, there are technological solutions for those of us too rushed or too lazy to write everything down. Most of the databases that you might use to find many of your materials—whether books or articles—will also allow you to save the complete citations in any of the standard writing styles. And many will generate records suitable for a bibliography program. Bibliography software is extremely useful for storing accurate and complete lists of materials you have read, whether you ended up using them in your current paper or not. They also allow you to store keywords with each record, which we know is helpful. And since you can download the citations and copy them into files with a few keystrokes, you have little opportunity to introduce typos. Your university library may offer free or reduced-cost software for this, and many programs can be downloaded for little or no money anyway. You can try out a few and decide for yourself.

First, though, we need to think about how we use all of these notes.

New work is built on a foundation of old work. We take the best of what is currently known and weave it together to form the solid ground on which to place our own, new, contributions. The content notes that I described earlier are not such a foundation. To push the metaphor a little more, they are the materials from which we construct that foundation.

Let's imagine that I am starting a study of teen drug use. Clearly, some of my background literature would come from the field of juvenile delinquency studies, from which I would learn of the statistical distributions of different forms of youthful criminal behavior, the nature of interventions and their success and failure rates, and criminological theories for such behavior. All of this is a start, but little of it would be exactly on my topic. The youths I'm studying aren't necessarily thieves or thugs, gang members, or even dropouts. Most of them are probably suburban stoners. But the delinquency literature is one pillar.

There is a rich social-psychological research literature on adolescence. One can get lost in such a broad field, soaking up thousands of pages of new information. For the sake of efficiency, I would need to limit my reading with the strategic use of additional keywords. I would obviously read about

Pillars

teen drug use, but also teen drinking and probably teen smoking as well. This body of research would provide another pillar, with theories and data about the nature and causes of adolescent behaviors that are viewed as "antisocial." Notice that "antisocial" behavior will overlap with some of what the delinquency literature calls "criminal" behavior. Relating the two to each other, or separating them in a useful way, is part of my job as the writer of my own research paper.

A third pillar for this work might come from research on families. There might be household-level data that I would want to consider. Of course, the drug of choice among youths varies by socioeconomic status. Powdered cocaine is more popular among people who can afford it, while crack cocaine is accessible to low-income consumers. Heroin goes in and out of fashion, while marijuana remains the perennial favorite among casual users. I would certainly want to know more about who is typically using what in order to both plan and describe my research.

Finally, at least for purposes of this discussion, there are classic works that simply have to be included if I'm going to make any sort of conceptual argument about my topic. If I want to investigate youth drug use in relation to *anomie*, then I will have some discussion of Durkheim. If I want to address the social context in which the drugs are used, or the meaning of the act to the users, then I would certainly start with Norman Zinberg's (1984) *Drug, Set, and Setting*.

With all of this research literature consumed and reduced to notes, I have my materials. But I still don't have my foundation. Simply listing all of the different viewpoints that all of this past work has claimed or demonstrated would produce more confusion than clarity. Results in one source, taken at face value, contradict the results of another. Each of the sources addresses some small part of my study, but none of them directly answer my question. (Notice that if one of them did answer my question, and I accepted that answer as valid and complete, then there would be no justification for me to do my work at all. We're supposed to use our work to go beyond our sources.) So how do I use my notes?

Let's recall the purpose of writing a literature review. You provide the background needed to educate your readers enough so that they can understand and follow what you are doing, and so that they can appreciate the need for your work. The review of past research: brings them up to speed; introduces and explains the major concepts with which you are working; does not introduce concepts that you don't need; and provides the motivation for your new research (Galvin, 1999). Ideally, by the time individuals have finished reading your background section, they should be on the edge of their seats wanting to know what you have found.   *1, 2, 3*

There are many ways to write a literature review section. A few of the things you might try to do when writing yours are as follows:

1. Dispel myths. Among the myths of drug use are that we could eliminate it entirely if we had just the right policies and strategies. Yet studies indicate that drug use is universal, across all sorts of times and places, under all regime types and through all kinds of economic and social conditions.

2. Explain competing conceptual frameworks. Some drug use studies center on the issue of blame. Are the users bad people? Are their parents so? Have their schools failed them? Other studies look at control efforts, police budgets, and enforcement technologies. So one set of readings is concerned with the problems of supply, while others are all about demand.

3. Clarify the focus of your own work. I might, for example, explain the unique features of a symbolic interactionist approach to state that I am interested in understanding the meaning of the act (drug use) from the perspective of the user, not from the perspective of parents or politicians.

4. Justify assumptions. Drug use patterns are cyclical. The popularity of specific drugs rises and falls endlessly. By using government data on drug sales and arrests, I can back up my claim that declines in use of one drug are usually accompanied by increases in the use of others. Therefore, I might reject a local mayor's claim that his own policies toward drug control are responsible for the recent decline in whatever drug is going out of favor.

outline of Lit Review

The main point is that your literature review section is like an essay on the background to your topic. It has an introduction, in which you explain what your topic is and what you are reviewing. It has a point, which is to support your research question and your design. There is the body of the paper, in which you present the information that defines the background to your work. Therefore, you can start with an outline as you might for a larger paper. And this is where you start to map out a strategy for putting your content notes to use. You can lay out the major claims of the literature, decide what order to address them in, and begin to write out notes about what you want your readers to understand about the material. Ultimately, you would produce a coherent essay that flows from the introduction to the conclusion, touching on the various works of the field along the way.

Notice how completely unlike a junior high school book report this final essay is. No one, honestly, no one wants to read your content summaries.

Your papers are not strengthened by a long diversion into listing a bunch of things that you have read. All of that content summary was for you, to make it easier for you to write the real literature review part.

TRYING IT OUT

There are a number of ways you can practice aspects related to the planning of research. A few suggestions follow that should provide an opportunity to gain some experience. Although these are useful experiential activities, they should not be confused with actually conducting research.

Suggestion 1   Using your favorite search engine on the Web, look up "Family Research Council." Now take a look at the research data available at several of the hits that the search has found. Consider the merits of the documents on each of these sites. Does the material seem biased? Does the material sound reasonable? How heavily would you rely on this information in a report or research?

Suggestion 2   Locate the Index to the Social Sciences in a college or university library. Use the index to find 10 sources of reference material for a potential study on homelessness. Now go to the Web and using your favorite search engine enter the search term "homelessness" and locate 10 additional reference items. Compare the two sets of materials.

micro/methods exercise

Theory, Reality, and the Social World

Larry Reynolds and Nancy Herman-Kinney (2003, p. 1045) suggest that "interactionists have often been described, and sometimes describe themselves, as fundamentally 'unscientific,' doubtful of the possibility of an objective truth." In some ways, this is a true statement, but at the same time, it misses the very nature of the perspective: its flexibility and diversity. That orientation also ignores the fact that many interactionists who question quantitative purist approaches see themselves as very scientific because they adopt various systematic processes and employ rigorous standards when gathering information (data). While many argue for a subjective and interpretive approach to human behavior, other interactionists strive to build a science of human conduct that is much more a social realist approach built on natural science criteria. More recently, Denzin and Lincoln (2008, pp. 8–9) remarked:

This is true of all science

Qualitative research as a set of interpretative activities, privileges no single methodological practice over another. As a site of discussion or discourse, qualitative research is difficult to define clearly. It has no theory or paradigm that is distinctly its own....multiple theoretical paradigms claim use of qualitative research methods and strategies, from constructivists to cultural studies, feminism, Marxism, and ethnic models of study. Qualitative research is used in many separate disciplines...it does not belong to a single discipline.

Thus, tensions exist between systematic and rigorous standards and more phenomenological, subjective, and interpretative discovery. Further, a variety of disciplines each claims methodological involvement with qualitative strategies, orientations, and techniques—if not control or ownership. These tensions are frequently apparent in qualitative writings and raise the questions: "How can one be objective while still being subjective?" How can so many disciplines each use the same strategies to undertake research? To be certain, I cannot fully answer these questions in this methods book. However, as may already be becoming clear, I too walk that slender tightrope between objectivity and subjectivity in terms of how one goes about designing his or her research study. Moreover, since this book is directed to the social sciences in general, and not a specific discipline, I too have embraced the notion that these strategies do not require links to a particular substantive discipline in order to be effective. One good way to begin is to clearly understand the distinctions between objective and subjective reality, or what can be described as the distinction between *cognitive reality* and *physical* or *sensory reality*, and their relationship with theory.

In cognitive reality—the thoughts that you can conjure in your mind—anything is possible; however, in sensory reality very clear limitations exist. For example, if you close your eyes, you should have little trouble imagining yourself standing on a railroad track with a train engine speeding toward you. Now, in your mind, you can raise your hands in front of your chest and imagine that as the train is about to strike, you can hold it at bay, as if you were a super being. Yet, in the sensory world, you would be unwise to attempt a similar feat. Sensory reality is the world around you. It is the world filled with smells, tactile surfaces, loud sounds, beautiful or unpleasant sights, and the tastes of sweets, sours, tarts, and spices (Praetorius, 2000; Stone, 2001).

Social scientists tend to move smoothly from one reality to the other during the early phases of a research study. After all, when you conceive an idea for your research, you are operating in the cognitive realm. When you turn to a review of the literature, you slide into the sensory world, but just long enough to formulate concepts and work with theory to develop a doable research question or series of research aims—then back to sensory reality, where you will need to frame your newly created research question or problem.

Framing Research Problems

Research problems direct or drive the research enterprise. How you will eventually conduct a research study depends largely on what your research questions are. It is important, therefore, to frame or formulate a clear research problem statement. Remember, the research process begins with an idea and only a rough notion of what is to be researched. As you have been reading through and collecting information from the literature, these rough questions have become clearer and theoretically more refined.

Let us return to the earlier research idea: What is the relationship between college and drinking among American males? After reading through some of the literature, you might begin to refine and frame this idea as a problem statement with researchable questions:

Problem Statement. This research proposes to examine alcohol-drinking behaviors in social settings among college-age American males.

Research Questions. A number of questions are addressed in this research including (although not limited to) the following:

1. What are some normative drinking behaviors of young adult American males during social gatherings where alcohol is present?
2. How do some young adult American males manage to abstain from drinking (e.g., avoidance rituals) while in social situations where alcohol is present?
3. How do young adult American males define appropriate drinking practices?
4. How do young adult American males define problem drinking?

These questions did not just happen spontaneously. They were influenced by the literature about drinking practices among Americans. They resulted after the investigator began thinking about what issues were important and how those issues might be measured. This required the researcher to consider various concepts and definitions and perhaps to develop operationalized definitions.

Operationalization and Conceptualization

When someone says, "That kid's a delinquent," most of us quickly draw some mental picture of what that is, and we are able to understand the meaning of the term *delinquent*. If, however, someone were to ask, "How would you define a delinquent?" we would probably find that some people think about this term differently from others. For some, it may involve a youth under the legal age of adult jurisdiction (usually between 16 and 18 years of age) who commits law violations (Bynum & Thompson, 1992). For others, a delinquent may be simply defined as a youthful law violator (Thornton & Voigt, 1992). Still others may require in their definition some notion of a youth who not only breaks a law but who is also convicted in court of this law violation (Siegel & Welsh, 2008). In other words, there are a number of possible definitions for the concept *delinquent*.

If you, as a researcher, are interested in studying the behavior of delinquent girls, you will first need to clearly define *delinquent*. Because humans cannot telepathically communicate their mental images of terms, there is no way to directly communicate which possible meaning of delinquent you have in mind. To ensure that everyone is working with the same definition and mental image, you will need to *conceptualize* and *operationalize* the term. This process is called *operationally* defining a concept.

Operational definitions concretize the intended meaning of a concept in relation to a particular study and provide some criteria for measuring the empirical existence of that concept (Frankfort-Nachmias & Nachmias, 2007; Leedy & Ormrod, 2004).

In operatively defining a term or concept, you, as a researcher, begin by declaring the term to mean whatever you want it to mean throughout the research. Although it is important for your readers to understand what you mean when, for example, you use the concept delinquent, they need not necessarily agree with that definition. As long as they understand what you mean by certain concepts, they can understand and appraise how effectively the concept works in your study. You may even use your literature review to introduce other working definitions of the concept in order to distinguish your definition from these. Researchers routinely introduce changes in the formal definitions of their concepts, building on the accomplishments of past work, refining our tools in pursuit of the nuances of our study topics. Different definitions may coexist, each highlighting a particular aspect of the concept. The important thing is to let your readers know what you mean when you refer to the concept.

Once defined, the concept needs some way to be measured during the research process. In quantitative research, this means creating some index, scale, or similar measurement indicator intended to calculate how much of or to what degree the concept exists. Qualitative investigators also need agreement over what a concept means in a given study and how that concept is to be identified and examined. How will the researcher gather empirical information of data that will inform him or her about that concept?

measurement vs. examined

Consider, for example, the concept *weight*. As a researcher, you might define the concept *weight* as the amount of mass an object possesses in terms of pounds and ounces (measured at g_0). Now everyone holds the same concrete meaning and mental image for the concept *weight*. How shall we measure weight as a social concept? Operationally, weight can be determined by placing an object on a scale and rounding to the nearest ounce. This operational definition clearly tells others what the concept is designated to mean and how it will be measured. Of course, this technical definition tells us nothing about the socially relevant concepts of "ideal weight," or "underweight or overweight," and is clearly insufficient to talk about body image and the marketing of weight-loss programs. There are medical definitions of "obesity," which inform our social definitions of the concept, up to a point. As social researchers, we also need to know where the perceptions of obesity and the impact of obesity on other behaviors depart from the medical measures of one's body-mass index. But on its own, removed from any social context, we know what weight is.

Unfortunately, not all concepts are as easy to define as weight or as easy to measure. Polit and Hungler (1993) and Polit and Beck (2007), for example, suggest that many concepts relevant to research in nursing are not operationalized simply. For instance, in nursing research, the quality of life for chronically ill patients may be defined in terms of physiological, social, and psychological attributes. If the nurse researcher emphasizes the physiological aspects of quality of life for chronically ill patients in his or her definition, the operationalized component may involve measuring white blood cell counts or oxygen output, assessing invasive surgical procedures or ventilation procedures, measuring blood pressure, and so forth.

If, on the other hand, quality of life for chronically ill patients is defined socially, the operationalized elements of the definition would need to measure family or social support, living arrangements, self-management skills, independence, and similar social attributes. Likewise, if the nurse researcher uses a more psychological conceptualization, the operationalized measures would be directed along the lines of the patients' emotional acceptance of chronic illness.

Let's try another illustration of defining and operationalizing. Say you are interested in studying to what degree or extent people are religious. To begin, you must define the concept *religious*. For this example, *religious* will be defined as how actively one is involved with his or her religion. In a sense, we would wish to know how important religion is to one's life on a daily or larger basis. Next, you must decide what kinds of information inform others about someone's active involvement in religion. After consulting the literature, you decide that you know how religious someone is by knowing whether that person believes in a divine being, attends organized religious services on some regular basis, prays at home, reads religious materials, celebrates certain religious holidays, readily declares membership in a particular religion, participates in religious social organizations, and contributes to religious charities.

In effect, you, the researcher, are saying, "I can't immediately apprehend a person's religiousness, but I can think about what elements seem to go into making up or representing observable behaviors that I understand and associate with the meaning of *religious.*" By obtaining information regarding the subset of observable attributes delineated earlier to represent religious, you can study the concept of religiousness, or *religiosity.* As you think about the observable attributes of religiosity—or of any other concept—you should again peruse the literature. By spiraling back into the literature stage, you can seek ways in which others have examined the concept. You may borrow some of these previous attributes, or you may create others.

In some forms of qualitative research, the investigator is not as rigorously concerned with defining concepts in operational terms as outlined here. This is because some forms of interpretative and phenomenological research seek to discover naturally arising meanings among members of study populations. However, in many cases of qualitative research, failure to define and operationalize concepts will spell disaster. If, as a researcher, you have not made clear what your concepts mean, your results may be meaningless in terms of explanatory power or applicability. If you have not thought about how data will be collected to represent attributes of the concept, it will be very difficult for you to determine answers to research questions. And if you have not worked with the literature in developing relevant meanings and measurable attributes, it will be impossible for you to see how eventual results fit into this extant body of knowledge.

Your next problem, then, is to determine exactly how information about various attributes will be obtained. As you reach this point, you move one foot forward toward the design stage of the research enterprise. Naturally, your other foot will remain in the literature stage.

Designing Projects

The design for a research project is literally the plan for how the study will be conducted. It is a matter of thinking about, imagining, and visualizing how the research study will be undertaken (Green & Thorogood, 2007; Leedy & Ormrod, 2004; McTavish & Loether, 2002). Or as Valerie Janesick (1994, 1998) metaphorically describes it, design is the *choreography* that establishes the *research dance.*

It's often unclear what information goes into a research design, and at what level of detail. One possibly useful rule of thumb is that you should write your plan with enough specificity that you could turn it over to several different people to implement, and they would all be able to do more or less the same study. For example, consider a research design that stated, "I will recruit a representative sample of subjects from the community for the interviews." Really, it only states that sampling matters. It doesn't tell us how to define the community, what makes people representative, or even how many subjects to aim for. In contrast, the statement, "I will identify two key informants from the neighborhood, and, using snowball sampling, recruit 15 subjects from each informant's personal network" defines goals and criteria for inclusion. It tells the reader what you actually intend to do.

Research design involves particular requirements, and this book offers guidelines for achieving them. Nonetheless, planning is also a matter of personal style, as Berg illustrates with this story: "My daughter Kate once planned a trip to Vienna to study for a month and to tour various countries in Europe for several weeks. As part of her planning, she arranged her lodgings in each country, the purchase of a Euro-pass, and tickets to several plays and operas all in advance and via the Internet. She even determined she could travel from Spain to France on a night train and thereby save on the cost of a hotel room. Her meal expenses were worked out to the last penny, and she even carried a list of things people had indicated they would like her to bring back for them as souvenirs. My son, on the other hand, took a trip to Palm Desert with a friend. I asked him the name of the hotel where he was staying, and he said he had no idea, but his friend did. I asked if he knew which city in Palm Desert he would be in, and again, he told me, 'I have no clue.' I asked if he was bringing any cash, and he said, 'That would probably be a good idea, huh? Thanks for reminding me. I'll stop at the bank on my way out of town.' This example illustrates that when you have two different people, you often have two different styles of planning. My daughter is meticulous about planning every minute of her trips. My son is a bit looser about details. Designing a research project can similarly run the gamut of being very well planned and organized or more loosely designed. Some researchers, such as Robert Bogdan and Sari Knopp Bilken (2002, p. 49), recommend that you 'hang loose.' I, on the other hand, support a more intentional and planned approach—or at least an approach that falls somewhere between a detailed plan and no plan at all."

In either case, the design stage of research involves a series of important decisions about the research idea or question(s). What types of information will be gathered and through what forms of data-collection technologies? Where will the research be undertaken, and among what group or groups of people (questions of site, setting, and sample)? When conducting research,

Planned but open (see Diagram)

you must decide whether to use a single data-collection strategy or to combine several strategies (data triangulation). Will you undertake the study alone or with the assistance of others (multiple investigator triangulation)? You must consider whether the study will be framed by a single overarching theory or by several related theories (theoretical triangulation). How much will the project cost in terms of time and money, and how much can you actually afford? Are the data-collection strategies appropriate for the research questions being addressed? What will the data (physically) look like once they have been collected? How will the data be organized and analyzed?

In effect, during the design stage, you, the investigator, sketch out the entire research project in an effort to foresee any possible glitches that might arise. If you locate a problem now, while the project is still on the drafting board, there is no harm done. After the project has begun, if you find that concepts have been poorly conceived, that the wrong research questions have been asked, or that the data collected are inappropriate or from the wrong group of people, the project may be ruined.

In addition, the researcher must consider what Morse and Richards (2002) call the pacing of the project. By *pacing*, Morse and Richards (2002, p. 66) mean planning the sequence of various components of the study and the movement between data gathering and data analysis. This planning requires considerable decision making during the design stage and the flexibility to make additional changes during the course of the research: Once you select a data-collection strategy, say field observations, when do you start? Once you have begun, when do you stop? Should you include interviews along with your field observations, even though you did not originally plan to do so? All of these decisions affect the pace, duration, and design of your research.

Researchers in the social sciences typically conduct research on human subjects. The design stage is a time when you, the researcher, must consider whether ethical standards and safeguards for subjects' protection are adequate. You must make certain that subjects will be protected from any harm. Chapter 3 discusses issues of research ethics in detail. For now, regard the design stage as the time when ethical proprieties such as honesty; openness of intent; respect for subjects; issues of privacy, anonymity, and confidentiality; the intent of the research; and the willingness of subjects to participate voluntarily in the study are appraised.

Concept Mapping

For many inexperienced researchers, the development of a research design, creation of a theoretical framework, or even development or use of existing theories can be a very daunting task. At this juncture, therefore, I want to introduce

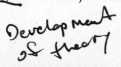

a tool that can assist you in this process and that can also clarify confusions about a particular research design plan or theoretical framework you may want to use. This tool is referred to as *concept mapping* or occasionally *mind mapping* (Kane & Trochim, 2006; Maxwell, 2005; Novak, 1990). A concept map is a technique that allows you to better understand the relationships between ideas, concepts, plans of action, and the like by creating a pictorial representation of these ideas, or plans, and their connections. Concept maps allow you to visualize specific connections between ideas or activities you are thinking about, or to connect new ideas to knowledge that you already possess about a theory or concept. In effect, a concept map permits you to better organize your ideas and plans as you develop your research design or theoretical frame. It is quite literally your *drawing board* for working through research and theoretical plans.

Most sources suggest that the original idea of concept maps can be traced to the work of Joseph Novak (Novak, 1990; Novak & Gowin, 1995) and his colleagues at Cornell University during the 1970s—first to explore the way students learned science and then as a tool for teaching science (Maxwell, 2005; Walker & King, 2002). To the casual observer, a concept map looks like a pretty standard flowchart; it is drawn with boxes or circles called *nodes*, connections between various nodes represented by *lines,* and sometimes arrows, and *labels* that identify what each node is and what the relationships are as represented by the lines. Together, these nodes, lines, and labels represent *propositions* or elements of meaning. Figure 2.2 shows a simple concept map for considering a theoretical framework for a study on health professionals' perceptions of obese patients.

Concept maps have been used in educational settings as a learning strategy, an instructional strategy, a strategy for curriculum planning, and a means of student assessments. In recent years, concept maps have also been integrated into many nursing programs and assist in the development of patient care programs (Carpenito-Moyet, 2007); in evaluation research, concept maps are frequently used to assist in developing plans (designs) for evaluating programs and organizations (Kane & Trochim, 2006). Similar schematic diagramming strategies have been offered in the social sciences by Miles and Huberman under the general rubric of "conceptual frameworks" (Huberman & Miles, 1994, pp. 18–22), by Anselem Strauss as an "integrative diagram" (Strauss, 1987, p. 170), and by Maxwell as literal cognitive maps (Maxwell, 2005, pp. 46–48).

As Figure 2.2 illustrates, a concept map provides a means for organizing and thinking about the researcher's notions about some subject or theoretical premise in a graphic or pictorial manner. This tool is particularly useful for social scientists in developing and detailing ideas and plans for

Figure 2.2 Concept Map of Concepts Pertaining to Social and Health
Professional Perceptions of Obese Teens

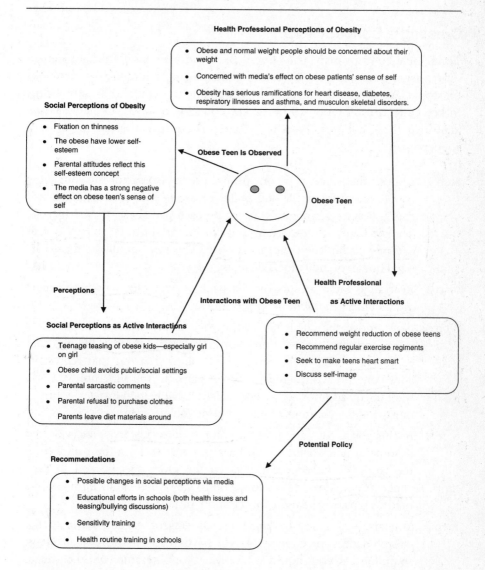

research. It is especially valuable when researchers want to involve relevant
stakeholder groups in the act of creating the research project, as when conducting participatory research efforts (see *Action Research* in Chapter 7).
It should be noted that typically one does not draft and complete a concept map all in one setting. Even the draft of the concept model shown
in Figure 2.2 is largely a first draft that could be refined as the researcher

Add to Syllabus

developed additional information or narrowed his or her focus on specific issues. How then, you may be asking, do you go about creating a concept map?

Creating a Concept Map

To create a concept map, you should first read widely on your subject, in short, begin examining the literature and amassing relevant documents on the topic. As you read through these documents, you should also begin to keep a record of about 10 or 12 key concepts or ideas. Once you have identified these concepts, you may follow these several steps to create a concept map:

Step 1: List out the concepts on one page. I use my laptop for this, but some people are more tactile and prefer to use post-it notes or small pad pages, writing a separate concept on each pad sheet or post-it page. The medium isn't important, but it is important to be able to look at and move all of the concepts at once. This step should yield a good-sized bunch of individual concepts.

Step 2: Rearrange the concepts on the page so you move from the most abstract ideas to the most specific ones.

Step 3: Now, move the concepts on the page under separate columns, or create separate piles of notes so that ideas go directly below other related ideas. This stage gives you a physical layout that represents your conceptual arrangement of the parts. At this juncture, you also want to add additional concepts or labels that help to explain, connect, or expand the columns or piles of ideas you are creating.

Step 4: At this point, you can move the columns into clusters of ideas located at some distance from each other, such that you can draw lines from the larger or broader concepts to the more specific and focused concepts and ideas. This allows you to view where your tight clusters of ideas separate from the looser, more distant interrelations.

Step 5: You are now ready to begin the process of making sense of the clustered ideas and connections you have created in the previous steps. In doing this, you should again review your literature and then begin to assign descriptive labels to the connections among the clusters of concepts or ideas. These terms and labels should explain or identify the relationships you see between these clusters of concepts or ideas.

Step 6: You may want to separately describe examples, or even illustrations (pictures, cartoons) of actions that belong with and may illuminate the concepts and concept clusters.

Step 7: Now, you should reorganize the concepts so that the relationships among them are visually apparent. You may want to create a flowchart using various shapes (circles, squares, rectangles, etc.) to depict the arrangement of the concept and/or idea clusters and connective lines, as in Figure 2.2.

Step 8: The final step is really a refining stage. You may want to show your cognitive plan to others knowledgeable about the general subject area or others working on your research team. From their comments, you may make changes and/or additions to your overall concept map.

One of the great benefits of concept mapping is that it distinguishes between concepts that depend on one another and ones which are distinct but related. For example, if you were to work out a concept map for socioeconomic status (SES), you would certainly need to work in qualitative and quantitative factors that indicate social status and those that indicate economic status. Income is part of SES, so you would need some measure for that. But you wouldn't say that income *relates to* SES, because they are part of the same concept. Many of my students, recognizing that racial categories relate to SES in the United States, also try to fit race into their conceptualization. But race is a separate variable, one which can only be compared to SES because the two are different things.

The final concept map, as suggested previously, may go through a series of further refinements as others review the draft or as you review additional pieces of literature. In addition to the overall design of the research, you will also need to consider other elements, including, for example, the nature of the research setting and the appropriateness of your subjects.

Setting and Population Appropriateness

During the research phase of a project, the investigator must consider a rationale for identifying and using a particular setting as a data-collection site (Marshall & Rossman, 2006). Decisions must also be made regarding who will collect the data and who will comprise the research study population. While choices may be numerous, some advice is in order. First, it is best to be practical. Select a site or setting that is reasonable in size and complexity so the study can be completed within the time and budget you have available. It is also wise to consider your own level of skill, which as a novice researcher is likely to be limited and your confidence somewhat uncertain. The study site or setting should be a location where:

1. Entry or access is possible.
2. The appropriate people (target population) are likely to be available.

3. There is a high probability that the study's focuses, and processes, people, programs, interactions, and structures that are part of the research question(s) will be available to the investigator.
4. The research can be conducted effectively by an individual or individuals during the data-collection phase of the study.

Also, don't use a shopping mall, unless your study is about shopping.

The research question is generally regarded as the primary guide to the appropriate site or setting selection (Flick, 2006; Leedy & Ormrod, 2004; Marshall & Rossman, 2006; Silverman, 2006). For example, if the research question has to do with why some battered women remain with their battering spouses, the data-collection site must be a safe place related to battered women, such as a shelter for battered women and children. If you want to know more about women who leave their husbands, try family court. To understand popular *representations* of battering, look to television, newspapers, and magazines. Or, if your research concerns effective intervention strategies, contact mediation centers and family counseling services.

In many cases, the decision to use a particular research site is tied closely to obtaining access to an appropriate population of potential subjects. Poor study site selection and poor sample decisions may weaken or ruin eventual findings (National Research Council, 2005). You must be careful to identify an *appropriate* population, not merely an easily accessible one. For instance, let's say you wanted to conduct a study investigating the opinions or practices of Native Americans. One easy way of locating a site and population might be to turn to college students. After all, college students are easy to locate on college campuses. They are likely to be willing to take part in an interview—either out of curiosity or to help out another student. But you must ask the question: What pertinent information will the average non–Native American college student have regarding how Native Americans think, perceive their social world, or practice their particular lifestyles? In other words, if you want to know about Native Americans, then you need to locate a setting where Native Americans can be accessed. That point may seem obvious, but we still encounter studies of the impact of new policies that are conducted among voters who don't actually have any knowledge of the policy, or studies of race relations that only gather data from members of one racial group. The subjects in these groups may well have opinions about the topics without actually possessing relevant knowledge or experience.

Sometimes researchers identify what they believe to be an appropriate study population, but they cannot immediately see where an appropriate setting might be for data collection. For example, several years ago, Berg had a student interested in conducting a study about fear of crime among the blind.

On the surface, this sounds like a good research topic. The problem arose when Berg asked him how (and where) he planned to access such a population of potential subjects.

The student reported that he had discussed his need to access blind people to conduct a study of their perceptions of fear of crime with another faculty member. The faculty member—who was obviously not terribly versed in research methods—suggested that the student simply go to one of the large introductory classes and divide the class in half. Then he suggested that the student have half the class place blindfolds over their eyes and spend a period of time walking around campus (ushered by one of the other nonblind-folded students). Following this experience, the students could switch off, so both groups experienced *blindness*. Next, the class could be administered a pencil-and-paper survey about their fear of crime, having now experienced the precariousness of not being able to see. The student immediately recognized that this would not be an appropriate setting or sample for his study. Wisely, however, he did not argue with the faculty member but rather thanked him and explained that he wanted to conduct a more qualitative study. (See "Disengaging," in Chapter 6.)

The student then did some background research and came up with an actual plan. He indicated that he intended to attend a summer camp for the blind sponsored by several nonprofit agencies. He had learned that the population of the camp came from the entire state and that no one who wanted to attend was ever turned away (those who could not afford to pay were awarded camp scholarships). Thus, the camp contained a population from various socioeconomic strata, races, ages, and both men and women. The student spent the summer and was able to conduct both nearly 60 interviews and some limited participant observation (Rounds, 1993). The quality of the research depended on the appropriateness of the research setting.

Another problem may arise when one must pay a fee for accessing certain types of settings, such as oral history archives that may charge a fee for use, or a fee for reproduction of various interviews (Ritchie, 2003). Most archives do not charge merely for a researcher examining materials they house, but may charge if the researcher plans on publishing long lengths or excerpts of material from an interview housed in the archive. Cost may also become a factor for seemingly "public" settings, such as sporting events. There was a time when a student researcher could go to all of their local professional team's home games for a month to observe the crowd, but such a study now would require a large grant. Most bars don't charge for entry, but costs can add up for a researcher trying to "participate" in the setting. Situations such as these require one to reconcile the benefits of the particular source materials (the particular archive or location as a research setting), possible alternative settings, and the costs.

Sampling Strategies

The logic of using a sample of subjects is to make inferences about some larger population from a smaller one—the sample. Such inferences succeed or fail according to how well the sample *represents* the population. In large quantitative studies, the investigator is keenly concerned with probability sampling. The concept of *probability sampling* is based on the notion that a sample can be selected that will mathematically represent subgroups of some larger population (Shaughnessy, 2008; Vito, Kunselman, & Tewksbury, 2008). The parameters required for creating these probability samples are quite restrictive but allow the investigator to make various inferential hypothesis tests (using various statistical techniques). The most commonly discussed probability sample is the *simple random* sample. The simple random sample most closely approximates the ideals in probability sampling. To accomplish a simple random sample, each element in the full population must have an equal and independent chance of inclusion in the eventual sample to be studied. Simple random sampling typically begins with a full listing of every element in the full population to be investigated (see Figure 2.3).

The social sciences often examine research situations in which one cannot select the kinds of probability samples used in large-scale surveys and which conform to the restricted needs of a probability sample. Many populations can be described, but not enumerated or listed. Some populations are deliberately hidden, while others may simply be difficult to locate. In these situations, investigators rely on *nonprobability samples.*

In nonprobability sampling, the investigator does not base his or her sample selection on probability theory. Rather, efforts are undertaken (1) to create a kind of quasi-random sample and (2) to have a clear idea about what larger group or groups the sample may reflect. Nonprobability samples offer the benefits of not requiring a list of all possible elements in a full population and the ability to access otherwise highly sensitive or difficult-to-research study populations. For example, it would be very difficult to undertake a study of active prostitutes, because it would be virtually impossible to create a list of all of the prostitutes in a given area. At best, one might create a listing of all the known (convicted) prostitutes. Thus, frequently in the social sciences, a researcher is presented with interesting and potentially important research questions that cannot be answered by a probability sampling technique. From the perspective of qualitative research, nonprobability sampling tends to be the norm. The following sections describe the four most common types of nonprobability samples.

Convenience Samples   The convenience sample is sometimes referred to as an *accidental* or *availability sample* (Babbie, 2007; Mutchnick & Berg, 1996; Polit & Beck, 2007). This category of sample relies on available subjects—those

Figure 2.3 Probability Sampling Strategies

Simple Random Sampling. Typically, this procedure is intended to produce a representative sample. The process draws subjects from an identified population in such a manner that every unit in that population has precisely the same chance (probability) of being included in the sample.

Systematic Random Sampling. The use of a systematic sample provides a convenient way to draw a sample from a large identified population when a printed list of that population is available. In systematic sampling, every nth name is selected from the list. Usually the interval between names on the list is determined by dividing the number of persons desired in the sample into the full population. For example, if a final sample of 80 was desired and the population list contained 2,560 names, the researchers would divide 2,560 by 80. The resulting 32 becomes the interval between names on the list. It is important, however, to begin the list at some random starting place. Frequently, researchers select a number between 1 and 20 (usually taken from a random numbers table) and begin at that location on the list and then stop at every nth name—in our example, at every thirty-second name on the list.

Stratified Random Sampling. A stratified sample is used whenever researchers need to ensure that a certain sample of the identified population under examination is represented in the sample. The population is divided into subgroups (strata), and independent samples of each stratum are selected. Within each stratum, a particular sampling fraction is applied in order to ensure representativeness of proportions in the full population. Thus, sampling fractions in some strata may differ from those of others in the same sample. Stratified samples can be used only when information is available to divide the population into strata.

who are close at hand or easily accessible. For example, it used to be fairly common for college and university professors to use their students as subjects in their research projects. This technique has been used all too frequently and has some serious risks associated with it (Gilligan, 1982). Specifically, often a researcher is interested in studying characteristics or processes that college students simply are not equipped to offer information about. Consider again, for example, the suggested use of blindfolded students to study fear of crime among the blind.

Under certain circumstances, this strategy is an excellent means of obtaining preliminary information about some research question quickly and inexpensively. For example, if an investigator were interested in examining how college students perceive drinking and drunkenness, he or she could easily make use of a convenience sample of college students. If, on the other hand, the researcher was interested in studying self-images among blue-collar workers, he or she could not use this convenience sample of college students and simply ask them to pretend that they are blue-collar workers when answering the researcher's questions. In other words, convenience samples must be evaluated very carefully for their appropriateness of fit for a given study.

Purposive Samples   This category of sampling is sometimes called *judgmental sampling* (Hagan, 2006). When developing a purposive sample, researchers use their special knowledge or expertise about some group to select subjects who represent this population. In some instances, purposive samples are selected after field investigations on some group in order to ensure that certain types of individuals or persons displaying certain attributes are included in the study. Despite some serious limitations (e.g., the lack of wide generalizability), purposive samples are often used by researchers. Laquinta and Larrabee (2004), for example, used a purposive sample to examine the lived experiences of a small sample of patients with rheumatoid arthritis. The results were a rich and textured description of what it is like to live with rheumatoid arthritis, as well as a number of nursing practices related to care quality.

Snowball Samples   Another nonprobability sampling strategy, which some may see as similar to convenience sampling, is known as snowball sampling, chain referral sampling (Biemacki & Waldorf, 1981; Owens, 2005; Penrod, Preston, Cain, & Stark, 2003), or respondent-driven sampling (Heckathorn & Jeffri, 2003). Snowballing is sometimes the best way to locate subjects with certain attributes or characteristics necessary in the study. Snowball samples are particularly popular among researchers interested in studying various classes of deviance, sensitive topics, or difficult-to-reach populations (Lee, 1993).

The basic strategy of snowballing involves first identifying several people with relevant characteristics and interviewing them or having them answer a questionnaire. These subjects are then asked for the names (referrals) of other people who possess the same attributes they do—in effect, a chain of subjects driven by the referral of one respondent of another.

If you wanted to learn more about, say, drug use or theft by nurses, the use of some sort of probability sample would seem out of the question. But, through use of a few informants, field investigations, or other strategies, the researcher might identify a small number of nurses with these characteristics. By asking these first subjects for referrals of additional nurses, the sample eventually "snowballs" from a few subjects to many subjects (e.g., Dabney & Berg, 1994; Wright, Decker, Redfern, & Smith, 2006).

Quota Samples   A quota sample begins with a kind of matrix or table that creates cells or stratum. The researcher may wish to use gender, age, education, or any other attributes to create and label each stratum or cell in the table. Which attributes are selected will have to do with the research question and study focuses. The quota sampling strategy then uses a nonprobability method to fill these cells. Please note that I said "method," not "methods." Each category in the overall sample must be filled using the same recruitment strategy in order for the resulting groups to be comparable. Next, the researcher needs to determine the proportion of each attribute in the full-study population (Babbie, 2007). For instance, let's say a researcher wants to study perceptions of violence among people in the United States, with a special interest in people over age 65. Census data would provide the researcher with reasonable estimates of people over age 65, as well as various categories under age 65. The research could create various age cohorts—people over 65, 45–65, 25–44, and under 25. Next, the researcher could determine the proportion of people in each of these age groups. Following this, the investigator could select a region of the country and sample people in that area, identifying the same proportion of people for each age cohort as identified in the census data.

All is data

Data Collection and Organization

As you begin visualizing how the research project will unfold, you must also imagine what the data will look like. Will raw data be audiotape cassettes that result from long interviews? Will the data comprise dozens of spiral notebooks filled with field notes? Will the data include photographs or video recordings? Will they entail systematic observational checklists or copies of files containing medical or criminal histories? Could data actually be the smudges left on a polished counter or glass display case? Just what will the research data look like?

   The next question to be answered is, What do you do with the data to organize them and make them ready for analysis? As Morse and Richards (2002, p. 100) point out, "the volume of data that qualitative researchers must manage is enormous. Researchers tell stories of 'drowning in data,' of stacking piles of data in their basements, or of not being able to use their dining room table for several months while the process of analysis is ongoing." It is frequently at this point in the research enterprise that many students fall flat on their faces and find themselves hopelessly lost, even after having taken several research courses. While most research courses and textbooks are excellent at describing the basic structures of research, few move the student into the areas of data organization and analysis. Typically, the results are that students come up with excellent ideas for research, conduct solid literature reviews, produce what sounds like viable research designs, and may even collect massive amounts of data. The problem arises, however, at this juncture: What do you do with all that collected data?

If you were doing quantitative research, there might be an easy answer to the question of organization and analysis. You would reduce the data to spreadsheet form and enter them into a database. Then, using a packaged statistical program for the social sciences, you would endeavor to analyze the data. Lamentably, qualitative data are not as quickly or easily handled. A common mistake made by many inexperienced or uninformed researchers is to reduce qualitative data to symbolic numeric representations and quantitatively computer-analyze them. As Berg and Berg (1993) stated, this ceases at once to be a qualitative research and amounts to little more than a suspect variation of quantitative data collection and analysis.

How qualitative data are organized depends in part on what the data look like. If they are in textual form, such as field notes, or can be made into textual form, such as by transcribing a tape-recorded interview, they may be organized in one manner. If they are video, photographic, or drawn material, they will require a different form of organization and analysis. But regardless of the data form, you must consider this issue during the design stage of the process. Again, this points to the spiraling effect of research activities. If you wait until data have actually been collected to consider how they are to be organized for analysis, serious problems may arise. For example, you may not have planned for adequate time or financial resources. Or you might collect data in such a way that they should be systematically organized, coded, or indexed as they were collected and not after the fact. In any event, you must direct thought toward how data will be organized and analyzed long before you begin the data-collection process.

Typically, the recently collected raw data are not immediately available for analysis. Rather, the raw data require some sort of organizing and processing before they can actually be analyzed. Field notes, for example, may fill hundreds of pages of notebooks or take up many megabytes of space on disk. These notes need to be edited, corrected, and made more readable, even before they can be organized, indexed, or entered into a computer-generated text analysis program file. Recorded interviews must be transcribed (transformed into written text), corrected, and edited also before being somehow indexed or entered into a text-based computer analysis program. The volume of pages of qualitative raw data can sometimes be quite daunting to the inexperienced researcher.

Thus, understanding how data can be organized and managed is very important. This directs our attention to notions of data storage and retrieval.

Data Storage, Retrieval, and Analysis

A clear and working storage and retrieval system is critical if one expects to keep track of the reams of data that have been collected, to flexibly access and use the data, and to assure systematic analysis and documentation of the data. In this way the study can, in principle, be verified through replication.

Auerbach and Silverstein (2003), Huberman and Miles (1994), and Marshall and Rossman (2006) all argue that data management and data analysis are integrally related. There are, in fact, no rigid boundaries between them. The main concerns are as follows:

1. A system that ensures high-quality accessibility to the data.
2. Documentation of any analysis that is carried out.
3. Retention and protection of data and related analysis of documents after the study has been completed.

From the perspective of this book, and in keeping with the preceding three issues, data analysis can be defined as consisting of three concurrent flows of action: data reduction, data display, and conclusions and verification (see also Huberman & Miles, 1994, pp. 10–12).

Data Reduction   In qualitative research, data reduction does not necessarily refer to quantifying nominal data. Qualitative data need to be *reduced* and *transformed* (coded) in order to make them more readily accessible, understandable, and to draw out various themes and patterns. Data reduction acknowledges the voluminous nature of qualitative data in the raw. It directs attention to the need for focusing, simplifying, and transforming raw data into a more manageable form. Frequently, data reduction occurs throughout the research project's life. For example, as in-depth interviews are completed and hours of audiotapes are created, the interviews are also transcribed into print by word-processing programs and/or computer-based textual analysis formats. As the project continues, further elements of data reduction will occur (written summaries, development of grounded themes, identification of analytic themes, consideration of relevant theoretical explanations, etc.). This data-reduction and transformation process occurs throughout the span of the research.

Coded to draw out themes & patterns

Data Display   The notion of data display is intended to convey the idea that data are presented as an organized, compressed assembly of information that permits conclusions to be analytically drawn. Displays may involve tables of data; tally sheets of themes; summaries or proportions of various statements, phrases, or terms; and similarly reduced and transformed groupings of data. These displays assist the researcher in understanding and observing certain patterns in the data or determining what additional analysis or actions must be taken. As with the activity of data reduction, the development of displays is not really a separate step but rather a component of the analysis process.

Conclusions and Verification   The last analysis activity I will discuss is conclusion drawing and verification. Throughout the research process, the investigator has been making various informed evaluations and decisions about the study and the data. Sometimes these have been made on the basis of material found in existing literature (as the researcher spirals back and forth to the literature). Sometimes these evaluations and decisions have arisen as a result of data as they are collected (based on observations in the field, statements made during interviews, observations of patterns in various documents, etc.). Yet, experienced researchers do not make definitive conclusions during these preliminary periods in the research process. Rather, they hold an open and perhaps even a skeptical point of view. In fact, some of the tentative outcomes have aided in data-reduction and data-display activities. Eventually, after the data have been collected, reduced, and displayed, analytic conclusions may begin to emerge and define themselves more clearly and definitively.

Verification is actually a twofold consideration. First, conclusions drawn from the patterns apparent in the data must be confirmed (verified) to assure that they are real and not merely wishful thinking on the part of the researcher. This may be accomplished by the researcher carefully checking the path to his or her conclusion (i.e., retracing the various analytic steps that led to the conclusion). Or, it may involve having another researcher independently examine the displays and data to see if he or she will draw comparable conclusions, a kind of intercoder reliability check.

Second, verification involves assuring that all of the procedures used to arrive at the eventual conclusions have been clearly articulated. In this manner, another researcher could potentially replicate the study and the analysis procedures and draw comparable conclusions. The implication of this second verification strand implies that qualitative analysis needs to be very well documented as a process. In addition to its availability to other researchers, it permits evaluation of your analysis strategies, self-reflection, and refinement of methods and procedures.

Dissemination

Once the research project has been completed, it is not really over. That is, doing research for the sake of doing it offers no benefit to the scientific community or to the existing body of knowledge it might inform. Research, then, is not complete until it has been disseminated. This may be accomplished through reports submitted to appropriate public agencies or to funding sources. It may include informal presentations to colleagues at brown-bag lunches or formal presentations at professional association meetings. It may involve publishing reports in one of a variety of academic or professional journals. Regardless of how the information is spread, it must be disseminated if it is to be considered both worthwhile and complete. Chapter 12 explains how you may go about disseminating your research results. For the purposes of designing research projects, it is important to bear in mind that this stage of the research process is integral to the whole.

TRYING IT OUT

There are a number of ways you can practice aspects related to the planning of research. A few suggestions follow that should provide an opportunity to gain some experience. Although these are useful experiential activities, they should not be confused with actually conducting research.

Suggestion 3   Identify six concepts and operationally define each. Be sure to consult relevant literature before terms are defined. Do not make up definitions. When operatively defining how each concept will be measured, be certain these operations conform to both relevant literature and the qualitative paradigm.

Suggestion 4   Run a Web search on the term *asthma*. Now check on the different resources that may be available if you add the search terms "peer reviewed" or "magazine."

REFERENCES

Auerbach, C., & Silverstein, C. B. (2003). *Qualitative Data: An Introduction to Coding and Analysis.* New York: New York University Press.
Babbie, E. (2007). *The Practice of Social Research* (11th ed.). Belmont, CA: Wadsworth.
Ball, R. A., & Curry, G. D. (1995). The logic of definition in criminology: Purposes and methods for defining "gang." *Criminology 33*(2), 225–245.

Berg, B. L., & Berg, J. (1993). A reexamination of triangulation and objectivity in qualitative nursing research. *Free Inquiry in Creative Sociology 21*(1), 65–72.

Biemacki, P., & Waldorf, D. (1981). Snowball sampling: Problems and techniques of chain referral sampling. *Sociological Methods & Research 10*(2), 141–163.

Bogdan, R., & Knopp Bilken, S. (2002). *Qualitative Research for Education* (4th ed.). Boston, MA: Allyn and Bacon.

Brown, P. (1998). *Catskill Culture: A Mountain Rat's Memories of the Grand Jewish Resort Area.* Philadelphia, PA: Temple University Press.

Brown, P. (2002). *In the Catskills. A Century of Jewish Experience in the Mountains.* New York: Columbia University Press.

Bynum, J. E., & Thompson, W. E. (1992). *Juvenile Delinquency: A Sociological Approach.* Boston, MA: Allyn and Bacon.

Carpenito-Moyet, L. J. (2007). *Understanding the Nursing Process: Concept Mapping and Care Planning for Students.* Philadelphia, PA: Lippincott Williams & Wilkins.

Dabney, D. A., & Berg, B. L. (1994). Perceptions of drug and supply diversion among nurses. *Free Inquiry in Creative Sociology 22*(1), 13–22.

Denzin, N. K. (1978). *Sociological Methods: A Source Book* (2nd ed.). New York: McGraw-Hill.

Denzin, N. K., & Lincoln, Y. S. (2008). *The Landscape of Qualitative Research* (3rd ed.). Los Angeles, CA: Sage.

Flick, U. (2006). *An Introduction to Qualitative Research* (3rd ed.). Newbury Park, CA: Sage.

Frankfort-Nachmias, C., & Nachmias, D. (2007). *Research Methods in the Social Sciences* (7th ed.). New York: Worth Publishing.

Galvin, J. (1999). *Writing Literature Reviews: A Guide for Students of the Social and Behavioral Sciences.* Glendale, CA: Pyrczak Publishing.

Gilligan, C. (1982). *In a Different Voice.* Cambridge, MA: Harvard University Press.

Green, J., & Thorogood, N. (2007). *Qualitative Methods for Health Research.* Thousand Oaks, CA: Sage.

Hagan, F. E. (2006). *Research Methods in Criminal Justice and Criminology* (7th ed.). Boston, MA: Allyn and Bacon.

Heckathorn, D. D., & Jeffri, J. (2003). Social movements of jazz musicians. In Changing the Beat: A Study of the Work Life of Jazz Musicians, Volume III: Respondent-Driven Sampling: Survey Results by the Research Center for Arts and Culture. *Research Division Report* 43, pp. 48–61. National Endowment for the Arts, Washington, DC.

Huberman, M. A., & Miles, M. B. (1994). Data management and analysis methods. In N. Denzin & Y. S. Lincoln (Eds.), *Handbook of Qualitative Research.* Thousand Oaks, CA: Sage.

Janesick, V. J. (1994). The dance of qualitative research design. In N. Denzin and Y. S. Lincoln (Eds.), *Handbook of Qualitative Research.* Thousand Oaks, CA: Sage.

Janesick, V. J. (1998). *Stretching Exercises for Qualitative Researchers.* Thousand Oaks, CA: Sage.

Kane, M., & Trochim, W. M. K. (2006). *Concept Mapping for Planning and Evaluation* (Applied Social Research Methods Series Vol. 50). Thousand, Oaks, CA: Sage.

Laquinta, M. L., & Larrabee, J. H. (July–September 2004). Phenomenological lived experiences of patients with rheumatic arthritis. *Journal of Nursing Care Quality 19*(3), 280–289.

Lee, R. M. (1993). *Doing Research on Sensitive Topics.* Newbury Park, CA: Sage.

Leedy, P., & Ormrod, J. E. (2004). *Practical Research: Planning and Design* (8th ed.). Upper Saddle River, NJ: Prentice Hall.

Lune, H., Pumar E., & Koppel, R. (eds.) (2009). *Perspectives in Social Research Methods and Analysis. A Reader for Sociology* (3rd ed.). Thousand Oaks, CA: Sage Publications.

Marshall, C., & Rossman, G. B. (2006). *Designing Qualitative Research* (4th ed.). Newbury Park, CA: Sage.

Maxfield, M. G., & Babbie, E. (2007). *Research Methods for Criminal Justice and Criminology* (5th ed.). Belmont, CA: Wadsworth.

Maxwell, J. A. (2005). *Qualitative Research Design: An Interactive Approach* (2nd ed.). Thousand Oaks, CA: Sage.

McTavish, D. G., & Loether, H. J. (2002). *Social Research: An Evolving Process* (2nd ed.). Boston, MA: Allyn and Bacon.

Merton, R. K. (1968). *Social Theory and Social Structure* (Rev. and Enlarged ed.). New York: Free Press.

Morse, J. M., & Richards, L. (2002). *Read Me First: For a User's Guide to Qualitative Methods.* Thousand Oaks, CA: Sage.

Mutchnick, R. J., & Berg, B. L. (1996). *Research Methods for the Social Sciences: Practice and Applications.* Boston, MA: Allyn and Bacon.

National Research Council (2005). *Access to Research Data: Reconciling Risks and Opportunities.* Washington, DC: National Academy of Sciences.

Neuman, W. L. (2000). *Social Research Methods: Qualitative and Quantitative Approaches.* Boston, MA: Allyn and Bacon.

Novak, J. D. (1990). Concept mapping: A useful tool for science education. *Journal of Research in Science Teaching 27*(10), 937–950.

Novak, J. D., & Gowin, D. B. (1995). *Learning How to Learn.* New York: Cambridge University Press.

Owens, B. (February 2005). *Personal Communication at the Western Society of Criminology Meeting,* Oahu, Hawaii.

Penrod, J., Preston, D. B., Cain, R. E., & Stark, M. T. (2003). A discussion of chain referral as a method of sampling hard-to-reach populations. *Journal of Transcultural Nursing 14*(2), 100–107.

Polit, D. F., & Beck, C. T. (2007). *Nursing Research: Generating and Assessing Evidence for Nursing Practice.* Philadelphia, PA: Lippincott Williams & Wilkins.

Polit, D. F., Beck, C. T., & Hungler, B. P. (2003). *Nursing Research: Principles and Practice* (7th ed.). Philadelphia, PA: Lippincott Williams & Wilkins.

Polit, D. F., & Hungler, B. P. (1993). *Essentials of Nursing Research.* Philadelphia, PA: Lippincott Williams & Wilkins.

Popper, K. R. (1968). *Conjectures and Refutations: The Growth of Scientific Knowledge.* New York: Harper and Row.

Praetorius, N. (2000). *Principles of Cognition, Language, and Action.* Netherlands: Kluwer Academic Publishers.

Punch, K. F. (2006). *Developing Effective Research Proposals* (2nd ed.). London: Sage.

Reynolds. L. T., & Herman-Kinney, N. J. (2003). *Handbook of Social Interactionism.* New York: Rowman & Littlefield.

Ritchie, D. A. (2003). *Doing Oral Histories* (2nd ed.). New York: Oxford University Press.

Rounds, D. (1993). Perceptions of crime and victimization among individuals with legal blindness and severe visual impairment: An exploratory study. Doctoral dissertation. Department of Criminology, Indiana University of Pennsylvania, Indiana, PA.

Shaughnessy, J. J. (2008) *Research Methods in Psychology* (8th ed.). New York: McGraw-Hill.

Siegel, L. J., & Welsh, B. C. (2008). *Juvenile Delinquency: Theory, Practice, and Law* (11th ed.). Belmont, CA: Wadsworth Publishing Company.

Silverman, D. (2006). *Interpreting Qualitative Data* (3rd ed.). Thousand Oaks, CA: Sage.

Stone, J. (2001). Behavioral discrepancies and the role of constructural processes in cognitive dissonance. In G. B. Moskowitz (Ed.), *Cognitive Social Psychology* (pp. 41–59). Mahwah, NJ: Lawrence Erlbaum Associates, Inc., Publishing.

Strauss, A. L. (1987). *Qualitative Analysis for Social Scientists.* New York: Cambridge University Press.

Taylor, S. J., & Bogdan, R. (1998). *Qualitative Research Methods* (3rd ed.). New York: John Wiley and Sons.

Thornton, W. E., Jr., & Voigt, L. (1992). *Delinquency and Justice* (3rd ed.). New York: McGraw-Hill.

Turner, J. H. (1989). *Theory Building in Sociology: Assessing Theoretical Cumulation.* Newbury Park, CA: Sage.

Vito, G. F., Kunselman, J., & Tewksbury, R. (2008). *Introduction to Criminal Justice Research Methods: An Applied Approach.* Chicago, IL: Charles C. Thomas Publishers.

Walker, J. M. T., & King, P. H. (2002). Concept mapping as a form of student assessment and instruction. Presented at the annual meeting of the American Society of Engineering Education Conference and Exposition, Quebec, Canada.

Wright, R., Decker, S. H., Redfern, A. K., & Smith, D. L. (2006). A snowball's chance in hell: Doing fieldwork with active residential burglars. In J. Mitchell Miller & Richard Tewksbury (Eds.), *Research Methods: A Qualitative Reader.* Upper Saddle River, NJ: Pearson/Prentice Hall.

Zinberg, N. E. (1984). *Drug, Set, and Setting: The Basis for Controlled Intoxicant Use.* New Haven, CT: Yale University Press.

Chapter 3

Ethical Issues

OCIAL SCIENTISTS, PERHAPS TO a greater extent than the average citizen, have an ethical obligation to their colleagues,
their study populations, and the larger society. The reason
for this is that social scientists delve into the lives of other human beings. From
such excursions into private social lives, various policies, practices, and even
laws may result. Thus, researchers must ensure the rights, privacy, and welfare
of the people and communities that form the focus of their studies.

During the past several decades, methods of data collection, organization,
and analysis have become more sophisticated and penetrating. As a consequence,
the extent or scope of research has greatly expanded. With this expansion has
come increased awareness and concern over the ethics of research and researchers.

To a large extent, concerns about research ethics revolve around various
issues of harm, consent, privacy, and the confidentiality of data (ASA, 1997;
Punch, 1994, 2005). This chapter considers these important ethical concerns
as associated with research in general and with qualitative research in particular.

Among the fundamental tenets of ethical social scientific research is
the notion of *do no harm*. This quite literally refers to avoiding physical and
emotional (psychological) harm. As Babbie (2007) suggests, few people would
seriously disagree with this basic concept, in principle. Sometimes, however, it
is difficult to follow absolutely in practice—difficult but not impossible.

Researchers eager to gain access to some population that might otherwise be difficult to reach may pride themselves on their clever plans to locate
a hidden population without recognizing the ethical implications of their
actions if they involve deception or invasions of privacy, for example. Some
overly zealous researchers, while realizing that certain of their practices may
be unethical, nonetheless plunge forward, justifying their actions under the
excuse that it isn't illegal! And some otherwise sensible researchers, desperate to
produce some results before their funding runs out, might feel the pressure

to cut some corners. Most often, I strongly suspect, ethical failures occur due to carelessness, or the simple fact of not having worked out all the details of one's research design.

Many experienced researchers can tell with regret war stories about having violated some tenet of ethics in their less-experienced years. The transgression may have involved allowing some gatekeeper to manipulate subjects to take part in a study (under veiled threat of some loss of privilege), or it may have involved some covert investigation that resulted in subtle invasions of privacy. In any case, these now experienced researchers are still likely to feel somewhat embarrassed when they think about these instances—at least one hopes they do.

Often, glaring violations of ethical standards are recognized nearly as soon as the researchers have conceived them. Frequently, during planning stages, particularly when conducting research together with a colleague, ethical problems are identified and worked through. This is not to say that practices that might appear unethical to others outside the study are always eliminated. Rather, the process, like much of qualitative research, is a negotiation, a trade-off for the amount of access to subjects the researchers are willing to accept in exchange for the amount of ethical risk they are willing to take.

It is not difficult to understand that injecting unknowing subjects with live HIV (the AIDS virus) is unethical. It may not be quite as easy to see that studying drug dealers and then turning over their addresses and field notes as evidence to the police is also unethical. This latter example is somewhat more difficult to see because a law-abiding attitude is probably so well ingrained in most researchers that the logical response seems obvious—namely, if citizens can prevent criminal behavior, they have a moral obligation to do so. However, precisely because such tensions between logic and ethics exist, careful consideration of ethical issues is critical to the success or failure of any high-quality research involving humans.

The first portion of this chapter examines some of the historical background of research ethics, including some of the major events that influenced current ethical research practices. Ethical elements commonly considered important when researchers involve human subjects in their research are then addressed.

Research Ethics in Historical Perspective

Contemporary discussions on research ethics run a wide gamut from highly procedural approaches (trying to find the right set of rules) to highly conceptual, such as feminist, postmodern or postcolonial concerns with the objectification of "the subject" in research or the institutionalization of the dominant group's version of reality. Regardless of one's orientation or thoughts on specific elements of ethical behavior and practice, there is general agreement in the literature that current concerns with research ethics grew out of biomedical research, particularly the ghoulish torture and dismemberment perpetrated under the guise of medical research by Nazi physicians and scientists during World War II. For instance, in the name of science, physicians exposed subjects to freezing temperatures, live viruses, poisons, malaria, and an assortment of untested drugs and experimental operations (Berger, 1990; Burns & Grove, 2000; Hagan, 2006; Trochim, 2001). This wartime medical research led to the formation of the Nuremberg Code in 1949. This code established principles for research on human subjects, most notably, that subjects must *voluntarily consent* to participate in a research study (Wexler, 1990, p. 81).

This ethical canon became the foundation of the Declaration of Helsinki, adopted by the World Health Organization in 1964 and revised in 1975 (Levine, 1986). It was also the basis for the "Ethical Guidelines for Clinical Investigation" adopted by the American Medical Association in 1966 (Bower & de Gasparis, 1978). Yet, as Katz (1972) has indicated, years later and thousands of miles away from the bloodstained walls of Nazi operating rooms, extremely risky—sometimes fatal—research was being carried out on unknowing patients here in the United States. Consider, for example, the case of two research physicians at the Brooklyn Jewish Chronic Disease Hospital, who during the mid-1960s injected a suspension containing live cancer cells into 22 unsuspecting elderly patients (Levine, 1986). Although media and public pressure brought an end to the experiment, neither physician was ever prosecuted on any sort of criminal charge (Hershey & Miller, 1976).

Interestingly, before the 1960s, few laws regulated the research process. Consequently, no legal redress was available to subjects, even if they had been wronged by a behavioral scientist. Highly questionable practices in research throughout the late 1950s and 1960s repeatedly demonstrated the need for regulation and control of studies involving human subjects.

For instance, the U.S. Public Health Service once conducted a study that is regarded by many as the most glaring violation of ethical practices. This project has come to be called the Tuskegee Syphilis Study (Brandt, 1978; Gray, 2002; Hagan, 2006; Jones, 1993). This project, which spanned more than 40 years, was a longitudinal study whose purpose was to identify a population of syphilitic black men and to observe in these subjects, over a period of time, the consequences of untreated syphilis. One of the study's original creators is attributed as having made the following prophetic statements about the project: "It will cover us with mud or glory when completed" (Jones, 1993, p. 112). Today many would likely agree that the project did indeed cover the researchers and the U.S. Public Health Service with mud.

Although the researchers on the study did not themselves infect the subjects, once the study had begun, the investigative team actively interfered with the lives and health of the subjects without their consent (Jones, 1993). The study began in 1932 when no cure for syphilis existed. After a cure (penicillin) was identified in the 1950s, the research team actively sought to keep the existence of the treatment from their subjects. This included offering free so-called treatment and health services to the sample of men, as well as contacting local African American physicians and instructing them not to treat (for syphilis) any of the 400 men involved in the study.

To ensure that an autopsy could be done on any subject who died during the experiment, the team offered free burial services. Surviving family members typically were unaware that free burial was conditional on allowing an autopsy. The study ended in 1972 after it was exposed by the news media, and public pressure forced officials to terminate the study. Yet the study had not been conducted in secret until then. Questions were raised in the 1960s, leading to endorsements of the project by the Centers for Disease Control and the American Medical Association (CDC, 2009). Following the public exposure of the study in 1971, the Department of Health, Education, and Welfare (the parent agency of the U.S. Public Health Service) appointed a panel that concluded that the research had been "ethically unjustified." The study was ended at that point in time.

On May 16, 1997, 65 years after it had begun—and 23 years after it had ended—President Clinton publicly apologized to the families of the subjects and the surviving subjects in the Tuskegee Syphilis Study (Clinton, 1997). In his remarks, President Clinton stated the following:

> The eight men who are survivors of the syphilis study at Tuskegee are a living link to a time not so very long ago that many Americans would prefer not to remember, but we dare not forget. It was a time when our nation failed to live up to its ideals, when our nation broke the trust with people that is the very foundation of our democracy. It is not only in remembering that shameful past that we can make amends and repair our nation, but it is in remembering that past that we can build a better present and better future. And without remembering it, we cannot make amends and we cannot go forward.

It would be comforting to imagine that this one study was an aberration, a one-time failure of epic proportions, but this is not the case. In fact, it was recently discovered that a second syphilis study was conducted in Guatemala by researchers working for the U.S. government (Reverby, 2011). While the Guatemalan study lasted only two years, it was in many ways more egregious in its design. Mental patients, prisoners, and soldiers were deliberately exposed to syphilis (with the cooperation of infected prostitutes) in order to test the effectiveness of penicillin. Significantly, both of these studies targeted people of color. Although the government's official apologies in 1997 and 2010 were an important step toward repairing the breach of faith inflicted on these communities, the "negative legacy" of the Tuskegee study continues to impede researchers' efforts to conduct an assortment of research projects, particularly those involving minorities (Shalala, 1997). As Harlan Dalton noted in the 1980s, efforts to study and prevent the transmission of HIV among African Americans had to fight against "the deep-seated suspicion and mistrust many of us feel whenever whites express a sudden interest in our well-being" (Dalton, 1989, p. 211).

Stanley Milgram's (1963) experiment on authority and control is one of the most famous cases of influential research that would no longer be considered ethically justified. Influenced by the Nuremberg Trials, in which accused Nazi war criminals famously defended their actions as "just following orders," Milgram became interested in learning about the tendency to obey authority figures. To observe this phenomenon, he told voluntary "assistants" that they were to help teach another person, supposedly another volunteer subject, a simple word-association task. The other volunteer, however, was actually another investigator on the study while the supposed assistants were the real subjects. The experiment was designed to push the subjects to perform acts that they felt were wrong merely because they were under orders to do so, and despite the fact that they would suffer no loss if they refused.

The subject/teacher was instructed by Milgram to administer an electric shock to the learner (the confederate in an adjacent room) whenever the learner made a mistake. The subject/teacher was told that this electric shock was intended to facilitate learning and should be increased in intensity progressively with each error. Many of the subjects obediently (in fact, gleefully) advanced the shock levels to potentially lethal levels. Others objected or resisted vocally before complying with the project director's instructions. Either way, the majority continued to administer the supposed shocks well into the danger zone.

In reality, the supposed learner received no shocks at all. Rather, each time the subject/teacher administered a shock, a signal indicated that the learner should react as if shocked. The harm done was emotional, not physical. The deception aroused considerable anguish and guilt in the actual subjects. As fascinating and important as it is to learn that people can be pressured into harming or even potentially killing others through the power of simple authority relations, it is not something that one wants to actually experience or learn about one's self in that way. Milgram debriefed the subjects, explaining that they had not actually harmed others. Nonetheless, they had already sat there pressing the shock button while an innocent stranger screamed in pain.

In another study, regarded by many social scientists to be as controversial as the Milgram study, Philip Zimbardo (1972) sought to examine the interaction patterns between inmates and guards. His experiment involved a simulated prison where groups of paid volunteers were designated as either inmates or guards. For this study, Zimbardo constructed a model jail facility in the basement of one of the university buildings at Stanford. The design of the study called for those subjects assigned to the inmate role to be arrested by actual police officers, charged with serious crimes, booked at a local station, and brought to the "jail" facility on campus. The guards were other paid volunteers who were garbed in uniforms and were issued nightsticks. The study was intended to run for a two-week period, during which time Zimbardo expected to watch the subjects act out their various roles as inmates and guards. However, within the first 24 hours, as guards became increasingly abusive and inmates grew more hostile toward their keepers, verbal altercations began to break out between several of the inmates and guards, escalating to a physical altercation between one of the guards and inmates. Within 48 hours, the inmates had begun planning and executing their first escape, while others had to be released from the study due to stress and mental anguish. Despite these extreme and unexpected events, Zimbardo did not call off the experiment until the sixth day. Even then, as he described it, it was pressure from his girlfriend at the time that convinced him not to continue (Granberg & Galliher, 2010). Authority, when perceived as legitimate, impacts research practices in other less direct ways as well. Dean Champion (2006, pp. 518–519) recounts another research study of questionable ethics. This study, commonly known as the CIA's ARTICHOKE program, was undertaken by the Central Intelligence Agency (CIA) of the U.S. government. The study sought to uncover ways to control peoples' behavior. According to Champion (2006, p. 519):

> A CIA memo dated January 25, 1952, indicated that a program, ARTICHOKE was underway and that its primary objectives were the evaluation and development of any methods by which we can get information from a person against his will and without his knowledge.

One component of the study was to control peoples' behavior through use of drugs and chemicals that could create psychological and physiological changes. These included the use of electroshock, LSD, hypnosis, and various drugs thought to induce memory loss and amnesia. Apparently, these drugs and activities were administered to unwitting citizens and members of the armed forces. These harmful acts were designed by a government agency, but carried out by professional social and behavioral scientists.

In 1963, the CIA was forced to deal with the public disclosure of its efforts after several news agencies carried stories about this study. Naturally, the study was brought to a close. However, professional organizations such as the American Psychological Association and the American Sociological Association sought explanations for how ARTICHOKE could have been carried on for so long without the public being informed about its existence (Champion, 2006). Even today, many social scientists continue to question how the CIA could have enlisted so many psychologists and other social scientists to assist them in this rather blatantly unethical course of action in the ARTICHOKE study. Did they think their actions were appropriate, or were they just following orders?

Laud Humphreys' (1970) study of casual homosexual encounters, called *Tearoom Trade*, raised questions about other forms of harm to research subjects. Humphreys was interested in gaining understanding not only about practicing homosexuals but also about men who lived heterosexual lives in public but who occasionally engaged in homosexual encounters in private. In addition to observing encounters in public restrooms in parks (tearooms), Humphreys developed a way to gain access to detailed information about the subjects he covertly observed.

While serving as a watch queen (a voyeuristic lookout), Humphreys was able to observe the sexual encounters and to record the participants' license plates. With those, he was able to locate the names and home addresses of the men he had observed. Next, Humphreys disguised himself and deceived these men into believing that he was conducting a survey in their neighborhood. The result was that Humphreys managed to collect considerable amounts of information about each of the subjects he had observed in the tearooms without their consent.

Shortly after the publication of Humphreys' work in 1970, there was a considerable outcry against the invasion of privacy, misrepresentation of researcher identities, and deception commonly being practiced during the course of research. Many of the controversies that revolve around Humphreys' research remain key ethical issues today. Paramount among these issues are the justifications that the subject matter was of critical importance to the scientific community and that it simply could not have been investigated in any other manner. This justification relies in part on the fact that since people were legally prosecuted for homosexuality in 1970, and would have lost their jobs and marriages as well, he could hardly have expected voluntary cooperation. Yet, for exactly those reasons, voluntary cooperation is necessary. The researcher alone cannot decide what risks other people should confront.

Naturally, this begs the question of how to weigh the potential benefit of a research project against the potential harm. This utilitarian argument essentially

Figure 3.1 The Research Risk/Benefit Scale

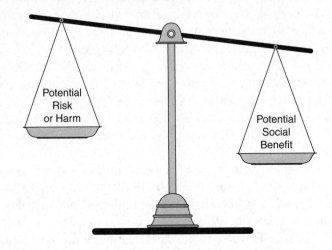

sets up a kind of scale in which risk and harm are placed on one side and benefits are placed on the other side (see Figure 3.1). If the determination is that the amount of benefit outweighs the amount of potential risk or harm, then the research may be seen from an ethical point of view as permissible (Christians, 2008; Taylor, 1994). This notion, of course, assumes that there is no potential serious risk of harm, injury, or death possible for any research subject.

In the case of Humphreys' study, there are many researchers who maintain that the social, legal, and psychological policy changes that have resulted far outweigh any minor invasions of privacy. This is not to suggest that there are not other researchers who argue that the research was unethical no matter how great the benefits have been.

From Guidelines to Law: Regulations on the Research Process

Early attempts within the American political system to devise rigorous biomedical experimentation guidelines failed. One major reason was the inability to develop a single code of ethics that, as Bower and de Gasparis (1978, p. 5) put it, "could cover with equal adequacy and flexibility the entire range of biomedical experimentation." However, in 1966, the U.S. Surgeon General issued what may have been the first official rules concerning all Public Health Service (PHS) research. This statement specified that any research financially supported by the PHS was contingent on a review by an institutional committee. The committee was charged with the responsibility of ensuring that study procedures would not harm human subjects and that subjects were informed of any potential risks (and benefits) from their participation.

Several revisions of this general policy occurred from 1967 to 1969. Finally, in 1971, the U.S. Department of Health, Education, and Welfare (DHEW) published a booklet entitled *The Institutional Guide to DHEW Policy on Protection of Human Subjects*, which extended the requirement of an institutional review committee to all DHEW grant and contract activities involving human subjects. In addition, this booklet required researchers to obtain *informed consent* from subjects before including them in the research.

In 1974, the National Research Act was passed by Congress, and the National Commission on Protection of Human Subjects of Biomedical and Behavioral Research was created by Title II of this law. The National Research Act directed all institutions that sponsored research to establish institutional review committees, today more commonly called *institutional review boards* (IRBs). Locally based in-house IRBs were now charged with the responsibility of carefully reviewing any proposed research that involved human subjects.

Among several other issues, IRBs were expected to ensure that research investigators had considered both potential risks and benefits to subjects, that important scientific knowledge could be derived from the project, that legally informed consent would be obtained from each subject, and that the rights and interests of subjects were protected (Liemohn, 1979; W.H.O., 2002).

Another important piece of research-related legislation is the education amendments of 1974. These laws, better known as the Buckley Amendment (also called the Family Educational Rights to Privacy Act), were intended to protect the privacy of parents and students (Holden, 1975; U.S. Department of Education, 2007). In essence, these laws limited access to official records concerning (and identifying) an individual, and they prohibited release of such personal information (with some exceptions) to anyone else without written consent of the student (and the parent in the case of minors).

Finally, the Privacy Acts of 1974 offered additional legal assurances against invasive research on human subjects. This legislation was primarily designed to protect citizens from large private corporations and federal institutions and from the release of potentially erroneous information and records. In addition, however, it provided individuals with judicial machinery for redressing indiscriminate sharing of personal information and records without prior written consent—including when obtained by deceptive researchers. A fair number of these regulations are informally overseen by institutional review boards. Let us consider IRBs in greater detail.

Institutional Review Boards

Whenever someone brings up the topic of institutional review boards, he or she runs the risk of evoking strong feelings among social science researchers. Among the negatives: Some researchers see IRBs as handcuffs impeding their search for scientific answers to social problems. Some researchers simply believe that contemporary IRBs have grown too big for their breeches and that they tend to overstep their perceived purpose and limits. Other researchers say IRBs are staffed with clinicians unable to understand the nuances of certain social scientific styles of research, particularly qualitative research. Indeed, there are many who view IRBs as villains rather than as necessary—let alone virtuous—institutions. While many researchers view IRBs in less than positive terms, few today doubt that IRBs are necessary. Recent research on the topic among ethnographers indicates that most find the review process fair and appropriate, though some still question the extent to which the reviews contribute to either research or human subjects' protection (Wynn, 2011). Ideally, IRBs should be seen as a group of individuals who selflessly give their time and expertise to ensure that human subjects are neither physically nor emotionally injured by researchers, thereby also assisting researchers in preparing their work.

In the academic community of the new millennium, research continues to uphold its position as a critically important element. Fundamentally, and some-what altruistically, research still holds the promise of important revelations for collective thinking and changes for the better in society. At a more pragmatic level, social science research offers the academician opportunities for publication that, in turn, form the rungs in academic promotion and tenure ladders. Furthermore, the new millennium has brought with it a wave of new ethical challenges with the advent of Internet-based research and widespread surveillance data. With these new challenges many researchers are vividly reminded of the problems that are today apparent in the research studies of the recent past that exploited human subjects in deplorable ways. The question that remains unanswered, however, is this: Exactly what are the institutional review boards' duties in the new millennium?

IRBs and Their Duties

Among the important elements considered by IRB panels is the assurance of informed consent. Usually, this involves requirements for obtaining written informed consent from potential subjects. This requirement, which is mostly taken for granted now, drew heavy critical fire from social scientists when it was first introduced (Fields, 1978; Gray, 1977; Meyer, 1977). Although strategies for obtaining informed consent have been routinized in most research, some difficulties and criticisms persist. Qualitative researchers, especially those involved in ethnographic research, have been particularly vocal. Their concerns often pertain to the way that formal requirements for institutional review and written informed consent damage their special field-worker–informant relationships (Berg, Austin, & Zuern, 1992; Lincoln, 2008; Taylor & Bogdan, 1998).

The National Commission for the Protection of Human Subjects, created by the National Research Act of 1974, reviewed its own guidelines (Department of Health, Education, and Welfare, 1978a) and offered revisions that addressed some of these concerns (*Federal Register*, 1978). The revisions are more specific about the role the IRB should play than previous documents were. For example, the *Federal Register* states that board members may be liable for legal action if they exceed their authority and interfere with the investigator's right to conduct research. These revised guidelines also recommend that the requirement for written informed consent could be waived for certain types of low-risk styles of research.

Because their research procedures are more formalized and require contacts with subjects, the more limited and predictable characteristics of quantitative methodologies are generally simpler to define. As a result, the specific exemptions for styles of research that can be expedited through IRBs largely are quantitative survey types, research involving educational tests (diagnostic, aptitude, or achievement), and qualitative approaches that don't require contact with individuals such as observation in public places and archival research (Department of Health, Education, and Welfare, 1978b).

The temporary (usually single visit) and formal nature of most quantitative data-gathering strategies makes them easier to fit into federal regulations. In survey research in particular, confidentiality is also rather easy to ensure. Written consent slips can be separated out from surveys and secured in innovative ways. It becomes a simple task to ensure that names or other identifiers will not be connected in any way with the survey response sheets.

Qualitative research, especially ethnographic strategies, presents greater challenges to IRBs. Presumably, most qualitative researchers make every effort to comply with federal regulations for the protection of human subjects. However, strict compliance is not always easy. In order to ensure consistency, lists of names are sometimes maintained even when pseudonyms are used in field notes. Furthermore, the very nature of ethnographic research makes it ideal for studying secret, deviant, or difficult-to-study populations. Consider, for example, drug smugglers (Adler, 1985), burglars (Cromwell, Olsen, & Avary, 1990), or crack dealers (Jacobs, 1998). It would be almost impossible to locate sufficient numbers of drug smugglers, burglars, or crack dealers to create a probability sample or to administer a meaningful number of survey questionnaires. Imagine, now, that you also needed to secure written informed-consent slips. It is not likely that anyone could manage these restrictions. In fact, the researcher's personal safety might be jeopardized even by announcing his or her presence (overt observation). It is similarly unlikely that you would have much success trying to locate a sufficient number of patrons of pornographic DVD rentals to administer questionnaires. Yet, observational and ethnographic techniques might work very well (see, e.g., Tewksbury, 1990).

Many qualitative researchers have arrived at the same conclusion about the relationship between researcher and subjects in qualitative research—namely, that the qualitative relationship is so different from quantitative approaches that conventional procedures for informed consent and protection of human subjects amount to little more than ritual (Bogdan & Biklen, 1992, 2003). For example, Tewksbury (1990) located voluntary participants for a study of sex and danger in men's same-sex, in-public encounters by posting notices on social service agency bulletin boards, college campuses, and through personal contacts (a variation of snowballing, discussed in Chapter 2). Berg and colleagues (2004) located a population of Latino men who have sex with men (MSMs) in an HIV outreach support group and worked with outreach workers who already had rapport with these MSMs to invite them to take part in an interview study. In effect, the qualitative researcher typically has a substantially different relationship with his or her subjects, and one markedly distinct from the more abstract and sterile relationship most quantitative researchers have with theirs.

In the kind of research for which these guidelines have typically been written, subjects have very circumscribed relationships. The researcher presents some survey or questionnaire to the subjects who in turn fill it out. Or the researcher describes the requirements of participation in some experiment, and the subject participates. In these quantitative modes of research, it is a fairly easy task to predict and describe to the subject the content of the study and the possible risks from participation. As Janice Morse noted, at some institutions, the IRB requires distribution of a "Bill of Rights" whenever a subject is included in an experiment (Morse, 1994, p. 338).

With qualitative research, on the other hand, the relationship between researcher and subject is frequently an ongoing and evolving one. Doing qualitative research with subjects is more like being permitted to observe or take part in the lives of these subjects. At best, it may be seen as a social contract. But, as in all contracts, both parties have some say about the contents of the agreement and in regulating the relationship. Although it is not difficult to predict possible risks in quantitative survey studies, this task can be quite a problem in some qualitative research projects.

Consider, for example, a study in which a researcher seeks to observe the gambling behavior of people while drinking alcohol at taverns (McSkimming, 1996). Can the researcher actually determine whether people who are drinking alcohol and gambling as part of their social worlds will be at risk because the researcher is present in the same tavern watching them? Certainly, any time people consume alcohol and engage in something as volatile as gambling there is the potential for violence. From the standpoint of the IRB, a declaration from the researcher that there is no greater risk to subjects because the researcher is present observing their behaviors is likely to be sufficient; in short, the research project itself does not increase or cause risk. Of course, this does nothing to diminish the usual risk of these behaviors.

Consider also a study similar to McSkimming's. In Tomson Nguyen's (2003) study, the researcher sought to examine illegal gambling in a Vietnamese café. Nguyen visited a café known to be a location where local Vietnamese residents went to play illegal poker machines. While he had the permission of the café owner to be there, none of the players were aware of his intention to observe their gambling for a research study. Again, in itself, Nguyen's presence in the café did not alter the risks to these gamblers' (or the café owner's) of being apprehended by police should there be a raid. But the IRB to which Nguyen submitted took considerable convincing that this project would not in some way harm subjects.

Some researchers, confronted with the daunting task of convincing IRBs that their risk management strategies are sufficient, have thrown in the towel and simply stopped researching controversial topics. That is, these researchers may have taken the position that not all topics are appropriate for academic study, or worse, the pragmatic position that it is not "safe" for one's career to try to pursue certain questions. This, however, could lead to a serious problem. If, over the course of years, the impact of institutional review highly encouraged some forms of research while discouraging others, then eventually large segments of the social world will all but disappear from view as researchers learn to avoid them. Consider, for example, how we could ever design effective interventions to reduce the spread of sexually transmitted diseases if we didn't study the whole spectrum of sexual behaviors. By extension, it would be impossible to protect sexually active teenagers, whose exposure and transmission rates are particularly high, if we could not do research among such teens. Yet, basic requirements for the protection of minors would require us to get written permission from the teens' parents before beginning our work. But even the act of informing parents that we are studying sexual activities would put the potential subjects at risk of harm. A degree of creative innovation is required to address such questions.

Clarifying the Role of IRBs

Having raised concerns about the negative impact of IRBs, it is worth remembering that the practice of review arose from some serious and widespread failures on the part of researchers to protect subjects on their own. Formal procedures to protect people is an essential part of the research process. Initially, IRBs were charged with the responsibility to review the adequacy of consent procedures for the protection of human subjects in research funded by the U.S. DHEW. This mandate was soon broadened to include a review of all research conducted in an institution receiving any funds from DHEW—even when the study itself did not (Burstein, 1987; Department of Health and Human Services, 1989).

Part of the IRBs' duties was to ensure that subjects in research studies were advised of both the potential risks from participation and also the possible benefits. This task seems to have evolved among some IRBs to become an assessment of risk-to-benefit ratios of proposed studies. In some cases, this is based on an IRB's impression of the worth of the study. In other cases, this may be based on the IRB's presumed greater knowledge of the subject and methodological strategies than potential subjects are likely to possess (Bailey, 1996; Burstein, 1987). Thus, in many cases, IRBs, and not subjects, determine whether the subject will even have the option of participating or declining to participate in a study, by refusing to certify research that does not seem important to them.

According to the *Code of Federal Regulations* (CFR, 1993, Article 45, Part 46, 101–110), there are a number of research situations that do not require a full-blown institutional review. These projects are subject to what may be termed an *expedited review*. Expedited reviews may involve a read-through and determination by the chair or a designated IRB committee member rather than review by the full committee. Usually, studies entitled to an expedited review are evaluations of educational institutions that examine normal educational practices, organizational effectiveness, instructional techniques, curricula, or classroom management strategies (see also CFR, 2008).

Other types of research subject areas may receive an expedited review or no review, depending on the specific institutional rules of a given university or research organization. These areas include certain survey procedures, interview procedures, or observations of public behavior. The CFR provisions that exclude research areas from review state the following:

1. The information obtained is recorded in such a manner that the participants cannot be identified.
2. Any disclosure of the participants' response outside the research cannot reasonably identify the subject.

3. The study and its results do not place the participant at risk of criminal or civil liability, nor will it be damaging to the participant's financial standing, employability, or reputation (e.g., an observational study in which subjects are not identified).
4. The research will be conducted on preexisting data, documents, records, pathological specimens, or diagnostic specimens, provided these items are publicly available or if the information is recorded by the investigator in such a manner that subjects cannot be identified.

In effect, the governmental regulations as established by the CFR allow certain types of research to be undertaken without any review by an IRB and rather depend on the professional codes or ethics of the researcher or on the various more restrictive rules of a particular university or research organization.

Today, researchers have claimed that many IRBs have further extended their reach to include evaluation of methodological strategies, not, as one might expect, as these methods pertain to human subject risks but in terms of the project's methodological adequacy. The justification for this, apparently, is that even when minimum risks exist, if a study is designed poorly, it will not yield any scientific benefit (Berg et al., 1992; Lincoln, 2008).

Some researchers complain that IRBs have begun to moralize rather than assess the potential harm to subjects. As an example, consider the following situation that arose during an IRB review of a proposal at a midsized university on the East Coast. The project was designed to examine ethnographically the initiation of cigarette smoking and alcohol consumption among middle school and high school youths. The design called for identified field researchers to spend time in public places observing youths. The idea was to observe how smoking and alcohol fit into the social worlds of these youths.

Several IRB committee members were extremely concerned that ethnographers would be watching children smoking and drinking without notifying their parents of these behaviors. During a review of this proposal with the investigator, these committee members argued that it was unthinkable that no intervention would be taken on the part of the field-workers. They recommended that the researchers tell the youths' parents that they were engaging in these serious behaviors. The investigator explained that this would actually be a breach of confidentiality and potentially expose the subjects to serious risk of corporal punishment.

One committee member asked, "What if the youth was observed smoking crack; wouldn't the field-worker tell his or her parents then?" The investigator reminded the committee that these observations were to be in public places. The field-workers did not have a responsibility to report to the parents what their children were doing—no matter how potentially unhealthy it may be.

The investigator further explained that there was no legal requirement to inform on these subjects, and, in fact, to do so would make the research virtually impossible to conduct. The committee member agreed that there may be no legal requirement but went on to argue that there certainly was a moral one!

Eventually, a compromise was struck. The researcher agreed to include a statement in the proposal indicating that if the field-workers observed what they believed were children engaging in behavior that would likely result in immediate and serious personal injury or imminent death, they would intervene. Of course, such a statement seemed unnecessary for the researcher, because it was already agreed on by the research team. It did, however, appease the committee members who continued to grumble that the parents should be informed about their children's behavior.

The conflict in this case did not arise from the normal and required actions of the review board, but from the fact that the IRB's role may be open to a variety of interpretations by individuals. That is, it appears (to us) that the researcher had a better understanding of the nature of human subjects' protections than one member of the review committee did. We can therefore consider this situation to be an individual error, not a systemic problem. Yet, given the fact that issues of risk, benefit, and harm are all matters of interpretation, such conflicts can crop up at any time.

Active versus Passive Consent

Another controversial question concerns the use of active versus passive informed consent by parents of children involved in research, particularly research conducted on the Internet. Active consent may be defined as the "formal written permission by an informed parent or legal guardian that allows a child to participate in a research project" (Deschenes & Vogel, 1995). Passive consent is usually based on the assumption that parental permission is granted if parents do not return a refusal form after being informed about the study's purpose (Chartier et al., 2008; Deschenes & Vogel, 1995; Eaton, Lowry, Brener, Grunbaum, & Kahn, 2004).

Even the federal government has gotten into the picture. In 1995, it began considering a bill that would require active consent for research involving children. If this legislation had passed, it would have put a considerable damper on the research undertaken by many educational researchers.

In the past, researchers who have employed an active consent style have reported that it yields unacceptably low response rates. This translates into the underrepresentation of relevant study subjects, often the very ones involved in or at risk from the study behaviors (Kearney et al., 1983; Severson & Ary, 1983; Thompson, 1984).

To avoid excluding relevant study subjects, many researchers have turned to the passive consent method (Ellickson & Hawes, 1989; Ross, 2006). The moral question here rests on the argument that passive procedures do not fully inform parents about the research or give them sufficient opportunities to refuse participation. Some researchers question whether parents have actually intentionally decided to allow their child to participate and have consciously not sent in the refusal notice. In this case, one might interpret nonresponse as more of an indicator of indifferent attitudes toward research—but not necessarily consent.

Yet active consent requirements may be too stringent for many qualitative research endeavors. This is especially true when qualitative projects implement a series of diligent data safeguards, such as removal of identifiers, to ensure confidentiality. Carefully designed passive consent procedures can avoid various negative consequences of active consent, while still ensuring parents are being informed.

The use of active consent begs the question of how extensive it must be and how it should be implemented in qualitative research. For example, if an investigator is interested in observing the interactions between children at play and during their studies, how extensive would the active consent need to be? Certainly, if observations are being made in a classroom, all of the parents would need to be notified, but would all have to actively agree before the researcher could enter the room? If one parent said no, would that mean that the child could not be included in the researcher's notes or that the research could not be undertaken? If the researcher wanted to observe this class of children on the playground, would he or she need the active consent of the parents of every child in the school?

In 2002, the issue of active and passive consent made headlines when New Jersey passed a law stating that all research undertaken in New Jersey schools requires the active consent of parents. Put quite simply, if parents do not say yes, their child cannot take part in the research (Wetzstein, 2002). The controversy originated for New Jersey students and parents in 1999 when a survey containing over 156 questions was administered to more than 2,000 public middle school and high school students in Ridgewood, New Jersey. The survey asked teens about their sexual activity, birth control use, drug and alcohol use, cigarette smoking habits, binge eating, depression, suicide, stealing, physical violence, and relationships with family members and friends (Viadero, 2002).

The problem with such active consent requirements, as previously indicated, is that 20–30 percent of parents typically fail to return the consent forms. This can result in serious problems with study samples, causing researchers to drop certain schools from their studies because of low response rates from potential subjects' parents.

Again, these concerns do seem to direct themselves more to quantitative than to qualitative research studies. To a certain extent, a qualitative research effort might find it less problematic to not have all the parents' consent and to simply exclude children whose parents have not provided their permission for, say, an interview. It is not as simple, however, to exclude youths from observational studies. Thus, if an investigator desires to undertake this type of research, under the New Jersey law of active consent, he or she would not be able to do so. Naturally this suggests, once more, the push toward what some might call "research of the sterile and mundane."

Active versus Passive Consent in Internet Research

The Internet is an enormously comprehensive electronic archive of materials representing a vast array of social artifacts reflecting peoples' opinions, concerns, life stories, activities, and lifestyles. Materials on these sites can be a rich source of data for social scientists interested in understanding the lives, experiences, and views of people. As discussed later in this book, there are a number of ways researchers can access and use data via the Internet. Among the several ways data can be solicited via the Internet are electronic surveys and electronic interviews (Bachman & Schutt, 2007; Eysenbach & Wyatt, 2002). Dillman (2000) suggests the e-mail survey is one method by which researchers can provide potential subjects with an instrument to complete via e-mail address and ask them to return the completed device. In terms of consent, one can certainly send along the survey with a description of the study and a statement to be checked off to indicate *informed consent.* If you have ever checked the "I have read and understood the terms and conditions" checkbox on a Web site before downloading a file, then you have given this sort of informed consent. Whether you took the time to read the "informed" part or not is up to you.

Web surveys, according to Bachman and Schutt (2007), are a variation on this data-collection strategy. Surveys are placed either on a server controlled by the researcher or at a Web survey firm, and potential respondents are invited to visit the Web site and complete the instrument. A description of the study can be provided, and the act of the subject going to the site and completing the survey can serve as a variation on passive consent.

Electronic interviews (see Chapter 4): Once the interviewer and subject agree and informed consent is obtained either in person or online, electronic interviews can be undertaken through the use of private chat rooms where both the interviewer and the subject interact in real time, asking and answering questions over the Internet. Again, with regard to informed consent, information about the study can be transmitted to the subject's e-mail, and agreement to take part in the interview can be obtained at that time or, to maintain anonymity, during the course of the interview, once the interviewer directs the subject to the chat space. The inclusion of the Internet in qualitative research certainly opens innovative doors for research strategies. However, it also presents new problems for IRBs. Members of IRBs must deal with an assortment of ethical and even moralistic problems. A reasonable question to ask is this: Who in his or her right mind would want to serve on such a panel? This, however, brings us to the question of exactly who does serve on the review boards.

Membership Criteria for IRBs

The federal regulations specify that "each IRB shall have at least five members with varying backgrounds to promote complete and adequate review of research activities commonly conducted by the institution" (CFR, 1993, p. 7; CFR, 2008). There are also provisions that IRBs should not be composed entirely of women, men, single racial groups, or one profession. Furthermore, each IRB should contain at least one member whose primary work does not include the sciences or social sciences (e.g., lawyers, ethicists, or members of the clergy). However, federal guidelines do not articulate how to select or locate IRB members, what research qualifications members should have, what lengths members' terms should be, or how to establish an IRB chairperson. The federal regulations do require that "assurances" be submitted to the Office for Protection from Research Risks, National Institutes of Health.

Among these assurances must be a list of IRB members' names, their "earned degrees; representative capacity; indications of experience such as board certifications, licenses, etc." (CFR, 1993, p. 6). While no suggestion is given about what types of degrees people should have in order to sit on the IRB, the allusion to board certification or licenses does convey the notion of clinicians rather than social scientists. The diversity of backgrounds on most IRBs ensures that, almost any, project proposals that are submitted for review will be evaluated by at least one person with appropriate expertise in that area, as well as a few without such expertise. It's a tricky balance.

There are no simple rules for establishing IRBs that are able to ensure both safety to human subjects and reasonably unhampered research opportunities for investigators. As the serious ethical infractions that occurred before the advance of IRBs demonstrate, social scientists left to their own designs sometimes go astray. On the other hand, researchers may be correct in their stance that IRBs left to their own devices may grow too restrictive. Nonetheless, IRBs should be able to operate in concert with researchers rather than in opposition to them. Social scientists need to become more involved in the IRB process and seek ways to implement board goals and membership policies that are responsive to changing times, social values, and research technologies.

Ethical Codes

During the past several decades, changing social attitudes about research as well as changing legislation have led professional associations to create codes of ethical conduct. For example, the American Nurses' Association developed *Human Rights Guidelines for Nurses in Clinical and Other Research* (1975). The American Sociological Association produced its code of ethics during the early 1980s (American Sociological Association, 1984, 1997). Ethical guidelines for psychologists emerged in the American Psychological Association (1981) in a document entitled "Ethical Principles of Psychologists" and again in a document entitled "Ethical Principles in the Conduct of Research with Human Participants" (1984). The American Society of Criminology has not formally adopted a code of ethics; however, the society's Web site links to numerous other societies' ethical codes (http://www.asc41.com/ethicspg.html). Hagan (2006) has suggested that most criminologists and criminal justice researchers tend to borrow from cognate disciplines for their ethical guidelines. Paramount among these borrowed ethical tenets is the avoidance of harm to human subjects.

Some Common Ethical Concerns in Behavioral Research

Among the most serious ethical concerns that have received attention during the past two decades is the assurance that subjects are voluntarily involved and informed of all potential risks. Yet, even here there is some controversy.

In general, the concept of voluntary participation in social science research is an important ideal, but ideals are not always attainable. In some instances, however—such as the one illustrated by Humphreys' (1970) study—violating the tenet of voluntary participation may appear justified to certain researchers. Typically, such justifications are made on the basis of an imaginary scale described as tipped toward the ultimate social good as measured against the possible harm to subjects.

Another argument against arbitrary application of this notion of voluntary participation concerns the nature of volunteering in general. First, if all social research included only those persons who eagerly volunteered to participate, little meaningful understanding would result. There would be no way of determining if these types of persons were similar to others who lacked this eagerness to volunteer. In other words, both qualitative and aggregated statistical data would become questionable.

Second, in many cases, volunteer subjects may in reality be coerced or manipulated into volunteering. For instance, one popular style of sample identification is the college classroom. If the teacher asks the entire class to voluntarily take part in a research project, there may be penalties for not submitting even if the teacher suggests otherwise. Even if no punishments are intentionally planned, if students believe that not taking part will be noticed and might somehow be held against them, they have been manipulated. Under such circumstances, as in the case of the overeager volunteers, confidence in the data is undermined. Many universities disallow faculty to use their own students as research subjects for just this reason.

Babbie (2007) similarly notes that offering reduced sentences to inmates in exchange for their participation in research—or other types of incentives to potential subjects—represents yet another kind of manipulated voluntary consent. For the most part, inmate research is disallowed by IRBs in the United States. As Martin, Arnold, Zimmerman, and Richard (1968) suggested, voluntary participation in studies among prisoners results from a strange mix of altruism, monetary gain, and hope for a potential way of enhancing their personal prestige and status.

Both of these scenarios suggest that voluntary participation may not always be completely voluntary, and therefore they raise questions about the validity of certain subject pools. The same concerns may be offered as justifications for collecting data without consent. If consenting students or prisoners are qualitatively different from nonconsenting ones, then only a study of both together would be truly representative. This is a dangerous and difficult approach to take, and one which can appear to be a crass attempt to undermine human subjects protections. Yet, for some research projects, aggregated data about particular populations, such as students or inmates, may be collected from the institution without either the direct involvement of individual subjects or any means to trace specific data back to them. To reiterate the point, however, such an approach must be carefully managed and precisely justified.

A third rationalization for not gaining the voluntary consent of subjects was suggested by Rainwater and Pittman (1967). They believed that social science research enhanced accountability in public officials. Consequently, research in many public institutions must be conducted covertly (thus, without voluntary participation on the part of subjects) if it is to be meaningful—and in some instances if it is to be conducted at all. In many cases, data about public figures are mostly public, and transparency policies and freedom of information laws allow public access to much of the workings of public agencies. It is sometimes unclear, however, whether a social scientist ought to pursue data that have not been deemed public. Social research serves an accountability function; but we are not investigative journalists.

Some researchers argue that voluntary participation actually may conflict with the methodological principle of *representativeness* and representative sampling (Schutt, 2006). Carrying this notion to its logical conclusion, one might argue that if a researcher gives people a choice about participating in a survey study, certain types would decline at disproportionate rates (those with great wealth, non-English-speaking persons, people from certain ethnic or cultural backgrounds, privacy advocates, anti-government activists, etc.). Certainly, compulsory participation in research creates a host of additional ethical concerns and would not likely be seriously considered by even the most statistically pure of heart researcher. Further, and particularly in light of modern and somewhat more critically influenced orientations, certain invasions of privacy and manipulations of research subjects are likely to occur mostly among fairly powerless segments of society and organizations; this too raises some very serious ethical concerns over who one should include in a study. On the one hand, researchers might justify this invasion as the conduct of do-gooders who focus on such disadvantaged groups as drug users, the unemployed, the mentally impaired, and the poor because social service agencies are interested in helping people with social problems. On the other hand, researchers can create as strong a case for social agencies' desires to get a firmer grip on these disadvantaged groups, and certainly government agencies, by using ethical social science research strategies to formulate policies (Engel & Schutt, 2005).

Regardless of the justification, because of their lack of political, social, and financial power, these disadvantaged groups are more accessible to researchers than more powerful groups are. In consequence, researchers must consider whether our study populations are the most appropriate for our work, or simply available. To the extent that we do study certain groups opportunistically, we should ask ourselves whether doing so has political or other implications. Are we inadvertently supporting, rather than questioning, existing divisions of power and privilege? Do our research questions inherently support some political agenda, regardless of our actual findings? Even if we are confident that whatever disadvantaged groups are the best ones for our research, we must still be responsive to these concerns and clearly explain to subjects the rights and responsibilities of both the researchers and the participants.

No hard-and-fast answers exist for resolving the dilemma of voluntary participation. Researchers must balance how voluntary subjects' participation will be against their perceptions of personal integrity; their responsibilities to themselves, their profession, and their discipline; and the ultimate effects for their subjects. In other words, in the end, researchers must define for themselves what is ethical in research.

Covert versus Overt Researcher Roles

The question of voluntary participation virtually begs another question, namely, what role a researcher should take when conducting research: an *overt* and announced role or a *covert* and secret role? This concern is largely one that confronts researchers using ethnographic strategies such as observing people in their natural settings (see also Chapter 6 on *Ethnographic Field Strategies*). Many textbooks refer to Gold's *typology of naturalistic research* (Denzin & Lincoln, 2005; Marks & Yardley, 2004; Punch, 2005). Briefly, Gold's typology offers four roles for the researcher: complete participant, participant as observer, observer as participant, and complete observer. These roles are described as follows:

- *Complete participant:* In this case, the researcher seeks to engage fully in the activities of the group or organization under investigation. Thus, this role requires the researcher to enter the setting covertly as a secret or hidden investigator. For example, a researcher might enter a subcultural group in this manner without making his or her intent to conduct research known to the people involved in the group under investigation. Among the advantages to this role is that more accurate information is likely to flow permitting the researcher to obtain a fuller understanding of the interactions and meanings that are held important to those regularly involved in this group in this setting. This is the most covert role, and therefore the one most likely to introduce risks to the subjects and the researcher.
- *Participant as observer:* When the researcher adopts this role, he or she is accepting an overt or announced role as a researcher. In this case, the researcher formally makes his or her presence and intentions known to the group being studied. This may involve a general announcement that he or she will be conducting research, or a specific introduction as the researcher meets various people who participate in the setting. This strategy carries its own problems related to the ability of the researcher to develop sufficient rapport with participants, and the potential that the researcher will *go native*; that is, become so immersed in the activities, issues, and meanings of the group that he or she has difficulty maintaining an objective researcher's perspective on these activities, issues, and meanings.
- *Observer as participant:* Researchers donning the role of the observer as participant move away from the idea of participation but continue to embrace the overt role as an investigator. Often, this role involves a single site or setting visit, along with the use of interviews, and may

call for relatively more formal observation (e.g., examination of the organizational structure of a business or group, and written policies, rather than the organization or group's norms and practices). These replace the more informal observation or participations usually associated with other researcher observational roles. This strategy runs the risk of the researcher failing to understand some of the subtleties and nuances between participants involved in this organization or group; consequently, the researcher may miss or fail to adequately appreciate certain informal norms, roles, or relationships.

- *Complete observer:* When a researcher uses the complete observer role, it too tends to be an overt and announced role as a researcher. In this case, however, the researcher typically remains in the setting for a prolonged period of time, but is a passive observer to the flow of activities and interactions. For example, the researcher may sit in the rear of a classroom and observe training of police recruits during academy training classes. From this vantage, the researcher can freely move in and around the setting and participants while observing the recruits and the instructors—but not while serving or masquerading as either.

Between 1969 and 1971, Dan Rose (1988) conducted covert research, where he effectively used a *complete participant* researcher's role in order to ethnographically study a black neighborhood in Philadelphia, Pennsylvania. As part of his effort, he moved with his wife into the area and took a job as an auto mechanic in a small private garage. His decision to enter the setting covertly was based on his desire to avoid affecting the natural flow of information from the cultural scenes he expected to observe in the neighborhood—in essence to avoid researcher reactivity. When he wrote up his narrative, Rose indicated his own conflicted personal feelings about entering the field in this deceptive manner; but he also indicates that he saw the advantages to using this complete immersion into the neighborhood. In general, Rose suggests that entrance into the field as an announced ethnographer tends to focus on the interests of the researcher, rather than those of the people in the natural setting (the setting participants) and the flow of interactions from the cultural activities that occur in that setting.

Patricia Adler, for example, explained her attempt to strike a balance between overt and covert researcher roles (Adler, 1985, pp. 17, 27):

In discussing this issue [whether to overtly or covertly investigate drug trafficking] with our key informants, they all agreed that we should be extremely discreet (for both our sakes and theirs). We carefully approached new individuals before we admitted that we were studying them. With many of these people, then, we took a covert posture in the research setting.... Confronted with secrecy, danger, hidden alliances, misrepresentations and unpredictable changes of intent, I had to use a delicate combination of overt and covert roles.

Researchers may seek to justify taking a complete participant (covert researcher's role) approach by claiming that entry to some groups is very important to learn more about these groups and would otherwise be impossible if their true intentions were known (Miller, 1998; Miller & Tewksbury, 2001, 2005). As a covert participant/observer whose scientific intentions are unknown by the setting participants, access to and flow of information from these participants is possible. Taking what may be termed an *ethical relativist* position, researchers may claim to believe they have a scientific right to study any group whether this group is interested in being studied or not; provided this researcher furthers scientific understandings (Engel & Schutt, 2005; Nason-Clark & Neitz, 2001).

Another justification sometimes offered by researchers taking this ethical relativist stance is that subjects alter their behaviors once they learn that they are being studied; thus, covert research strategies avoid this type of *Hawthorne effect* (discussed in Chapter 6).

Many researchers, however, strenuously oppose covert research or any sort of deception of subjects on both ethical and pragmatic grounds. This sort of *ethical absolutist* perspective argues that researchers have no *right* to invade peoples' privacy under the color of scientific research, and that the deliberate deception of participants regarding the researcher's true intentions can always potentially cause harm to the subjects (Banks, 2004; Engel & Schutt, 2005; Nason-Clark & Neitz, 2001).

There is also the problem, particularly when conducting covert field research on deviant groups, that one will necessarily break the law (Adler, 1985; Becker, 1963; Carey, 1972; Tunnell, 1998). Again, Patricia Adler (1985, p. 23) provides an excellent illustration of the various levels of illegality one might become guilty of:

This [law violation] occurs in its most innocuous form from having "guilty knowledge": information about crimes that are committed. Being aware of major dealing and smuggling operations made us an accessory to their commission, since we failed to notify the police. We broke the law, secondly, through our "guilty observations," by being present at the scene of a crime and witnessing its occurrence.... Lastly, we broke the law through our "guilty actions," by taking part in illegal behavior ourselves. Although we never dealt drugs (we were too scared to be seriously tempted) we consumed drugs and possessed them in small quantities.

Kenneth Tunnell (1998, p. 208) made a similar observation:

> Whenever we as researchers gain entry into the world of deviants and person-
> ally learn the activities of hustlers, thieves, and drug peddlers, for example, we
> become privy to information normally accessible only to occupants of such
> trades. A resultant problem, and one described by other ethnographers, is that
> legal authorities may learn of the research and exact damning information from
> researchers.

Although deception may be seen as a minor ethical violation by some
investigators, it remains a serious breach of ethical conduct for others (Barnbaum & Byron, 2001; Kelman, 1967). Esterberg (2002, p. 52) states that
she believes that covert research is almost never ethical, although she admits
that some deception may at times be necessary. The decision about whether
to assume an overt or a covert researcher role, then, involves a negotiated and
balanced weighing of the potential gains against the potential losses.

Regardless of which stance one embraces, or seeks to justify, it is important that one *does not* violate his or her own sense of ethical tenets. If one, for
example, cringes at the thought of undertaking a study of young children who
shoot heroine, or of men who molest prepubescent young girls, it matters
little whether the research is designed using covert or overt strategies for data
collection; what matters is that the material subject rubs against the potential
researcher's ethical beliefs. One's personal sense of ethics will certainly change
over one's life course as he or she matures, experiences various dark and light
sides of life, and learns more about various ways of life. It is very important,
however, that one be in tune with the limits to his or her ethical boundaries
prior to deciding one any researcher role or beginning any research project.
Failure to accurately estimate one's own ethical limits may result in a ruined
research project regardless of whether data are collected covertly or overtly.

The orientation supported in this text is that there are situations in which
covert research is both necessary and ethically justified, but that they are far
from routine. The determination depends on what you are studying, how
you plan to conduct the study, and what you plan to do with the results. For
example, powerful and elite groups in society are difficult to access; consequently, social scientists tend to avoid them and concentrate their research
efforts on more powerless groups (Hertz & Imber, 1993; Miller, 1998;
Taylor & Bogdan, 1998). To be sure, there are far more studies of poor people
than there are of politicians, nurses than doctors, employees of corporations
than CEOs of corporations, the working class than celebrities, and so forth.
Researchers reveal the faults and frailties of these *undergroups*, while the
powerful and elite go unscathed. Open and announced research in such
circles is typically constrained by bargains designed by the subjects to protect

their own interests. In some cases, to which a researcher should never agree, a study subject may only agree to participate in exchange for the right to edit the researcher's notes. Covert strategies of research may be the only means by which to investigate the powerful and elite. Such research, then, may well be morally and ethically justified. Nonetheless, the orientation supported here is to be cautious about the use of deception. I am especially cautious about outright deception of anyone merely for the sake of conducting a study, that is, only adding another *research notch* to an investigator's metaphoric gun handle, or simply to expedite the research, or because the research study will allow one to complete a degree requirement.

Other concerns related to decisions about ethical research practices can more easily be detailed and considered. Elaboration of each of these elements may assist researchers (particularly the inexperienced) in determining how to deal with ethical concerns in research. These elements include informed consent and implied consent, confidentiality and anonymity, securing the data, and objectivity and careful research design.

New Areas for Ethical Concern: Cyberspace

During the past decade, many areas of social scientific inquiry have benefited by extending their data-collection strategies to include the Internet. For instance, surveys have managed to take advantage of the geographical reach offered by the Web, as well as the fact that data can potentially be collected all hours of the day and night. Qualitative researchers can also take advantage of various benefits afforded by the Web. For instance, focus groups (to be discussed in detail in Chapter 5) can be formed via the Internet to simultaneously undertake data collection among small groups composed of individuals in several distant locations. Oral historians are now able to reach archives located on the Web in minutes, whereas previously it might have taken days or weeks to reach their sources (Frisch, 2008). What may be the most surprising thing about the current Web-based research is not that there have been so many egregious violations of ethics but that there appear to have been so few (Thomas, 1999). Although problems have been identified and various solutions have been offered, concerns about the potential use and misuse of the Internet continue to move scholars toward finding ways to maintain ethical integrity in research when using the Internet as a research tool (Hine, 2008).

One of the interesting ethical elements of Web-based research is that it is potentially far more anonymous than many other types of invasive data-collecting strategies. Thus, a greater sense of security and anonymity may be permitted for some research subjects. The investigator and the subject need not ever engage in face-to-face interactions, be concerned over being appropriately dressed, or even necessarily have concerns about the investigator's gender, thus removing several major traditional sources of researcher reactivity. For example, in a study by Nicola Illingworth (2001, par. 7.1), which examined women's views on assisted reproductive technologies, she found the use of what she terms *computer-mediated communications* provided an effective means for collecting her data. As she explained it:

> Firstly, online participation offered personal anonymity in a very emotive field. Secondly, because of the sensitive nature of this research, a number of respondents emphasized their reluctance to participate had this research been conducted in a more conventional, face-to-face setting.

Of course, from a qualitative researcher's point of view, this absence of face-to-face engagement could also be considered a loss of potential data (in the various forms of visual cues and symbolic information contained in grimaces, winces, body movements, and the like).

There are at least two areas of potential ethical concern which are produced by the freedom and anonymity created by Web-based data-collection strategies. These include greater needs to protect children and the need for debriefing subjects (Nosek, Banafi, & Greenwald, 2002).

Protection for Children

Whether or not the research being undertaken on the Internet is designed to include children, one must be mindful that children are out there. In a standard interview or focus group, the investigator is likely to notice a child's response when the research is designed for adults. On the other hand, merely asking the subject's age over the Internet does not necessarily ensure a truthful response. There are several precautions that one can take, however, to better ensure that participants are adults when using a Web-based data-collection strategy. First, recruit potential participants from list servers, chat rooms, Web sites, and organizations having an adult target audience.

Second, avoid using cutesy images or cartoons on the survey Web site in order to increase its appeal to adults and reduce its entertainment value to children. This might seem obvious, but we tend to design our outreach strategies with our target audiences in mind, and to not think as much about how other audiences might respond.

Third, like some adult Web sites, you can require that the participant register with an *adult check* system prior to entering the research Web site.

Although this procedure generally requires the subject to enter a credit card number and/or a driver's license, the individual's identity is kept confidential from the researcher. The obvious drawback to this restriction, of course, is that many would-be participants will leave abruptly rather than enter a credit card or driver's license number over the Web—no matter how secure you make the site.

Fourth, you might include a brief set of screening questions that is likely to tap into the memory of an adult but not likely to be common information known by most children. For example, you might ask where the Los Angeles Dodgers played before they moved to Los Angeles (answer: Brooklyn), or you might ask what color Howdy Doody's hair was (answer: red), or even who sang "Alice's Restaurant" (answer: Arlo Guthrie). Although these screening questions may not be foolproof, (particularly as the answers may be found online), they are an added safeguard intended to better ensure that the average minor will not be allowed to take part in the research. If a few adults cannot answer your questions and are eliminated as a result, following such a procedure may still be in the best interest of protecting children and maintaining the ethical integrity of the research as a whole.

Debriefing the Subjects

It is not uncommon during the course of a face-to-face interview or a focus group interview to notice when a subject is becoming upset, agitated, or otherwise unsettled. However, given the nature of the Internet (and the loss of symbolic visual cues), it is not equally possible. Therefore, in the interest of ensuring no harm to participants, it is important to debrief the subjects and to determine if they require any assistance, counseling, or explanations for questions they have been asked during the course of the interview. The problems here include the innate difficulties of the technology itself. Internet participants may become involuntarily disconnected because of their server timing out, a server crash, their computer locking up or crashing, a program error, or even a power surge or outage. Or they may voluntarily and abruptly withdraw from participation because they become bored, angry, frustrated, or even simply because their doorbell or phone rings. Whatever the cause, early withdrawal from the study is a threat not only to the quality of the research but also to the ability of the researcher to adequately debrief the subject and ensure that no harm has come to the participant.

There are a number of precautions the investigator can take to improve the likelihood of providing subjects with a debriefing. First, to ensure debriefing (even if it requires little more than to ask if the subject is okay or has any questions) it may be a good idea to secure the participant's e-mail address at the beginning of the study (Nosek et al., 2002). This, of course, assumes that the research is not anonymous.

Second, the Web site might include an *exit study* button clearly apparent on each page of the study, which might automatically direct participants to a debriefing page or a page outlining how to get directly in touch with the researcher if they have any concerns or questions.

Third, the researcher could provide his or her own e-mail address at the beginning of the interview and indicate that subjects should feel free to contact him or her if they have any concerns after completing the interview or at a later time should they need to discontinue the interview suddenly.

Fourth, if the Web site is not already a chat room-based medium (which works well for both interviews and focus group strategies), subjects might be directed to a chat room to have a real-time conversation with the interviewer about any concerns or questions they have.

Informed Consent and Implied Consent

Issues surrounding informed consent grow out of the concern to avoid—or at least identify and articulate—potential risks to human subjects. Risks associated with participation in social scientific research include exposure to physical, psychological, or social injury.

Informed consent means the knowing consent of individuals to participate as an exercise of their choice, free from any element of fraud, deceit, duress, or similar unfair inducement or manipulation. In the case of minors or mentally impaired persons, whose exercise of choice is legally governed, consent must be obtained from the person or agency legally authorized to represent the interests of the individual.

In most institutionally sponsored research, consent must be ensured in writing. Typically, *informed consent statements* contain a written statement of potential risks and benefits and some phrase to the effect that these risks and benefits have been explained. As a rule, these statements are dated and signed by both the potential subject and the researchers or their designated representative. It is usual for the researcher to briefly explain the nature of the research in this informed consent document, as well as offer an assurance of confidentiality and protection of the participant's anonymity. An example of a formal informed consent form is shown in Figure 3.2.

There are chiefly two rationales behind the requirement to obtain signed informed consent statements. First, they systematically ensure that potential subjects are *knowingly* participating in a study and are doing so of their own

Figure 3.2 Example of Informed Consent Form

You are being asked to take part in a research study concerning the use of graphic images in government-funded anti-smoking campaigns.

This study is being conducted by the <name of college> department of sociology and department of public health. The principle investigator is <name>. Questions about this study may be directed to <name> at <contact information>. Questions or comments about your rights as a study participant may be directed to the institutional review board at <other contact info>.

You have been selected to take part in this research by random selection from a list of addresses within walking distance of <a local landmark>. Your participation is important to this research and we appreciate your taking the time to help.

You will be asked to view a series of images, some of which may show damaged lungs, throats and other body parts in graphic detail. You may find these images disturbing. You will be asked to discuss these images, as well as questions about your lifestyle habits including diet, exercise, smoking and drinking. In addition, you may be asked questions about your family's health and habits.

Your responses will be kept confidential by the researchers, and no one outside of the research team will see them. No individually identifying information will be reported. Names, dates and locations will be suppressed or pseudonyms will be used.

Your participation is voluntary. You do not have to provide any information that you do not wish to provide, or answer any questions that you prefer not to answer. If, at any time, you decide not to continue, you may simply say so and the interview will be terminated. At the conclusion of the interview, you will be given a Metrocard to cover your travel costs. You will receive this whether you complete the interview or not.

By signing below, you indicate that you have read and understood what is being asked of you, and that you consent to participate.

Participant:

_____   _____   _____
       name   *signature*   *date*

Interviewer:

_____   _____   _____
       name   *signature*   *date*

choice. Second, signed consent slips provide IRBs a means by which to monitor (by examining signed statements) the voluntary participation of subjects. Typically, signed informed consent slips are maintained by the researcher in a secure location for a period of three years. After this time, they should be destroyed.

Obtaining a signed informed consent slip, as may be obvious, presents in itself a slight ethical dilemma. A written record of the subjects' names (and frequently their addresses as well) means that a formal record of participants exists. In order to preserve privacy, these slips are usually kept under very careful guard by the principal investigator(s) and are revealed to IRBs only if questions arise concerning ethical practices in a given study.

Sometimes in large-scale survey questionnaire studies, separate signed informed consent slips are eliminated and replaced with implied consent. *Implied consent* is indicated by the subject taking the time to complete the lengthy questionnaire. In these circumstances, explanations of the study's purpose and potential risks and benefits are provided at the beginning of the survey.

A similar kind of implied consent can replace a signed consent statement when researchers conduct tape-recorded in-depth interviews. In this instance, the interviewers fully explain the nature of the project and the potential risks and benefits at the beginning of each interview. Next, the interviewers ask the subjects if they understand the information and are still willing to take part in the interview. Affirmative responses and completed interviews serve the purpose of implying consent in the absence of a signed consent slip. The benefit of this particular style of informed consent is the elimination of any record of the subjects' names. This procedure is particularly helpful when interviewing people who might otherwise refuse to take part in a study. To a large measure, this type of implied consent is related to the next topic—namely, confidentiality and anonymity.

Warning! Many inexperienced researchers, and not a few experienced ones, have difficulty deciding how much information constitutes *informed* consent. This difficulty frequently presents itself in one of two ways, each of which seriously undermine the research process.

Under-sharing. I have often seen research proposals written by students or others in which the investigator states that "there are no risks from participating in this study." Such a statement is almost guaranteed not to be true, and will rarely pass an IRB review. I expect that much of the time the researcher really means to say that "there are very few risks involved, most of them are pretty trivial, and I have already thought of how to handle them so that it won't be a problem." With a few careful changes in wording, that could almost be your statement of risk. Specifically, you need to *inform* your subjects of your intentions: What topics will you discuss? What actions will they be expected to perform? Who will view, read, or hear their parts? The informed consent statement identifies potential risks or harms, and specifies the means by which the risks are being managed.

Over-sharing: This one is kind of subtle. The subjects need to know what will be asked of them, but they don't need to know why. More to the point, if you reveal your actual hypothesis in the consent statement, then you have already invalidated the research. Consider an example. I might be interested in whether voters who hold "liberal" or "conservative" positions on one item, such as crime control, are likely to actually invoke liberal or conservative philosophies when explaining their positions. That is, are they really liberals or conservatives, or do they come to these specific positions by some other path of reasoning or values? For a consent statement to conduct interviews, I do need to tell subjects that I will be asking them to discuss and explain their positions on certain questions that might be considered politically controversial. But I do not need to tell them that I am trying to relate those positions to specific ideological positions. If I were to tell them that, then I would be leading the subjects to answer in the way that I expect, rather than just letting them talk. This would undermine the whole study. For reference, this same point applies to naming your study. A consent statement titled "The Persistence of Hidden Racism," for example, will kill the project before it even begins.

Confidentiality and Anonymity

Although *confidentiality* and *anonymity* are sometimes mistakenly used as synonyms, they have quite distinct meanings. *Confidentiality* is an active attempt to remove from the research records any elements that might indicate the subjects' identities. In a literal sense, *anonymity* means that the subjects remain nameless. In some instances, such as self-administered survey questionnaires, it may be possible to provide anonymity. Although investigators may know to whom surveys were distributed, if no identifying marks have been placed on the returned questionnaires, the respondents remain anonymous.

In most qualitative research, however, because subjects are known to the investigators (even if only by sight and a street name), anonymity is virtually nonexistent. Thus, it is important to provide subjects with a high degree of confidentiality.

Researchers commonly assure subjects that anything discussed between them will be kept in strict confidence, but what exactly does this mean? Naturally, this requires that researchers systematically change each subject's real name to a pseudonym or case number when reporting data. But what about changing the names of locations? Names of places, stores, or streets, in association with a description of certain characteristics about an individual, may make it possible to discover a subject's identity (Babbie, 2007; Gibbons, 1975; Morse & Richards, 2002). Even if people are incorrect about their determination of who is being identified, the result may nonetheless make people wary of cooperating in future research. Researchers, therefore, must always be extremely careful about how they discuss their subjects and the settings (Hagan, 1993, 2006; Hessler, 1992). It is also common to assure confidentiality in the formal informed consent form (see preceding discussion and Figure 3.2).

Keeping Identifying Records

It is not unusual for researchers, particularly ethnographers, to maintain systematically developed listings of real names and pseudonyms for people and places. As discussed in detail in Chapter 6, the use of such systematic lists ensures consistency during later analysis stages of the data. However, the existence of such lists creates a potential risk to subjects. Although court battles may eventually alter the situation, social scientists are presently unable to invoke professional privilege as a defense against being forced to reveal names of informants and sources during criminal proceedings. John Van Maanen (1983) once refused to turn over subpoenaed materials in a case of alleged police brutality on the questionable grounds of *research confidentiality*; he did not indicate that his efforts were successful. In other words, under normal conditions, lists of names and places can be subpoenaed along with other relevant research notes and data.

Strategies for Safeguarding Confidentiality

In effect, researchers may be placed in an ethical catch-22. On the one hand, they have a professional obligation to honor assurances of confidentiality made to subjects. On the other hand, researchers, in most cases, can be held in contempt of court if they fail to produce the subpoenaed materials. Still, investigators can take several possible steps to safeguard their reputations for being reliable concerning confidentiality.

First, as discussed in Chapter 6, researchers may obtain a Federal Certificate of Confidentiality. Under provisions set forth as conditions of award, investigators cannot be forced to reveal notes, names, or pertinent information in court. Unfortunately, few of the many thousands of researchers who apply are awarded a Federal Certificate of Confidentiality.

A second tack, which is more effective, is to avoid keeping identifying records and lists any longer than is absolutely necessary. Although this may not prevent the courts from issuing a subpoena and verbally questioning investigators, the likelihood of this occurring is reduced in the absence of written records. In the mid-1980s, a court case resulted in a federal judge ruling in favor of a sociologist's right to protect subjects by refusing to release his field notes to a grand jury investigating a suspicious fire at a restaurant where he worked and conducted covert research (Fried, 1984). This case, however, has yet to result in significant changes in judicial attitudes about the nature of research and field notes. Certainly, the potential for legal problems is likely to persist for some time.

Because of the various precedents and differing state statutes, speculating or generalizing about how a particular case may be resolved is impossible (see Boruch & Cecil, 1979; Carroll & Knerr, 1977). For instance, Rik Scarce (1990) published a book based on his research on animal rights activists entitled *Ecowarriors: Understanding the Radical Environmental Movement.* In 1993, Scarce was ordered to appear before a grand jury and asked to identify the activists involved in his research. In order to maintain the confidentiality he had promised these individuals, Scarce refused to reveal who they were. Scarce was held in contempt and confined to jail for 159 days. Even if researchers choose to risk imprisonment for contempt, the fact that there exists a moral obligation to maintain their promise of confidentiality to the best of their ability should be apparent.

Securing the Data

Although court-related disclosures provide particularly difficult problems, they are rare cases. A more likely—as well as more controllable—form of disclosure comes from careless or clumsy handling of records and data. In other words, researchers must take intentional precautions to ensure that information does not accidentally fall into the wrong hands or become public.

Researchers frequently invent what they believe are unique strategies to secure pieces of research information. More often than not, though, these innovations simply represent attempts to separate names or other identifiers from the data. Regardless of whether you store data in multiple locations or place them in metal boxes inside locked closets or a locked desk drawer, precautions against accidental disclosure must be taken.

Precautions should also be taken to ensure that research-related information is not carelessly discussed. Toward this end, signing a *statement of confidentiality* is common for each member of a research team. This is sometimes referred to as a *personnel agreement for maintaining confidentiality* (see Figure 3.3). These statements typically indicate the sensitive nature of the research and offer a promise not to talk to anybody about information obtained during the study.

While it is true that a signed statement of confidentiality is not likely to stand up in court if an investigator is subpoenaed, it does provide at least some assurance that personnel on the research team will not indiscriminately discuss the study.

Figure 3.3 Personnel Agreement for Maintaining Confidentiality

Name:_____

Position:_____

I recognize that, in the course of my participation as an investigator on the study "Drinking and Texting," I may gain access to subject information that must be treated as confidential and disclosed only under limited conditions. I agree that:

1. I will not reference or reveal any personal or identifying information outside of the context of this study.

2. I will only use this information in the manner described in the study's approved human subjects research application.

3. I will not disclose information except where required by law to do so.

4. I will take all reasonable and necessary precautions to ensure that the access and handling of information are conducted in ways that protect subject confidentiality to the greatest degree possible. This includes maintaining such information in secured and locked locations.

Signature:_____   Date:_____

Objectivity and Careful Research Design

A researcher may use an assortment of complicated measures to ensure confidentiality, but perhaps the most effective strategy is to think through the project carefully during the design stage. During the design stage of any study, the researcher can safely consider what actions must be taken to safeguard the identities of subjects as well as the data once it is collected, used, and stored.

In addition to these general safeguard issues, nurse researchers may have other ethical problems to consider because some of their research endeavors overlap into the biomedical realm. Polit and Hungler (1995, pp. 132–133), for example, outline a number of research problems and potential ethical dilemmas that each may involve. Two of these sample problems follow (Polit & Hungler, 1995, p. 132):

Research Problem

How empathic are nurses in their treatment of patients in intensive care units?

Ethical Dilemma

To address this question, the researcher would likely want to observe nurses' behavior while treating patients. Ethical research generally involves explaining the study to participants and obtaining their consent to participate in the study. Yet, if the researcher in this example informs the participating nurses that their treatment of patients will be observed, will their behavior be "normal"? If the nurses' behavior is altered because of their awareness of being observed, the entire value of the study would be undermined.

Research Problem

What are the feelings and coping mechanisms of parents whose children have a terminal illness?

Ethical Dilemma

To answer this question fully, the researcher may need to probe intrusively into the psychological state of the parents at a highly vulnerable time in their lives; such probing could be painful and even traumatic. Yet, knowledge of the parents' coping mechanisms could help to design more effective ways of dealing with parents' grief and anger.

As these examples suggest, some research situations place the researcher in an ethical bind. On the one hand, researchers want to advance scientific knowledge and understanding in the most rigorous manner possible. On the other hand, they must be careful not to violate the rights of subjects or to place them in harm's way.

Even if researchers can protect subjects from harm during the course of research, they must also consider what happens thereafter as a direct result of the research. Particularly when conducting policy-laden research on various drug- or crime-involved subjects, what investigators learn from these subjects may change the subjects' lives—and not necessarily for the better. Disseminating results that provide law enforcement agencies with improved techniques for interception could be construed as causing harm to the subjects (Lakoff, 1971; Ruane, 2005).

In addition to deciding against a given project during the design stage, researchers may consider possible ways of protecting the interests of subjects both during and following the actual study. By carefully considering possible harm to subjects in advance, researchers can sometimes avoid personal embarrassment and breaches of confidentiality.

The practice of researchers ensuring confidentiality in order to obtain the cooperation of subjects is likely to continue. It is quite important, therefore, that novice researchers recognize the potential tension between what might be called *academic freedom* and enforcement of the laws of the land. As Hofmann (1972) pointed out, social scientists must be responsible—and accountable— for their actions. With this firmly in mind, researchers ultimately may continue to question whether their ethical practices are justified by their ends. The ethical justification of research must be considered situationally, case by case (Israel & Hay, 2006).

I started this chapter by pointing out how great the impact of our research could be on people's lives, and how harmful that could be if we are not careful. I hope the cases described here have made that clear. In closing, however, I feel the need to present a different angle on the same matter. When we conduct our research, and particularly when we conduct fieldwork, we are taking from others in order to benefit ourselves. That is, we impose our curiosity, our goals, our nosiness into other people's lives. We take their time, and we reduce important elements of their lives to our data. Yes, in the long run, we hope that our efforts will benefit society in some way. In the short run, however, all of this giving on the part of our informants serves our professional needs, to complete studies, write reports, and publish papers. We have to respect the trust that our informants place in us. Poor ethical conduct is not just a professional liability. It is an antisocial act against strangers who have gone out of their way to help us.

TRYING IT OUT

You have been asked to sit on an institutional review board to consider a doctoral student's planned dissertation project. The summary for this research follows:

> My proposed research will involve an observational study of children's classroom behavior, and the effect of praise on student performance. I propose to use sixth-grade students in a local public school. I plan to enter the setting as a student teacher (the teacher of record will be told what my real purpose is). I will then divide the class into two separate groups. One group of children I will

frequently compliment and praise for being smart, clever, intelligent, and good students. The other group I will largely ignore, or when pressed, comment that they are doing an adequate job. I will collect field notes on how members of each group tend to interact with each other and their teacher. I will additionally collect discrete data (their various exam and essay scores for the class) to see if my use of positive labels affects their class performance.

After reading the foregoing summary of the proposal, answer the following questions:

1. What are some of the important ethical concerns to consider regarding this proposed research project?
2. If you were the researcher, what might you do to respond to the comments made in question 1?
3. What safeguards should the researcher take to protect the subjects in this particular study?

REFERENCES

Adler, P. A. (1985). *Wheeling and Dealing*. New York: Columbia University Press.
American Nurses Association (1975). *Human Rights Guidelines for Nurses in Clinical and Other Research*. Kansas City, MO: American Nurses Association.
American Psychological Association (1981). Ethical principles of psychologists. *American Psychologist 36*(6), 633–638.
American Psychological Association (1984). *Ethical Principles in the Conduct of Research with Human Participants*. Washington, DC: American Psychological Association.
American Sociological Association (1997). *Code of Ethics Policies and Procedures of the ASA Committee on Professional Ethics*. Washington, DC: American Sociological Association. Available online at http://asanet.org/about/ethics/COPE.cfm.
American Sociological Association (March 1984). *Code of ethics*. Washington, DC: American Sociological Association.
Babbie, E. (2007). *The Practice of Social Research* (11th ed.). Belmont, CA: Wadsworth.
Bachman, E., & Schutt, R. K. (2007). *The Practice of Research in Criminology and Criminal Justice* (3rd ed.). Thousand Oaks, CA: Sage.
Banks, C. (2004). *Criminal Justice Ethics: Theory and Practice*. Thousand Oaks, CA: Sage.
Bailey, C. A. (1996). *A Guide to Field Research*. Thousand Oaks, CA: Pine Forge Press.
Barnbaum, D. R., & Byron, M. (2001). *Research Ethics Text and Readings*. Upper Saddle River, NJ: Prentice Hall.
Becker, H. S. (1963). *Outsiders: Studies in the Sociology of Deviance*. New York: Free Press.
Berg, B. L., Austin, W. T., & Zuern, G. A. (March 1992). Institutional review boards: Who, what, where, and why? Paper presented at the annual meeting of the Academy of Criminal Justice Sciences, Pittsburgh.
Berg, B., Sañudo, F., Hovell, M., Sipan, C., Kelley, N., & Blumberg, E. (2004). The use of indigenous interviewers in a study of Latino men who have sex with men: A research note. *Sexuality and Culture 8*(1), 87–103.

Berger, R. L. (1990). Nazi science: The Dachau hypothermia experiments. *New England Journal of Medicine 322*(20), 1435–1440.

Bogdan, R., & Biklen, S. K. (1992). *Qualitative Research for Education* (2nd ed.). Boston, MA: Allyn and Bacon.

Bogdan, B., & Biklen, S. K. (2003). *Qualitative Research for Education* (4th ed.). Boston, MA: Allyn & Bacon.

Boruch, R. F., & Cecil, J. (1979). *Assuring the Confidentiality of Social Research Data.* Philadelphia, PA: University of Pennsylvania Press.

Bower, R. T., & de Gasparis, P. (1978). *Ethics in Social Research.* New York: Praeger.

Brandt, A. M. (December 1978). Racism and research: The case of the Tuskegee syphilis study. *Hasting Center Report 9*(6), 21–29.

Burns, N., & Grove, S. (2000). *The Practice of Nursing Research* (4th ed.). Philadelphia, PA: W. B. Saunders.

Burstein, A. G. (February 1987). The virtue machine. *American Psychologist 42*(2), 199–202.

Carey, J. T. (1972). Problems of access and risk in observing drug scenes. In J. D. Douglas (Ed.), *Research on Deviance.* New York: Random House.

Carroll, J. D., & Knerr, C. (1977). The confidentiality of research sources and data. Testimony presented to the Privacy Protection Study Commission. Washington, DC.

CDC (2009). U.S. Public health service syphilis study at Tuskegee. Washington, DC, Centers for Disease Control and Prevention. Retrieved [January 21, 2011] from http://www.cdc.gov/tuskegee/timeline.htm.

Champion, D. J. (2006). *Research Methods for Criminal Justice and Criminology* (3rd ed.). Upper Saddle River, NJ: Pearson/Prentice Hall.

Chartier, M., Vander Stoep, A., McCauley, E., Herting, J. R., Tracy, M., & Lymp, J. (March 2008). Parental permission: Implications for the ability of school based depression screening to research youth at risk. *Journal of School Health 78*(3), 129–186.

Christians, C. G. (2008). Ethics and politics in qualitative research. In N. K. Denzin & Y. V. Lincoln (Eds.), *The Landscape of Qualitative Research* (pp. 185–220). Los Angeles, CA: Sage.

Clinton, W. (1997). Remarks by the President in apology for study done in Tuskegee. Press release. Washington, DC: Office of the Press Secretary, The White House.

Code of Federal Regulations (1993). Protection of Human Subjects. Article 45, Part 46, Sections 101–110. Washington, DC: Office of the Federal Register, National Archives and Records Administration.

Code of Federal Regulations (January 2008). Protection of Human Subjects. Title 1, Volume 1. Washington, DC: Office of the Federal Register, National Archives and Records Administration.

Cromwell, P. F., Olsen, J. N., & Avary, D. W. (1990). *Breaking and Entering: An Ethnographic Analysis of Burglary.* Thousand Oaks, CA: Sage.

Dalton, Harlon L. (1989). "AIDS in blackface." *Daedalus 118*(3), 205–227.

Denzin, N., & Lincoln, Y. S. (2005). *The Sage Handbook of Qualitative Research* (3rd ed.). Thousand Oaks, CA: Sage.

Department of Health and Human Services (1989). Code of Federal Regulations (45 CFR 46). Protection of Human Subjects. Washington, DC: National Institutes of Health, Office for Protection from Research Risks.

Department of Health, Education, and Welfare (1978a). Report and Recommendations on Institutional Review Boards, Pub. No. (05) 78–008. Washington, DC.

Department of Health, Education, and Welfare (1978b). Belmont Report. Pub. no. (05) 78–0012. Washington, DC.

Deschenes, L. P., & Vogel, R. E. (1995). Ethical and practical issues in school-based research: A case study of active consent. Paper presented at the annual meeting of the American Society of Criminology, Boston.

Dillman, D. (2000). *Mail and Internet Surveys: The Tailored Design Method* (2nd ed.). New York: John Wiley and Sons.

Eaton, D. K., Lowry, R., Brener, N. D., Grunbaum, J. A., & Kahn, L. (2004). Passive versus active parental permission in school-based survey research: Does the type of permission affect prevalence estimates of risk behaviors. *Evaluation Review 28*(6), 564–577.

Ellickson, P. L., & Hawes, J. A. (1989). An assessment of active versus passive methods for obtaining parental consent. *Evaluation Review 13*(1), 45–55.

Engel, R. J., & Schutt, R. K. (2005). *The Practice of Research in Social Work*. Thousand Oaks, CA: Sage.

Esterberg, K. G. (2002). *Qualitative Methods in Social Research*. Boston, MA: McGraw Hill.

Eysenbach, G., & Wyatt, J. (2002). Using the Internet for surveys and health research. *Journal of Medical Internet Research 4*(2), 13–20.

Federal Register (November 30, 1978). Protection of human subjects: Institutional review boards, 943 FR 56174. Washington, DC: U.S. Government Printing Office.

Fields, C. M. (March 12, 1978). Universities fear impact of rules to protect research subjects. *Chronicle of Higher Education*, pp. 5–6.

Fried, J. P. (April 8, 1984). Judge protects waiter's notes on fire inquiry. *New York Times*, p. A47.

Frisch, M. (2008). Three dimensions and more: Oral history beyond the paradoxes of method. In S. Nagy Hesse-Biber & P. Leavy (Eds.), *Handbook of Emergent Methods* (pp. 221–238). New York: The Guilford Press.

Gibbons, D. C. (February 1975). Unidentified research sites and fictitious names. *American Sociologist 10*, 32–36.

Granberg, D. O., & Galliher, J. F. (2010). *A Most Human Enterprise: Controversies in the Social Sciences*. Lanham, MD: Lexington Books.

Gray, B. G. (1977). The functions of human subjects review committees. *American Journal of Psychiatry 134*, 907–909.

Gray, F. D. (2002). *The Tuskegee Syphilis Study: The Real Story and Beyond*. Montgomery, AL: River City Publishing.

Hagan, F. E. (1993). *Research Methods in Criminal Justice and Criminology*. New York: Macmillan.

Hagan, F. E. (2006). *Research Methods in Criminal Justice and Criminology* (7th ed.). Boston, MA: Allyn and Bacon.

Hershey, N., & Miller, R. (1976). *Human Experimentation and the Law*. Germantown, MD: Aspen.

Hertz, R., & Imber, J. B. (1993). Fieldwork in elite settings: Introduction. *Journal of Contemporary Ethnography 22*(1), 3–6.

Hessler, R. M. (1992). *Social Research Methods*. New York: West Publishing.

Hine, C. (2008). Internet research as emergent practice. In S. Nagy Hesse-Biber & P. Leavy (Eds.), *Handbook of Emergent Methods* (pp. 525–541). New York: The Guilford Press.

Hofmann, G. (1972). The quest for relevance: Some implications for social research. *ET AL. 3*, 50–57.

Holden, C. (1975). Privacy: Congressional efforts are coming to fruition. *Science 188*, 713–715.

Humphreys, L. (1970). *Tearoom Trade: Impersonal Sex in Public Places.* Chicago, IL: Aldine.

Illingworth, N. (2001). The Internet matters: Exploring the use of the Internet as a research tool. *Sociological Research Online 6*(2). Retrieved [June 28, 2011] from http://www.socresonline.org.uk/6/2/illingworth.html.

Israel, M., & Hay, L. (2006). *Research Ethics for Social Scientists: Between Ethical Conduct and Regulatory Compliance.* London: Sage.

Jacobs, B. A. (1998). Researching crack dealers: Dilemmas and contradictions. In J. Ferrell & M. S. Hamm (Eds.), *Ethnography at the Edge: Crime Deviance and Field Research* (pp. 160–177). Boston, MA: Northeastern University Press.

Jones, J. H. (1993). *Bad Blood: The Tuskegee Syphilis Experiment.* New York: Free Press.

Katz, J. (1972). *Experimentation with Human Beings.* New York: Sage.

Kearney, K. A., Hopkins, R. H., Mauss, A. L., & Weisheit, R. A. (1983). Sample bias resulting from a requirement for written parental consent. *Public Opinion Quarterly 47*, 96–102.

Kelman, H. C. (1967). The human use of human subjects: The problem of deception in social psychological experiments. *Psychological Bulletin 67*(1), 1–11.

Lakoff, S. A. (1971). Knowledge, power, and democratic theory. *Annals 394*, 5–12.

Levine, R. J. (1986). *Declaration of Helsinki. Ethics and Regulations of Clinical Research* (2nd ed.). Baltimore, MD: Urban and Schwarzenberg.

Liemohn, W. (1979). Research involving human subjects. *Research Quarterly 50*(2), 157–163.

Lincoln, Y. V. (2008). Institutional review boards and methodological conservatism. In N. K. Denzin & Y. V. Lincoln (Eds.), *The Landscape of Qualitative Research* (pp. 221–243). Los Angeles, CA: Sage.

Marks, F., & Yardley, L. (2004). *Research Methods for Clinical and Health Psychology.* Thousand Oaks, CA: Sage.

Martin, D. C., Arnold, J. D., Zimmerman, T. F., & Richard, R. H. (1968). Human subjects in clinical research—A report on three studies. *New England Journal of Medicine 279*, 1426–1431.

McSkimming, M. J. (1996). Gaming and gambling in Tavern life. Doctoral dissertation. Department of Criminology, Indiana University of Pennsylvania, Indiana, PA.

Meyer, R. E. (August 1977). Subjects' rights, freedom of inquiry, and the future of research in the addictions. *American Journal of Psychiatry 134*(8), 899–903.

Milgram, S. (1963). Behavioral study of obedience. *Journal of Abnormal and Social Psychology 67*(37), 1–378.

Miller, J. M. (1998). Covert participant observation: Reconsidering the least used method. In P. Tontodonato & F. E. Hagan (Eds.), *The Language of Research in Criminal Justice.* Boston, MA: Allyn and Bacon.

Miller, J. M., & Tewksbury, R. (2001). *Extreme Methods: Innovative Approaches to Social Science Research.* Boston, MA: Allyn and Bacon.

Miller, M. J., & Tewksbury, R. (2005). *Research Methods: A Qualitative Reader.* Upper Saddle River, NJ: Pearson/Prentice Hall.

Morse, J. M. (1994). *Critical Issues in Qualitative Research Methods.* Thousand Oaks, CA: Sage.

Morse, J. M., & Richards, L (2002). *Read Me First: For a User's Guide to Qualitative Methods.* Thousand Oaks, CA: Sage.

Nason-Clark, N., & Neitz, M. J. (2001). *Feminist Narratives and the Sociology of Religion*. Walnut Creek, CA: Alta Mira Press.

Nosek, B. A., Banafi, M. R., & Greenwald, A. G. (2002). E-research: Ethics, security, design, and control in psychological research on the Internet. *Journal of Social Issues 58*(1), 161–172.

Nguyen, T. H. (2003). Video gambling Vietnamese cafés: An observational study of "Hot Line" machines in Southern California. Unpublished Masters Thesis, Department of Criminal Justice, California State University, Long Beach, CA.

Polit, D. F., & Hungler, B. (1995). *Nursing Research: Principles and Methods* (6th ed.). Philadelphia, PA: Lippincott, Williams & Wilkins.

Punch, M. (1994). Politics and ethics in qualitative research. In N. K. Denzin & Y. S. Lincoln (Eds.), *Handbook of Qualitative Research* (pp. 83–98). Thousand Oaks, CA: Sage.

Punch, K. F. (2005). *Introduction to Social Research: Quantitative and Qualitative Approaches*. London: Sage.

Rainwater, L., & Pittman, D. J. (1967). Ethical problems in studying a politically sensitive and deviant community. *Social Problems 14*(4), 357–365.

Reverby, S. M. (2011). "Normal Exposure" and Inoculation Syphilis: A PHS "Tuskegee" Doctor in Guatemala, 1946–1948. *Journal of Policy History 23*(1), 6–28.

Rose, D. (1988). *Black American Street Life: South Philadelphia 1969–1971*. Pennsylvania, PA: University of Pennsylvania Press.

Ross, L. F. (2006). *Children in Medical Research: Access Versus Protection*. New York: Oxford University Press.

Ruane, J. M. (2005). *Essentials of Research Methods: A Guide to Social Science Research*. Malden, MA: Blackwell Publishing.

Scarce, R. (1990). *Ecowarriors: Understanding the Radical Environmental Movement*. Chicago, IL: Noble Press.

Schutt, R. (2006). *Investigating the Social World: The Process & Practice of Research* (5th ed.). Thousand Oaks, CA: Pine Forge Press.

Severson, H., & Ary, D. (1983). Sampling bias due to consent procedures with adolescents. *Addictive Behaviors 8*, 433–437.

Shalala, D. E. (June 17, 1997). Ethics in human subjects research—action. Memorandum from the Secretary of Health and Human Services, Washington, DC.

Taylor, R. B. (1994). *Research Methods in Criminal Justice*. New York: McGraw-Hill.

Taylor, S. J., & Bogdan, R. (1998). *Introduction to Qualitative Research Methods: A Guidebook & Resource*. New York: John Wiley and Sons.

Tewksbury, R. (1990). Patrons of porn: Research notes on the clientele of adult bookstores. *Deviant Behavior 11*(3), 259–272.

Thomas, J. (Spring 1999). Balancing the ethical conundrums of Internet research—an existential view from the trenches. *Iowa Journal of Communications 31*, 8–20.

Thompson, T. (1984). A comparison of methods of increasing parental consent rates in social research. *Public Opinion Quarterly 48*(4), 779–787.

Trochim, W. M. K. (2001). *The Research Methods Knowledge Base* (2nd ed.). Cincinnati, OH: Atomic Dog Publishers.

Tunnell, K. D. (1998). Honesty, secrecy, and deception in the sociology of crime: Confessions and reflections from the backstage. In J. Ferrell & M. S. Hamm (Eds.), *Ethnography at the Edge: Crime Deviance and Field Research* (pp. 206–220). Boston, MA: Northeastern University Press.

U.S. Department of Education. (2007). *Balancing Student Privacy and School Safety*. Washington, DC: U.S. Department of Education.

Van Maanen, J. (1983). The moral fix: On the ethics of fieldwork. In R. M. Emerson (Ed.), *Contemporary Field Research* (pp. 269–287). Boston, MA: Little, Brown.

Viadero, D. (February 27, 2002). New student-survey policy worries some researchers. *Education Week 21*(1), 8.

Wetzstein, C. (January 29, 2002). All that schools survey. *The Washington Times.*

Wexler, S. (1990). Ethical obligations and social research. In K. L. Kempf (Ed.), *Measurement Issues in Criminology* (pp. 78–107). New York: Springer-Verlag.

W.H.O. (2002). *International Ethical Guidelines for Biomedical Research on Human Subjects.* New York: World Health Organization.

Wynn, L. L. (2011). Ethnographers' experiences of institutional ethics oversight: Results from a quantitative and qualitative survey. *Journal of Policy History 23*(1), 94–114.

Zimbardo, P. G. (1972). Pathology of imprisonment. *Society 9*(6), 4–6.

Chapter 4

A Dramaturgical Look at Interviewing

NTERVIEWING MAY BE DEFINED simply as a conversation with a purpose. Specifically, the purpose is to gather information. The interviewer asks questions and the interviewee, called the informant, provides the answers. What could be easier?

Unfortunately, the question of *how* to conduct an interview is not so simple. Is interviewing an art, a craft, a contest of wills, or something entirely different? Interview training manuals vary from long lists of specific do's and don'ts to lengthy, abstract discussions on empathy, intuition, and motivation. The extensive literature on interviewing contains numerous descriptions of the interviewing process. In some cases, being a good interviewer is described as an innate ability or quality possessed only by certain people. Interviewing, from this perspective, has been described as an art rather than a skill or a science (Fontana & Frey, 1998; Grobel, 2004). In earlier approaches, interviewing was described as a game in which both the researcher and the informant received intrinsic rewards for participation (Benny & Hughes, 1956; Holmstrom, cited in Manning, 1967). In contrast to this ineffable sensibility, interviewing was described by others as a technical skill you can learn in the same way you might learn how to change a flat tire. In this case, an interviewer is like a laborer or a hired hand (Roth, 1966). Contemporary sources describe interviewing as some sort of face-to-face social interaction, although exactly what distinguishes this type of interaction from others is often left to the imagination (Leedy & Ormrod, 2001, 2004; Salkind, 2008; Warren & Karner, 2005).

To be sure, there is some element of truth to each of these characterizations. Anybody can be instructed in the basic orientations, strategies, procedures, and repertoire (to be discussed later in this chapter) of interviewing. Gorden (1992), for example, offers a clear, step-by-step description of how to go about the process of interviewing. To a large extent, Gorden and others offer the basic rules of the game (see, e.g., Seidman, 2006) in which the object of one player is to extract information, but it is not assumed that the object of the other is to withhold it. Furthermore, there is assuredly something extraordinary (if not unnatural) about a conversation in which one participant has an explicitly or implicitly scripted set of lines and the other participant does not. To judge any of these characteristics exclusively, however, seems inadequate. Just as some artists and actors are perceived by their peers to be exceptional while others in the field are viewed as mediocre, so can this assessment be made about interviewers. The previous characterizations have served little more than to circumscribe what might be termed the possible range of an interviewer's ability; they have not added appreciably to the depth of understanding about the process of interviewing or how you might go about mastering this process.

This chapter is devoted to the latter effort and draws on the symbolic interactionist paradigm—the stream of symbolic interaction more commonly referred to as *dramaturgy*. An interview, then, may be seen as a performance in which the researcher and subject play off of one another toward a common end.

Dramaturgy and Interviewing

This chapter attempts to illustrate dramaturgy's beneficial effects on interviewing beyond the interviewer training stage. Discussions will include types of interview structures, interview guidelines, the interviewer roles (social roles played by the investigator), rapport, reactivity, and accessing difficult or sensitive materials.

It has been suggested by Denzin (2001, p. 26) that we inhabit a performance-based, dramaturgical culture. Indeed, even in research, the line between performer and audience sometimes blurs, and the whole process becomes a dramatic performance. So-called "reality-based" television shows have significantly influenced what we now consider entertainment and what we consider real, blurring the lines between performance and everyday life. Research is swept along with the other aspects of culture, and it too is significantly affected by the blurring of lines between performance and reality. Researchers entering into the field take on defined "social roles" in relation to their informants. They "perform" certain kinds of interactions through their interviews. Nonetheless, there should be no fiction to the encounter. You, the researcher, enter into the interview as yourself, needing to know certain things from others, who we hope will answer honestly as themselves. What, then, is the performative aspect?

Research, particularly field research, is sometimes divided into two separate phases—namely, data collection (getting in) and data analysis (Shaffir, Stebbins, & Turowetz, 1980). *Getting in* is typically defined as various techniques and procedures intended to secure access to a setting, its participants, and knowledge about phenomena and activities being observed (Friedman, 1991, 2007). *Analysis* makes sense of the information accessed during the getting-in phase. This is a useful distinction for teaching, but not the most accurate description of the process. Viewing data collection instead as an interpretive performance blurs the boundaries between these two phases—assuming they ever really existed. As an active interviewer, you need to consider the meanings of the information you are gathering from each question as you prepare the question to follow.

Nonetheless, this chapter will clarify the two phases and consider each phase separately, even as they run into one another. In the case of the former, getting in means learning the ropes of various skills and techniques necessary for effective interviewing (Bogdan & Biklen, 2006; Gorden, 1992; Lofland, Snow, Anderson, & Lofland, 2005). Regarding the latter, as this chapter will show, there are a number of ways you may go about making sense out of accessed information. This topic will be explored in greater depth in Chapter 11.

Let us look at the process of interviewing, specifically the notion of interviewing, as an "encounter" (Goffman, 1967), or as a "social interaction" (Fontana & Frey, 1998). All discussions of interviewing are guided by some model or image of the interview situation, and here interviewing is perceived as a "social performance" (Goffman, 1959), organized around the premise that interviewing is best accomplished if guided by a dramaturgical model.

Dramaturgy involves the elements and language of theater, stagecraft, and stage management. This theoretical perspective is derived in part from the symbolic interactionists' general assumption that humans perceive and interact in reality through the use of symbols. Drama, then, is a mode of symbolic action in which some individuals act symbolically for others who watch symbolically. In the case of the former, the term used to describe acting individuals is usually simply *actors*. In the case of the latter, the reference typically is *social audience* or simply *audience*. The actors convey meaning through coded words and deeds. The audience understands these meanings by decoding them.

The symbolic action that passes between actor and audience is called a *social performance* or simply a *performance*. In this chapter, the language of dramaturgy is applied metaphorically to a concrete situation—namely, the interview. The dramaturgical orientation offered in this chapter is similar in some ways to what Douglas (1985) terms *creative interviewing*. Creative interviewing involves using a set of techniques to move past the mere words and sentences exchanged during the interview process. It includes creating an appropriate climate for informational exchanges and for mutual disclosures. This means that the interviewer will display his or her own feelings during the interview as well as elicit those of the subject. The dramaturgical model of interviewing presented here is also similar to what we refer to as performance-based or, simply, performance interviews. Performance interviews (Butler, 1997; Mienczakowski, 1995, 2000), then, can be situated in the complex system of discourse, where traditional, everyday, and avant-garde meanings of theater, film, video, ethnography, performance, text, and audience come together and inform one another (Denzin, 2001). Performance methods differ from other qualitative methods because of the unique sense of performance. In performance, there is immediacy in the literal interview performance, whereas, such immediacy is lacking in the one-dimensional transcript of a traditional interview (Leavy, 2008).

Also similar to the dramaturgical perspective presented here is what Holstein and Gubrium (1995, 2004) call *active interviewing*. From their perspective, the interview is not arbitrary or one-sided. Instead, the interview is viewed as a meaning-making occasion in which the actual circumstance of the meaning construction is important (Holstein & Gubrium, 1995, 2004). The proposed dramaturgical model differs most from the active interview in its emphasis on the interviewer *using* the constructed relationship of the interviewer and subject to draw out information from the subject. The various devices used by the dramaturgical interviewer, therefore, move this orientation slightly closer to the creative interviewing model and the more reflexive performance interview.

Types of Interviews

Before we make any decisions about the dramaturgical style that we wish to adopt for any given interview, we must select its basic type: the standardized (formal or highly structured) interview, the unstandardized (informal or nondirective) interview, and the semistandardized (guided-semistructured or focused) interview. The major difference among these different interview structures is their degree of rigidity with regard to presentational structure. Thus, if we cast them onto an imaginary continuum of formality, they would look a little like the model in Figure 4.1.

The Standardized Interview

The *standardized interview*, as suggested in Figure 4.1, uses a formally structured "schedule" of interview questions, or script. The interviewers are required to ask subjects to respond to each question, exactly as worded.

Figure 4.1 Interview Structure Continuum of Formality

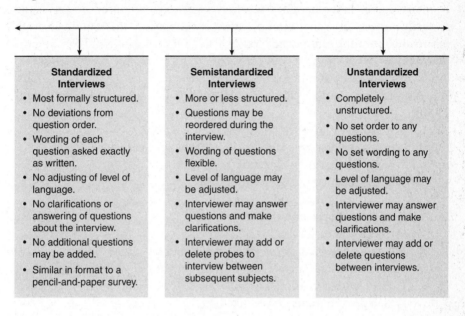

Standardized Interviews	Semistandardized Interviews	Unstandardized Interviews
• Most formally structured.	• More or less structured.	• Completely unstructured.
• No deviations from question order.	• Questions may be reordered during the interview.	• No set order to any questions.
• Wording of each question asked exactly as written.	• Wording of questions flexible.	• No set wording to any questions.
• No adjusting of level of language.	• Level of language may be adjusted.	• Level of language may be adjusted.
• No clarifications or answering of questions about the interview.	• Interviewer may answer questions and make clarifications.	• Interviewer may answer questions and make clarifications.
• No additional questions may be added.	• Interviewer may add or delete probes to interview between subsequent subjects.	• Interviewer may add or delete questions between interviews.
• Similar in format to a pencil-and-paper survey.		

The rationale here is to offer each subject approximately the same stimulus so that responses to questions, ideally, will be comparable (Babbie, 2007). Researchers using this technique have fairly solid ideas about the things they want to uncover during the interview (Flick, 2006; Merriam, 2001; Schwartz & Jacobs, 1979). In other words, researchers assume that the questions scheduled in their interview instrument are sufficiently comprehensive, and sufficiently simple, to elicit from subjects all (or nearly all) information relevant to the study's topic(s). They further assume that all questions have been worded in a manner that allows subjects to understand clearly what they are being asked. Stated in slightly different terms, the questions are usually short and simple. Finally, they assume that the meaning of each question is identical for every subject. These assumptions, however, remain chiefly "untested articles of faith" (Denzin, 1978, p. 114). However, to the extent that standardized interviews are applied to relatively straightforward matters of fact, these assumptions seem safe.

In sum, standardized interviews are designed to elicit information using a set of predetermined questions that are expected to elicit the subjects' thoughts, opinions, and attitudes about study-related issues. A standardized interview may be thought of as a kind of survey interview. Standardized interviews, thus, operate from the perspective that one's thoughts are intricately related to one's actions in the sense that one measures tangible facts, such as actions, without further probing questions about informants' thoughts or interpretations. Standardized interviews are frequently used on very large research projects in which multiple interviewers collect the same data from informants from the same sample pool. This format is also useful for longitudinal studies in which the researcher wishes to measure, as closely as possible, exactly the same data at multiple points in time.

A typical standardized interview might look like this diet history (Berg, 1986):

1. When is the first time you eat or drink on a typical day?
2. What is the first thing you eat?
3. When is the next time you eat or drink?
4. What do you eat or drink?
5. When is the next time you eat or drink?
6. What do you eat or drink?
7. What else do you eat or drink on a typical day?
8. How many times a week do you eat eggs? Cheese? Milk? Fish? Beef? Pork? Beans? Corn? Grits? Bread? Cereal? Ice Cream? Fruits? Vegetables?
9. Which protein foods do you like best?
10. Which protein foods do you not eat?
11. What foods do you like to eat between meals?

The Unstandardized Interview

In contrast to the rigidity of standardized interviews, *unstandardized interviews* are loosely structured and are located on the imaginary continuum (as depicted in Figure 4.1) at the opposite extreme from standardized interviews. While certain topics may be necessary and planned, the actual flow of the conversation will vary considerably according to the responses of each informant. No specific questions need to be scripted. As much as possible, the interviewer encourages the informant to lead the conversation. In place of an "interview schedule," researchers prepare a looser set of topics or issues that one plans on discussing, possibly with a preferred order in which to address them. These "interview guidelines" serve as notes, or possibly a checklist, for the interviewer. One way or another, by whatever route you and your informant follow, the guidelines indicate the subject matter that you intend to cover.

Naturally, unstandardized interviews operate from a different set of assumptions than those of standardized interviews. First, interviewers begin with the assumption that they do not know in advance what all the necessary questions are. Consequently, they cannot predetermine a complete list of questions to ask. They also assume that not all subjects will necessarily find equal meaning in like-worded questions—in short, that subjects may possess different vocabularies or different symbolic associations. Rather than papering over these individual differences, by forcing each interview down the same path, an unstandardized interview encourages and pursues them. The individual responses and reactions are the data that we want. The unstandardized interview process is much more like a regular conversation in which the researcher responds to the informant as much as the other way around.

In an unstandardized interview, interviewers must develop, adapt, and generate questions and follow-up probes appropriate to each given situation and the central purpose of the investigation. The prepared guidelines keep the conversation heading in the right direction while the details are generated in the verbal exchange itself. The interview is therefore like an improvised performance in which the performers have agreed in advance on the underlying themes and purposes, but left the details to be worked out in the moment.

Loosely structured interviews are sometimes used during the course of field research to augment field observations. For example, Diane Barone (2002) undertook a field study that examined literacy teaching and learning in two kindergarten classes at a school considered to be at risk and inadequate by the state. Barone conducted observations in the classrooms and wrote weekly field notes. In addition, however, she included ongoing informal interviews with the teachers throughout the yearlong study. Such unstructured interviews, or conversations, permit researchers to gain additional information about various phenomena they might observe by asking questions. Unstandardized interviews, however, are not restricted to field research projects, as illustrated by content analysis study undertaken by Horowitz and her associates (2000). In this study, the researchers were interested in examining the sociocultural disparities in health care. Toward this end, the investigators examined the contents of health care and health articles with regard to racial, ethnic, and socioeconomic disparities. In addition to this more archival approach, they also included informal interviews with research, policy, and program experts to assist in developing a framework of programs that addressed disparities (Horowitz, Davis, Palermo, & Vladeck, 2000). Thus, the informal interviews provided important information for these investigators along with the data culled from various published and unpublished articles and documents.

Unstructured interviews are optimal for dynamic and unpredictable situations, and situations in which the variety of respondents suggests a wide variety of types of responses. Consider the following two hypothetical answers to the same question.

Interview 1

Interviewer: What do you plan to do when this job draws to a close?

Respondent: Well, I have a few options that I'm looking into, but I might just use the downtime to finish my training certification.

Interview 2

Interviewer: What do you plan to do when this job draws to a close?

Respondent: Why do you need to know that?

There are times when the basic framework of questions that you might have prepared only serve to open the doors to an entirely different discussion. With an unstructured approach, that can lead to a successful interview of surprising richness.

Whereas highly structured interviews assume that the researchers and informants share a system of meaning, researchers undertaking loosely structured interviews typically seek to learn the nature of the informants' meaning system itself.

The Semistandardized Interview

As drawn in Figure 4.1, the *semistandardized interview* can be located somewhere between the extremes of the completely standardized and the completely unstandardized interviewing structures. This type of interview involves the implementation of a number of predetermined questions and special topics. These questions are typically asked of each interviewee in a systematic and consistent order, but the interviewers are allowed freedom to digress; that is, the interviewers are permitted (in fact, expected) to probe far beyond the answers to their prepared standardized questions.

Again, certain assumptions underlie this strategy. First, if questions are to be standardized, they must be formulated in words familiar to the people being interviewed (in vocabularies of the subjects). Police officers, for example, do not speak about all categories of persons in a like manner. Research among police in the 1980s identified special terms they used including "scrots" (derived from the word *scrotum*), used as a derogatory slur when describing an assortment of bad guys; "skinners," used to describe rapists; "dips" to describe pickpockets; and "clouters," used to describe persons who break into automobiles to steal things. Of course such informal language changes with subsequent generations, and varies considerably across places, so most of the examples given here would be hopelessly out of date in a contemporary interview, possibly undermining the researcher's credibility. Hence, it is often useful to adapt your actual wording to the context of the interview.

Questions used in a semistandardized interview can reflect an awareness that individuals understand the world in varying ways (Gubrium & Holstein, 2003). Researchers, thus, seek to approach the world from the subject's perspective. Researchers can accomplish this by adjusting the level of language of planned questions or through unscheduled probes (described in greater detail in the following interview excerpt) that arise from the interview process itself.

One study of Latino men who have sex with other men (Berg et al., 2004; Zellner et al., 2008) used semistandardized interviews. Although many of the primary questions asked to each of the 35 subjects derived from the predetermined schedule, the men's perceptions were often more fully elaborated after being asked an unscheduled probe. For example, after being asked a question, the subject might have responded with a brief "yes" or "no." In order to elicit additional information, the interviewer would then ask, "And then?" or "Uh huh, could you tell me more about that?" or some similar simple inquiry.

On other occasions the interviewer might have asked another full question seeking additional information. An example of these scheduled and unscheduled probes from interview number 14 illustrates this (Berg, 2002). All questions were asked and answered in Spanish and later translated into English.

Interviewer [Scheduled Question]:   How about your family, do they know about your sexual activities?

Subject: Yes, yes, they do know how I am, how I see myself. But they do not like it. On some occasions they tell me that they are going to send me to Mexico. They wanted to bribe me, but that is why I work, so I do not have to depend on them economically.

Interviewer [Scheduled Question]:   What do your parents (brothers, sisters, etc.) think about your participation with sex between same masculine genders?

Subject: Okay, my parents found out because I told my sister that I was homosexual, because one of my father's brothers had raped me. My sister then told my father and my parents supported me. If the rest of my family does not support me, I do not care, just as long as my parents accept me, that is enough for me.

Interviewer [Unscheduled Probe]:   When your uncle raped you, did he know you were gay?

Subject: Yes.

Interviewer [Unscheduled Probe]:   How old were you at the time of the rape?

Subject: I was only eight years old when he raped me.

Interviewer [Unscheduled Probe]:   Yes, and then? (pause)

Subject: I was eight years old when my uncle raped me, we were at the ranch, my mother and father went to make a phone call to my brothers who were in the United States so I was left alone with him. I already showed signs of being gay, my uncle took off my clothes, hit me and raped me. I still do not know why he did this to me; after all we were family. He threatened me, and told me to not say anything or he was going to hurt my parents. But at age thirteen I exploded, I could not keep it in any longer, so I told my sister what was happening. It was already the second time he had raped me. My sister was crying, she hugged me and said that she loved me. She then told my father and he made me confront my uncle. My father thought I was lying to him, but my uncle could not lie; he lowered his head and admitted that he had raped me. My father questioned him on why he did it and his response was that I wanted to do it with a homosexual. But I always ask myself, "Why me?"

Interviewer [Unscheduled Probe]:   How old was your uncle?

Subject: He was twenty-six years old and I was eight the first time he raped me. I already knew I was homosexual, but I would have preferred to experience that with the person that I loved, not by being raped. That gets me so upset and I will never forget it. I do not even wish for it to happen to my worst enemy.

The interviewer's prepared questions and notes could not have anticipated this turn in the conversation. Yet, to "stick to the script" would involve ignoring a topic that is clearly central to this informant's understanding of the subject being discussed. One could not understand this man's feelings, meaning systems, or other concerns without following the conversational leads that he offered.

In another study, the investigators used a semistandardized interview to draw out the lives and professional work experiences of 12 women, all of whom began working in parole or corrections between 1960 and 2001 (Ireland & Berg, 2006, 2008). The interview focused on various aspects of each woman's experiences working in a largely male-dominated occupation and how they perceived the respect they received—or did not receive—from their male counterparts and the parolees. The flexibility of the semistructured interview allowed the interviewers both to ask a series of regularly structured questions, permitting comparisons across interviews, and to pursue areas spontaneously initiated by the interviewee. This resulted in a much more textured set of accounts from participants than would have resulted had only scheduled questions been asked.

The Data Collection Instrument

The interview is an especially effective method of collecting information for certain types of research and, as noted earlier in this chapter, for addressing certain types of assumptions. Particularly when investigators are interested in understanding the perceptions of participants or learning how participants come to attach certain meanings to phenomena or events, interviewing provides a useful means of access. However, interviewing is only one of a number of ways researchers can obtain answers to questions. The determination of which data-gathering technique to use is necessarily linked to the type of research question being studied.

For instance, Becker (1963) suggested that if you were interested in knowing how frequently a subject smokes marijuana (how many times daily, weekly, monthly, etc.), then you could effectively use a questionnaire survey. Indeed, the objective feel of an anonymous survey may both encourage more respondents to respond and reduce the likelihood of them exaggerating or downplaying their use patterns. If, however, you were interested in the sensation of marijuana smoking (the emotion-laden sensory experience as perceived by the subject), a more effective means of obtaining this information might be an open-ended interview (Mutchnick & Berg, 1996). This is the kind of question that requires some thought, some back and forth with an interviewer, to help the informant arrive at an answer.

A similar consideration is necessary when you determine what sort of structure an interview should have. For example, Rossman (1992) used semistructured interviews in his examination of the development of Super-fund community relations plans (Superfunds are federal funds offered to assist communities in environmental cleanup activities). In such large-scale public studies, interviews have to be somewhat standardized, for comparability. And researchers need to create the research structure that others, paid interviewers, might follow. But too much standardization can be counter-productive. Rossman (1992, p. 107) explains:

> Because of the nature of the information collected, applied researchers who develop community relations plans are best advised to use interviews and inter-viewers. Questionnaires lack the flexibility that is required to capture the subtle character of risk definition, especially a risk that is often defined ambiguously within a community. Risks such as those associated with Superfund sites are a major part of the community's social structure, but are less crystallized than risk associated with crime, or even natural environmental risk.

Conversely, in my work on community responses to HIV, unstructured inter-views allowed me to first question and later abandon some of the assumptions that had guided my initial study design. As I expressed it at the time (Lune, 2007, p. 184), I had begun with the expectation that groups pursued different forms of action due to different ideological and/or pragmatic priorities.

> Happily, I had chosen to start each interview with personal questions about the background and "career" trajectory of each of my informants. What I learned from that was that HIV/AIDS work was, for most of my informants, a calling and not a career. They did not divide the field in separate categories of function. They did not argue over the "right way" to do what they did. … Most of the people whom I interviewed or emailed back and forth with were more like voluntary firefighters in an endless summer of wildfires. They went where they were needed, and they stayed as long as they could.

Similarly, Ellis, Kiesinger, and Tillmann-Healy (1997, p. 121) wanted to gain a more reflexive and intimate understanding of women's emotional experiences and, therefore, decided to use an interactive approach and a more or less unstructured interviewing style:

> [We] view interviewing as a collaborative communication process occurring between researchers and respondents, although we do not focus on validity and bias. For us, interactive interviewing involves the sharing of personal and social experiences of both respondents and researchers, who tell (and sometimes write) their stories in the context of a developing relationship.

Thus, when determining what type of interview format to use, you must consider the kinds of questions you want to ask and the sorts of answers you expect to receive. This line of thought naturally leads to consideration of how to create questions and interview guidelines.

Guideline Development

The first step to interview preparation has already been implied: Researchers must determine the nature of their investigation and the objectives of their research. This determination provides the researchers with a starting point from which to begin writing guidelines for the interview, if not an actual script. We refer to the prepared materials through which the data collection is organized as the data collection "instrument." Examples include an actual survey form for surveys, the schedule of questions for highly standardized interviews, or the researcher's guidelines for less standardized interviews. In the remainder of this section I will discuss the development of interview guidelines.

A good place to begin is with a kind of *outline*, listing all the broad categories you feel may be relevant to your study. This preliminary listing allows you to visualize the general format of the guidelines. Next, researchers should develop sets of questions relevant to each of the outlined categories.

I typically suggest that the researcher begin by listing out (kind of as a freewriting exercise) all of the conceptual areas that may be relevant to the overall topic under investigation. For example, let's imagine you are seeking to investigate collegiate drinking. You can begin with a short list of topics and ideas that you expect would relate to your subject. After reviewing some of the literature on this topic, you will almost certainly need to refine your list. Let's imagine that you decide that the following general areas (conceptual areas) will need to be explored in the interview: demographics, family drinking practices, leisure activities, school achievements, personal drinking practices, and involvement in organizations. After listing each of these major conceptual areas in what amount to separate columns, you can begin to list under each, general areas of inquiry—not necessarily specific questions, but items that may be formed into specific questions. Let's consider the first three conceptual areas listed earlier (the areas listed are not necessarily exhaustive of all that might be listed).

Demographics	Family Drinking Practices	Leisure Activities
Age	Parental drinking	Extracurricular activities
Education	Sibling drinking	Sports involvements
Ethnicity	Grandparent drinking	Social activities
Religious affiliation	Extended family members	Television viewing
Family members	drinking	Video/computer game
Finances	Family drinking situations	playing at home
	Family drinking concerns	Game playing outside
		of home
		Reading

For a nonstandardized interview, this table alone may serve as your interview guidelines. The researcher enters into the conversation with this set of crucial topics that need to be addressed. How they are covered may vary from one interview to the next. Since we use nonstandardized interviews to discover how informants think and feel about a topic, rather than just the answers to our questions, it is important not to force the conversation down the paths of our own choosing. Nonetheless, we need to cover certain topics, and therefore to remain aware of which subjects occur "naturally" through the interview, and which we must "force" into it before we finish.

A semistandardized interview requires more structure. Having developed your table of conceptual areas, as mentioned earlier, you can begin to create relevant questions for each of the items listed under each major conceptual heading. You may adopt a preferred (standardized) wording for certain measures. In the case of Demographics, in the preceding example, you might create the following questions: "What is your date of birth?" for Age, "What would you say is the highest level of education you have completed?" for Education, and so forth. You may notice that each of these questions is written in a rather colloquial fashion. This is intentional and allows for a more flowing and conversational interview interaction. Depending on your informant's response, you may choose to follow some or all of these matter-of-fact questions with a more probing one. You may have to refine, change, shorten, or reword these questions later; but for now, it allows you to begin getting a sense of how many questions you will be asking for each conceptual area in order to collect the data that you need.

Question Order (Sequencing), Content, and Style

The specific ordering (sequencing), phrasing, level of language, adherence to subject matter, and general style of questions may depend on the backgrounds of the subjects as well as their education, age, and so forth. Additionally, researchers must take into consideration the central aims and focuses of their studies. For studies in which a certain amount of personal or potentially uncomfortable information is included, it is often best to begin with the easy material and work up to the more challenging questions. This allows informants to become comfortable with the interview process before deciding how much they are really willing to share. On the other hand, when the central focus of the interview is a sensitive topic, whether it involves difficult moral decisions, stigmatized behaviors, illegal activities, or the like, this gradual approach may feel manipulative. Often it is better to get to the point quickly so that your informants fully understand what sort of interview this is meant to be. The risk is that some of them will drop out almost immediately, and that you won't be able to use their data. The benefit, however, is that the participation you receive from the rest is deliberate, knowledgeable, and unforced.

From my perspective, there are no hard and fast rules or rigid recipes for sequencing questions in an interview schedule. However, as many writers recommend, I usually begin with questions that will be fairly easy for the subject to answer, and which are largely questions that are not sensitive or threatening (Grinnell & Unrau, 2005; Trochim, 2005). In my experience, demographic questions are frequently about educational levels, date of birth, location of residence, ethnicity, religious preferences, and so forth. Many of these sorts of demographic questions are regularly asked of people in their work or school lives and are likely to receive quick responses with no sense of threat or concern on the part of the interviewee. The underlying rationale for this sort of a question sequencing is that it allows the interviewer and the participant to develop a degree of rapport before more serious and important questions are asked. As well, it fosters a degree of commitment on the part of the interviewee, since he or she will have already invested some time in the interview by answering these easy to answer questions. Of course, you do not want to delay getting into the more important material for too long. At the least, you risk establishing a pattern of short questions and short answers that may discourage deeper responses when you need them. At worst, as noted earlier, informants may feel ambushed or coerced when you finally get past the easy part and spring some more threatening questions on them. The following suggests a general sequencing of types or categories of questions for a semistandardized interview:

1. Start with a few easy, nonthreatening (demographic) questions.
2. Next begin with some of the more important questions for the study topic (preferably not the most sensitive questions)—the questions should stick to a single concept or topic.
3. More sensitive questions can follow (those related to the initiated topic).
4. Ask validating questions (questions restating important or sensitive questions, worded differently than previously asked).
5. Begin the next important topic or conceptual area of questions (these may include the more or most sensitive questions).
6. Repeat steps 3 and 4, and so on through your major topics.
7. End by returning to any key concepts that you might have had to bypass or skim through when they first came up.

It is also important to note that each time you change from one topical area to another, you should use some sort of a transition. This may be a clear statement of what is coming next, such as: "Okay, now what I'd like to do is ask some questions about how you spend your leisure time." Or, "The next series of questions will consider how your family feels about drinking." The logic here is to assure that the interviewee is aware of what specific area he or she should be thinking about when answering questions. Such transitions allow the interviewer to lead the direction of the conversation without taking too much initiative away from the informant.

In order to draw out the most complete story about various subjects or situations under investigation, four types or styles of questions should be included in one's interview repertoire and possibly written into the interview instrument: essential questions, extra questions, throwaway questions, and probing questions.

Essential Questions   *Essential questions* exclusively concern the central focus of the study. They may be placed together or scattered throughout the survey, but they are geared toward eliciting specific desired information (Morris, 2006). For example, Glassner and Berg (1980, 1984) sought to study drinking patterns in the Jewish community using a standardized interview format. Consequently, essential questions addressing this specific theme were sprinkled throughout the 144-structured-question instrument. For instance, among a series of questions about friends and people the family feels proud of, the following question was introduced: "Has anyone in the family ever thought anyone else drank too much?" Later during the interview, among general questions about ceremonial participation in the Jewish holiday of Passover, the interviewer systematically asked:

> There is a question that we are a little curious about, because there seems to be some confusion on it. During the Passover story, there are seven or eight places it speaks about lifting a glass of wine. And there are three or four places which speak directly of drinking the wine. In some people's homes they drink a cup each time, and in some people's homes they count a sip as a cup. How is it done in your home?

Another regularly scheduled question asked during this segment of the interview is, "Another question that interests us is, what becomes of the cup of wine for Elijah [ceremonially poured for the Angel Elijah]?" Later, during a series of questions centering on Chanukkah observance styles, the interviewer asked: "What drinks are usually served during this time?"

Separating these essential questions, however, were numerous other essential questions addressing such other research concerns as ritual knowledge and involvement, religious organization membership, leisure activities, and so on. In addition, there were three other types of questions intended for other purposes.

On the other hand, while my study of community organizing in response to HIV (Lune, 2007) relied on semistandardized interviews, I entered into each with a list of crucial topics. Then, as I neared the end of each interview, I ould consult my list (either physically in the early interviews or mentally once I'd gotten used to them) and ensure that all the key data were collected. Often, after a long mostly nonstandardized conversation I would say something along the lines of "that covers most of what I needed to know, but there are a couple of specific questions that I want to ask before we end." In this way, I could ensure that every interview, no matter how loose, touched on the same central issues.

Extra Questions   *Extra questions* are those questions roughly equivalent to certain essential ones but worded slightly differently. These are included in order to check on the reliability of responses (through examination of consistency in response sets) or to measure the possible influence a change of wording might have. For example, having earlier asked an informant something general, like "how well do you get along with members of your family," you might want to return to the subject by asking, "Are there people in your family who you particularly look forward to seeing, or seriously dread seeing?"

Throwaway Questions   Frequently, you find throwaway questions toward the beginning of an interview guideline instrument. *Throwaway questions* may be essential demographic questions or general questions used to develop rapport between interviewers and subjects. You may also find certain throwaway questions sprinkled throughout a survey to set the interviewing pace or to allow a change in focus in the interview. Throwaway questions, as the term implies, are incidental or unnecessary for gathering the important information being examined in the study. Nonetheless, these throwaway questions may be invaluable for drawing out a complete story from a respondent.

On occasion, throwaway questions may serve the additional purpose of cooling out the subject (Becker, 1963; Goffman, 1967). On these occasions, a throwaway question (or a series of them) may be tossed into an interview whenever subjects indicate to the interviewers that a sensitive area has been entered. The interviewer offhandedly says something to the effect of, "Oh, by the way, before we go any further, I forgot to ask you. . . ." By changing the line of questions, even for only a few moments, the interviewer moves away from the sensitive area and gives the interviewee a moment to cool down. This change in focus from sensitive issues to simple facts may also help to remind your informants that your goal is to collect information, not challenge, judge, or argue with them. (Of course, as the interviewer you also need to remember that, and avoid reacting emotionally to statements with which you disagree.)

Probing Questions   *Probing questions*, or simply *probes*, provide interviewers with a way to draw out more complete stories from subjects. Probes frequently ask subjects to elaborate on what they have already answered in response to a given question—for example, "Could you tell me more about that?" "How long did you have that?" "What happened next?" "Who else has ever said that about you?" or simply, "How come?" For example, if an informant is telling stories about things that happened without much examination of the meanings of the events, the interviewer can toss in the occasional "how did that work out for you?" or "why not?" to encourage more reflection from the informant. Along similar lines, Lofland and Lofland (1984, p. 56) wrote the following:

> In interview[s] . . . the emphasis is on obtaining narratives or accounts in the person's own terms. You want the character and contour of such accounts to be set by the interviewees or informants. You might have a general idea of the kinds of things that will compose the account but still be interested in what the interviewees provide on their own and the terms in which they do it. As the informants speak, you should be attentive to what is mentioned and also to what is not mentioned but which you feel might be important. If something has been mentioned about which you want to know more, you can ask, "You mentioned_____; could you tell me more about that?" For things not mentioned, you might ask, "Did_____?" or "Was_____a consequence?"

In standardized or semistandardized interviews, researchers incorporate a structured series of probes triggered by one or another type of response to some essential question. In nonstandardized interviews, it is still worthwhile to anticipate patterns of responses and to have in mind the kinds of probes that will encourage further elaboration, often by echoing back to the informant ideas that they have offered up themselves. Probes, then, are intended to be largely neutral. Their central purpose is to elicit more information about whatever the respondent has already said in response to a question.

Wording of Questions   In order to acquire information while interviewing, researchers must word questions so that they will provide the necessary data. Thus, you must ask questions in such a manner as to motivate respondents to answer as completely and honestly as possible. As in the saying about computers, "garbage in, garbage out," so it is in interviewing. If the wrong questions are asked, or if questions are asked in a manner that inhibits or prevents a respondent from answering fully, the interview will not be fruitful—garbage will come out.

We can think of our questions as invitations to the informants to speak their minds. While we do want to encourage full and truthful responses, we must never become either interrogators or therapists. We are, ideally, interested listeners. The truth is that we conduct interviews in order to learn what people think, not to tell them what we think. Most people, I assume, will readily see the problem with a set of interview guidelines written by a student of mine one time, beginning with "Have you ever had an abortion," optionally followed by the probe "How could you?" But there are many subtle ways in which a question can discourage informants. The goal is often to seem both warmly human and cooly nonjudgmental.

Communicating Effectively

Perhaps the most serious problem with asking questions is how to be certain the intentions of the questions have been adequately communicated. Researchers must always be sure they have clearly communicated to the subjects what they want to know. The interviewers' language must be understandable to the subject; ideally, interviews must be conducted at the level or language of the respondents. Some interviewers may view this as a matter of "dumbing down" the questions for nonspecialists, but one must not forget the part about educating oneself about the context, concerns, language use, slang, and histories of the groups that we recruit into our studies ("smarting up?").

When developing surveys that will be applied to a large and diverse general population, many researchers choose what may be termed the *zero-order level of communications.* In such instances, the words and ideas conveyed by survey questions are simplified to the level of the least sophisticated of all potential respondents. Although this should tend to minimize potential communication problems with a range of respondents, it may also create some problems: This approach is somewhat condescending, and may easily come across that way. The more sophisticated respondents may also react negatively to questions asked in too simplistic a manner. When you are investigating a homogeneous subculture, this problem becomes somewhat less critical. However, when interviewing a cross section of subjects on the same topic, you may need to consider varying levels of language.

Similarly, you must allow for special languages (both real and symbolic) that certain groups may use. For example, in the Glassner and Berg (1980, 1984) study, the interviewer needed to be moderately versed in Yiddish idioms in order both to conduct many of the interviews and to assist transcribers in accurately reproducing interview transcripts. In another instance, when Berg and Doerner (1987) conducted a study of volunteer police officers, the interviewer needed a general understanding of "cop speak," the jargonized symbolic language frequently used by police officers as illustrated earlier in this chapter. Of course, should you encounter specialized terms or local slang that you don't understand, you can always turn that into an opportunity to explore your informant's meaning system. For example, I have often found it effective to say, "I am not familiar with that phrase; can you explain it to me," or words to that effect. Such strategies, however useful, should not be relied on as a substitute for being prepared.

It is important during the course of the interviews that the interviewer shares meanings for terms commonly held by members of the research population. This sometimes goes beyond mere language barriers. For example, in a study of Latino men who have sex with men (Berg et al., 2004) regarding risk factors associated with men who have sex with other men (MSM), one obstacle was that the subjects spoke Mexican street Spanish. Another was that within the MSM community, certain words and terms are used with specific connotations. To the average outsider, these terms hold one meaning, but to the MSM community member such terms hold a dramatically different meaning. It was important, therefore, that the researchers be versed in these special words and terms.

The last point was underscored by Murray (1991), who suggested that researchers must be aware of what he referred to as *language codes* in linguistics. These may include widely shared idioms, such as various phrases used in Black English and Chicano or Mexican "street Spanish," professional jargon, ethnic expressions that are commonly dropped into English language conversations (or non-English, depending on where you are), and even popular cultural references. I would not go so far as to say that a contemporary researcher needs to be fluent in texting abbreviations, but some of the most basic shorthands are entering into conversation as subtle variations on "standard" word usage. If the interviewer is not knowledgeable about a group's special language use, various nuances of dialect may be lost during the interview.

A Few Common Problems in Question Formulation

Several other problems arise when constructing interview questions. Among the more serious ones are affectively worded (leading) questions, double-barreled questions, and overly complex questions.

Affectively Worded Questions

Affective words arouse in most people an emotional response that is usually negative. Although these questions may not be intended as antagonistic, they nonetheless can close down or inhibit interview subjects (McGivern, 2006). For instance, the word *why*, in American culture, tends to produce in most people a negative response. One possible explanation has to do with the punitive connotation of this question, as in "Why did you do that wrong thing?" Consequently, when subjects mention some form of conduct or an attitude and are then asked by the interviewers, "Why?" they may not respond accurately or completely. On the other hand, if asked in response to these same statements, "How come?" they may offer more thorough responses in a relaxed manner.

Kinsey, Pomeroy, and Martin (1948) similarly found that when affective topics were considered, neutralizing the sense of the questions (reducing their affects) improved the likelihood of a full answer. They cited, as an example, asking subjects in a study of human sexuality, "Do you masturbate?" Virtually all the initial respondents answered immediately, "I never masturbate." Yet, when the question was reworded—"About how many times a week would you say you masturbate?"—suddenly many respondents were willing to offer responses. The second version of the question tends to neutralize or normalize the affect (sensitivity) of the question. Asking how often one masturbates implies that others do so as well, thereby reducing the affect of the word and concept *masturbate*. (Apart from the issue of question wording, it also matters who is asking and how the subject perceives them. As an instructor, I would not allow a lone female college student to interview men about their sexual practices, including masturbation. It would invite risks to the students and generally threaten the validity of the responses.)

There are also strategies for neutralizing the threat inherent in certain topics. For example, it is unlikely that you would elicit helpful answers from police officers if you were to ask them, "What steps would you take to protect yourself from liability if you made a mistake during an arrest?" The question itself implies that the informant has or would both make mistakes and try to cover them up. Furthermore, the topic potentially involves illegal activities. On the other hand, consider the following question: "If a fellow officer admitted to you that he or she had made a mistake during an arrest, it would raise a host of questions about how to handle it. Some of those questions involve the officer's liability. How do think you might advise them in order to protect themselves in this respect, separate from all of the other issues that need to be considered?" Such a question makes the issue more abstract, removes the personal risk, and still admits that the whole hypothesis involves treading some dangerous waters. The point is that there are valid pieces of information that we might want which refer to threatening contexts. We have to think about ways to take the question out of that context in order to remove or reduce the threat in order to get at the information.

The Double-Barreled Question

Among the more common problems that arise in preparing guidelines or schedules is the double-barreled question. This type of question asks a subject to respond simultaneously to two issues in a single question. For instance, one might ask, "How many times have you smoked marijuana, or have you only tried cocaine?" It should be noticed that the two issues in this single question are slightly unrelated. In the first clause, the question asks the frequency of marijuana usage. The second clause confuses the issue and asks whether marijuana or cocaine has ever been used by the subject. By lumping the two together, the researcher is creating a false dichotomy—the idea that it has to be one or the other—without providing any opportunity for an informant to separate the two. This "error" is sometimes introduced deliberately in "push polls," where the goal is to force respondents to give a particular desired answer. In that situation, the question might resemble this: "Do you favor collecting DNA samples from teachers, or do you not care what happens to other people's children?" Often, however, the error is accidental and less obvious.

The logical solution to the double-barreled question, of course, is to separate the two issues and ask separate questions. Failure to separate the two issues may yield some answers, because people tend to be obliging during interviews and may answer almost anything they are asked, but analysis of a response to a double-barreled question is virtually impossible.

Complex Questions

The pattern of exchange that constitutes verbal communication in Western society involves more than listening. When one person is speaking, the other is listening, anticipating, and planning how to respond. Consequently, when researchers ask a long, involved question, the subjects may not really hear the question in its entirety. Their response, then, may be only to some small portion of a greater concern woven into the complex question. Thus, keeping questions brief and concise allows clear responses and more effective analysis of the answers. In my experience, if you ask a subject about two things at once, he or she will tell you about the second of them, losing sight of the first.

Pretesting the Schedule

Once researchers have developed their instrument and are satisfied with the general wording and sequencing of questions, they must pretest the schedule. Ideally, this involves at least two steps. First, the schedule should be critically examined by people familiar with the study's subject matter—technical experts, other researchers, or persons fitting the type to be studied. This first step facilitates the identification of poorly worded questions, questions with offensive or emotion-laden wording, or questions revealing the researchers' own biases, personal values, or blind spots.

The second step in pretesting before the instrument can be used in a real study involves several practice interviews to assess how effectively the interview will work and whether you will obtain the information you seek. You should record and transcribe the practice interviews, and compare the transcripts to the interview guidelines. Make note of any point at which you had to clarify or repeat a question; you may want to modify the wording. At what points, if any, did your subjects become reticent, angry, defensive or otherwise upset? Those sections might need to be moved, reworded, regrouped, or more carefully introduced. There might be follow-up questions that you found useful in more than one interview. They should probably be added to the guidelines. In general, look for evidence that your research subjects were more or less motivated, more or less likely to go off topic, or likely to give very short answers. Most importantly, look for signs that your questions had a different meaning to your subjects than that which you intended. Finally, you should code the practice interviews as you would any "real" data and attempt to analyze the patterns of responses. (See chapter 11 for more on text analysis.) Ask yourself whether, if you had more data like this, you would know how to answer your research question.

A careful pretest of the instrument, although time consuming in itself, usually saves enormous time and cost in the long run.

Long versus Short Interviews

Interviewing can be a very time-consuming, albeit valuable, data-gathering technique. It is also one that many uninitiated researchers do not fully understand. This is particularly true when considering the length of an interview. Many quantitative researchers who dabble at interviewing are convinced that interviews must be short, direct, and businesslike. Some who use interviews over the telephone even recommend keeping them to no more than about five minutes (Hagan, 1995). As a result, one issue surrounding interviews is exactly how long or short they should be.

There are several ways to answer this question, but all will immediately direct your attention back to the basic research question(s). If potential answers to research questions can be obtained by asking only a few questions, then the interview may be quite brief. If, on the other hand, the research question(s) are involved or multilayered, it may require a hundred or more questions. Length also depends on the type of answers constructed between the interviewer and the subject. In some cases, where the conversation is flowing, a subject may provide rich, detailed, and lengthy answers to the question. In another situation, the subject may respond to the same question with a rather matter-of-fact, short, cryptic answer.

Obviously, the number of questions on the interview schedule is at least partially related to how long an interview is likely to take. On the average, an interview schedule with 165 questions is likely to take longer than one with only 50 questions. Yet, there are several misconceptions about long interviews that sometimes creep into research methods class lectures. For instance, some researchers believe that most subjects will refuse to engage in an interview once they know it may last for two or more hours. Others maintain that subjects may not remain interested during a long interview, and it will end in a withdrawal. Or, conversely, some researchers believe that short interviews do not provide any useful information. In fact, I am certain that such conditions do occasionally occur. However, they do not represent binding rules or even terribly viable guidelines.

Interviews, unlike written surveys, can be extremely rewarding and interesting situations for both the interviewer and the subject. Believing that subjects would quickly weary with a written survey containing 175 questions may be true. I for one believe such a situation is boring. However, talking with an interviewer about things that matter to the interviewee, and doing so in a way that provides him or her with appropriate feedback, often provides subjects with a kind of intangible yet intrinsic reward. It is common for subjects to comment after a long interview that they did not actually realize so much time had already passed. I liken this to reading a good book. At some time or another, most of us have begun reading some exciting or engaging novel and not realized that hours had actually passed. So it is with a well-run long interview. Even after several hours, there is often a feeling that only minutes have passed.

Certain types of research lend themselves to longer interviews than others. For example, when one conducts a *life history*, the researcher is interested in the life events of those being interviewed (Rubin & Rubin, 1995). In this case, the interview may go on for a very long time, perhaps carrying over to several separate sessions on different days. On the other hand, the interview may involve a single topic and require only a brief interview situation.

Length is a relative concept when conducting interviews. Some topics and subjects will produce long interviews while others will create short ones. Furthermore, different styles of interviewing, such as interactive or interpretive orientations, that require the development of a *relationship* between researcher and subject, may last not only long durations but also multiple sessions (Hertz, 1995; Kvale, 1996; Miller, 1996). What is important to remember is that simply because an interview contains many questions or only a few does not in itself immediately translate into a long or short interview.

Telephone Interviews

Related to the question of interview length is the role of telephone interviews in qualitative research. Telephone interviews are not a major way of collecting qualitative data. To be sure, telephone interviews lack face-to-face nonverbal cues that researchers use to pace their interviews and to determine the direction to move in. Yet, researchers have found that, under certain circumstances, telephone interviews may provide not only an effective means for gathering data but also in some instances—owing to geographic locations—the most viable method. In fact, the primary reason that one might conduct a qualitative telephone interview is to reach a sample population that is in geographically diverse locations. For example, if an investigator is interested in studying how nursing home directors define elder abuse, he or she might consider conducting in-person interviews with some sample of nursing home directors. However, given that nursing home facilities may be at some distance from one another, as well as from the location of the interviewer, conducting interviews by telephone may be a logical resolution.

Qualitative telephone interviews are likely to be best when the researcher has fairly specific questions in mind (a formal or semistructured interview schedule). Qualitative interviews are also quite productive when they are conducted among people with whom the researcher has already conducted face-to-face interviews or with whom he or she may have developed a rapport during fieldwork (Rubin & Rubin, 1997). There are several important, necessary steps to accomplish a qualitative telephone interview. First, the investigator must establish legitimacy; next, the researcher must convince the potential subject that it is important for the subject to take part in the research; and finally, the researcher must carefully ensure that the information he or she obtains is sufficiently detailed to contribute meaningfully to the study.

This first step can be accomplished in several ways. For example, the interviewer might mail a letter to the prospective subject explaining the nature of the research and that the subject will be called to set an appointment for the actual interview. The letter should be on official letterhead and may contain supportive documentation (letters of support from relevant or significant people in the community, newspaper stories about the researcher or the study, etc.).

The second step will arise when the investigator initially contacts potential subjects and attempts to convince them to take part. This call will actually accomplish several things. It will allow the subjects to ask questions and raise any concerns they might have about the study or their participation. It will also provide an opportunity for the investigator to gain some sense of the individual and to begin developing a kind of relationship and rapport as well as an opportunity to convince the individual to participate in the study if the individual is resistant.

These calls should be made during normal working hours and researchers should *break the ice* by introducing themselves and ascertaining whether the individual has received the letter and accompanying materials. Calls should be made approximately 1 week to 10 days following the mailing of the letters of introduction. After the initial introduction, the researcher might ask if the individual has any questions. Next, using a polite and friendly but firm affirmative statement, the researcher should ask, "When would it be convenient for me to call you back to conduct the interview?" Recognize that not all subjects will immediately agree to take part, and the researcher may need to do a little convincing. This may offer the additional benefit of forging a rapport with the subject.

Advantages of the Telephone Interview

Hagan (2006) outlines a series of advantages associated with undertaking telephone interviews. These include reduced staff requirements, a method by which the investigator can easily monitor ongoing interviews to assure quality and avoid interviewer bias, and the ability to reach widespread geographic areas at an economical cost. In addition, interviews can be recorded via an inexpensive patch between the telephone and the recording instrument. If a digital recorder is used, the interview can later be transcribed in the traditional fashion or downloaded into a computer and converted to text (which may need light editing) by a speech-to-text program (Halbert, 2003). Some researchers argue that telephone interviews and surveys, because they provide a kind of instant anonymity, are effective for obtaining hard-to-locate individuals or when asking highly sensitive questions (Champion, 2006; Hagan, 2006).

Disadvantages of the Telephone Interview

There are, of course, disadvantages to using telephone interviews, which for many researchers outweigh the potential advantages. For example, some people have no telephone, and others have unlisted numbers—both groups are effectively eliminated as potential interviewees. Also excluded from the subject pool are those who screen their calls through caller ID or an answering machine and avoid taking calls from researchers. From a symbolic interactionist perspective, an important disadvantage is that current telephone technology generally lacks the ability for the interviewer and interviewee to use full channels of communication. In other words, neither can read visual cues offered by the other (either those unintentional cues by the respondent or those intentionally transmitted by the interviewer).

Computer Assisted Interviewing

Computer-based tools may be integrated into the interview process in multiple ways. Here, I discuss two approaches. One is through the use of interview-specific software tools commonly referred to as *Computer Assisted Telephone Interviewing* (CATI) and *Computer Assisted Personal Interviewing* (CAPI). Each of these tools have long been used in traditional survey research, but both also have potential qualitative applications. The second approach is to adapt everyday Internet-based communications programs for use in interviewing.

Computer Assisted Telephone Interviewing (CATI)

When conducting qualitative telephone interviews, CATI can be very useful. Earl Babbie (2004, p. 265) offers an excellent image of the basic process. He states the following:

> Imagine an interviewer wearing a telephone headset, sitting in front of a computer terminal and its video screen. The central computer has been programmed to select a telephone number at random and dials it. (Random-digit dialing avoids the problem of unlisted telephone numbers.) On the video screen is an introduction ("Hello, my name is . . .") and the first question to be asked ("Could you tell me how many people live at this address?").

When the subject answers the telephone, the interviewer begins with an introduction, explains the purposes of the study, and invites the person to take part. Once the subject consents to participate, the interview begins. As the subject answers each question, the interviewer immediately types the response into the computer. In computer-assisted, *pencil-and-paper* surveys, the interviewer chiefly asks the questions, lists the possible answers, and then inputs the subject's responses.

In a qualitative version of CATI, the interviewer asks open-ended questions and types in the full accounts offered by the subject. The advantages to this version include skipping the need to later transcribe the data and allowing the information to be immediately input into a textual data manager (a computer program designed for qualitative textual analysis) or to be coded. Naturally, this requires an interviewer who is skilled in typing and is able to take the equivalent of dictation. However, because not all interviewers have this typing capacity and because it can become quite expensive to hire and train someone to do this, an investigator might opt to employ a system known as *Voice Capture*. This process involves digitally recording the voice of the subject during the course of interview. Later, this recording can be transcribed, but during the course of the interview the subject is permitted to speak openly and freely with an added sense of anonymity, since the interviewer does not know who the subject is or what he or she looks like. Again, there is the obvious loss of visual cues because of the absence of face-to-face contact. This can be rectified with CAPI.

Computer Assisted Personal Interviewing

Like CATI, CAPI employs a computer to provide the questions and capture the answers during an interview. In this case, the interviews are conducted face-to-face, thereby restoring the visual cues lost during a typical CATI-type interview. Again, the process can involve either the interviewer asking the questions and typing in the response (as with dictation) or the use of Voice Capture or a similar type of system to record the answers. There is also a second style of computer-assisted interviewing called *Computer Assisted Self-Administered Interviewing* (CASI). In this version of the process, the subject is provided with a computer (a laptop or access to a desktop computer) and allowed to read the interview schedule and type in his or her responses. Again, the advantages to this strategy include having the data ready to be placed into a data manager or coded, as well as offering the subject privacy while responding (there is no interviewer present while the subject types his or her answers).

The disadvantages, unfortunately, are numerous and include the fact that some people cannot type and will take a long time to hunt and peck at the keyboard. Some people may feel self-conscious about being poor spellers or writers, or just not like to write and, thus, use only very brief responses rather than fluid full accounts. Other subjects may be in a hurry and choose to either skip questions or write only very short answers to save time. Some subjects may be weak readers or illiterate, further complicating the process. For this last category of subjects, some advances have been offered. Turner and his associates (1998), for example, have employed what they coined *Audio-CASI* (Audio Computer Assisted Self-Interview) as a strategy. This technique similarly employs a laptop computer with the questions on it and the ability of the subject to provide answers, but in addition this technique uses a headset and an audio version of the survey that is played for the subject to hear. Although Turner and colleagues (1998) used this technique with a survey-type questionnaire, the same process could be adapted for a more open-ended qualitative interview.

Web- and E-mail-Based In-Depth Interviews

Computer-based conversations can take place either synchronously or asynchronously. *Synchronous environments* include real-time chat rooms, instant messenger protocols, and real-time threaded communications. Such environments provide the researcher and respondent an experience similar to face-to-face interaction insofar as they provide a mechanism for a back-and-forth exchange of questions and answers in what is almost real time. In some cases, computer-linked video cameras can be used to allow the researcher and respondent to actually see one another.

While this type of interview interaction is not identical to a more traditional face-to-face interview, it does approach it in a number of ways. For example, when a respondent answers a question, the interviewer has the ability to ask probing questions to elicit additional information or to run in an entirely different direction, similar to the interviewer's ability in a face-to-face interview. Consequently, a researcher can delve as deeply as he or she chooses into an area either structured into the interview schedule or arising spontaneously in the course of the interview exchange.

Asynchronous environments include the use of e-mail, message boards, and privately hosted bulletin posting areas. Asynchronous environments are commonly used by investigators undertaking survey-based research (Bachman & Schutt, 2003; Champion, 2006). Bampton and Cowton (2002, p. 1) suggest that qualitative researchers can also take advantage of what they term the "e-interview." They describe the benefits of conducting e-mail-based qualitative interviews:

> The asynchronicity of the e-interview has several consequences. There can be pauses in face-to-face interviews, of course, but in an e-interview the delay in interaction between researcher and subject can range from seconds (virtually real time) to hours or days. In our own research some of the replies came back surprisingly quickly, but the important thing is that the interviewee was not committed to replying promptly. In this lies one of the major benefits of the e-interview, in that busy subjects—and busy researchers, for that matter—do not have to identify a mutually convenient time to talk to each other. Nor do they each need to find a single chunk of time in which to complete the

full interview, since as an interview—rather than something more akin to an e-mailed questionnaire—there should normally be more than one episode of question and answer. Indeed, such iterations are fundamental to the communication having the dialogic or conversational characteristics of a good interview.

For many people throughout the world, the use of e-mail has become a common and comfortable activity. Transferring this comfort to the interview situation, then, can similarly provide a benefit for qualitative interviewing (Stromer-Galley, 2003). Another advantage of the e-interview is that e-mail questions transmitted to an individual are effectively private: No one else online can add to, delete, or interrupt the exchange.[1]

Setting meeting times for interviews and conquering distance problems have long been problems when conducting qualitative interviews. E-mail interviews eliminate these issues by permitting subjects to answer in their own time and literally from across the country or even the world. Lindlof and Taylor (2002) also suggest that fatigue can be a problem in lengthy interviews, and this too is eliminated in the e-interview.

Asynchronous environments such as e-mail and bulletin boards naturally have drawbacks when it comes to conducting qualitative interviews. The obvious drawback is the loss of visual cues—both those that occur between interviewer and respondent as part of the conversational flow of the interview and those that serve as social markers in the interactionary process (e.g., age, gender, race, dress style). Also lacking is the spontaneity of probing and chasing down interesting topics that inadvertently arise in the course of the interview. Finally, interview subjects are limited to those who have access to both a computer and an e-mail account, as well as to those who are literate enough to express themselves in an e-mail format.

While I am not arguing that the e-interview should replace the face-to-face interview in all future research endeavors, it seems prudent to include this and other technological data-collecting strategies in the arsenal of lines of action for conducting qualitative research.

TRYING IT OUT

Suggestion 1   Imagine that you are designing an interview-based research project on the topic of where people get their news and information. Create a list of major conceptual areas that need to be covered in the interview. For each area, list 3–5 specific data items that you would need to measure. Create a semistructured interview guideline for at least 6 such items.

Conducting an Interview: A Natural or an Unnatural Communication?

Everyone actually has received some training and has experience in interviewing. Children, for example, commonly ask their parents questions whenever they see or experience something different, unusual, or unknown. In school, students ask their teachers questions and respond to questions put to them by teachers. People regularly observe exchanges of questions and answers between teachers and other students, siblings and parents, employers and employees, talk show hosts and guests, and among friends. Thus, one might assume that since everyone has received tacit training in both asking questions (sending messages) and answering questions (receiving messages), the research interview is just another natural communication situation. But the research interview is not a natural communication exchange.

Beyond acquiring the ability to send and receive messages while growing up in society, people also learn how to avoid certain types of messages. Goffman (1967) has termed this sort of avoidance *evasion tactics*. Such tactics may involve a word, phrase, or gesture that expresses to another participant that no further discussion of a specific issue (or in a particular area) is desired. Conversely, people also usually acquire the ability to recognize these evasion tactics and, in a natural conversational exchange, to respect them. This sort of deference ceremony (Goffman, 1967, p. 77) expresses a kind of intrinsic respect for the other's avoidance rituals. In return, there is the unspoken expectation that this respect will be reciprocated in some later exchange.

As anyone who has ever conducted an interview or watched a political debate already knows, this sort of deference ceremony simply cannot be permitted during the course of a research interview. In fact, a subject's evasion tactics during the course of an interview are among the most serious obstacles to overcome—but overcome them you must! At the same time, you do not want to jeopardize the evolving definition of the situation, the potential rapport with the subject, or the amount of falsification and gloss a subject may feel compelled to use during the interview. As Gorden (1987, p. 70) suggested, "If all respondents said nothing, responded with truth, or said 'I won't tell you!' the task of the interviewer would be much simpler. Unfortunately, the respondent can avoid appearing uncooperative by responding voluminously with irrelevancies or misinformation, and this presents a challenge to the interviewer." In other words, the interviewer must maneuver around a subject's avoidance rituals in a manner that neither overtly violates social norms associated with communication exchanges nor causes the subject to lie.

Qualitative interviews may appear to be similar to ordinary conversations in some ways, but they differ in terms of how intensely the researcher listens to pick up on key words, phrases, and ideas (Rubin & Rubin, 2004). They differ also in terms of the kinds of nonverbal cues that the investigator will watch for in order to effectively identify the interviewee's emotional state, deference ceremonies, and even lies. One way these obstacles can be handled is through use of the dramaturgical interview.

The Dramaturgical Interview

There are a number of necessary terms and elements connected with under-standing the dramaturgical interview and learning how to maneuver around communication-avoidance rituals. Central to these is the differentiation between the *interviewer's role* and the *roles an interviewer may perform*. As De Santis (1980, p. 77) wrote, the interviewer may be seen as "playing an occupational role," and "society can be expected to have some knowledge, accurate or inaccurate, about the norms which govern the role performance of various occupations." For instance, in our society, one might expect a farmer to wear jeans, not a fine three-piece suit, while working in the field (or relaxing at home). Similarly, one can expect certain things about appearance, manner, style, and language connected with other occupational roles, including that of an interviewer.

The implication is that preconceived notions do exist among interviewees, but these notions are malleable. There can also be preconceived notions of subjects on the part of interviewers. Whether acknowledged or not, "There is always a model of the research subject lurking behind persons placed in the role of interview respondent" (Holstein & Gubrium, 1995, p. 7). For exam-ple, in a study seeking to examine the isolation and vulnerability of elders, Cherry Russell (1999) found that her preconceived understandings of older people affected how she planned to research them, and this preconceived notion negatively affected the study. Because a subject's and an interviewer's preconceptions about one another may be based on both correct and incorrect information, the actual conception of the interviewer role rests on the defini-tion of the situation established during the course of the interview itself.

In a number of sources on interviewing, the interviewer's role is discussed in terms of *biasing effects* or *reactivity* (Babbie, 2007; Chadwick et al., 1984). But the role of the interviewer is not necessarily established in granite, nor do the interviewer and interviewees operate within a vacuum! It is, therefore, within the capacity of an interviewer to affect even the preconceived notions that subjects may have about the interviewer's role.

Many roles are available to an interviewer. Regardless of any preconceived notion and expectation about the interviewer's role as perceived by the interviewee, it is possible (within certain limits) for the interviewer to shape, alter, and even create desired role images. Gorden (1987, p. 213) described this as *role-taking*. He explained that "role-taking is a conscious selection, from among one's actual role repertory, of the role thought most appropriate to display to a particular respondent at the moment."

As explained in the next section, by changing roles, the interviewer can also circumvent many of the avoidance tactics an interviewee might otherwise effectively use.

Interviewer Roles and Rapport

The model of the dramaturgical interview is intended to convey the notion of a very fluid and flexible format for conducting research interviews. With regard to rapport, which can be defined as the positive feelings that develop between the interviewer and the subject, it should not be understood as meaning there are no boundaries between the interviewer and the subject. The model of the dramaturgical interview should be interpreted as a conversation between two people centered on one person's perceptions on the events of daily life, but, as Kvale (1996, pp. 5–6) similarly explains, "It is not a conversation between equal partners." The dramaturgical interview should not be a dialogue, with more or less equal time allocated to each participant, because the whole point is to obtain information from the subject. In many ways, the ideal situation would be to assist the subject in conveying almost a monologue on the research topic. When this is not possible, the dramaturgical interview provides pathways to help the subject to offer his or her accounts.

To accomplish this, the interview must rely on the establishment and maintenance of good rapport. Just as no two people in society are exactly alike, no interviewer and his or her subject are exactly alike. However, if the interviewer is able to establish some sense of common ground, then one avenue of rapport building could be opened. For example, during the course of the Berg et al. (2004) study of risk factors associated with men who have sex with other men, one of the interviewers, Jose (a pseudonym), regularly made reference to the fact that he was a member of the MSM community. A second interviewer, Rosa, a heterosexual Latina, found common ground by referring to familiar Mexican cultural elements and events she and the subjects both understood. Similarly, in a study of Appalachian women and domestic violence, Patricia Gagne found common ground by alluding to her own experiences in an abusive relationship (Tewksbury & Gagne, 1997).

It is important to note that the interviewer does not necessarily always have to possess similar characteristics or experiences to that of the subjects—although some degree of understanding would certainly be a good thing to possess. In some situations, such as a study of the Ku Klux Klan, it would be challenging to send an African American in to conduct interviews. On the other hand, simply sending a Caucasian would not guarantee rapport, though it is a step in that direction. That is, the interviewer certainly would not have to subscribe to the subjects' social or political views. And one certainly should not pretend to do so. But it helps if the interviewer does not appear to be immediately at odds with the subjects.

Let us not exaggerate the importance of shared experiences. There are many ways to establish rapport. In my own interviews with active and former drug users involved in syringe exchange (Lune, 2002), for example, I drew upon my own lack of experience to emphasize the unique expertise of my informants. As a nonuser myself, I turned to them for the inside story. For the most part, these interview subjects were happy to educate me. Presumably, I would only have made myself look both foolish and disrespectful if I had tried to pass as an experienced user.

A number of feminist approaches to research in the social sciences seek to emphasize the importance of building rapport with the respondents in order to achieve a successful interview outcome. Toward this end, some feminist researchers have argued that interviewers must be willing to offer self-disclosures of personal information and develop genuine relationships with their interviewees beyond the boundaries of the roles of interviewer and interviewees (Cotterill, 1992; Oakly, 1981). This gives way to what may be referred to as a participatory model of interviewing (Lyons & Chipperfield, 2000). Participatory models of interviewing address the power differential between the researcher and the subject, thereby creating a nonhierarchical, nonmanipulative research relationship. Unfortunately, most interview situations, and notably the dramaturgical model, require the interviewer to maintain a certain amount of intentional control over the interview process—no matter how deferential, open, or self-disclosing he or she might choose to be during the course of the interview or when developing rapport. Openness on the part of the interviewer helps to smooth over this imbalance, but does not eliminate it.

Much of the literature on interviewing, especially in relation to the concepts of reactivity and rapport, suggests that the interviewee's conception of the interviewer centers around aspects of appearance and demeanor. Overt, observable characteristics such as race, gender, ethnicity, style of dress, age, hairstyle, manner of speech, and general demeanor provide information used by an interviewee to confirm or deny expectations about what an interviewer ought to be like. The negative reactive effects of an interviewer's observable social characteristics and personal attributes are extensively discussed in the literature on interviewing (see Burns & Grove, 1993; De Santis, 1980; Gorden, 1987; Nieswiadomy, 2002; Patton, 2002). In each source, however, the emphasis is on the effect an interviewer's characteristics have on obtaining the interviewee's consent to participate in an interview. Another theme emphasized in the literature is the potential bias arising from the effects of the interviewer's attributes.

There is little question that, as Stone (1962, p. 88) stated, "Basic to the communication of the interview meaning is the problem of appearance and mood. Clothes often tell more about the person than his conversation." Is it really sufficient merely to look the part? If a man dons an ermine cape and robe, places a gold crown on his head, attaches a perfectly sculpted crepe beard to his face, and regally struts about, is this a guarantee that he will perform *King Lear* in a convincing or even adequate fashion? Certainly I could not have improved my access to drug-injecting clients of syringe exchanges by dressing up (or dressing down) as whatever I imagined a drug user ought to look like. It is far better to dress as a professional researcher and approach my subjects from an honest place. To be sure, the interviewer's appearance, accreditation, sponsorship, and characteristics are important to interviewing. All of these, of course, are within the absolute control of the interviewer. Had I put on my best suit—the one I keep for weddings and funerals—before going out into the field, I would have had a much harder time sitting down to a long interview at a syringe exchange program where many of the clients, and staff, live on the edge of poverty. Even when you dress as who you are, you are making strategic decisions about your presentation of self. Attributes of appearance are in many ways analogous to the old door-to-door vacuum cleaner salesman's trick of placing a foot between the open door and its jamb—a trick that neither ensured a sale nor prevented the injury of the salesman's foot as the door was slammed shut.

The Role of the Interviewee

It is important to keep in mind that throughout the interview process, there are two individuals involved: the interviewer and the interviewee. While this text and others spend considerable time discussing the role of the interviewer, little, if any, direct attention is given to the impression-management activities of the interviewee (Collins, Shattell, & Thomas, 2005). In our everyday conversations with others, it is common to consider how each party in the conversation seeks to present his or her best face, so to speak. But, it is less common to think about such impression management going on in the interview relationship between the interviewer and the interviewee (Dingwall, 1997).

Individuals who agree to take part in an interview usually have a complex set of reasons for doing so. Perhaps they expect to gain some sort of therapeutic benefit or are curious about the topic to be addressed. They may desire to share some personal experiences they have not felt comfortable sharing with others before, or their reason may be as mundane as a desire to spend time with someone because they are lonely, or to get the sandwich and coffee the interviewer has provided. Each of these is an element, or facet, of the interviewee that he or she may want to either show or shield from the interviewer. Particularly because social scientists may be interviewing various criminals, abusers, or victims of abuse, or people otherwise engaged in deviant acts, the interviewee may desire to construct himself or herself in the most positive (or perhaps most negative) light possible in relation to the study topic (Rapley, 2001).

While interviewees often experience a kind of intangible gratuitous reward as a consequence of talking with a trained listener, they may also experience considerable apprehension about how the interviewer perceives them or the behaviors they are discussing (Collins et al., 2005; Thomas & Pollio, 2002). The solution, then, is for the interviewer to become somewhat more reflexive in his or her efforts throughout the interaction and to become a more *self-conscious performer* during the interview.

The Interviewer as a Self-Conscious Performer

The performance of the interviewer, as illustrated in the preceding anecdotes, is not at all haphazard. Actions, lines, roles, and routines must be carefully prepared and rehearsed in advance and, thus, constitute a *self-conscious performance*.

The literature on interviewing techniques often describes interviewers who react spontaneously to responses offered by interviewees in areas not scheduled on the interview instrument. Interviewers are described as using their insight and intuition to formulate the next question or probe almost instinctively. However, even though following up subject areas initiated by interviewees is important (even when the areas may not have been seen as relevant during the interview's design stage), the notion that interviewers respond spontaneously is faulty. The use of terms such as *intuition* likewise seems loose and inaccurate.

Goode and Hatt (1952, p. 186) voiced a similar concern more than 50 years ago. They stated, "This is an unfortunate term [intuition] since for many it possesses overtones of vagueness, subjectivity and even mysticism."

Perhaps a more accurate understanding of the meaning of interviewer's intuition is what Archer (1980) called *social interpretations*. The process of social interpretation, although not fully understood, is nonetheless evidenced by convincing empirical research (see Archer & Akert, 1980). Even when interviewers are presented with a unique response by an interviewee, it is highly unlikely that a similar (spontaneously created) action or statement is required from the interviewers. In the majority of interview situations, even novice interviewers will use some version of social interpretation and draw on a response taken from their repertoire of tactics (discussed in detail in a following section). Lincoln and Guba (1985) similarly mentioned the effects of tacit knowledge with regard to nonverbal cues relevant to communications between senders and receivers—in other words, subtly and often implicitly learned pieces of knowledge that trigger associations between actions and meanings.

Social Interpretations and the Interviewer

Social interpretations are defined as the affected messages transferred from one acting individual to another through nonverbal channels. These nonverbal channels include body gestures, facial grimaces, signs, symbols, and even some phonemic sounds such as tongue clicks, grunts, sighs, and similar visible indicators of communication (physical proximity between participant actors, their blocking, etc.).

Nonverbal channels include a variety of diverse elements. Each of these elements, taken individually, provides only a fragment of the information necessary for an accurate social interpretation. When rendered in combination, they provide sufficient cues and clues to convey clear messages and social meanings. These nonverbal channels of communication, together with more obvious verbal channels, make up the conversational interaction situation or what has been called *full-channel communication.*

Social interpretations are not instinctive but learned and can be accurately made in a matter of seconds (Archer & Akert, 1980). Social interpretations are formed by observing the complex presentation of clues in real-life situations, from filmed versions of these interactions or from still photographs in which even the nonverbal channels have been frozen in motionlessness as well as silence.

Throughout the interview process, the interviewer and the interviewee simultaneously send and receive messages on both nonverbal and verbal channels of communication. This exchange is in part a conscious social performance. Each participant is aware of the other's presence and intentionally says something and/or acts in certain ways for the other's benefit. However, to some extent, the interactions in an interview are also *unconscious,* which does not necessarily mean *unintended.* Unconscious behaviors should be understood as second-nature behaviors. An illustration of this sort of second-nature (automatic) interaction can often be observed when someone answers the telephone. The telephone voice is frequently almost melodic, even when only moments before the same voice may have been raised in angry shrieks directed toward a spouse or child. The social performance, of course, is for the benefit of whoever has just telephoned. Following the call, this individual's voice may again be raised in tones of anger—just as quickly and unconsciously.

Whenever interviewers realize they have trespassed on some unpleasant area of a respondent's life or an area the respondent does not want to talk about, it is not simply due to intuition or insight. This realization is derived from a social interpretation of the messages sent by the interviewee. The ways interviewers respond to these messages, however, will have a profound effect on the quality of the interview as a whole. For example, if interviewers ignore what they have interpreted as a very sensitive area and plunge ahead, they may force the respondent to lie, change the subject, not respond, or withdraw from the interview. If, on the other hand, interviewers do defer to the avoidance rituals used by the respondent, they may lose valuable information necessary to the study.

However, if an interviewer, in response to the clues, offers some demonstration that he or she has received the message and will at least, to some extent, respect the interviewee's desires, the interview will probably continue. It is also likely that the interviewer will be able to direct the respondent back to this sensitive area at a later point in the interview.

The use of social interpretations as described earlier certainly resembles Goffman's (1967) deference ceremony. There are, however, several critical distinctions, perhaps the most significant being that the deference is often only temporary.

It has been suggested previously that throughout the performance, you as an interviewer must be conscious and reflective. You must carefully watch and interpret the performance of the subject. Your interpretations must be based on the cues, clues, and encoded messages offered by the interviewee. Included in the information these interactions supply may be the communication of a variety of moods, sentiments, role portrayals, and stylized routines, which represent the interviewee's script, line cues, blocking, and stage directions. You, the interviewer, then must play several other roles simultaneously with that of interviewer. You must participate as an actor but must serve as director and choreographer as well.

Before we continue on, we need to make note of a very important area of misunderstanding concerning social interpretations. The discussion mentioned earlier is entirely about the need for the interviewer to observe and interpret nonverbal communications *in order to manage the interview process.*

One's awareness of the interview subject's moods, attitudes, and other non-verbal responses is crucial to avoiding errors that would derail the interview. Nonetheless, the data that you are collecting through your interviews are the words of the subject, not your impressions of their gestures and tone of voice. Should your interpretations of a subject's body language lead you to question the accuracy or honesty of some statement, the proper response is to ask more questions, or even to ask the subject if they are uncomfortable with the topic. I believe that few readers would consider your work valid were you to report that the subject stated X, but that you aren't counting that answer because you didn't believe the subject. Our job is to draw out the most and the best information we can from our respondents, not to decide for ourselves what they *really* meant.

The Interviewer as Actor   As an actor, you must perform your lines, routines, and movements appropriately. This means that in addition to reciting scripted or unscripted lines (the interview guidelines), you must be aware of what the other actor (the interviewee) is doing throughout the interview. You must listen carefully to line cues in order to avoid stepping on the lines of the interviewee (interrupting before the subject has completely answered a question). In addition, as actor, you must remain nonjudgmental regardless of what the interviewee may say. If you want people to openly talk about their feelings and views, you must refrain from making any negative judgments—either verbally or through visual cues. The best way to accomplish this is to accept people for who and what they are; avoid making judgments of their actions, beliefs, or lifestyles, even in your mind. This might mean that there are certain people whom you should not interview because you, personally, cannot suspend your judgment of them.

The Interviewer as Director   At the same time as you are performing as actor, you must also serve as director. In this capacity, you must be conscious of how you perform lines and move as well as of the interviewee's performance. As an interviewer, you must reflect on each segment of the interview as if you were outside the performance as an observer. From this vantage point, you must assess the adequacy of your performance (e.g., whether you are responding correctly to line cues from the interviewee and whether you are handling avoidance messages appropriately). This may include demonstrating both verbally and visually that you are empathic to things the interviewee has said. An approving nod or a brief comment, such as "I understand what you mean" or "I see," may offer sufficient positive reinforcement. You can also, carefully, communicate that you consider some response to be unfinished, or insufficient, and that you are waiting for more elaboration.

The Interviewer as Choreographer   The various assessments made in the role of director involve a process similar to what Reik (1949) described as "listening with the third ear." By using what you have heard (in the broadest sense of this term) in a self-aware and reflective manner, you as interviewer manage to control the interview process. As a result, as choreographer, you can effectively block (choreograph) your own movements and gestures and script your own response lines.

From this dramaturgical perspective, you as interviewer do not respond to any communication, verbal or nonverbal, scheduled (on the interview) or initiated by the subject, by means of spontaneous intuition or innate insight. Instead, the entire interview performance is a self-conscious social performance. You and the interviewee are constantly in the process of performing and evaluating your own and each other's performance. Using these assessments, both participants are able to adjust scripts and movements in response to messages sent and received throughout the interview.

The Interviewer's Repertoire

Interviewers make adjustments throughout the interview consisting largely of switching from one role to another or altering their style of speech, manner, or set of lines. These devices comprise the interviewer's *repertoire*. Interviewers seldom genuinely improvise a spontaneous technique or strategy during the course of an actual interview. Certainly, a new technique would hardly be recommended unless the repertoire of standard strategies has already been exhausted.

Preparation is a major guideline in interviewing. This is not to say that you should not actively pursue a topic initiated by the interviewee. However, even when interviewers pursue unplanned leads, they still can do it in a consistently planned, rather than novel, fashion. At the very least, interviewers should be prepared with a series of basic questions that may be triggered by virtually any possible topic area. These questions, very simply, include "Who with?" "Where?" "How come?" "How often?" "How many?" and a variety of similar questions relevant to the specifics of the study. In other words, during the design stages of the research, one must think about the possibility that unanticipated subject areas might arise. Consequently, even the unanticipated can be planned for!

For example, although one of the major foci in the Jewish drinking study conducted by Glassner and Berg (1980, 1984) was alcohol use, we were also interested in our subjects' possible involvement in other drugs. However, this interest was incidental, and we were thus only interested in drug use if the subjects raised the issue. For example, whenever a subject initiated a discussion connected with marijuana use, regardless of where in the structured interview it occurred, the interviewer pursued the topic through use of a series of systematically scripted questions. Following the completion of the question series, the interviewer returned to the place in the interview schedule from which he had digressed. The use of a consistent and systematic line of questions for even unanticipated areas is particularly important for reliability and for possible replication of a study. This is especially true when interviewing from a dramaturgical perspective. Since interviewers as actors, directors, and choreographers may not be able to provide future researchers with detailed descriptions of the various character portrayals, routines, and devices they used during individual interview performances, it is crucial that, at least, a comparable script exists.

The idea of interviewers possessing a repertoire of prepared lines, routines, and communication devices sometimes conjures up the image of a little black bag of dirty tricks. It should not. As suggested earlier in this chapter, the research interview is not a natural communication interaction. When interviewing, it is necessary to remain in control of the interaction. Similarly, the interviewers' ability to move gracefully into and out of a variety of characterizations should not be seen as phony behavior. The characterizations are also components of the interviewers' repertoire, and they provide interviewers with the means of effectively conducting research interviews without violating social norms or injuring subjects.

An interviewer's ability to accurately read lines and cues offered by an interviewee and to play effectively to them is not some insincere ploy intended only to obtain desired information. Quite the contrary—if these were the only objectives, there would be no reason to vary roles and/or characters to adjust to the subject's responses. The various tactics and characterized roles used by dramaturgical interviewers allow interviewees to feel more comfortable. The performance is, thus, not a phony one. As Zurcher (1983, p. 230) wrote the following:

> Why do we select a particular role for enactment? Why do we conform to some roles and modify or create others? What influences our choices or strategy for resolving role conflict or marginality? Why do we accept some identities and reject others? The circumstances of the social setting and the socialization process in which we find ourselves instrumentally affect the character of our role selections and enactments.

Extending Zurcher's notions on role enactments, one can see that in many situations, character projections present effective opportunities to develop or increase rapport. For example, one rapport-building tool that can be used before beginning an interview is *chatting* (Berg & Glassner, 1979; Douglas, 1985; Silverman, 2004). By briefly speaking with the subject on nonstudy-related issues, the interviewer develops rapport with the interviewee even before the interview has begun. It is an opportunity, also, for the interviewee to adjust his or her projection of self in an effort to be more comfortable with whatever impression he or she chooses to manage (Rapley, 2001).

As Goffman (1967) aptly stated, the initial self-projection of the interviewers commits them to being what and who they purport to be. Thus, when interviewers identify themselves as such, namely, as research interviewers, they are committed to portraying a convincing characterization of this role. How they develop the character is variable and dependent on the other participant(s) in the interview performance.

As the interview unfolds from the initial encounter, various modifications, alterations, and adaptations used by the interviewer may be added to the initial projection of the interviewer's character. It is essential, of course, that these additions neither contradict nor ignore earlier character developments or the initial projection of self. Instead, these additions should be built on previous expressions of the interviewer's projected image.

Interviewers' Attitudes and Persuading a Subject

Attitudes toward the interview process strongly affect the quality of the resulting research. One interesting and fairly common assumption novice interviewers make is that subjects will not discuss certain topics with them. Interestingly, however, once subjects have been persuaded to participate in an interview, they often tell far more intimate details than the interviewers would ever want to know.

The problem actually involves helping novice interviewers get over the first few nervous moments when they attempt to persuade potential subjects to take part in the research. Naturally, if everybody always happily participated in research projects, there would be no problem for novice interviewers. Unfortunately, people often resist or are skeptical and need to be convinced.

When they meet this sort of resistance, novice interviewers are often panic-stricken. Nervousness is to be expected, especially if you are unprepared. On the other hand, countless interviewers have already encountered this situation and have developed a number of effective responses. Knowledge of these responses should both reassure novice interviewers and provide a means of persuading the majority of resistant individuals to take part in a research project.

Some individuals will not cooperate regardless of how persuasive one is or how they are approached. Backstrom and Hursh (1981) offered a variety of typical statements by skeptical potential subjects, along with sample responses. As they suggest, subjects tend to ask, "Why me and not someone else?" and insist, "I simply don't have the time." For example, a potential subject might ask, "Why [or how] was I picked?" The best answer is a simple and direct one: For example, "You were chosen by chance according to a random selection procedure."

It is also sometimes necessary to convince subjects that what they have to say is important. For instance, a common response from a potential subject is, "I don't know too much about [whatever the subject is]; maybe you should interview someone else." Again, simplicity is the key: "It isn't what you know about [whatever the subject is], just what you think about it. I'm interested in your opinions."

If potential respondents insist that they simply have no time, researchers may be faced with a somewhat more difficult problem. Several strategies may be necessary. First, depending on the actual length of time required for the interview, interviewers may volunteer to conduct it during late evening hours (if that is convenient for the subject). Or they may suggest conducting the interview in several segments, even during lunch breaks at the work site, if that is possible. Frequently, if interviewers simply indicate that they realize time is an important commodity and they really appreciate the sacrifice the potential subject will be making, some accommodation will be made. In the Glassner and Berg (1980, 1984) study, for example, interviews were conducted at the homes of individuals or in their offices and periodically began as late as 11:30 at night or as early as 5:30 in the morning. In other words, it is important to be flexible.

Developing an Interviewer Repertoire

One final question that naturally arises is how neophyte interviewers develop their repertoires. People do not usually wake up one morning and suddenly decide that they are going to run out and conduct research using interviews to collect data! People also do not become expert interviewers immediately after reading books on interviewing. Interviewing requires practice. Whether first attempts at conducting interviews are called pilots, role-playing, pretests, practice interviews, mock interviews, or any other euphemism, they all mean interviews. Certainly, reading about how to interview, particularly ethnographic accounts, offers new interviewers some necessary strategies and tactics. However, without actually conducting interviews, students cannot manage to develop appropriate repertoires.

Perhaps the most effective way to learn how to interview is by role-playing with more experienced interviewers. Although many sources on interviewing recommend role-play, few specify that at least one participant should be experienced. To have two inexperienced interviewers role-play with each other seems analogous to having two neurosurgeons teach each other plumbing. It is particularly fruitless, furthermore, to have neophyte interviewers assume the role of interviewees. Although it would be impossible for even the most experienced interviewer to characterize all the different kinds of individuals and sorts of responses neophytes will encounter in the field, it is, however, far less likely that inexperienced researchers could perform the role of interviewee adequately. It is, however, possible for experienced interviewers to draw on their actual past performances and to develop composite characterizations of different interviewee types. By working with these projected characterizations in the process of a mock interview, students are afforded an opportunity to acquire various lines and routines necessary for maintaining control over the entire interview performance.

Techniques to Get New Researchers Started

Sometimes, during the course of an interview, you will notice that the interviewee answers only in single-word responses or in very short statements. In order to create more complete and detailed interviews (to literally draw out the depth), interviewers must use various strategies and devices from their repertoire. In an effort to give new interviewers a few techniques to start their repertoire, I will address the uncomfortable silence, echoing, and letting people talk.

Uncomfortable Silence   The technique of uncomfortable silence involves consciously creating a long, silent pause after asking the interviewee a question, even if the interviewee offers only a word or a cryptic response. Indeed, Kvale (1996) also pointed to the possible utility of silence as a strategic device to enhance data collection. Specifically, he suggested that interviewers employ silence to further the interview in a manner analogous to that used by therapists. "By allowing pauses in the conversation the subjects have ample time to associate and reflect and then break the silence themselves with appropriate information" (Kvale, 1996, pp. 134–135).

In normal conversational interactions, particularly in Western society, people have a difficult time with silence while talking with someone. The natural reaction when such a silence continues for a prolonged period is for interviewees to say something. In some cases, they will repeat their brief answer. In other cases, they will provide additional and amplifying information. In still other situations, they will state, "I have nothing else to say," or some similar comment. Rarely, however, will they simply sit silently for too long. I recommend that this period of silence extend only for a maximum of 45 seconds. Try to count slowly to yourself ("one, Mississippi, two Mississippi," and so forth) while offering the interviewee good eye contact.

Echoing   There is a tendency in interviewing to try and communicate that you understand what the interviewee is talking about. Some sources will even recommend that the interviewer periodically state "I know what you mean," or "that happened to me too" (Taylor & Bogdan, 1998, p. 100). I will argue that this can be disastrous, especially for a new interviewer, because it is unlikely that a novice will make a short statement and leave it at that. The danger (and to a large extent the more natural conversational response) is that the interviewer will discuss in detail his or her similar experience, shifting the focus from the interviewee to the interviewer. This does not effectively convey that the interviewer is paying attention to the interviewee. Instead, it says, "Listen to me. I have something more important to say than you do."

However, it is important to convey the idea that you as interviewer are hearing what is being said and that you are genuinely listening and understand. This can be accomplished through echoing what the interviewee has just said. For example, consider the following exchange.

Jack: When I first tried using marijuana, I felt really scared. I was, like, really out of control. I was all alone and I really didn't like how it felt.

Interviewer: That must have been a scary feeling.

Jack: Yeah, I was not really interested in trying marijuana again too soon. At least, I wasn't going to do it alone. I figured it would be better with a group of friends.

Although the interviewer has added nothing new to the exchange, he or she has conveyed that he or she was listening. In turn, the interviewee is encouraged to continue.

Letting People Talk   From a dramaturgical perspective, this actually means the interviewer must not *step on the interviewee's lines.* In other words, avoid unintentional interruptions. People speak at different paces and with varying breathing and pausing rates. Just because a subject has made a 1-sentence statement and paused does not mean he or she may not intend to continue with 8 or 10 more sentences. The interviewer must assess the way a subject tends to answer questions and adjust his or her own pace and desire to ask probing questions. Inexperienced interviewers frequently cut off their interviewees simply because they are anxious to get through their schedule of questions. This can be a serious mistake that will radically reduce the quality of the resulting interview. The answer is this: *Let people talk!* Better to be a little slow at first with your questions than to constantly cut off interviewees by stepping on their lines.

Taking the Show on the Road

After neophyte interviewers have become novices and have developed their repertoire, they are ready to play their role before an audience. Just as a musical show seldom opens on Broadway until it has played in smaller cities such as Boston or New Haven, novice interviewers should also not run immediately into the field. Broadway productions take the show on the road in order to obtain feedback from critics and audiences. In a similar manner, novice interviewers must try out their performances in front of an audience of competent critics, who may include experienced interviewers or the kinds of people they may be interviewing for a given study. Try your material out in Peoria first, and if it plays there, then take it on the road.

   This sort of going on the road should allow interviewers to polish their performances. The most effective way to accomplish this is a dress rehearsal—that is, conducting an interview as if it were the real thing. This will also provide the novice with an opportunity to try out various strategies for drawing out fuller and more complete details. Following this dress-rehearsal period, novice interviewers should be ready to enter the field.

The Ten Commandments of Interviewing

Borrowing an idea from Salkind (2008), I have constructed the following 10 points or 10 commandments of interviewing. I believe they nicely summarize the basic rules for conducting a decent interview. Better interviews will result only from practice and interviewer's self-development.

   1. *Never begin an interview cold.* Remember to spend several minutes chatting and making small talk with the subject. If you are in the subject's home, use what's there for this chatting. Look around the room and ask about such things as photographs, banners, books, and so forth. The idea here is to set the subject at ease and establish a warm and comfortable rapport.

2. *Remember your purpose.*   You are conducting an interview in order to obtain information. Try to keep the subject on track, and if you are working with an interview schedule, always have a copy of it in front of you—even though you should have your questions memorized.

3. *Present a natural front.*   Even though your questions are memorized, you should be able to ask each one as if it had just popped into your head. Be relaxed, affirmative, and as natural as you can.

4. *Demonstrate aware hearing.*   Be sure to offer the subjects appropriate nonverbal responses. If they describe something funny, smile. If they tell you something sad, look sad. If they say that something upset them, try to console them. Do not present yourself as uninterested or unaware.

5. *Think about appearance.*   Be sure you have dressed appropriately for both the setting and the kind of subject you are working with. Generally, business attire is most appropriate. If you are interviewing children, a more casual appearance may be more effective. Remember to think about how you look to other people.

6. *Interview in a comfortable place.*   Be sure that the location of the interview is somewhere the subject feels comfortable. If the subject is fearful about being overheard or being seen, your interview may be over before it ever starts.

7. *Don't be satisfied with monosyllabic answers.*   Be aware when subjects begin giving yes-and-no answers. Answers like these will not offer much information during analysis. When this does occur, be sure to probe for more.

8. *Be respectful.*   Be sure the subject feels that he or she is an integral part of your research and that any answer offered is absolutely wonderful. Often subjects will say things like, "You don't really want to know how I feel about that." Assure them that you really do!

9. *Practice, practice, and practice some more.*   The only way to actually become proficient at interviewing is to interview. Although this book and other manuals can offer guidelines, it is up to you as a researcher to develop your own repertoire of actions. The best way to accomplish this task is to go out and do interviews.

10. *Be cordial and appreciative.*   Remember to thank the subject when you finish and answer any questions he or she might have about the research. Remember, you are always a research emissary. Other researchers may someday want to interview this subject or gain access to the setting you were in. If you mess things up through inappropriate actions, you may close the door for future researchers.

Know Your Audience

If you have ever attended the live performance of a pretty good comedian, you may have noticed that he or she seemed to know the audience. The comedian seemed to know how much *blue material* the audience wanted and would tolerate. He or she even may have used local names of people or places in the routine. In fact, in the case of really good comedians, they may even have incorporated certain local *insider* jokes during the course of the routine. All of these things were because the comedian had taken the time to prepare and get to know the audience.

When interviewing, it is likewise advisable to *know your audience*. In this case, however, it means understanding the group or groups from which you draw your subjects. During the past several years, we have worked with a number of Asian and Middle Eastern graduate students. They are a constant reminder to me that it is very important to understand the culture of your research subjects. Often the kinds of questions that we in the West take for granted create significant cultural dilemmas for certain groups.

For instance, one of Berg's graduate students was developing a dissertation project to examine delinquency in Taiwan. The student, who was Chinese, began developing questions from information he found in the literature.

Among the original questions we discussed was what seemed to be a fairly innocuous one: "About how often do you date?" The student explained that he could not ask Chinese adolescents this question. He went on to explain that proper Chinese adolescents do not date as Westerners think about dating. In other words, an adolescent boy and girl would never go off on their own to the movies, or roller-skating, or any other *traditional date*. In fact, such an activity would be viewed by most proper adults as indecent, since dating tends to have sexual connotations in Taiwan. Furthermore, it would be impolite to ask adolescents such a question. He also explained that this did not mean that Taiwanese adolescents did not have their own form of dating. This variation in dating might be called *group dating*. In this form, five or six male friends will meet five or six girls at a skating rink—not so much by chance as by design. Once there, the groups tend to pair off, but they would never describe *this as a date*.

The solution to this problem was to craft a question that asked whether the youths ever intentionally went to certain locations with friends of the same gender to meet with groups of friends of the opposite gender.

The point is to understand the culture of the subjects you work with. It is of critical importance that when you develop interview schedules the language as well as the nature of the questions remain inoffensive. In the ever-shrinking electronic world we currently live in, it is becoming more and more possible to conduct comparative research projects. As a result, many researchers are dealing with a wide variety of different and literally foreign cultures. It is critical, then, that you carefully plan out the types of questions you want to ask and the types of individuals you use to conduct interviews in these situations. In short, know your audience before your performance!

Curtain Calls

In concluding this section on learning the ropes of dramaturgical interviewing, it is important to note that some individuals may never achieve the status of highly skilled interviewer. However, just as there are B-movie actors who make their entire careers by acting in dozens of low-budget films and never achieve stardom, so too can there be effective B-movie interviewers. Put simply, some individuals will be able to obtain sufficient information from an interview to conduct viable research, yet will not be considered stars.

Other individuals will completely fail to conduct interviews successfully. These individuals fail to become even B-level interviewers not because of interpersonal limitations but because of their failure to achieve a self-aware performance. These individuals are unable to adapt their scripts and blocking in order to accommodate the interviewee while continuing to maintain effective control over the interview process. Of course one can learn and improve. But sometimes it is better to simply find your strengths and go with those.

Analyzing Data Obtained from the Dramaturgical Interview

When novice interviewers have mastered to some extent interviewing strategies and practices and have conducted a number of interviews, the next problem is how to organize all the data accumulated in the interviews. How should the interviewers proceed with the task of taking many hours of tape-recorded interviews, for example, and analyzing them? Janice Morse (1994, p. 23) observed that despite the proliferation of qualitative research methodology texts, the process of data analysis remains fairly poorly described.

Although analysis is without question the most difficult aspect of any qualitative research project, it is also the most creative. Because of the creative component, it is impossible to establish a complete step-by-step operational procedure that will consistently result in qualitative analysis. Unlike quantitative research, qualitative analysis does not lend itself to this sort of certainty. One cannot pull out numbers (operationally reduce responses) from the interviews and expect to plug them into a qualitative analysis computer program— none exists! For these reasons, the following points are intended more as recommendations, tips, and hints on how to organize interview data rather than as a specific, rigid guide. Although some of the suggestions may suit certain projects nicely, the analysis of data is primarily determined by the nature of the project and the various contingencies built in during the design stages.

It is important to note that while qualitative analysis is sometimes thought to lack the precision assumed to be present in quantitative research, this is not necessarily the case. Good qualitative research, like good quantitative research, is based on calculated strategies and methodological rigor. Insights obtained from qualitative research can not only add texture to an analysis but also demonstrate meanings and understandings about problems and phenomena that would otherwise be unidentified. Qualitative analysis cannot be undertaken quickly, neatly, or lightly, but this should never be viewed as a liability or limitation. Instead, this characteristic of qualitative analysis is perhaps its greatest strength. When qualitative analysis is undertaken, certain priorities must be established, assumptions made during the design and data-collection phases must be clarified, and a particular research course must be set. Quantitative data are sometimes incorrectly leaf raked (particularly by computer programs) in order to find results, but qualitative analysis cannot be conducted in this manner.

From an interactionist position, interviews are essentially symbolic interactions. From the dramaturgical interview's perspective, these interactions can be described along the lines of performances. The social context of the interview, therefore, is intrinsic to understanding the data that were collected (Silverman, 1993, 2004).

Beginning an Analysis

Analysis of interview data cannot be completely straightforward or cut and dry, but it is still necessary to understand what to do when you reach this phase in the research. The most obvious way to analyze interview data is *content analysis*. Although you may certainly abstract reducible items from interview data in order to quantify them, your analysis immediately ceases to be qualitative. A comprehensive consideration of content analysis is the subject of Chapter 11. This section outlines how to organize and prepare for analyzing the data collected from depth interviews. In order to analyze data, you must first arrange them in some ordered fashion. In the next section, some suggestions about ordering data are offered.

Systematic Filing Systems

As Lofland and Lofland (1984) suggest, "First, and perhaps foremost is the establishment of some kind of filing system." By *filing*, Lofland and Lofland literally mean a physical (mechanical) means of maintaining and indexing coded data and sorting data into coded classifications. Files may involve placing material into boxes, file cabinets, or envelopes, or, preferably, computer files. The obvious purpose of a filing system is to develop a means by which to access various aspects of the data easily, flexibly, and efficiently. Of course, the central issue is what should be filed. In Chapter 11, a related and comprehensive examination of what Strauss (1987) called *open coding* is offered. In this chapter, however, it is assumed that each interview was recorded on tape and transcribed verbatim and is ready for a thorough reading and annotating of codable topics, themes, and issues.

To begin, you simply seek naturally occurring classes of things, persons, and events, and important characteristics of these items. In other words, you look for similarities and dissimilarities—patterns—in the data. But you must look for these patterns systematically!

Typically, a systematic indexing process begins as researchers set up several sheets of paper (yes, paper) with major topics of interest listed separately. Below these major interest topics are usually several other subtopics or themes. For example, Glassner and Berg (1980) began analysis with 16 separate major thematic topic sheets, each containing from 2 to 13 minor topics or subthemes (Berg, 1983, p. 24). A total of 80 specific subthemes were consistently sought, coded, and annotated on interview transcripts.

Ideally, this process should be accomplished by two or more researchers/coders, independently reading and coding each of several transcripts. This process is intended to establish the various topics to be indexed in the filing system. Using two or more independent coders ensures that naturally arising categories are used rather than those a particular researcher might hope to locate—regardless of whether the categories really exist. The degree of agreement among the coders is called *inter-rater reliability* (IRR). If the IRR is high, then your coding system is working. If low, then you need to re-examine your categories and definitions. As well, you need to look carefully at each case in which the coders disagree. The consequence of this process, if correctly executed, is a precise, reliable, and reproducible coding system.

These *index sheets* should contain some type of code identifying the transcript in which it has been located, the page number of the specific transcript, and a brief verbatim excerpt (no more than a sentence). Traditionally, codes used to identify transcripts are pseudonyms or case numbers (randomly assigned). A typical index sheet might look something like the one in Table 4.1. Additionally, I like to color code the major code categories, and to highlight the corresponding section of text in the transcript file using that color. Note that while this helps me to find the relevant test sections, it remains important to actually write down the page numbers.

Table 4.1 Alcohol Use [Major Topic/Theme]

	Subthemes	
Beer	*Wine*	*Hard Liquors*
#12, pp. 3–6: I only drink beer when I am with my. . . .	#6, pp. 2–4: I love the taste of wine, but I hate beer.	#7, pp. 22–25: When I'm feeling real up, I'll have a drink.
#6, pp. 2–4: (see wine) #9, pp. 3–4: Whenever I am really warm, like in the summer, I'll have a beer.	#5, p. 8: I only drink wine during the ceremonies, you know, the religious ceremonies.	#5, p. 23: I almost never drink liquor, just that one I told you about.

As implied in the preceding example, every subtheme is annotated from each transcript. When more than one subtheme is mentioned in the same passage, it is nonetheless shown under each subtheme (see the entries for #6 under the headings *Beer* and *Wine*). Cross-referencing in this fashion, although extremely time consuming during the coding stage, permits much easier location of particular items during the later stages of analysis.

When every interview transcript has been read and index sheets have been appropriately annotated, researchers should have a comprehensive means for accessing information. Additionally, the index sheets provide a means for counting certain types of responses in order to suggest magnitudes in response sets or for beginning content analysis of various specific themes.

Short-Answer Sheets

In addition to developing a comprehensive filing and indexing system, researchers may want to create a *quick response* or short-answer sheet to include in their files. Particularly when conducting standardized interviews, it is possible to complete brief responses for each of the questions asked as you read through and code each transcript. In essence, the questions become the interview schedule, and coders simply write short responses for each. Frequently this can be accomplished by reducing many of the responses to either affirmative (yes), negative (no), no clear response (unclear), or a very brief excerpt (no more than one sentence) including page reference.

Short-answer sheets are included primarily for convenience. They can be stored in separate files or with each interview transcript. They summarize many of the issues and topics contained in each transcript (respondent's income, age, gender, occupation, etc.). Since answers for which more detail was provided have been captured and coded in the indexing sheet procedure, these short-answer sheets offer another type of cross-reference summary.

Analysis Procedures: A Concluding Remark

Stacy (1969) had suggested that the collection of qualitative data is often so extensive that researchers can feel that their jobs must be complete when they have gathered it all in. This conclusion, of course, is far from accurate. As they listen to the interviewees, researchers frequently develop many interesting (and sometimes unreliable) impressions about possible patterns. After the interviews are completed, however, researchers must closely examine potential patterns to see what findings actually emerge directly from the data. Such grounded findings, emerging from the data themselves, are frequently among the most interesting and important results obtained during research, even though they may have gone unnoticed during the data-collecting phase. Your final set of code categories will contain both the ones you expected and the ones you discovered in the analysis. Procedures used to identify these grounded concepts and patterns are discussed in greater detail in Chapter 11.

TRYING IT OUT

Naturally, a certain amount of mental effort is required to learn the skills necessary for conducting effective interviews. These mental juices may have been flowing as you read this chapter on interviewing. But, as previously mentioned, there is no substitute for practice. You will have to go out and conduct several interviews. There are many public places where you can practice interviewing. Consider, for example, conducting several unstructured interviews with people at your local public library, on a busy downtown street corner, or even while feeding pigeons in a public park.

You might also consider testing your semistructured instrument (either individually or as a class) from earlier in this chapter. These instruments can then be used as practice schedules during interviews either among classmates or in public places. Some possible topics include how the threat of AIDS may have affected dating practices, whether all workers should be subject to urine analysis as a condition of employment, or whether elementary and secondary school teachers should be required to pass competency examinations as conditions of their retention in schools. Or, simply select a topic from the headlines of the local newspaper. Remember, your purpose is to practice interviewing skills, not to derive actual scientific empirical research. Each of the suggestions offered here measures people's opinions about social policies and practices, not details about the practices themselves.

Good interviewers work on improving their listening skills. The better an interviewer hears what is being said by the subject, the more effectively he or she can play the interviewer role. Classrooms are excellent places to practice aware hearing techniques. In our culture, we have a tendency to interrupt speakers in order to interject our own views or comments. It is, in fact, quite difficult for novice interviewers to learn that they cannot say such things as, "Oh yeah, I did that once," or "That's really something, but have you ever tried . . .," or similar interruptions. Remember, when interviewing, the ideal is to have the subject speaking 80–90 percent of the time. When interviewers take up too much of the conversation, little research information is gained.

It is likewise important to demonstrate to the subject that you are really listening—*aware listening*, as it may be called. This means you are not thinking about your next question or about how smart you can make yourself look with some comment—the usual style of natural conversational exchange.

Try the following in order to practice aware listening skills: The instructor pairs off all the students in the class. Each pair is positioned so that their seats are facing each other, but not too close together. The teacher arbitrarily assigns a listener and a speaker in each pair. Now the teacher asks each speaker to talk for 30 seconds on some mundane topic—for example, "my favorite color," "my favorite food," or "the best day in my life." The instructor times this exercise and, after 30 seconds have elapsed, calls out "Stop!" At this point, the *listener* repeats verbatim everything he or she heard. This includes using first person singular ("I" statements) if the original speaker used them.

Following this, the participants reverse roles. The original speaker becomes the listener and vice versa. The teacher again times a 30-second mundane-topic exchange. After this is complete, the time is increased to 60 seconds, and the teacher suggests a slightly more personal topic, such as "the most embarrassing thing that ever happened to me," "something I really like about myself," "something I would change about myself if I could," or "something I dislike about myself."

It is important to be sure you do not make any verbal statements, responses, or comments when in the role of the listener. You may make non-verbal gestures, such as a nod or use of eyes or eyebrows, to show appropriate response to statements.

When you have completed the exchanges, consider the following questions:

1. Did your body language change during the exchanges? For example, did you move closer or further apart? Did you cross or uncross your legs or arms?
2. Did the level of sound change at all when you went from the mundane question to the more revealing personal one?
3. Was there less (if any) giggling and movement during the more self-revealing questions as compared with the mundane questions?
4. Was it difficult to sit silently and concentrate on listening?

NOTES

1. Slight risk does exist, of course, should these e-mails be transmitted via a wireless network. A well-versed hacker could conceivably hijack the entire communication. The likelihood of this occurring is rather small, and encrypting wireless transmissions would even further reduce the risk.

REFERENCES

Archer, D. (1980). *Social Intelligence.* New York: Evans.

Archer, D., & Akert, R. M. (1980). The encoding of meaning: A test of three theories of social interaction. *Sociological Inquiry 50* (3–4), 393–419.

Babbie, E. (2004). *The Practice of Social Research* (10th ed.). Belmont, CA: Wadsworth.

Babbie, E. (2007). *The Practice of Social Research* (11th ed.). Belmont, CA: Wadsworth.

Bachman, E., & Schutt, R. K. (2003). *The Practice of Research in Criminology and Criminal Justice* (2nd ed.). Thousand Oaks, CA: Pine Forge Press.

Backstrom, C. H., & Hursh, G. D. (1981). *Survey Research.* New York: John Wiley and Sons.

Bampton, R., & Cowton, C. J. (2002). The e-interview. *Forum: Qualitative Social Research 3*(2), 165–174.

Barone, D. (2002). Literacy teaching and learning in two kindergarten classrooms in a school labeled at-risk. *The Elementary School Journal 102*(5), 415–442.

Becker, H. S. (1963). *Outsiders: Studies in the Sociology of Deviance.* New York: Free Press.

Benny, M., & Hughes, E. C. (1956). Of sociology and the interview: Editorial preface. *American Journal of Sociology 62,* 137–142.

Berg, B. L. (1983). Jewish identity: Subjective declarations or objective life styles. Doctoral dissertation, Syracuse University, Syracuse.

Berg, B. L. (2002). Risk factors associated with Latino men who have sex with other men. Interview number 14. Unpublished interview.

Berg, B. L., & Doerner, W. G. (November 1987). Volunteer police officers: An unexamined aspect of police personnel. Paper presented at the annual meeting of the American Society of Criminology, Montreal, PQ.

Berg, B. L., & Glassner, B. (1979). Methodological strategies for a study of Jews and drinking. Paper presented at the annual meeting of the American Sociological Association, Boston, MA.

Berg, B., Sañudo, F., Hovell, M., Sipan, C., Kelley, N., & Blumberg, E. (2004). The use of indigenous interviewers in a study of Latino men who have sex with men: A research note. *Sexuality and Culture 8*(1), 87–103.

Berg, J. P. (1986). Dietary protein intake: Compliance and knowledge in hemodialysis patients. Master's thesis, University of Florida, Gainesville.

Bogdan, R., & Knopp Biklen, S. (2006). *Qualitative Research for Education* (5th ed.). Boston, MA: Allyn and Bacon.

Burns, N., & Grove, S. K. (1993). *The Practice of Nursing Research* (2nd ed.). Philadelphia, PA: W. B. Saunders.

Butler, J. (1997). *Excitable Speech: A Politics of the Performative.* New York: Routledge.

Chadwick, B. A., Bahr, H. M., & Albrecht, S. L. (1984). *Social Science Research Methods.* Englewood Cliffs, NJ: Prentice Hall.

Champion, D. J. (2006). *Research Methods for Criminal Justice and Criminology* (3rd ed.). Upper Saddle River, NJ: Pearson/Prentice Hall.

Collins, M., Shattell, M., & Thomas, S. P. (2005). Problematic interviewee behaviors in qualitative research. *Western Journal of Nursing Research 27*(2), 188–199.

Cotterill, P. (1992). Interviewing women: Issues of friendship, vulnerability, and power. *Women's Studies International Forum 15*(5–6), 593–606.

De Santis, G. (1980). Interviewing as social interaction. *Qualitative Sociology 2*(3), 72–98.

Denzin, N. K. (1970). *Sociological Methods: A Sourcebook*. Chicago, IL: Aldine.

Denzin, N. K. (1978). *The Research Act* (5th ed.). New York: McGraw-Hill.

Denzin, N. K. (2001). The reflexive interview and a performative social science. *Qualitative Research 1*(1), 23–46.

Dingwall, R. (1997). Accounts, interviews, and observations. In G. Miller & R. Dingwall (Eds.), *Context and Method in Qualitative Research* (pp. 51–65). Thousand Oaks, CA: Sage.

Douglas, J. D. (1985). Creative interviewing. In L. T. Reynolds & N. J. Herman-Kinney (Eds.), *Handbook of Symbolic Interactionism*. New York: Rowman & Littlefield.

Ellis, C., Kiesinger, C. E., & Tillmann-Healy, L. M. (1997). Interactive interviewing: Talking about emotional experiences. In R. Hertz (Ed.), *Reflexivity and Voice* (pp. 119–149). Thousand Oaks, CA: Sage.

Flick, U. (2006). *An Introduction to Qualitative Research* (3rd ed.). Thousand Oaks, CA: Sage.

Fontana, A., & Frey, J. (1998). Interviewing: The art of science. In Norman K. Denzin & Yvonna S. Lincoln (Eds.), *Collecting and Interpreting Qualitative Materials*. Thousand Oaks, CA: Sage.

Friedman, J., & Orru, M. (1991). Organizational access to research settings: Entering secondary schools. *The American Sociologist 22*(2), 117–136.

Glassner, B., & Berg, B. L. (1980). How Jews avoid alcohol problems. *American Sociological Review 45*(1), 647–664.

Glassner, B., & Berg, B. L. (1984). Social locations and interpretations: How Jews define alcoholism. *Journal of Studies on Alcohol 45*(1), 16–25.

Goffman, E. (1959). *The Presentation of Self in Everyday Life*. Garden City, NJ: Doubleday.

Goffman, E. (1967). *Interaction Ritual*. New York: Anchor Books.

Goode, W. J., & Hatt, P. K. (1952). *Methods in Social Research*. New York: McGraw-Hill.

Gorden, R. L. (1987). *Interviewing* (4th ed.). Chicago, IL: Dorsey Press.

Gorden, R. L. (1992). *Basic Interviewing Skills*. Itasca, IL: F. E. Peacock Publishers.

Grinnell, R. M., & Unrau, Y. A. (2005). *Social Work: Research and Valuation*. New York: Oxford University Press.

Grobel, L. (2004). *The Art of the Interview: Lessons from a Master of the Craft*. New York: Three River Press.

Gubrium, J. F., & Holstein, J. A. (2003). *Postmodern Interviewing*. Thousand Oaks, CA: Sage.

Hagan, F. (1995). *Research Methods in Criminal Justice and Criminology* (4th ed.). New York: Macmillan.

Hagan, J. E. (2006). *Research Methods in Criminal Justice and Criminology*. Boston, MA: Allyn and Bacon.

Halbert, S. C. (2003). Rhythm and reminiscence: Popular music, nostalgia, and storied self. Senior Thesis, Department of Sociology, University of Houston. Cited by

Carol A. B. Warren and Tracey X. Kamer (2005, p. 153) in Discovering Qualitative Methods. Los Angeles, CA: Roxbury.

Hertz, R. (1995). Separate but simultaneous interviewing of husbands and wives: Making sense of their stories. *Qualitative Inquiry 1*(4), 429–451.

Holstein, J. A., & Gubrium, J. F. (1995). *The Active Interview*. Thousand Oaks, CA: Sage.

Holstein, J. A., & Gubrium, J. F. (2004). The active interview. In D. Silverman (Ed.), *Qualitative Research: Theory, Method, and Practice* (2nd ed.). Thousand Oaks, CA: Sage.

Horowitz, C. R., Davis, M. H., Palermo, A. S., and Vladeck, B. C. (2000). Approaches to eliminating sociocultural disparities in health. *Health Care Financing Review 21*(4), 57–75.

Ireland, C., & Berg, B.L. (2006). Women in parole: Gendered adaptations of female parole agents in California. *Women & Criminal Justice 18*(1–2), 131–150.

Ireland, C., & Berg, B. L. (August 2008). Women in parole: Respect and rapport. *International Journal of Offender Therapy and Comparative Criminology 52*(4), 474–491.

Kinsey, A. C., Pomeroy, W. B., & Martin, C. E. (1948). *Sexual Behavior in the Human*. Philadelphia, PA: W. B. Saunders.

Kvale, S. (1996). *Interviews: An Introduction to Qualitative Research Interviewing*. Thousand Oaks, CA: Sage.

Leavy, P. (2008). Performance-based emergent methods. In N. Hesse-Biber & P. Leavy (Eds.), *Handbook of Emergent Methods*. New York: The Guilford Press.

Leedy, P., & Ormrod, J. E. (2001). *Practical Research: Planning and Design* (7th ed.). Upper Saddle River, NJ: Prentice Hall.

Leedy, P., & Ormrod, J. E. (2004). *Practical Research: Planning and Design* (8th ed.). Upper Saddle River, NJ: Prentice Hall.

Lincoln, Y. S., & Guba, E. G. (1985). *Naturalistic Inquiry*. Beverly Hills, CA: Sage.

Lindlof, T. R., & Taylor, B. C. (2002). *Qualitative Communication Research Methods* (2nd ed.). Thousand Oaks, CA: Sage.

Lofland, J. A., & Lofland, L. H. (1984). *Analyzing Social Settings: A Guide to Qualitative Observation and Analysis*. Belmont, CA: Wadsworth.

Lofland, J. A., Snow, D. A., Anderson, L., & Lofland. L. H. (2005). *Analyzing Social Settings: A Guide to Qualitative Observations and Analysis* (4th ed.). Belmont, CA: Wadsworth.

Lune, H. (2002). Weathering the storm: Nonprofit organization survival strategies in a hostile climate. *Nonprofit and Voluntary Sector Quarterly 31*(4), 463–483.

Lune, H. (2007). *Urban Action Networks: HIV/AIDS and Community Organizing in New York City*. Boulder, CO: Rowman and Littlefield.

Lyons, L., & Chipperfield, J. (Spring–Summer 2000). (DE) constructing the interview: A critique of the participatory model. *Resources for Feminist Research*, 33–49.

Manning, P. K. (1967). Problems of interpreting interview data. *Sociology and Social Research 15*(3), 302–316.

McGivern, Y. (2006). *The Practice of Market & Social Research*. Upper Saddle River, NJ: Prentice Hall Publishing.

Merriam, S. B. (2001). *Qualitative Research and Case Study Applications in Education*. San Francisco, CA: Jossey-Bass.

Mienczakowski, J. (1995). The theatre of ethnography: The reconstruction of ethnography into theatre with emancipatory potential. *Qualitative Inquiry 1*(3), 360–375.

Mienczakowski, J. (2000). Ethnodrama: Performed research—limitations and potential. In P. Atkinson, A. Coffey, S. Delemont, J. Lofland, & L. Lofland (Eds.), *Handbook of Ethnography*. London: Sage.

Miller, M. (1996). Ethics and understanding through interrelationship: I and thou in dialogue. In R. Josselson (Ed.), *Ethics and Process in the Narrative Study of Lives* (Vol. 4, pp. 129–147). Thousand Oaks, CA: Sage.

Morris, T. (2006). *Social Work Research Methods: Four Alternative Paradigms*. Thousand Oaks, CA: Sage.

Morse, J. M. (1994). *Critical Issues in Qualitative Research Methods*. Thousand Oaks, CA: Sage.

Murray, S. O. (1991). Ethnic differences in interpretive conventions and the reproduction of inequality in everyday life. *Symbolic Interaction 14*(2), 165–186.

Mutchnick, R. J., & Berg, B. L. (1996). *Research Methods for the Social Sciences: Practice and Applications*. Boston, MA: Allyn and Bacon.

Nieswiadomy, R. M. (2002). *Foundations of Nursing Research* (4th ed.). Upper Saddle River, NJ: Prentice Hall.

Oakly, A. (1981). Interviewing women: A contradiction in terms. In H. Roberts (Ed.), *Doing Feminist Research* (pp. 30–61). London: Routledge & Kegan Paul.

Patton, M. Q. (2002). *Qualitative Research and Evaluation Methods* (3rd ed.). Thousand Oaks, CA: Sage.

Rapley, T. J. (2001). The art (fullness) of open-ended interviewing: Some considerations on analyzing interviews. *Qualitative Research 1*(3), 303–323.

Reik, T. (1949). *Listening with the Third Ear*. New York: Farrar, Straus.

Rossman, E. J. (1992). The use of semistructured interviews in developing Superfund community relations plans. *Sociological Practice Review 3*(2), 102–108.

Roth, J. (1966). Hired hand research. *The American Sociologist 1*, 190–196.

Rubin, H. J., & Rubin, I. S. (1995). *Qualitative Interviewing: The Art of Hearing Data*. Thousand Oaks, CA: Sage.

Rubin, H. J., & Rubin, I. S. (1997). *Qualitative Interviewing: The Act of Hearing Data* (2nd ed.). Thousand Oaks, CA: Sage.

Rubin, H. J., & Rubin, I. S. (2004). *Qualitative Interviewing: The Art of Hearing Data* (2nd ed.). Thousand Oaks, CA: Sage.

Russell, C. (1999). Meanings of home in the lives of older women (and men). In M. Poole & S. Feldman (Eds.), *A Certain Age: Women Growing Older* (pp. 36–55). Australia: Allen & Unwin.

Salkind, N. J. (2008). *Exploring Research* (7th ed.). Englewood Cliffs, NJ: Prentice Hall.

Schwartz, H., & Jacobs, J. (1979). *Qualitative Sociology: A Method to the Madness*. New York: Free Press.

Seidman, I. (2006). *Interviewing as Qualitative Research: A Guide for Researchers in Education and the Social Sciences*. New York: The Teachers College Press.

Shaffir, W. B., Stebbins, R. A., & Turowetz, A. (1980). *Fieldwork Experience: Qualitative Approaches to Social Research*. New York: St. Martin's Press.

Silverman, D. (1993). *Interpreting Qualitative Data*. Thousand Oaks, CA: Sage.

Silverman, D. (2004). *Doing Qualitative Research* (2nd ed.). London: Sage.

Stacy, M. (1969). *Methods of Social Research*. New York: Pergamon.

Stone, G. P. (1962). Appearance and the self. In A. Rose (Ed.), *Human Behavior and Social Processes*. Boston, MA: Houghton Mifflin.

Strauss, A. L. (1987). *Qualitative Analysis for Social Scientists*. New York: Cambridge University Press.

Stromer-Galley, J. (2003). Depth interviews for the study of motives and perceptions of Internet use. Presented at the International Communication Association Conference, San Diego.

Taylor, S., & Bogdan, R. (1998). *Introduction to Qualitative Research Methods* (3rd ed.). New York: John Wiley and Sons.

Tewksbury, R., & Gagne, P. (1997). Assumed and presumed identities: Problems on self-presentation in field research. *Sociological Spectrum 17*(2), 127–156.

Thomas, S. P., & Pollio, H. R. (2002). *Listening to Patients: A Phenomenological Approach to Nursing Research and Practice*. New York: Springer.

Trochim, W. M. K. (2005). *Research Methods*. Cincinnati, OH: Atomic Dog Publishers.

Turner, C. F., Ku, L., Rogers, M., Lindberg, D. L., Pleck, J. H., & Sonenstein, F. L. (1998). Adolescent sexual behavior, drug use, and violence: Increased reporting with computer survey technology. *Science 280*, 867–873.

Warren, C., & Karner, T. (2005). *Discovering Qualitative Methods*. Los Angeles, CA: Roxbury.

Zellner, J. A., Blumberg, E. J., Daniel, J., Berg, B. L., Kelley, N. J., Sanudo, F., Sipan, C., Martinez-Donate, A., Carrizosa, C. M., & Hovell, M. F. (2008). Experiences of sexuality and homophobia in Mexico & the US among Mexican men who have sex men [forthcoming].

Zurcher, L. A. (1983). *Social Roles*. Beverly Hills, CA: Sage.

Chapter 5

Focus Group Interviewing

What are Focus Groups?

The focus group is an interview style designed for small groups of unrelated individuals, formed by an investigator and led in a group discussion on some particular topic or topics (Barbour, 2008). Using this approach, researchers strive to learn through discussion about conscious, semiconscious, and unconscious psychological and sociocultural characteristics and processes among various groups (Larson, Grudens-Schuck, & Lundy, 2004; Lengua et al., 1992; Stewart, Shamdasani, & Rook, 2006). This includes some amount of opinion research, though the approach is most appropriate for investigating motivations, decisions, and priorities. Group interviews are sometimes used to quickly and conveniently collect data from several people simultaneously; however, focus group interviews explicitly use group interactions as part of the data-gathering method. To be more specific, focus group interviews are guided or unguided group discussions addressing a particular topic of interest or relevance to the group and the researcher (Edmunds, 2000). It is, in this sense, nothing like a town-hall meeting.

Focus group interviews are a useful strategy either as a stand-alone data-gathering strategy or as a line of action in a triangulated project (see Chapter 2). Stewart and Shamdasani (1990, p. 15) offer a number of appropriate uses for focus groups interviews, including exploratory investigations into emerging areas of interest, research intended to generate new ideas or questions, and studying the language and slang used by a population group when talking about some phenomenon of shared interest. As discussed by David Morgan (1996), focus groups are also frequently used in combination with individual interviews as a kind of validity check on the findings and as a preparatory step in the design of survey instruments.

Each of these uses stress the *applied* nature of much focus group research, in which the group data-collection process serves some further application, such as program implementation, problem solving, or marketing. Focus groups also serve as important tools for *pure* research, studies in which we begin with a research question and use our primary data collection to answer it. This technique is most useful for research involving beliefs, impressions, and emotional concerns, rather than, for example, opinions, or actions. We will look at some examples of each of these later.

A typical focus group session consists of a small number of participants under the guidance of a facilitator, usually called the *moderator*. A skilled moderator can effectively draw out the feelings and ideas of the members of the group involved in the focus group interview (Stewart et al., 2006). Krueger (1994) suggests that for complex problems focus group size should be kept to no more than about seven participants.[1] Thus, larger groups of subjects may be divided into a series of smaller focus groups. There are a number of reasons why one should keep the size of the focus group small; chief among these is the ability to effectively elicit the breadth of responses that distinguish focus groups as a useful data-gathering strategy. Large groups are simply difficult to manage and can soon become unwieldy and may erode into several fragmented subgroups, further complicating control and understanding of the information offered by groups members (Break-well, Hammond, Fife-Schaw, & Smith, 2006). Other reasons include the ability to avoid one or two strongly motivated participants monopolizing the conversation, which becomes more difficult the larger the group is, and the more highly motivated individuals there are in the group. There is also the problem of a transcriber being able to properly associate a given speaker with his or her comments—much easier with a fewer number of individuals in each group. There is also the benefit of reducing *group think*, which involves several members of the group jumping on board a particular idea or series of comments about a given idea, attitude, or belief as the result of subgroup pressure.

Working with a Group

The moderator's job, like the standard interviewer's, is to draw out information from the participants regarding topics of importance to a given research investigation. The informal group discussion atmosphere of the focus group interview structure is intended to encourage subjects to speak freely and completely about behaviors, attitudes, and opinions they possess, but to stay on the subject (Gubrium & Holstein, 2001). Therefore, focus groups are an excellent means for collecting information from informants who might otherwise tend to go off on their own topics, such as young children and teens, as well as professionals in many fields, elected officials, and some elderly adults. Actually anyone who is easily distracted, somewhat egotistical, or just uncomfortable with the conversation might be prone to get off topic in a one-on-one conversation, but might not take control as readily in a group setting. More importantly, focus groups allow researchers to observe interactions and discussions among informants. The data collected during a group interview with seven participants are therefore a single unit of data from one group, not seven individual cases collected simultaneously. The heart of the data is in the group dynamic.

Focus group interviews also provide a means for collecting qualitative data in some settings and situations where a one-shot collection is necessary. Although one-shot data collections usually are associated with survey questionnaires, in some cases, focus group interviews may serve a similar purpose. Certain groups of interest to social scientists may remain available for study only for limited amounts of time. For example, say you are interested in studying battered women. You might decide that access to a sample of such women can be best obtained through a battered women's shelter. However, women typically remain in such shelters only for short periods of time, perhaps as little as a month. Now imagine there are 40 or 50 women residing in the shelter at any given time. Individual interviews would not be a practical strategy for data collection, considering the amount of time that would be required to conduct that many interviews. Focus group interviews, however, might work well. You could easily hold four or five sessions during the course of a single week and collect necessary research information.

Along with more traditional populations, then, semitransient ones such as prisoners; hospital, clinic, and HMO patients; students and children in special courses; migrant workers; parents at PTA or PTO meetings; and even conventioneers may be suitable for focus group interviews. Even the settings where these semitransient groups are found lend themselves to data-collection plans that are faster than traditional individual face-to-face interviews. That is, they gather. With good advanced planning, a researcher can travel to a place where members of the target population have already congregated to meet a preselected group in a suitable prepared office. Otherwise, bringing all of your informants together at the same time in your own research space may take a considerable amount of coordination.

Some Problems to Avoid in Focus Group Interviewing

There are a number of problems that researchers, especially inexperienced researchers, sometime fall victim to when undertaking focus group interviews. These problems can seriously reduce the quality of the resulting information from the focus groups and may even interfere in the moderator's ability to effectively elicit useful and relevant information. In the following section I outline and describe the problems and offer some recommendations for avoiding these obstacles.

1. **Running a Focus Group Because the Investigator Doesn't Know What Else to Do**. There are a wide variety of data-collecting techniques —certainly a number of these are discussed in this book. Focus group research, while sometimes appearing like a simple activity and easy to do, may be appealing for a researcher to use. However, the type of data one collects and the actual level of difficulty may not be what the investigator really needs to effectively undertake the study. For example, and similar to determining whether to undertake a paper-and-pencil survey or a depth interview, when a researcher actually is primarily interested in what some group does, or if they are involved in certain activities, the survey may be a better strategy than either the depth interview or a focus group. Conversely, if one is interested in why some group is interested in a particular activity, their attitudes about those involved in that activity, or even their beliefs about these activities or those involved in such behavior, a focus group may be a useful means for accessing this information.

2. **Being Too Vague About the Objectives of the Focus Group Interview.** Particularly since most focus groups use only a few questions as guides for the moderator to explore some area, subject, or topic, it is very important that the investigator be clear about what he or she is interested in examining during the course of the focus group interview. Similarly, it is important that these objectives are made crystal clear to the moderator (if this is not the actual investigator). Planning the objectives using a *cognitive map* (see Chapter 4) is one good method of assuring that you are clear on why you are using focus group research, as a strategy, and what sorts of questions you should be including during the course of the interview.

3. **Using Too Few Groups.** It is a serious error to plan on using focus group interviews because you can only identify a small group of individuals to serve as the sample. Focus group interviewing is not a remedy for a poorly planned sampling strategy. Often a researcher may use a series of several small focus groups, totaling 30 or more subjects in the full study. This can

allow for emergent results arising during the course of the research and the introduction of these topics in subsequent focus groups, as well as comparisons of results between groups (Morgan, Fellows, & Guevara, 2008). But don't be misled by the total. Five focus groups with a total of 30 participants equals 5 cases, not 30.

4. **Overreaching During Any Given Focus Group Interview.** Researchers need to be realistic about how many questions and how much coverage any given focus group can effectively handle. Most social research-based focus groups stay to a handful of questions, both to assure that these interviews only run for about 30–60 minutes, and to ensure sufficient coverage of information offered by the participants. It is sometimes difficult to gauge how many questions can be effectively explored during a given amount of time. Stewart et al. (2006) suggest that some of the factors that influence how much time a group may take on a subject may be associated with the group's composition. For example, a group composed of individuals with fairly homogeneous characteristics (a group of male elders, for example) may be able to move through many questions rather quickly; whereas, a very heterogeneous group of individuals (differing ages, genders, educational levels) or a group asked a series of questions with a number of different dimensions may labor long and hard over even a few questions. As a rule of thumb, then, the more complex, and/or emotionally charged a topic, or the greater the heterogeneity of expected views on a topic within a group, the fewer topics and specific questions that should be included.

Overreaching necessarily creates pressures on the moderator to speed up the process. In that case, the moderator may start to pressure participants to provide shorter answers, or to otherwise limit discussion. This undermines the focus group process considerably. In contrast, a skilled moderator generally seeks to draw more discussion and more detail from the participants. The goal, of course, is to encourage the participants to open up their answers and explore the topics.

In practice, most focus group interview guides or schedules typically consist of fewer than a dozen planned questions. Instead, the moderator is expected to use his or her judgment with regard to probes and adding various questions as situations and additional topics emerge. The moderator needs some elbow room to make that work.

5. **Overly Large Groups.** Some investigators may seek to limit the number of focus group sessions that may be necessary to include all the subjects in the sample; this is a mistake. This may allow for a greater amount of interaction, since there are more people to potentially offer their views

and attitudes. However, especially for an inexperienced moderator, this can create confusion and may result in more superficial results than might otherwise have been possible with a smaller group. Groups of six or eight participants are fairly easy to manage, and transcribers are typically able to correctly identify which of the participants said what from a recorded focus group interview. Larger groups are like large classes; a few people talk a lot while some of the others stare at their shoes or their phones.

6. **Too Much or Not Enough Influence from the Moderator.** Moderators must walk a careful tightrope drawn between complete hands off and guidance or steering of participants. The moderator should plan on moving through all of the planned topics and/or questions, but must also have the latitude to move off the plan to various areas that may spontaneously and serendipitously arise during the course of the focus group. On the other hand, the moderator must also keep the session moving forward and not spend all of the time delving into a single topic or question when there are several topics or a series of questions planned for a given session.

7. **Professional Moderators Tend to Get Professional Results.** Many inexperienced researchers read about focus group interviews, decide that is the way they should collect their data, and choose to act as the moderator themselves. This can sometimes be a serious mistake. Professional moderators have skills with regard to keeping participants on point (see item number 6 mentioned previously) while not overstaying on a particular topic or subject. This provides for a breadth and depth of topical coverage that an amateur moderator might not be able to successfully achieve. Certainly, an inexperienced researcher should not jump head first into the focus group interview waters, so-to-speak. If you are planning on using this strategy, you should begin by practicing with several sessions that will not be used for your research. This may involve using some other set of topics and questions and almost any group of people, but it should provide the inexperienced moderator with some necessary experience. Practicing pacing of topics and questions, handling resistant or overzealous participants, and drawing out information from participants require practice. Inexperienced researcher interested in undertaking focus group research should consult the *moderator's guide* offered later in this chapter.

8. **Bullies.** The moderator cannot force the group dynamic to work in any particular fashion. But often there will be a tendency for some participants to dominate the discussion while others back off. Without being too heavy handed, the moderator must create a discussion context that is inviting to all participants. As with any interviewing, this is a learned skill that looks like an art when it is done well.

A focus group is a guided, collective conversation. As with interviews, the primary data are the words and phrases offered by the informants in response to questions. But a group is not simply several individuals in the same place together. The data produced by this method of interviewing represent the ideas and interactions of the group as an entity unto itself. When focus groups are administered properly, there are extremely dynamic interactions among and between group members that can stimulate discussions during which one group member reacts to comments made by another. This group dynamism has been described as a "synergistic group effect" (Stewart et al., 2006; Sussman, Burton, Dent, Stacy, & Flay, 1991). The resulting synergy allows one participant to draw from another or to *brainstorm* collectively with other members of the group. A far larger number of ideas, issues, topics, and even solutions to a problem can be generated through group discussion than through individual conversations. Indeed, it is this group energy that distinguishes focus group interviews from more conventional styles of one-on-one, face-to-face interviewing approaches.

By this time, some readers are asking themselves one central question about focus group interviews: If focus group interviews are so compelling, why haven't they been more widely used in the social sciences? The answer to this question requires a little background on how focus group interviews have evolved over the past 60 or so years.

The Evolution of Focus Group Interviews

As a research technique, focus group interviews or discussions have existed since the beginning of World War II (Libresco, 1983; Merton, 1987). At that time, military psychologists and civilian consultants used group interviews to determine the effectiveness of radio programs designed to boost army morale. Although social scientists did originally make active use of this technique, until recently, it was more extensively used and developed by marketing researchers.

At the 1986 meeting of the American Association for Public Opinion Research (AAPOR), Robert K. Merton described his introduction to focus group interviewing (Merton, 1987). Merton explained that in November 1941, he was invited to dinner at the home of a colleague, Paul Lazarsfeld, who had just been asked by the Office of Facts and Figures—predecessor to the Office of War Information and later the Voice of America—to test responses to several radio morale programs.

Lazarsfeld invited Merton to attend a session and witness how audience responses were tested. Merton (1987, p. 552) explains his first reactions:

Merton was intrigued by this strategy for gathering information about people's attitudes. Lazarsfeld persuaded Merton to work with him on the radio response project (Merton, 1987). Later, Merton, with Patricia Kendall (1946), published an article in the *American Journal of Sociology* entitled "The Focused Interview." In 1956, Merton published a book by the same title (Merton, Fiske, & Kendall, 1956). The book sold only a few thousand copies and quickly went out of print (Merton, 1987). And, in many ways, so did the technique of focused group interviews go out of print for many of the social sciences.

Focus group interviews found a home within the confines of marketing research. In fact, focus groups remain the predominant form of qualitative research for marketing researchers (e.g., Bartos, 1986; Edmunds, 2000; Hayes & Tathum, 1989; Moran, 1986; Morgan, 1997). Today, with the technological advances made in computers and the Internet, marketing researchers, particularly including political campaign researchers, have expanded their focus group strategies to harness the power of the Web via the *virtual focus group*; and so too have social scientists (Bloor & Wood, 2006; Nucifora, 2000; Whiting, 2001).

For example, Adler and Zarchin (2002) used a virtual focus group strategy to identify a purposive sample of women who were on home bed rest for treatment of preterm labor. The investigators used e-mail to unite spatially and temporally separate participants in a text-based group discussion. This strategy provided a means for exploring the lived experiences of these women along the lines of the effect of bed rest on participants' including their transition into bed rest, loss of control and activities, changes in their identities and roles, coping and personal growth, transition off bed rest, and the effects of bed rest on relationships with others (their fetuses, children, husbands, and other members of their families).

Among most social scientists, however, little attention was paid to focus group interviewing as a technique until its reemergence during the 1980s (Hamel, 2001). During the 1980s and early 1990s, focus group interviewing conducted in the social sciences was sometimes labeled *group interviewing*. Yet, the basic elements of these group interviews closely resemble the purpose and procedures of focus group interviews. During this new millennium, it behooves social scientists to seriously begin looking toward the Internet as a means of securing and conducting a variation of marketing research's virtual focus group by improving on what some have already termed the *online focus group* (see, e.g., Clarke, 2000).

Advantages and Disadvantages of Focus Group Interviewing

Various sources in the literature describe a number of significant advantages associated with the use of traditional focus groups as a data-gathering strategy (see, e.g., Downs & Adrian, 2004; Edmunds, 2000; Marshall & Rossman, 2006; Salkind, 2008). A conglomeration of these various advantages suggests the following:

1. It is highly flexible (in terms of number of participants, groups, costs, duration, etc.).
2. It permits the gathering of a large amount of information from potentially large groups of people in relatively short periods of time.
3. It can generate important insights into topics that previously were not well understood.
4. It allows researchers to better understand how members of a group arrive at, or alter, their conclusions about some topic or issue and provides access to interactionary clues.
5. It can be used to gather information from transient populations.
6. It places participants on a more even footing with each other and the investigator.
7. The moderator can explore related but unanticipated topics as they arise in the course of the group's discussion.
8. Focus groups do not usually require complex sampling strategies.

There is also a set of accompanying disadvantages one can cull from the existing literature on focus groups:

1. The quality of the data is deeply influenced by the skills of the facilitator to motivate and moderate.
2. Focus groups lend themselves to a different kind of analysis than might be carried out with surveys or even individual interviews.
3. Focus group attendance is voluntary, and an insufficient number may attend a given planned session.
4. The length (duration) of each focus group needs to be fairly brief (ideally between 30 and 60 minutes, although longer focus groups do occur).
5. A limited number of questions can be used during the course of any focus group session.
6. Only group, not individual, responses are obtained in the results.

7. Dominant personalities may overpower and steer the group's responses unless the moderator is sufficiently active.
8. The researcher must be careful about how he or she uses (or attempts to generalize) information obtained from focus groups.

The information obtained from focus groups provides elements of data similar to those of traditional interviewing, direct observation, and even certain unobtrusive measures commonly used in qualitative research. Yet, I caution that focus group data does not actually offer the same depth of information as, for example, a long semistructured interview. Nor does it provide as much rich observational data as one might obtain, for instance, by observing a class of sixth graders on the playground over a period of several weeks. In effect, to best assess the benefits and limitations of focus group interviewing, we should actually compare it directly with several conventional qualitative data-collection approaches. The following sections undertake such a series of comparisons.

Focus Group Interviewing and Face-to-Face Interviewing

One important distinction between focus group and face-to-face interviewing is the ability to observe interactions about a discussion topic during the focus group session. Researchers can observe session participants interacting and sharing specific attitudes and experiences, and they can explore these issues. In truth, traditional interviewing styles permit a more detailed pursuit of content information than is possible in a focus group session. Traditional interviewing approaches, however, sacrifice the ability to observe interaction for greater amounts of detail on various attitudes, opinions, and experiences. As a consequence, researchers may never learn how subjects might have discussed these issues among themselves.

In many ways, it is the very give-and-take interactions characteristic of focus group interviews that lead to spontaneous responses from session participants. Hearing how one group member responds to another provides insights without disrupting underlying normative group assumptions. Meanings and answers arising during focus group interviews are socially constructed rather than individually created. Situations such as focus group interviews provide access to both actual and existentially meaningful or relevant interactional experiences. Such naturally arising glimpses into people's biographies are necessary for *interpretive interactionism* (Denzin, 1989).

As Rubin and Rubin (1995, p. 140) explained:

> In focus groups, the goal is to let people spark off one another, suggesting dimensions and nuances of the original problem that any one individual might not have thought of. Sometimes a totally different understanding of a problem emerges from the group discussion.

In the same way that face-to-face interviews should be understood as social interaction, focus group interviews should be seen in terms of group dynamics (Taylor & Bogdan, 1998). Because interactions between group members largely replace the usual interaction between interviewer and subject, greater emphasis is given to the subjects' viewpoints. As with informal interviewing, focus groups can sometimes be undertaken without preconceived questions, focus questions, or guidelines (Morgan, 1997). This can effectively eliminate the researcher's perspective from the resultant data. Conversely, should more guided responses be desired, focus group interviews, like individual ones, can be made more formal and structured.

David Morgan (2002, p. 148) offers a description of what he terms his "ideal focus group," which demonstrates the difference in flow between a face-to-face interview and a focus group session:

> The ideal group would start with an opening question that was designed to capture the participants' interest, so that they themselves would explore nearly all the issues that a moderator might have probed. Then, just as the allocated time for that question was running out, one of the participants in the ideal group would spontaneously direct the others' attention to the topic for the second question by saying something like, "You know what really strikes me is how many of the things we're saying are connected to..."

Naturally, such an ideal type of focus group is unlikely to unfold, especially when facilitated by a novice moderator. However, Morgan's illustration should serve as the model to strive toward in undertaking focus group interviews.

Another perceived benefit of focus group interviews is the belief by some that they are less expensive to conduct than individual interviews. This may be the case in some study situations but is not an accurate blanket rule. Much will depend on the way the investigator designed his or her study. (Design is discussed extensively in Chapter 2.) Certainly, if a researcher plans to pay subjects, hire a professional moderator, employ transcribers and coders, and purchase specialized equipment, costs could soar. On the other hand, costs could be low if the investigator conducted his or her own focus group interviews and did the data organization and analysis himself or herself.

A more relevant comparison between focus group interviewing and individual interviewing is time costs. As suggested earlier, focus group interviews can be undertaken among temporary or transient populations. This is because they require far less time than individual interviews do to involve the same number of participants. At the same time, of course, these focus group interviews will produce substantially less data than multiple individual interviews. Fern (1982), in a controlled experiment, showed that group interviews did not produce significantly more or better ideas than an equivalent number of one-on-one interviews. In fact, Fern found that the group interviews produced only about 70 percent as many original ideas as the individual interviews (those not duplicated in either the real group or the one-on-one interviews).

Sussman et al. (1991) found that subjects' responses tended to be more extreme in focus groups when compared to responses offered in survey questionnaires. Taken together with Fern's (1982) earlier work, this suggests that an interviewer must be willing to give up some degree of data precision in exchange for the interaction experience.

Focus Group Interviewing and Participant Observation

When you are involved with participant observation, you are able to observe the naturally unfolding worlds of the population under study. This includes those times when several parties in the field come together to spontaneously hold a conversation, discussion, or argument. This natural evolution, of course, is not present in the artificially created situation of the focus group. Focus groups frequently contain members who might never have come together were it not for the creation of the group. Furthermore, the facilitator or moderator can control the assembly, alter the pace of discussions, change the direction of comments, interrupt or stop conversations, and so forth. Focus groups, then, like other forms of interviewing, are not truly natural conversations.

If you are interested in observing behaviors and meanings as they emerge in their natural setting, you may find that the simulated conversations of focus groups are insufficient. More traditional forms of participant observations and various sorts of field ethnography might prove more fruitful. However, if you are interested in collecting data on a large range of behaviors, a wide variety of interactions, and comprehensive and open discussions about certain topics or issues, focus group interviews work well.

For the most part, focus group interviews are further limited by the fact that the bulk of the behavior is verbal. During the group sessions, you should take notes on various behaviors and physical expressions of participants. For example, subjects in focus groups may use body language, gestures, or other nonverbal clues to encourage, or intimidate, others while they are speaking. When a participant suddenly breaks off a comment, or shifts into a more confessional tone, your notes should indicate anything significant happening in the room that might have precipitated the change. However, these notes will represent only a small portion of the basic verbal data typically collected during a focus group interview. Videotaping helps, when possible.

Morgan (2002) suggests that focus groups are also useful when investigating research areas that do not have dense sets of observations readily available. In effect, researchers tend to conduct participant observation studies in settings where there is something available to observe. Organizations and organizational structures, social roles among group members, normative values among subcultures, and similar topics become typical fodder for participant observers. Topics like these seem especially well suited for the structure of participant observation. Yet topics of a more psychological, cognitive, or deep attitudinal nature seem less effectively studied through participant observation. Such topics could, however, be examined during focus group interviews.

Since both participant observation and focus groups seek to examine group interaction of some sort, there are many times and many topics in which either might be used. The decision you make when selecting one over the other, of course, is based on what you are willing to give up or trade off. You must be willing to trade off emergent observations in a natural setting for concentrated interactions in a short time frame. This is likely not the sort of decision that you will make strictly on the basis of financial and time costs. Largely, such decisions are made on the basis of the value placed on the advantages or disadvantages of each technique. Also, decisions will be affected by the research topic itself and the specific interests, values, background, and training of the investigator. Certainly, among many social scientists, focus group interviews remain tainted by their long-standing relationship with marketing and political research. This association may also have an impact on decisions about whether to use one technique over another.

Focus Group Interviewing and Unobtrusive Measures

One main advantage to unobtrusive measures is that, by definition, they do not require intrusion into the lives of participants by investigators. This is because most unobtrusive data have been created by people and left as either residue or erosion—but without the intention of leaving research data. Other data-collection strategies, including focus group interviews, are quite intentional and invasive.

In order to conduct focus group interviews, you must first locate some population from which to select participants. Next, you must contact potential participants and convince them that their participation is important and necessary. Finally, you must actually hold the focus group session. With most unobtrusive data strategies, no subjects need be involved during the actual course of the research. There are some types of unobtrusive data collection, however, in which subjects may be more actively involved than in others. For example, if researchers ask a group of individuals to intentionally create daily diaries, the lives of subjects have been intruded upon.

Unobtrusive data may include limited elements that provide insight into the cognitive or psychological lives of individuals. However, there is no interaction between subjects or between subject and investigator. Unlike focus groups, participant observation, or other forms of interviewing, unobtrusive strategies are passive rather than dynamic. If you are interested in examining how people have lived under certain circumstances or in specific settings, there may be a number of viable unobtrusive strategies available. Even if you wanted to know how people acted and their attitudes during some event or time, unobtrusive tactics could be used. But, by their very nature, unobtrusive data are often historical. That is, information is created at one time but identified as data at some later time.

Kramer (1983, pp. 3–4) has specifically called for the combined use of group sessions and diary research. In this case, Kramer refers to consciousness-raising groups: "Numerous studies have utilized the small group and consciousness-raising group…for information gathering, yet few have utilized the methodology as a complement to diary research." Reinharz (1992) described a computer group diary, a strategy that in some ways resembles an unobtrusive data strategy but is also akin to focus group interviewing. Reinharz tells how women graduate students in the department of sociology at Boston College established a computer-based group diary. Wikis and collectively authored blogs can also share interactive elements while creating a nonreactive record of events and impressions.

What the unobtrusive tactic of solicited diaries lacks in interaction can be adjusted through use of focus-group-like activities of a group diary. By sharing information, thoughts, and common problems and suggesting solutions one to the other, group diaries effectively become unguided focus groups. Their discourse, then, amounts to a similar synergistically created convergence of ideas and experiences. Such biographical information provides researchers with the structure of the writers' lives. Biographical experiences are culturally influenced and created. Every culture affects its members' self-perceptions and understanding about social roles, social institutions, and social structures. Group discussion reveals these shared assumptions and understandings.

Denzin (1989, p. 39) has suggested that biographical experiences have effects at two levels in a person's life: the surface level and the deep level. On the surface level, effects may be barely felt or noticed. They are often taken for granted and are nondisruptive. Picking up a container of milk on the way home from work might be an example. Effects at the deep level, however, strike at the core of an individual's life. They have a strong hold over us as individuals and affect how we behave, think, and understand things. Acceptance of our sexuality, self-hate, grief, and other deep-rooted epiphanies serve to illustrate deep-level life structures. Although unobtrusive strategies are quite good at identifying surface-level structures of life, most are not adequate for uncovering deep-level life structures.

Focus groups, on the other hand, provide avenues to understand a variety of deep structural elements. For instance, Twiggs (1994) and Grant (1993) suggested that focus groups can be used to evaluate the strengths and weaknesses of court cases and even to determine important issues in particular cases. Grant further suggests that information culled from focus groups may assist attorneys in selecting juries during *voir dire*.

Unobtrusive strategies and focus group interviews share an overlapping interest in the biographical experiences of group members. For the most part, unobtrusive measures remain in the realm of the surface level. On the other hand, focus group interviews possess the ability to effectively alternate between surface and deep levels. Decisions about whether to use unobtrusive measures or focus groups will be made for several reasons. The most obvious is the level of life structure you wish to examine. Another, again, may be financial. Here, however, you are likely to find that unobtrusive measures, like focus group interviews, can be created at fairly low cost. You might also consider innovatively combining the two, as in the group diary. Such a strategy allows both a variation on triangulation and a means for assessing both surface and deep levels of participants' lives.

The preceding comparisons between focus group interviews and certain more traditional strategies point out an important issue: Focus groups may be used either alone as a data-collection strategy or in combination with other techniques. In their simplest form, focus group interviews can be used as a sort of stand-alone data or primary data. This type of research is analogous to the kind of nontriangulated research you might accomplish using any single qualitative strategy.

Facilitating Focus Group Dynamics: How Focus Groups Work

Ideally, focus group procedures include a trained and practiced facilitator who asks a small group of individuals a series of open-ended questions. The moderator may use a single standard set of questions, asking each in turn, to stimulate discussion and conversation during a given session. The moderator may use the same set of questions during successive sessions. The questions may be more or less standardized depending on the needs of the research and the inclination of the investigator. For relatively inexperienced moderators, however, the quality and appropriateness of the questions may well depend on the quality of the data-collection instrument, also known as a *moderator's guide*.

The Moderator's Guide

The tasks of the moderator in a focus group are actually similar to those of the interviewer in face-to-face interviews. These tasks can be made more systematic (and somewhat easier for the novice) by preparing a procedural guide in advance of conducting the actual focus group. The procedures set out in the guide should eliminate some of the *fear of the unknown* that is perhaps apt to plague an inexperienced moderator of a focus group.

Preparation of the moderator's guide requires consideration of the level of language for the focus group. This may also include the language the interview will be conducted in. The guide should also provide a kind of outline or staging and the sequence of what the moderator should say and do. The moderator's guide should include the following:

1. Introduction and introductory activities
2. Statement of the basic rules or guidelines for the interview
3. Short question-and-answer discussions
4. Special activities or exercises
5. Guidance for dealing with sensitive issues

Introduction and Introductory Activities

As moderator, it is your job to explain to the subjects what the project is seeking and how a focus group operates. As well, you need to establish rapport with the subjects. The moderator's guide should include a basic description of the project (even though subjects may already have had the project's purpose explained in order to obtain informed consent). This can be a brief statement written out in the moderator's guide. It is also important to ask the group if they understand the project and their role in this research. Introductory activities also allow the subjects to meet you, understand what is expected of them, and become more comfortable. This can be accomplished by creating a series of simple activities intended to have each subject disclose a little something about himself or herself. For example, you might ask the group to go around the room and state their name, occupation, and one thing they think is special about themselves. Or you might ask subjects to tell about any leisure activities they might enjoy. This information provides a brief period of time for subjects to learn about one another and to begin feeling more comfortable in what is otherwise a fairly unnatural and potentially disconcerting situation among strangers.

Statement of the Basic Rules or Guidelines for the Interview

Although you do not want to simply list a bunch of rigid rules of conduct, you do want to establish some ground rules around the interactions during the focus group. You need to explain that you expect an open, polite, and orderly environment where everyone in the group will be encouraged to participate. If you plan to toss questions out to the full group, to be answered by anyone, tell the group that this will be your procedure. If you intend to ask each subject a question in turn, obtain a quick answer, and then open it up for discussion by the group—then, tell them this will be how the interview will proceed. Subjects need to know what to expect. The moderator should also tell participants that everyone may have a different opinion or answer to the questions and that you want to hear all of these opinions. It is a good idea to explain the reason for any recording device and its purpose, if one is present in the room. If the session is being recorded by a hidden camera, this too should be indicated to the group as well as why the camera is not in the room. For example, you might tell the group that the camera is hidden to avoid making them feel self-conscious.

Short Question-and-Answer Discussions

Most focus groups operate with a short series of discussions, sparked by questions asked by the moderator (Krueger, 1997; Krueger & Casey, 2000). These questions could be written out and listed in a similar manner to a semistructured interview guideline document (see Chapter 4). You may even plan out intentional probes to be used to facilitate more information in the event that there is little discussion after asking the initial questions. Experienced moderators are likely to deviate from such a schedule, as the dynamics of the group begin to animate the focus group experience, giving it a kind of life of its own. Less experienced moderators, however, may feel more secure having a script of questions to ask.

Special Activities or Exercises

Although many focus groups restrict their data collection to responses from a series of questions, some, especially those undertaken with children, may include drawing or role-playing exercises so that subjects may better express their views (Wright, 1994). It may also be helpful to the researcher to have a pencil-and-paper exercise to help validate the verbal responses that children are likely to offer (Wright, 1994). The major consideration for thinking about the inclusion of various additional exercises is age and maturity of subjects.

Exercises and activities also allow the moderator to determine what subjects individually know or believe without the influence of others in the group. One useful strategy is to have the subjects fill out a brief pencil-and-paper survey that is administered before the actual question-and-answer/discussion segment of the focus group begins (to be discussed later as an *extended focus group*). This prefocus group activity allows participants to think about and perhaps commit to certain ideas and attitudes about topics to be discussed during the group session (Wimmer & Dominick, 2006).

Guidance for Dealing with Sensitive Issues

As in any interviewing session, focus groups require the moderator to use sensitivity when dealing with certain subject matters. These typically include questions concerning alcohol or drug use, deviant behaviors, grief and loss, and certain mental health issues. In the focus group, one way to approach such sensitive issues is to begin with a general question for discussion that deals with the subject matter. For instance, let's assume you are interested in knowing about cigarette use by Asian American teenagers. Rather than saying immediately, "Tell me about your cigarette smoking habits," you might begin with a question such as, "What do you think about cigarette smoking?" In some cases, this slightly broader question may open the door for discussion in the group about individual participants' smoking habits—but without having placed anyone on the spot. If this does not occur, the more specific question may subsequently need to be asked.

Sensitive topics may also appear less threatening to participants when activities and tasks are incorporated into the focus group session. Among the activities one might use are free listing, rating or ranking of things being discussed, pictures to stimulate conversation, storytelling, projective techniques, and even some role-playing (Colucci, 2007). Bloor, Frankland, Thomas, and Robson (2002) suggest that focus groups may, in fact, be ideal situations for discussing sensitive topics, particularly when in the presence of friends, and colleagues, or with others similarly situated or involved in sensitive activities to themselves. Thus, focus groups may work very well, under certain circumstances when dealing with sensitive topics.

Basic Ingredients in Focus Groups

In a broader and more general sense than the specifics of a moderator's guide, it is possible to spell out some basic elements or ingredients required when conducting a focus group interview. Similar *checklists* have been suggested by Axelrod (1975), Byers and Byers (1996), Morgan (1997), Morgan and Scannell (1997), and Krueger and Casey (2000). These elements include the following:

1. *A clearly defined objective and/or research problem:* Is the focus group part of several other means for collecting data or is it being used as a stand-alone data-collection technique? Does the researcher have a clear understanding of the research problem and the questions to be used during the focus group session(s)?
2. *The nature of the group:* What are the group's characteristics? Is the group largely homogeneous or is it heterogeneous? Is it an appropriate group for the research question(s)? If you want to know about Sioux (Native American) culture, you simply cannot ask a random group of classmates.
3. *Atmosphere/environment and rapport:* As in any research project, the facilitator must assure confidentiality of information discussed during the focus group. However, the facilitator must create rapport between himself or herself and the group, as well as between group members. In other words, the researcher must make all of the group members feel comfortable talking openly in the group.
4. *An aware listening facilitator:* Facilitators, as with any interviewer, must listen to what the subjects are saying (see Chapter 4). It is important to have a schedule or agenda during the focus group;

however, it should never be so inflexible that interesting topics that spontaneously arise during the group discussion are shortchanged or unnecessarily truncated. Because of the nature of group dynamics, it is possible that topics and issues not originally considered by the researcher as important will emerge as very important.

5. *A well-organized and prepared facilitator:* Whether the facilitator intends to work with several specific questions or with several general topical areas, the facilitator should have a clear idea about how things will proceed. One sure way to kill a focus group discussion is to begin it without any direction or indication of what the flow of questions or topics will be. Often texts recommend that facilitators be highly trained and skilled leaders of focus groups (see, e.g., Krueger, 1994). Unfortunately, this is not always practical or possible. It, therefore, becomes even more important for an inexperienced researcher serving as facilitator to demonstrate clear organization and preparedness.

6. *Structure and direction but restrained contribution to the discussion:* Although the facilitator should guide the group's discussion, he or she should avoid offering opinions and substantive comments. With any interview, the ideal product is around 90 percent subjects and 10 percent researcher.

7. *Research assistance:* Many investigators use only a single researcher/ facilitator during the course of a focus group. This procedure sometimes occurs because of costs or time necessities. A more idyllic situation is to have someone serve as facilitator, while someone else sits and observes the group. This second researcher is able to create field notes about the group dynamics, as well as assist in identifying voices when it is time to transcribe the recording of the focus group interview. An even more effective record might be to videotape the focus group. Videotaping, however, is not always permissible or possible.

8. *Systematic analysis:* Whether the recording is a transcribed audiotape or a videotape of group sessions, the data must be analyzed using some systematic means. One style of analysis is analyzing the content of the statements made by subjects during the focus group (see Chapter 11). Whatever you do with the data, they should be clearly stated to ensure verifiability. This means that the analysis process should permit another researcher to arrive at similar conclusions using the same or similar documents and raw data (Krueger, 1994).

Often researchers employ a tactic called the *extended focus group*. This procedure includes a questionnaire administered to participants before the group session. The questionnaire generally includes material that will be discussed during the focus group session. Information from this questionnaire may assist both group members and the moderator. The questionnaires allow the participants to develop a commitment to a position before any group discussion begins (Sussman et al., 1991).

Information from these pregroup questionnaires may help to ensure that the moderator draws out minority opinions as well as more dominant ones (Wimmer & Dominick, 2006). In some ways, this is similar to the prejury selection questionnaire people commonly receive when called to serve on jury duty. These questionnaires elicit information that will allow the prosecuting and defense attorneys an opportunity to get to know potential jurors. When they ask questions of the jurors in a process called *voir dire*, they are guided by comments these people made in their questionnaires. Answers to their questions help the attorneys decide whom they do and do not want on the jury.

As one might expect, the use of the Internet has also managed to change the face of contemporary focus group techniques. Later in this chapter, I will discuss the use of a sounding concept related to that of the extended focus group, the time-extended focus group, and will draw out the specific distinctions.

One of the most difficult tasks for a moderator is controlling dominating respondents while simultaneously encouraging passive group members. This must be accomplished without embarrassing or completely shutting down the dominating participants. Often, like a traditional interviewer, moderators must rely on their ability to develop rapport with group members. If the moderator has been successful in developing a rapport, it may be useful in efforts to encourage the quiet members to participate.

Most researchers who use focus group techniques acknowledge that group influences can distort individual opinion. Some opinions may be more extreme and some may be less verbalized than others because of the group effects (Sussman et al., 1991). Having some idea about how individuals thought about certain topics before the group sessions start allows the investigator to gauge this group effect. This is not to say that material obtained during the group session is false. Quite the contrary; the opinions voiced during the session, even those that contradict pregroup questionnaires, merely demonstrate the impact of group dynamics. Additional information, confirmation or refutation of beliefs, arguments, discussion, and solutions heard during the group session shape participants' thinking. What results is a collective understanding, about issues discussed by the group.

Focus group data are *group data*. They reflect the collective notions shared and negotiated by the group. Individual interview data reflect only the views and opinions of the individual, shaped by the social process of living in a culture.

When you design a focus group interview study, your plans for participant selection must be undertaken very carefully. It should not be assumed that focus group samples necessarily are accidental or purposive. Even among marketing researchers, care is required to create samples that include subjects with necessary product user characteristics (Tynan & Dryton, 1989). For the more traditional social sciences, one should begin using standard strategies for sampling to create a sample pool. From this pool, the smaller focus groups may be formed.

For example, let us say you are interested in studying some aspects of the lives of incarcerated women. Perhaps you want to know how these women perceive their family role as mother, even though they are separated from their children (Moloney, 1997). In most states, there are few women's correctional facilities, often only one or two for the entire state. Thus, you easily can begin with a *census sample*[2] of women in prison to form the initial pool. Next, you might stratify this group into those who have children currently of juvenile status (under the age of juvenile jurisdiction) and those who do not. Using the group with children, you might now have a sample of 50 or 60 women. Assuming no rejections, you could randomly assign women in this group to five or six focus groups and conduct sessions in a fairly brief amount of time.

You can develop focus groups using other strategies to create the initial sample pool. This is particularly true if you are using focus group interviews as an additional line of action in a triangulated project. For example, when Karen Ryan and colleagues set out to explore why there were apparent "shortcomings . . . in the provision of palliative care for people with intellectual disabilities," they designed a mixed method approach combining focus groups with surveys. They further triangulated their research by targeting two groups of research subjects, health service workers who attend to those with intellectual disabilities and palliative care staff. Using surveys, the researchers asked subjects from each group to quantitatively rate their levels of experience, confidence, interest, and ability to manage the pain relief and comfort needs of terminal patients with intellectual disabilities. The surveys indicated that both groups of care providers were generally willing to provide the necessary services, but felt that they lacked training and experience to do so for this patient group. The researchers additionally organized 16 focus groups in which each group of participants were from one or the other of the target subjects. In this way they were able to explore the meanings,

Figure 5.1 Berg Sampling Strategy

	Males		Females	
	Younger Patients (under 45)	Older Patients (over 45)	Younger Patients (under 45)	Older Patients (over 45)
Serious Asthma Condition				
Moderate Asthma Condition				

concerns, and experiences of a mixed study sample that closely matched the survey respondent groups. The qualitative data both confirmed and explained the quantitative results. The Ryan article concluded with some general recommendations for alleviating the problem.

As illustrated earlier, samples for focus groups in the social sciences derive from a wide variety of types. Standard sampling procedures can improve the validity of group interview results. The main question that remains is, "When should a focus group strategy be used?" (Figure 5.1)

Although this is not its primary purpose, you might consider using a version of focus group interviews to pilot an interview schedule. In this instance, you would have members of the focus group read through the instrument under consideration. Next, the group would discuss the usual concerns researchers have about such research instruments: the level of language, comprehensibility of the questions, question order, affected wording of questions, and so forth.

As suggested throughout the examples offered in this chapter, there are numerous other occasions when a focus group could be used. This is, of course, true with many data-collection strategies. As suggested in the first chapter of this book, triangulation in qualitative research can be important to issues of validity. Whenever you can demonstrate corroboration of information you have obtained, you are on solid ground. Whether focus group techniques are used will depend on several issues. These issues have been mentioned in the preceding chapter, but they bear some reiteration.

First, you must decide whether information gathered through the focus group interview will inform the research questions. There is no point in conducting focus groups if the results are superfluous.

Second, you may want to consider aspects of time and cost effectiveness. Will focus group interviews allow you to obtain the best data for the time and money they will require?

Third, is the study population one that requires a faster data-collection strategy that might be provided by another technique? Naturally, this is related to the issue of your research questions as well as to the quality of the data. This may involve decisions about your willingness to make trade-offs between data precision and gains in data acquisition.

Finally, you should consider whether using focus groups might enhance a project by adding another line of action to the study. This additional line of action may, in fact, offer either corroboration of other data or insights into areas other data fail to illuminate.

Analyzing Focus Group Data

The information collected during the course of a focus group, like that collected during the course of a face-to-face interview, is *raw data*. The researcher's job is to prepare an analytic statement based on this collected raw data. Ideally, this assessment should be thoroughly grounded in the data. The first step is to transcribe the entire interview. This should be a verbatim transcription of each question asked by the moderator and each individual answer given by the focus group participants. It should include all probes asked by the moderator and various group members. It should also include any slang, dialects, or pauses offered by focus group members as they respond to the moderator and each other.

During the course of the focus group, either the moderator or a second observer working with the researcher should take copious notes. These might include various interactionary cues offered by individuals of the group (facial grimaces, head shakes, perhaps even side comments that might be lost in the transcription). These too will be useful along with the transcriptions when developing an analysis of the results of the focus group.

Taken together, the transcription and the observer notes provide a complete record of the discussion that unfolded during the focus group interview and will assist in analysis of this data. The next step is to analyze the content of the discussion to identify trends and patterns that reappear either within a single focus group or among a series of focus groups. Thus, the researcher undertakes a variation of content analysis (discussed in detail in Chapter 11), which begins by examining the text for similarly used words, themes, or answers to questions. Some system of indexing and retrieval of these terms and patterns must be used (see Chapter 11). The researcher should additionally consider the emphasis or intensity of respondents' comments (sometimes illustrated in observer notes). As well, the researcher should consider the consistency of comments and responses to probes both within a given focus group and across a series of focus groups.

The analysis of focus group data must take into account both the individual responses and the group interaction. As with any content analysis, we look at patterns in terms used, ideas expressed, associations among ideas, justifications, and explanations. With focus groups, however, we also need to examine the flow of ideas throughout the group. The analysis needs to attend to *consensus, dissensus,* and *resonance* (Lune et al., 2009). Consensus refers to points of agreement within the group. Did certain suggestions, ideas, or explanations go entirely unchallenged? Did the ideas recur among different speakers' responses? These ideas represent general points of agreement within your study sample. What about ideas or suggestions on which the group could not come to agreement? Are there points of disagreement where compromise or flexibility seems impossible? These ideas have stronger weight with the respondents than ideas around which they are willing to shift their positions. And finally, do certain expressions seem to "catch fire" within the group? Are there moments in the discussion where one participant expresses an idea that suddenly unites all (or nearly all) of the members? These are ideas or expressions that resonate within the study group and which may have a powerful influence on the thoughts or feelings of your study population in general.

There are several important rules of thumb for analyzing focus group data, which are quite different from the analysis of other textual data such as field notes or interview data:

- Avoid quantifying results or offering magnitudes; just because four of seven group members made a statement does not mean that 57 percent of the subjects agree on that statement. Such an assumption is quite meaningless and is not a finding in itself.
- Provide quotations to support your assessment of what the various trends and patterns of discussion are.
- Offer relevant characteristics of each group member prior to offering their quoted responses in order to provide a sense of three-dimensionality to group members (e.g., a 26-year-old single Latina mother of two stated...”). The operative phrase is "relevant characteristics," not random demographics.
- Make a point, or state a specific pattern, before offering quoted materials intended to demonstrate the point or pattern.
- Use quotes to illustrate, not prove. It does matter that everyone in your group prefers the yellow box over the green one, but it does not prove anything.

Confidentiality and Focus Group Interviews

One final issue requires discussion: the problem of confidentiality of information obtained through the use of focus group interviews. Although it is easy to ensure that the researcher will maintain confidentiality, what can be done among the participants? Ensuring confidentiality is critical if the researcher expects to get truthful and free-flowing discussions during the course of the focus group interview. If group members feel apprehensive or inhibited by fear of somehow being exposed, they will not fully disclose their feelings and perceptions.

In marketing research situations, this issue of confidentiality may not be viewed as terribly significant. After all, who really cares if the car manufacturer learns that someone thinks his or her automobile is ugly or fails to perform well? What difference does it make to have some cereal company learn that someone thinks the picture on the box is childish or the taste of the product is awful? Although executives need this information to improve product sales, none of these comments is very self-disclosing.

When focus groups are used for social scientific research, however, a different kind of information is obtained. A focus group interview among rapists, for example, could reveal very sensitive pieces of information. Discussion among obese focus group members may not be the kind of information members want to be identified with. Conversations among elementary school teachers about how they discriminate against particular ethnic groups or against girls could be very troublesome if revealed. Thus, certain procedures must be taken to ensure confidentiality.

The logical course to take is to have every member of the focus group sign a statement of confidentiality. In other forms of research, such as individual interviews, this is fairly common practice. The difference, however, is that in the individual interview, this contractual agreement is between researcher and subject. In the focus group situation, the agreement must be among *all* group members and the moderator/researcher. An example of such an agreement is offered in Figure 5.2.

Enforcement of this agreement, as with all confidentiality agreements in research, largely is one of honor rather than law. Use of this sort of document, however, does allow the participant an opportunity to think about issues of confidentiality. If a participant believes he or she will not be able to keep material confidential, this is the opportunity to withdraw. Similarly, if a group member is fearful about confidentiality, he or she can drop out of the group. Reminding participants of this is also part of the moderator's job.

Figure 5.2 Group Agreement for Maintaining Confidentiality

This form is intended to further ensure confidentiality of data obtained during the course of the study entitled [place title of research here]. All parties involved in this research, including all focus group members, will be asked to read the following statement and sign their names indicating that they agree to comply.

I hereby affirm that I will not communicate or in any manner disclose publicly information discussed during the course of this focus group interview. I agree not to talk about material relating to this study or interview with anyone outside of my fellow focus group members and the researcher [or moderator].

Name: _____

Signature: _____

Project Director's Signature: _____

Allowing concerned or unwilling subjects to withdraw is an important ethical element in all research. It is also important for the quality of your focus group data. Having an unwilling participant in the group could prove to be very disruptive or problematic for a moderator. The discussions, topics, and solutions the group might be able to develop could be seriously compromised.

Recent Trends in Focus Groups: Online Focus Groups

Online focus groups, like e-interviews (discussed in Chapter 4), can be conducted in one of two ways: *synchronously* or *asynchronously*. Synchronous sessions refer to sessions that are live. In other words, all participants take part at the same time. They can use a chat room or online conferencing program. Asynchronous sessions typically use e-mail, a Listserv, online discussion board, or mailing lists. The participants can read others' comments and contribute a comment themselves at any time, not necessarily when anyone else is participating (Adler & Zarchin, 2002; Murray, 1997; Rezabek, 2000). Asynchronous groups lack much of the group dynamic that typically characterizes focus group research, but it does allow participants time to think about their responses to the discussion, and to say as much as they want on the subject without fear of interruption or intimidation.

Another variation to the online focus group is what has come to be known as the *time-extended focus group* (see, e.g., Osiatynski & Wallace, 2005; Wrenn, Stevens, & Loudon, 2002). This style of focus group uses online communications technology, usually in a message board format, where questions can be posted and responded to either privately or for all to see; in a threaded message style, where questions can be asked and answered and all connected can view them; or even in a wiki community writing format, where focus group members can see questions and answers and can even simultaneously respond and post their impressions, answers, or other questions. The concept of extended time derives from the ability to leave these sessions online for prolonged periods of time. During that time, participants can add to, change, or comment on their or others' responses and statements.

As they did with focus groups in general, marketing researchers have jumped into the online focus group strategy with both feet. For example, Holly Edmunds (2000, p. 23), a leading scholar in the area of marketing research, summarizes the advantages in using the Internet for market research by stating that such online focus groups (a) cut costs; (b) have potential to reach a broad geographic scope; (c) provide access to hard-to-reach participants such as business travelers and professionals who have little time during normal hours to participate; and (d) provide for a convenient and a comfortable way of participating.

On the other hand, Tom Greenbaum (2003), another leading marketing research scholar, argues against the advent of online focus groups, listing a series of problems, including the loss of the role and authority of the moderator in online focus groups; the loss of the ability to feel and experience the atmosphere that arises during the course of an in-person focus group; the inability to effectively use group dynamics as an integral part of the overall focus group process; and the loss of attentiveness on the topic being discussed by the group when undertaken online.

In the social sciences, several researchers have successfully undertaken studies using various online focus group techniques (e.g., Adler & Zarchin, 2002; Moloney, Dietrich, Strickland, & Myerburg, 2003; Turney & Pocknee, 2005). It is a safe argument that for at least for some social scientists the near future holds online focus group interviews as a likely new data-collecting strategy. However, care must be taken to select participants who can comfortably participate in an electronic medium—that is, who already have a comfort level with technology—so that they can contribute and interact in the electronic focus group freely and clearly, resulting in their best contribution. Care must also be taken that the focus group is conducted and facilitated in a professional and efficient manner with efforts made to avoid the types of losses outlined by Greenbaum (2003). Procedures must be made clear and then followed by the facilitator and participants. Hopefully, this will result in a thorough discussion of the topic(s) by all involved, and important information will be revealed that can benefit the researcher.

Conclusion

The focus group interview is an innovative and evolving strategy for gathering what might otherwise be fairly difficult-to-obtain information. Recently reborn in the social sciences and revitalized in the past decade because of telecommunications and the Internet, the focus group interview promises to quickly become an integral part of data-collection technology among many qualitative researchers. It operates well as a stand-alone means for data collection or as an additional line of action. The limitations of focus group interviews in general, whether conducted in a traditional format or online, must be weighed against the advantages focus group interviewing may offer in a given research endeavor.

TRYING IT OUT

Suggestion 1 This suggestion is intended to allow students an opportunity to work in an unguided focus group. Divide the class into groups of approximately six or seven students. Each group begins discussing each of the following topics: how to select a course, how group members chose the college they are attending, and what types of vacations are best during spring break. Allow only 15 minutes or so for each topic. If possible, have each group tape-record its session. If recording isn't possible, have one or two members of each group take notes.

Suggestion 2 Develop a means for identifying participants for a focus group study on fear of crime among juveniles. Be certain you consider basic issues of sampling, including representation of both genders and a variety of ethnic groups, ages, and educational levels. Give thought to other descriptive variables that you might need to consider.

Suggestion 3 Create a moderator's guide for a focus group study on violence in high schools. Assume your sample will include high school students from your area.

NOTES

1. There is wide disagreement in the literature about what exactly constitutes a small group for focus group interviews. Some sources suggest 6–9 subjects (Pramualratana, Havanon, & Knodel, 1985, p. 205); others recommend 6, 7, or 8–10 group members (Bachman & Schutt, 2003, p. 243; Bogdan & Bilken, 2003, p. 101); still others claim that 6–12 participants may be the ideal size (Leedy & Ormrod, 2005; Lengua et al., 1992, p. 163). One thing seems certain: The more complex the research problem, the more effective it is to have a smaller size (perhaps, 5–7 people) focus group.

2. Census samples include all the people who fit a certain characteristic or who exist in a specific location. For instance, a nurse researcher might use such a sampling procedure to study all the patients being treated at a single hemodialysis center. Any potential subject who does not want to participate in the research falls into the researcher's rejection rate. Typically, this procedure is used when the total number of potential subjects is not very large.

REFERENCES

Adler, C. L., & Zarchin, Y. R. (2002). The "virtual focus group": Using the Internet to reach pregnant women on home bed rest. *Journal of Obstetric, Gynecologic, and Neonatal Nursing 31*(4), 418–427.

Axelrod, M. (1975). 10 essentials for good qualitative research. *Marketing News 8*, 10–11.

Bachman, R., & Schutt, R. K. (2003). *The Practice of Research in Criminology and Criminal Justice* (2nd ed.). Thousand Oaks, CA: Pine Forge Press.

Barbour, R. (2008). *Doing Focus Groups.* Thousand Oaks, CA: Sage.

Bartos, R. (1986). Qualitative research: What it is and where it came from. *Journal of Advertising Research 26*, RC3–RC6.

Bloor, M., Frankland, J., Thomas, M., & Robson, K. (2002). *Focus Groups in Social Research.* Thousand Oaks, CA: Sage.

Bloor, M., & Wood, F. (2006). *Keywords in Qualitative Methods: A Vocabulary of Research Concepts.* Thousand Oaks, CA: Sage.

Bogdan, R., & Knopp Bilken, S. (2003). *Qualitative Research for Education* (4th ed.). Boston, MA: Allyn and Bacon.

Breakwell, G. M., Hammond, S., Fife-Schaw, C., & Smith, J. A. (2006). *Research Methods in Psychology* (3rd ed.). Thousand Oaks, CA: Sage.

Byers, B., & Byers, P. Y. (March 1996). Focus group research and juries: Literature and applications. Paper presented at the annual meeting of the Academy of Criminal Justice Sciences, Las Vegas, NV.

Clarke, P. (2000). The Internet as a medium for qualitative research. Paper presented at the Web 2000 Conference, Johannesburg, South Africa.

Colucci, E. (2007). Focus groups can be fun: The use of activity oriented questions in focus group discussions. *Qualitative Health Research 17*(10), 1422–1433.

Denzin, N. K. (1989). *Interpretive Interactionism.* Applied Social Research Methods Series (Vol. 16). Newbury Park, CA: Sage.

Downs, C. W., & Adrian, A. D. (2004). *Assessing Organizational Communication.* New York: The Guilford Press.

Edmunds, H. (2000). *The Focus Group Research Handbook.* Thousand Oaks, CA: Sage.

Fern, E. F. (1982). The use of focus groups for idea generation: The effects of group size, acquaintanceship, and moderator on a response quality and quantity. *Journal of Marketing Research 19*, 1–13.

Grant, B. C. (1993). Focus groups versus mock trials: Which should you use? *Trial Diplomacy Journal 16*, 15–22.

Greenbaum, T. (April 2003). The case against Internet focus groups. *MRA Alert Newsletter.* Available online at http://www.groupsplus.com/pages/case2.htm.

Gubrium, J. F., & Holstein, J. A. (2001). *Handbook of Interview Research: Context and Method.* Thousand Oaks, CA: Sage.

Hamel, J. (2001). The focus group method and contemporary French sociology. *Journal of Sociology 37*(4), 341–354.

Hayes, T. J., & Tathum, C. B. (Eds.) (1989). *Focus Group Interviews: A Reader* (2nd ed., pp. 30–34). Chicago, IL: American Marketing Association.

Kramer, T. (Winter 1983). The diary as a feminist research method. *Newsletter of the Association for Women in Psychology*, pp. 3–4.

Krueger, R. A. (1994). *Focus Groups: A Practical Guide for Applied Research* (2nd ed.). Thousand Oaks, CA: Sage.

Krueger, R. A. (1997). *Developing Questions for Focus Groups.* Thousand Oaks, CA: Sage Publications.

Krueger, R. A., & Casey, M. A. (2000). *Focus Groups* (3rd ed.).Thousand Oaks, CA: Sage Publications.

Larson, K., Grudens-Schuck, N., & Lundy, B. (2004). *Can You Call It a Focus Group?* Ames, Iowa: Iowa State University Extension. Available online at http://www.extension.iastate.edu/publications/pm1969a.pdf.

Leedy, P. D., & Ormrod, J. E. (2005). *Practical Research: Planning and Design* (8th ed.). Upper Saddle River, NJ: Pearson/Prentice Hall.

Lengua, L. J., Roosa, M. W., Schupak-Neuberg, E., Michaeles, M. L., Berg, C. N., & Weschler, L. F. (1992). Using focus groups to guide the development of a parenting program for difficult-to-research, high-risk families. *Family Relations 41*, 163–168.

Libresco, J. D. (August–September 1983). Focus groups: Madison Avenue meets public policy. *Public Opinion*, pp. 51–53.

Lune, H., Enrique P., & Koppel, R. (Eds.) (2009). *Perspectives in Social Research Methods and Analysis. A Reader for Sociology.* Thousand Oaks, CA: Sage Publications.

Marshall, C., & Rossman, G. B. (2006). *Designing Qualitative Research* (4th ed.). Thousand Oaks, CA: Sage.

Merton, R. K. (1987). The focused interview and focus groups. *Public Opinion Quarterly 51*(4), 550–566.

Merton, R. K., & Kendall, P. L. (1946). The focused interview. *American Journal of Sociology 51*, 541–557.

Merton, R. K., Fiske, M., & Kendall, P. L. (1956). *The Focused Interview.* Glencoe, IL: Free Press.

Moloney, L. (1997). Women and children: Family perspectives among incarcerated women. Doctoral dissertation, Indiana University of Pennsylvania, Indiana, PA.

Moloney, M. F., Dietrich, A. S., Strickland, O., & Myerburg, S. (2003). Using Internet discussion boards as virtual focus groups. *Advances in Nursing Science 26*(4), 274–286.

Moran, W. T. (1986). The science of qualitative research. *Journal of Advertising Research 26*(3), RC16–RC19.

Morgan, D. (2002). Focus group interviewing. In J. F. Gubrum & J. A. Holstein (Eds.), *Handbook of Interview Research* (pp. 141–159). Thousand Oaks, CA: Sage.

Morgan, D. L. (1997). *Focus Groups as Qualitative Research* (2nd ed.). Thousand Oaks, CA: Sage.

Morgan, David L. (1996). Focus Groups. *Annual Review of Sociology*, Vol. 22, pp. 129–152.

Morgan, D. L., Fellows, C., & Guevara, H. (2008). Emergent approaches to focus group research. In S. N. Hess-Biber & P. Leavy (Eds.), *Handbook of Emergent Methods*. New York: The Guilford Press.

Morgan, D. L., & Scannell, A. U. (1997). *The Focus Group Guidebook*. Thousand Oaks, CA: Sage.

Murray, P. J. (1997). Using virtual focus groups in qualitative research. *Qualitative Health Research 7*(4), 542–554.

Nucifora, A. (2000). Internet is revolutionizing use of focus groups. *Orlando Business Journal 17*(17), 49.

Osiatynski, A., & Wallace, R. (2005). *Time-Extended On-Line Methodology: The Next Generation in Qualitative Research*. Arlington, TX: Decision Analyst, Inc.

Pramualratana, A., Havanon, N., & Knodel, J. (February 1985). Exploring the normative basis for age at marriage in Thailand: An example from focus group research. *Journal of Marriage and the Family 47*, 203–210.

Reinharz, S. (1992). *Feminist Methods in Social Research*. New York: Oxford University Press.

Rezabek, R. J. (2000). Online focus groups: Electronic discussions for research. *Forum: Qualitative Social Research 1*(1). Available online at http://www.qualitative-research.net/fgs-texte/1-00/1-00rezabek-e.htm.

Rubin, H. J., & Rubin, I. S. (1995). *Qualitative Interviewing: The Art of Hearing Data*. Thousand Oaks, CA: Sage.

Salkind, N. J. (2008). *Exploring Research* (7th ed.). Upper Saddle River, NJ: Prentice Hall.

Stewart, D. W., & Shamdasani, P. M. (1990). *Focus Groups: Theory and Practice*. Newbury Park, CA: Sage.

Stewart, D. W., Shamdasani, P. M., & Rook, D.W. (2006). *Focus Groups: Theory and Practice* (2nd ed.). Thousand Oaks, CA: Sage.

Sussman, S., Burton, D., Dent, C. W., Stacy, A. W., & Flay, B. R. (1991). Use of focus groups in developing an adolescent tobacco use cessation program: Collection norm effects. *Journal of Applied Social Psychology 21*, 1772–1782.

Taylor, S. J., & Bogdan, R. (1998). *Introduction to Qualitative Research Methods* (3rd ed.). New York: John Wiley and Sons.

Turney, L., & Pocknee, C. (2005). Virtual focus groups: New frontiers in research. *International Journal of Qualitative Methods 4*(2). Article 3. Retrieved [May 5, 2008] from http://www.ualberta.ca/~ijqm/english/engframeset.html.

Twiggs, H. F. (1994). Do-it-yourself focus groups: Big profits, modest cost. *Trial 30*(9), 42–117.

Tynan, A. C., & Dryton, J. L. (1989). Conducting focus groups: A guide for first-time users. In T. J. Hayes & C. B. Tathum (Eds.), *Focus Group Interviews: A Reader* (2nd ed., pp. 30–34). Chicago, IL: American Marketing Association.

Whiting, R. (July 30, 2001). Virtual focus groups. *Information Week*, p. 53.

Wimmer, R. D., & Dominick, J. R. (2006). *Mass Media Research* (8th ed.). Belmont, CA: Thomson/Wadsworth Publishing.

Wrenn, B., Stevens, R., & Loudon, D. (2002). *Marketing Research Text & Cases*. New York: Best Business Books, an Imprint of the Haworth Press, Inc.

Wright, P. A. (1994). Conducting focus groups with young children requires special considerations and techniques. Technical Assistance Bulletin. Rockville, MD: National Clearing House for Alcohol and Drug Information.

Chapter 6

Ethnographic Field Strategies

ETHNOGRAPHY HAS BEEN AROUND for a very long time, particularly as practiced by cultural anthropologists; however, social scientists differ sharply on both the conceptual meaning of ethnography and its applications. A technical definition would be "the study of culture," but that alone does not help us to distinguish ethnography as a research method from any other research in which culture plays a part. Researchers frequently use the term in seemingly different ways. Spradley (1979, p. 3), for example, offered that "ethnography is the work of describing a culture. The essential core of this activity aims to understand another way of life from the native point of view." Zigarmi and Zigarmi (1980) referred to ethnographers as virtually anyone who enters the natural setting in order to conduct *field research*, a concept that itself suffers from confused understanding (see Guy, Edgley, Arafat, & Allen, 1987). Some researchers, for example, Ellen (1984) and Stoddart (1986), suggest that ethnography involves the end product of field research—namely, the written accounts of observations. Other researchers, such as Warren and Karner (2005), tend to equate ethnography with participant observation and suggest it is the written accounts of these observers. Similarly, Babbie (2007) suggests that ethnography is a detailed and accurate description of some natural setting but offers no explanations. Some early ethnographic authorities, such as Agar (1973), Johnson and colleagues (1985), Preble and Casey (1969), and Weppner (1977), describe ethnography as an extremely effective method for studying illicit drug use and users. In an attempt to differentiate this style of research from anthropological ethnography, many such drug researchers have called this form *street ethnography* or *urban ethnography*. I use the term *organizational ethnography* to describe field research on the cultural dimensions of organizations (Lune, 2007). Leininger (1985, p. 33) coined the term *ethnonursing* to describe ethnography conducted by nurses, whereas Roper and Shapira (2000) and LoBiondo-Wood and Haber (2002) refer to this activity as *medical ethnographies*. Lofland (1996, p. 30) describes the strategy of *analytic ethnography* as follows:

> I use the term "analytic ethnography" to refer to research processes and products in which, to a greater or lesser degree, an investigator (a) attempts to provide generic propositional answers to questions about social life and organization; (b) strives to pursue such an attempt in a spirit of unfettered or naturalistic inquiry; (c) utilizes data based on deep familiarity with a social setting or situation that is gained by personal participation or an approximation of it; (d) develops the generic propositional analysis over the course of doing research; (e) strives to present data and analyses that are true; (f) seeks to provide data and/or analyses that are new; and (g) presents an analysis that is developed in the senses of being conceptually elaborated, descriptively detailed, and concept-data interpenetrated.

However, the various ways researchers speak about ethnography may amount to little more than terminological preferences. Agar (1986) came to this conclusion in his examination of the language differences among various ethnographers and ethnographic traditions in his book *Speaking of Ethnography*.

Nonetheless, the important point about the concept of ethnography, regardless of one's language and terminological preference, is that the practice places researchers in the midst of whatever it is they study. From this vantage, researchers can examine various phenomena as perceived by participants and represent these observations as accounts.

Wolcott (2008) captures the essence of most of these variations by defining ethnography as the science of *cultural description*. Clearly, ethnography is primarily a process that attempts to describe and interpret social expressions between people and groups. Or, as Geertz (1973) had suggested, the researcher's task is to convey *thick description*, such that a wink can be distinguished from a twitch, and a parody of a wink is distinguishable from an actual wink (see Wilcox, 1988, p. 458). The goal is to get at the meanings behind the acts.

Some researchers, Ellen (1984, 1987), for example, describe the ethnographic process as *subjective soaking*. According to Ellen (1984, p. 77), this occurs when the researcher "abandons the idea of absolute objectivity or scientific neutrality and attempts to merge himself or herself into the culture being studied." Other subjectivist and existential approaches have given rise to the notion of fieldwork as *transition*, in which cultural elements, including human ideas and perceptions, are considered *opaque texts*. From this vantage, the primary objective of ethnography is to read the text, which requires an understanding of the cultural context and meaning system in which the text is produced. The text, however, should be considered the literal textual context of the ethnographer's notebooks, memos, and the like. This orientation toward ethnography, then, can be understood as the product of interaction between the observer and the observed (Clifford, 1980). Along similar lines, some researchers seek to understand the worldviews of native inhabitants of social environments or what may be called the *emic view*. This emic or insider's view of the world can be contrasted with the *etic view* or outsider's worldview (Creswell, 1999, 2007; LoBiondo-Wood & Haber, 2002; Tedlock, 2000). Munhall (2006) explains that *etic* derives from the term *phonetic* and arises in the analysis produced by the researcher. The *etic* dimension of the research, then, operates in the understandings and latent meanings uncovered by the research in the course of the study. But these meanings and understandings are outside of the insider's (*emic*) general perceptions. Instead, these *etic* understandings are the products of interpretations of meaning, theoretical and analytic explanations and understandings of symbols as mediated through the researcher (an outsider).

The more traditional anthropological approach of ethnography, as represented by the works of Malinowski, Evans-Pritchard, and Boas, has been primarily concerned with this type of subjectivist translation. During the past 40 years, however, anthropological methods, like other sociological ones, have undergone considerable advancement, refinement, and change (see, e.g., Adler & Adler, 1987; Miller & Tewksbury, 2006; Tewksbury, 2001). Ellen (1984) and Agar (1996) both point out that these changes have produced no less than a quiet revolution, resulting in a *new ethnography*.

The field of the new ethnography, as suggested in the opening paragraphs of this chapter, has experienced considerable confusion, both conceptually and methodologically. One major result of adaptation to the new ethnography was a redefining of *ethnography* as a set of highly formal techniques designed to extract cognitive data (Ellen, 1984; Spradley, 1980; Van Maanen, 1982). Another consequence of this quiet revolution was what Spindler (1988) describes as the meteoric rise of *educational ethnography* during the 1980s. As Spindler (1988, p. 1) explained, "Ethnography has become virtually a household word in professional education, and it is the rare research project today that does not have somewhere in the table of operations at least one ethnographer and somewhere in the research design some ethnographic procedures."

During the past 25 years, this new ethnography has grown popular among nursing researchers (see, e.g., Leininger & McFarlane, 2002; Morse & Field, 1995). Frequently, one finds this technique referred to as *ethnonursing research* (Burns & Grove, 2000; Leininger & McFarlane, 2002; Polit & Hungler, 1995), which means conducting a study and analysis of some local or indigenous people's viewpoints, beliefs, and practices (the emic view) about nursing care behavior and processes as mediated by cultures. For example, Jennifer Fenwick, Lesley Barclay, and Virginia Schmied (1999) examined the context and nature of the interactions between health professionals and parents in two Australian level II nurseries. They found that, although the presence of mothers in the nursery was high, registered nurses remained the primary care-takers of the infants.

In the foreword to Ferrell and Hamm's (1998) work on ethnographies on crime and deviance, Patricia and Peter Adler characterized the evolutionary development of fieldwork as marked by an early (1920s) period of *impressionism* that emerged early in the Chicago school of urban research. Next came a period of *renaissance* (1946–1955), marked by a second generation of Chicago school researchers. This was followed by abstract *expressionism* during the 1960s and a shift of the ethnographic enterprise's sociological center to California, where focus was placed on deviant, alternative, countercultural, and illegal groups. Then, in the late 1970s, began the *dark ages* in deviant ethnographies, which grew to be full-blown in the 1990s. These were the years that institutional review boards (IRBs), funders, and others placed strangleholds on many ethnographic research endeavors. At the turn of the century, we entered a period of seeming *enlightenment*, a time when brave ethnographers were moving research into a new millennium. Currently, ethnography appears to be experiencing a renewed interest and healthy vigor.

The principal concern in this chapter is to examine the new ethnography as an effective research strategy. Van Maanen (1982, p. 103) suggested that ethnography has become the method "that involves extensive fieldwork of various types including participant observation, formal and informal interviewing, document collecting, filming, recording, and so on." It is not, however, the intent of this chapter to diminish the significant contribution made by the more traditional (textual) orientation. In fact, a section of this chapter on ethnography as a narrative style discusses the more traditional ethnographic orientation.

One other significant aspect of ethnography is the distinction sometimes made between *micro-* and *macroethnography* (sometimes referred to as *general ethnography*). One obvious difference is the scope of a given investigation. Macroethnography attempts to describe the entire way of life of a group. In contrast, microethnography focuses on particular *incisions* at particular points in the larger setting, group, or institution. Spradley (1980) differentiated types of ethnographies along a continuum of size and complexity of social units under investigation, and thereby, moves from the more microethnographic focus to the more macroethnographic (see also, Munhall, 2006). Typically, these specific points are selected because they in some manner represent salient elements in the lives of participants and, in turn, in the life of the larger group or institution.

A second fundamental difference between micro- and macroethnography is that the former analytically focuses more directly on the face-to-face interactions of members of the group or institution under investigation. By examining these interactions, their implications (or as Mehan [1978] suggests, their *outcomes*) can be considered. For example, Wolcott's (1973) *The Man in the Principal's Office* was intended to offer an accurate description of the real world of one elementary school principal and, by extension, to identify the various behaviors, attitudes, and processes shared by other elementary school principals.

In spite of various differences, both micro- and macroethnography share the overarching concern for assessing everyday community life from the perspectives of participants. From detailed examinations of people and their social discourse and the various outcomes of their actions, underlying principles and concepts can be identified. As a result, neither micro- nor macroethnography is fully understandable individually without some consideration of the other. For example, it would be impossible to understand the concept of classroom management in relation to the concept of learning without some consideration of how this relates to learning environments in general (see Allen, 1986).

This chapter is divided into five sections: Accessing a Field Setting: Getting In; Becoming Invisible; Other Dangers During Ethnographic Research; Watching, Listening, and Learning; and Disengaging: Getting Out.

Accessing a Field Setting: Getting In

As Leedy and Ormrod (2005, p. 137) suggest, "The first step in an ethnographic study is to gain access to a site appropriate for answering the researcher's general research problem or question." In effect, all field investigations begin with the problem of *getting in*. This particular problem should be addressed during the design stage of the research. It involves consideration of who the subjects are and the nature of the setting.

Robert Burgess (1991b, p. 43) suggested that access is "negotiated and renegotiated throughout the research process." He further observed that "access is based on sets of relationships between the researcher and the researched, established throughout a project."

The approach offered by Burgess is rather informal with an emphasis on making the most of circumstances as you find them. Relations in the field depend on multiple interactions with various people in the setting. Roger Vallance (2001) has a slightly different take on the matter. Vallance suggests that access should be sought through introduction and referrals. According to Vallance (p. 68):

> The essence of my contention can be summed up in the oft-quoted saying; *it is not what you know, but who(m) you know.* In a sense, this is analogous to snowballing: using one research participant to indicate others who can be equally or more informative. . . . Instead of using contacts to widen the sample as in snow-ball sampling, the suggestion here is to use one's contacts and relationships to gain the vital, initial entry into the field, where one can engage with possible research participants.

In an ideal situation, Vallance's suggestion is probably well taken—assuming the investigator is undertaking research in an area or on a topic in which he or she knows many people actively engaged in related work or activities or has reliable access to key personnel. This approach also works well for research in formal settings with a hierarchy of authority in which you would need contacts and introductions to move across the different levels. However, in many instances, researchers conduct studies in areas in which they simply do not know anyone who can serve as the kind of entrance guide or core to a *snowball* sample to be rolled through the project. For example, although a number of researchers have investigated burglary, few (if any) have themselves known active burglars prior to beginning their research (see, e.g., Cromwell & Nielsen, 1999).

Hertz and Imber (1993) similarly detail the problems associated with conducting field studies in *elite settings*. As they suggest, there are very few studies of elites because elites are by their very nature difficult to penetrate. Unlike some other segments of society, elites often are visible and fairly easy to locate. Yet, because they are able to establish barriers and obstacles and because they can successfully refuse access to researchers, many elites are difficult to study.

On the other hand, successful studies of elites frequently depend on personal networks and key informants, as Vallance describes. For example, Susan Ostrander describes the circumstances of her unusual access to internal documents, meeting, and private accounts of activities at the Boston Women's Fund, an elite and private philanthropic organization: "During the entire period of this research, I was a fully engaged member of this organization's board of directors, ending my term in 2002. During the past 15 years, I have served (and continue to serve) on various committees dealing with grants, program, strategic planning, retreat planning, and fund-raising" (2004, p. 31).

A cautionary note is in order before one trades on one's connections to get into private or elite settings. One of the salient aspects of all fieldwork is that it provides rich observational opportunities from an insider's perspective. Where and how one enters a field site both opens and closes off points of access on site. If one were studying boards of directors, for example, it would seem almost impossible to gain access without the support of at least one board member. If, on the other hand, one were researching labor relations, having the endorsement of upper management would necessarily raise questions about the loyalties and interests of the researcher. That is, employees might well hesitate to speak with an investigator who is strongly associated with the employers, particularly concerning labor relations.

Richard Tewksbury (2002, 2006) offers an interesting twist on an orientation originally offered by Joseph Styles (1979). Styles (1979, p. 151) referred to an *outsider* strategy of observation, which is not fully participatory but allows the researcher to appear available to participate. Tewksbury (2002) uses this approach to gain access to a gay bathhouse (a locale where men go seeking to have sex with other men). As Tewksbury explains it, the researcher's role becomes one of a *potential participant* in various activities of the natural setting. Tewksbury (2001, p. 6) explains this potential participant role as follows:

> [It] combines aspects of complete observation, complete participation and covert observational research designs. Whereas the researcher adopting a potential participant role seeks to appear to those being researched as a "real" setting member, the "science" activities are conducted in covert manners. To anyone noticing the potential participant, the researcher is a real member of the setting being studied. To the scientific community, the potential participant is a complete observer, acting in a covert manner *inside* the research environment.

Using this strategy, Tewksbury was able to enter the bathhouse, spend several hours circulating there, and chat freely among the patrons while conducting observations of their activities, movements, interactions, and use of physical features in the facility (Tewksbury, 2002).

How might you gain access to difficult-to-reach groups? As simplistic as it may seem, the answer lies in reading the literature. While various settings and groups are *difficult* to access, most are not impossible. Ostrander (1993) reported that she found it rather simple to gain access to upper-class women. She further suggests that sometimes a bit of luck, taking advantage of certain relationships, considerable background work, and making the right contacts frequently ease access to restricted groups. Ostrander also gained significant "insider" access to certain organizations through her dual roles as both researcher and complete participant, as described previously.

It is also important during the design stage of your research to consider several other important points. For example, because most ethnographic research involves human subjects, researchers must give considerable thought to ways they can protect the subjects from harm and injury. This is especially true when dealing with restricted groups or settings. You must be mindful not to either expose your informants to risk or bar future researchers' access by careless protection of subjects' rights and privacy. In addition, researchers must consider how they will go about gaining permission or consent of the subjects. Of course, this itself requires a decision about whether to enter the field as an announced researcher (overtly) or as a secret researcher (covertly). If covert, then many of us would feel that full participation is the setting would likely be unethical, but that nonparticipant observation is usually appropriate.

Ruth Horowitz (1983, p. 7) had to address all of these hazards to herself, her subjects, and the quality of her data as she sought entry among Latino gang members in Chicago in the 1970s.

> I had little choice but to acknowledge publicly the reasons for my presence on 32nd Street; not only do I differ in background from the 32nd Street residents but I had to violate many local expectations to gather the data I needed. For example, women do not spend time alone with male gangs as I did. Because I was an outsider I had to ask a lot of "stupid" questions—"Who are the guys in the black and red sweaters?" or "Why do you fight?" As anything but an acknowledged outsider I would have had a difficult time asking them. Moreover, while my appearance allowed me to blend into a youthful crowd, I sounded and looked sufficiently different so that most people who did not know me realized that I was not from the neighborhood.

Most sources on gaining access to the field agree on one thing: Whether it is a highly accessible or a very restricted setting, decisions made during the early stages of research are critical. This is true because such decisions will lay both the conceptual and methodological foundation for the entire project. This can be likened to what Janesick (1994, pp. 210–211, 2003, pp. 46–79) described as "choreographing the research design." In other words, just as an expressive dancer might ask, "What do I want to communicate through my dance?" an ethnographer must consider the question, "What do I want to learn from this study?" The act of entering the field must be a first step in a planned progress from entry to effective completion.

Toward this end, the decision to enter the field overtly or covertly as an investigator is important. Each style of entrance encompasses certain problems, and regardless of the style you choose, you must address these problems.

Similarly, with either style of entrance, researchers must consider that their very presence in the study setting may taint anything that happens among other participants in that setting. As Denzin (1970, pp. 203–204) suggested, "Reactive effects of observation are the most perplexing feature of participant observation, since the presence of an observer in any setting is often a 'foreign object.' The creation of the role of participant observer inevitably introduces some degree of reactivity into the field setting."

Spindler and Spindler (1988, p. 25) similarly expressed their concerns about intruding by participating in the "life of the school" during their research. As a partial solution, they strive to "melt" into the classroom as much as possible. This attempt to "become invisible" will be discussed in greater detail later in this chapter.

An argument can be made for both covert and overt stances when conducting ethnographic research. For instance, in studies about people who frequent so-called adult movie theaters and video stores, the identification of an observing ethnographer might result in little information about such persons. The activity itself is generally hidden, so it is likely that such an announcement would create uncontrollable reactivity to the presence of the researcher. That is, patrons would leave so as not to be observed. Similarly, nurses conducting ethnographic research with the intention of investigating drug theft practices of hospital staff members would likely create conflicts between themselves and others on the staff. Thus, a major argument for covert ethnographic research is the sensitivity of certain topics that might make it impossible to do research by other means. Of course, with covert research there are dangers as well, starting with the violation of the principle of voluntary consent by subjects, and including greater than usual risks to the researcher if he or she is found out. Naturally, in making a case for covert observation, you must also justify the undertaking of such research by some actual social or scientific benefit.

Scientific benefits notwithstanding, some serious ethical questions arise when covert research is conducted on human subjects. Among other concerns is the possibility that this type of research might abuse the rights and privacy of the research subjects, thereby causing them harm. For many scholars, there can be *no* justification for knowingly risking harm to subjects, and therefore no justification for deceptive practices or any research without participant knowledge. Certainly, I would not endorse covert student research.

At the same time, entering an ethnographic study as a known researcher has several benefits. For example, in his study of medical students, Becker (1963) noted that his status as an identified researcher allowed him to ask questions of various hospital personnel more effectively. Similarly, Berg, Ksander, Loughlin, and Johnson (1983), in a study of adolescent involvement in alcohol, drugs, and crime, suggest that by having entered the field overtly, they succeeded in locating guides and informants (discussed in detail later). Many of these adolescents might otherwise have thought the two field ethnographers were narcs—people who are or work for the police. Similarly, I have had the experience where my presence as a researcher disrupted normal activities because the subjects did not know that I was a researcher, and they too were concerned that I might be a cop. By establishing who we are and what we are doing in the field, ethnographers can improve the rapport with their subjects.

Because of the ethical concerns associated with covert studies and in light of heightened concern over falsification of research findings in scientific communities, this chapter primarily considers *getting in* as an overt activity. Issues commonly associated with determining a balance between covert and overt research techniques were more comprehensively considered in Chapter 3.

Reflectivity and Ethnography

Access and ethical concerns underscore that ethnography requires a reflective concern on the part of the researcher, or what some scholars refer to as *reflexivity* (Boyle, 1994, Hammersley & Atkinson, 2007). This reflexive characteristic implies that the researcher understands that he or she is part of the social world(s) that he or she investigates. Ethnography involves activities that fall somewhere between rigorous, dare I say, positivist approaches and more naturalistic reflections of the actual social worlds of the people being studied. Good ethnography requires that the researcher avoids simply accepting everything at face value but, instead, considers the material as raw data that may require corroboration or verification. We need good data, but we also need to avoid the temptation to imagine that we can observe "facts" without some process of shared interpretation. Ethnography is not about observing, but about understanding.

Ethnography, then, becomes a process of gathering systematic observations, partly through participation and partly through various types of conversational interviews (Werner & Schoepfle, 1987). Yet, it may additionally require the use of photography, computers, mapping, archival searches, and even assorted documents. Ethnographic analysis involves finding, interpreting, and explaining the patterns that emerge from all of these data sources. As previously noted, the researcher must see as an insider and think as an outsider.

Reflexivity further implies a shift in the way we understand data and their collection. To accomplish this, the researcher must make use of an internal dialogue that repeatedly examines *what the researcher knows* and *how the researcher came to know this*. To be reflexive is to have an ongoing conversation with yourself. The reflexive ethnographer does not merely *report findings as facts* but actively constructs interpretations of experiences in the field and then questions how these interpretations actually arose (Hertz, 1997; Saukko, 2003; Van Maanen, 1988). The ideal result from this process is reflexive knowledge: information that provides insights into the workings of the world *and* insights on how that knowledge came to be. Along similar lines to reflectivity is an approach known as *critical ethnography*.

Critical Ethnography

When one hears the term *critical* in reference to the social sciences, many people immediately think of the *Marxist critical perspective*, and, indeed, some feminist literature employs such an orientation; consider, for example, Hammer's (2002, pp. 43–83) discussion on *Culture Wars over Feminism*. But for most critical ethnographers, the term refers to a kind of advocacy orientation of the investigator's. This orientation is often attributed to a response to the contemporary trends in society with particular regard to power, prestige, privilege, and authority (Carspecken, 1996; Creswell, 2007; Madison, 2005). These structural attributes of society are viewed as marginalizing individuals who may be from various less influential classes, genders, educational levels, or even races. Thus, *critical ethnography* is an orientation where the researcher has a concern about social inequalities and directs his or her efforts toward positive change. Notions like "positive" change make some researchers nervous, implying as it does that the researcher brings a value system to bear on the research. But we do that anyway. Why study social problems, for example, if we have no concern to alleviate them? Theory, from this perspective, should do more than merely describe social life; it should advance or advocate for positive social change (Madison, 2005). For instance, critical ethnographers have studied classrooms in terms of an instructor's emphasis on encouraging males in the class to excel in sports or engineering while not similarly emphasizing this orientation for females in the class. The research question itself may be a matter of counting cases or observing patterns. Nonetheless, the motive for doing so includes the assumption that teachers who are made aware of such patterns are less likely to reproduce them. Thus, the major elements in a critical ethnography include an advocacy, or value-laden approach, that seeks to empower participants (and sometimes constituents represented by these participants) by challenging the status quo and addressing various concerns about power and control structures.

Thomas (1993) has suggested that critical ethnography and conventional ethnography are not incompatible, and that in fact, both share several important characteristics. For example, both rely on various types of qualitative data (interviews, focus groups, observations, etc.) and interpretations of these data using the same set of tools and procedures. Throughout the analysis of data, both critical and conventional ethnographic strategies adhere to the symbolic interactionist paradigm and potentially to the development of grounded theory (Glaser & Strauss, 1967; Strauss, 1987). Notwithstanding their similarities, there are also several important characteristics that distinguish critical from conventional ethnography.

At the most general level of distinction, *conventional ethnography* refers to the tradition of cultural descriptions and the analysis of various meanings or shared meanings through the interpretation of meaning. *Critical ethnography*, on the other hand, refers to a much more reflective approach through which the researcher chooses between various alternatives and makes *value-laden judgments* of meanings and methods in a conscious effort to challenge research, policy, and other forms of human activity. In essence, conventional approaches to ethnography may be said to examine and describe *what is*, whereas critical ethnographic approaches ask the question *what could be* (Thomas, 1993).

Thus, critical ethnography is not merely criticism about something, such as one might offer to a waiter if he or she bought out a meal that was too cold. Nor should one confuse critical ethnography with the broader and more general theory of capitalist or materialist society (e.g., a Marxian perspective). Critical ethnography *is* conventional ethnography, but with a clear purpose, and which intentionally seeks positive change and empowerment for participants.

The Attitude of the Ethnographer

The researcher's frame of mind when entering a natural setting is crucial to the eventual results of a study. If you strike the wrong attitude, you might well destroy the possibility of ever learning about the observed participants and their perceptions. According to David Matza (1969), one must enter *appreciating* the situations rather than intending to *correct* them. This sort of neutral posture allows researchers to understand what is going on around them rather than become either advocates or critics of the events they witness. In addition, appreciation does not require the interviewers to agree with or even to accept the perceptions of their subjects but to merely offer empathy.

Although many students might think it is unnecessary to suggest that ethnographers should conduct research with an appreciative attitude, in actuality, it is an important recommendation.

In Chapter 2 I had suggested that it would be difficult and impractical for a black researcher to study a white power movement, at least in terms of conducting observations and interviews. But does that mean that any white researcher can easily do so? To openly enter a field research site, such as an organization, a community, or a social movement, means that the researcher must define himself or herself to the subjects, up to a point. To conduct interviews, or even lengthy conversations, one needs to develop some kind of rapport with the subjects. Clearly, in a politically charged environment or a controversial cause, the subjects are likely to look for clues as to the researcher's attitude toward them. Ideally, researchers should be able to openly and honestly present themselves as neither an advocate for the group nor an opponent. At the very least we need to be honestly curious about the subjects' views and willing to consider them seriously. This is what empathy offers. We can want to hear what people are saying without needing to endorse it. And it is generally far better from both ethical and practical perspectives to state that you don't see things the same way than to pretend to be "one of them." Clearly, if you were to plan a study to determine what's wrong with some group or other, people would be suspicious of your ability to properly conduct your research.

At a casual glance, this idea of value neutrality in the field might appear to contradict the assumptions of critical ethnography. It does not, but it calls attention to an important distinction between attitude and values. If, for example, I undertook field research in classrooms due to a critical concern about the education system, that should not imply that I am a critic of teachers. In fact, I might hope that my research could assist teachers in their work. I can be neutral about any given classroom, positive about the role of education, and critical of the institutions through which it is administered. My research question is guided by my values, while my research action is guided by my research design. The next question, then, is which of these guides my writing when the study is complete.

The Researcher's Voice

Many researchers—both quantitative and qualitative alike—recommend that social science research maintain a *value-neutral position*. From this perspective, social scientists are expected to study the world around them as external investigators. This means neither imposing their own views nor taking any stands on social or political issues. This style of research tends to lend itself to a fairly positivist approach. A number of social researchers have argued against this façade of value neutrality. Among the more vocal have been feminist researchers (Hertz, 1997; Nagy Hesse-Biber, Leavy, & Yaiser, 2004; Reinharz, 1992; Ribbens & Edwards, 1998). Feminist-inspired sociologists have worked out a research orientation that is comfortable for both the researcher and the subjects. It tends to involve strategies that listen more and talk less, that humanize the research process, and that insist that the ethnographic researcher become both involved with his or her subjects and reflexive about his or her own thoughts. Some recent researchers have also sought to encourage the writing of self-reflective or *autoethnographies*, similar in concept to more traditional autobiographies (Ellis & Bochner, 1996; Tedlock, 2003).

Objectively, social scientists should recognize that research is seldom, if ever, really value neutral. After all, the selection of a research topic typically derives from some researcher-oriented position. As previously implied in this chapter, topic selection occurs because of an interest in the subject matter, because it is a politically advantageous area to receive grant monies, because of some inner humanistic drive toward some social problem, or because one has personal experiences or what Lofland (1996, p. 44) calls "deep familiarity" with the subject area. The fact is research is seldom undertaken for a neutral reason. Furthermore, all humans residing in and among social groups are the product of those social groups. This means that various values, moral attitudes, and beliefs orient people in a particular manner.

For instance, a person's selection of certain terms indicates the kind of influences that a person's social groups have on him or her. In research on illegal drug use, for example, researchers typically refer to the subjects as drug "abusers." While one might argue that illegal drug use is abuse, that sort of technical explanation would also need to encompass other forms of abuse, such as abuse of prescription medicines, misuse of over-the-counter drugs, and possibly abuse of alcohol. In fact, most of these studies concentrate on "street" drugs, and the term "abuse" is adopted normatively; researchers say abuse because it is normal to think of drug use this way. In adopting this technically imprecise term, researchers reproduce a value system that defines their subjects in a particular way prior to even entering the field. Reading this work, it is more difficult to empathize with, or otherwise under-stand, the research subjects. Yet, when we write about families, teachers, police, veterans, or just about anyone else, we do not burden them with demeaning labels.

More recently, and again following from feminist researchers' lead, my writing has begun to incorporate the use of first person singular. In other words, I use the word *I*. (More accurately, *we* use *I*, since this book has two authors each of whom write this way, separately.) Particularly when writing ethnographic reports, it began to be apparent (to me) that using the first person singular was more direct. Rather than saying, "The researcher began to recognize blah, blah, blah . . . ." it seemed more forthright to simply say, "I began to recognize. . . ." In this manner, a researcher can take both ownership and responsibility for what is being stated. Furthermore, one's writing style becomes far less cumbersome and often elimi-nates passive and convoluted sentences.

Along similar lines, the use of personal biography or deep familiarity with a subject has become more common and accepted by ethnographers. One excellent example is Phil Brown's exploration of the culture of the Catskill Mountains' resorts (Brown, 1996). The "Borscht Belt," as the area is known, is where mainly metropolitan Jews fled New York and New Jersey for a summer retreat (Brown, 1996). On the other side of the coin, it was a place where young, often Jewish, college students went to work in order to earn their way through school. A number of well-known and large hotels, bungalow colonies, and camps grew up during the 1940s, and the largely Jewish resort area flourished until about the 1970s. Brown (1996, p. 84) wrote from the perspective of an observer who grew up in the Catskill culture and from the orientation of first-person deep familiarity:

> I grew up in a family of "mountain rats," a Catskill term for those who lived and worked in "the Mountains" over many years. My parents began in 1948 as owners of a small hotel, Brown's Hotel Royal, on White Lake. . . . In 1948 the chef quit at the start of the season. Unable to find a replacement, my mother, Sylvia Brown, gave herself a crash course in cooking and never left the kitchen again. After our hotel went broke two years later, she spent the rest of her working years as a chef.

Maintaining the façade of neutrality prevents a researcher from ever examining his or her own cultural assumptions (Rubin & Rubin, 1995) or personal experiences. Subjective disclosures by researchers allow the reader to better understand why a research area has been selected, how it was studied, and by whom. If a nurse studies cancer patients and explains that his or her selection of this topic resulted after a family member contracted the disease, this does not diminish the quality of the research. It does, however, offer a keener insight about who is doing the research and why. It may even provide the reader with greater understanding about why certain types of questions were investigated, while others were not.

Similarly, when a researcher reveals that he or she was tempted to, or did, intervene in the lives of his or her subjects, the reader gets a different image of both the researcher and the research. It is likely that anyone who has ever undertaken drug research among children, at the very least, has been tempted to try to convince some child that using heroin or crack cocaine is not a good thing to do. From a strictly positivist value-neutral position, of course, one cannot do this. This activity is the work of social workers and not social scientists. From a softer, more humane perspective, however, it seems a reasonable activity along with the fieldwork. Having the researcher reveal that he or she did try to intervene or even the inner battle the researcher may have had resisting intervening is an important piece of information. This information allows the reader to better understand the true face of both the researcher and the study results.

Finally, presenting subjective disclosures, or giving voice to the researcher, provides insights into the world of research for the reader. Rather than merely heaping results, findings, and even analysis upon the reader, the researcher can share a small portion of the research experience.

Subjective Motivational Factors Frequently, qualitative studies report in considerable detail the autobiographical motivations that led investigators to conduct their research as they did. These sorts of "true confessions," as Schwartz and Jacobs (1979) called them, are apparently designed to describe the initial biases, values, and theoretical orientations that eventually produced the project. As Johnson (1975) suggested, some researchers may have been motivated or inspired to conduct research in the hopes that such a project would offer positive steps toward realizing some abstract ideal (e.g., advancing scientific knowledge, alleviating human misery, resolving some specific social problem).

External Motivating Factors Conversely, Punch (1986, p. 210) suggested that the gamut of possible personal motivational factors that leads investigators to conduct research of one type or another may not result from high ideals at all. A number of features—not articulated in the researcher's confessions—may have been critically influential in the decision to study a given phenomenon or to do so in a particular manner. Certainly, the personality of the researcher may have an effect. Not all investigators are willing to associate with certain types of deviant groups or enter into some specialized natural settings (e.g., investigating inmates in correctional institutions or drug addicts in the South Bronx).

Other simple factors, seldom discussed in detail yet perhaps responsible for much research, are geographic proximity and access opportunities. The Adlers (Adler, 1985), for example, indirectly explain that their study on drug dealers and smugglers arose almost serendipitously. After moving to California to attend graduate school and renting a condominium townhouse on the beach, they met a neighbor identified as Dave. Later, the Adlers learned that Dave was a member of a smuggling crew that imported "a ton of marijuana weekly and 40 kilos of cocaine every few months" (Adler, 1985, p. 14). The friendship that developed between Dave and the Adlers provided access to the world of high-level drug dealers and smugglers.

In a similar manner, Peshkin (1986) reports that he began his study of a fundamentalist Christian school largely as a matter of circumstance. As Peshkin (1986, p. 11) described it:

> By means of an event which my Christian friends would call providential, and everyone else I know would call coincidental, I came to my present study. The event: a midwinter blizzard, an evening class, and a student in need of a ride home. The student was the Reverend David Householder, whose son attended a local Christian school and who assured me, when I expressed a fascination with religious schools, that he would help in every way he could to arrange for me to study his son's school.

Certainly, there is something romantic and exciting about the image of an ethnographer spending time with potentially dangerous people in interesting, albeit grimy, bars, gambling houses, various hidden erotic worlds (see, e.g., Ferrell & Hamm, 1998; Lee, 2001; Tewksbury, 1995). Ethnography can be, as Lofland and Lofland (1984) describe it, an "adventure." Yet, it is also work; rigorous, time-consuming, and often boring, tedious work.

Many researchers study certain settings simply because of their convenience or special ease of accessibility. Later, they endeavor to justify their choice on the basis of some grand ideal or spurious theoretical grounds (Punch, 1986). It is similar to a kind of verbal exchange that Harry Wolcott uses at the beginning of his second chapter in his book on ethnography (Wolcott, 2008, p. 15):

> *First Ethnographer:*   Where are you going to do your fieldwork?
> *Second Ethnographer:*   I don't know yet.
> *First Ethnographer:*   What are you going to study?
> *Second Ethnographer:*   That depends on where I go.

The logic here, I would hazard, is that some researchers may have specific purpose in their research settings and the explorations of certain groups, while others seem to kind of float more like flotsam and jetsam, landing wherever that may and then trying to figure out what they have.

What many of these researchers apparently fail to recognize is that everyday realities are heavily influenced by human feelings, and presentation of these feelings is legitimate! One may choose a research setting or group to research, then, for a number of both objective and/or subjective reasons; but regardless of the subjective *emotional feelings* or objective *intellectual* or *analytic* motivations, all are legitimate.

The omission of the ethnographers' feelings for and about their research inevitably creates what Johnson (1975, p. 145) described as "the fieldworker as an iron-willed, steel-nerved, cunning Machiavellian manipulator of the symbolic tools of everyday discourse." Including some indication of why researchers have undertaken a particular project along with the methodological procedure provides a means for making the research come alive, to become interesting to the reading audience. Research is interesting, as Lofland, Snow, Anderson, and Lofland (2006, p. 136) indicate, when the separation of cognitive and emotional aspects of research is an attempt to avoid distortion in the research; nonetheless, cognitions are an integral aspect to meaning. Further, researchers tend to separate these two elements for two reasons: First, it tends to simplify the expository task, and second, it is consistent with both recent or rediscovered elements of reflectivity by social scientists and recognition that emotion is a central aspect to human life.

Unfortunately, in their attempt to objectify their research efforts, many investigators ignore, omit, or conceal their feelings as such emotions are not typically considered capable of independent verification by others. Yet it is important to remember that overrationalized, highly objectified, nearly sterile methodological accounts of fieldwork efforts are not complete descriptions of the research enterprise. Mentions of researchers' personal feelings are not wholly absent from the research literature, but they are still relatively rare and are frequently made anecdotally rather than with a substantive purpose in mind (Johnson, 1975).

Gaining Entry

Gaining entry, or getting in, to a research locale or setting can be fraught with difficulties, and researchers need to remain flexible concerning their tactics and strategies (Bogdan & Knopp Bilken, 2003; Lofland et al., 2006; Shenton & Hayter, 2004). Knowledge about the people being studied and familiarity with their routines and rituals facilitate entry as well as rapport once the researcher has gained entry. Understanding a group's *argot* (specialized language), for example, may assist an investigator not only in gaining entry but also in understanding what is going on once he or she has access. In some instances, the researcher may hold some special relationship with members of a group he or she seeks entry to or may himself be a member of that group (see, e.g., Brown, 1996, Ostrander, 2004).

Timothy McGettigan (2001) describes his experience and expectations about gaining entry for his study of the Green Tortoise (a young adult adventure bus). McGettigan (2001, par. 3.2) explains:

> One of the unique features of the Green Tortoise is that "getting in," or what Wax (1971) refers to as "the first and most uncomfortable stage of fieldwork," is equally difficult for all. Field researchers often study well-established groups, and, prior to initiation, they can appear hopelessly inept. . . . However, on the Tortoise there was no pre-established community. Instead, all of the passengers were cast into the role of bungling outsiders.
>
> In fact, developing a cohesive in-group is one of the principal features of Tortoise journeys. Adventure travel on the Tortoise is predicated upon cram-ming overbooked passengers onto old, refurbished buses and taking them on long trips without precise itineraries. Because the buses are usually very crowded (e.g., there were 42 people on this journey), passengers are forced to violate many of the niceties of conventional crowd behavior. Sean, a German man on his sixth adventure trip, noted that a common saying on the Green Tortoise

is "Move your meat, lose your seat." Nevertheless, I was alarmed throughout the first few days because of how often I bumped into others and invaded their space—no matter how ill-defined.

In spite of various ethnographers' personal accounts, as a starting point it is wise, especially for the beginning researcher, to begin in the library and to locate as much information about the group, organization, or neighborhood as possible before attempting entry. You might also begin, as Vallance (2001) suggests, by considering your friends and social networks to see if anyone you know can offer a *referral* into the group you intend to study. But in many instances, the library will be your best resource. Even when there is little literature on a specific topic, there is often considerable work on some related area.

Developing Research Bargains   Gaining entry into various settings also is affected by the kinds of arrangements or *bargains* made between researchers and subjects. Many researchers' accounts about how they gained entry to their research settings include descriptions of negotiating access with a highly visible and respected individual who held a position of rank, authority, or respect among others in the group (Calhoun, 1992; Guy et al., 1987; Leinen, 1993; Whyte, 1955). Another approach to this problem is to create *research teams* that include, as members, *insiders* from the group or groups to be studied (see, e.g., Jones, 1995; Tewksbury, 1997).

Gatekeepers   Gatekeepers are people or groups who are in positions to grant or deny access to a research setting (Feldman, Bell, & Berger, 2003; Hagan, 2006). Gatekeepers may be formal or informal watchdogs who protect the setting, people, or institutions sought as the target of research. Such individuals often hold pivotal positions in the hierarchy of the group or organization one seeks to study; although they may not be high up the hierarchical ranking, they are nonetheless in positions to stymie the researcher's ability to gain access. For example, secretaries are typically key gatekeepers in organizational settings. Secretaries can make a researcher's life easy or difficult. Yet, the social status of a secretary in most organizations is likely not as high as that of the individual for whom he or she works. Bartenders are often informal gatekeepers to the social world of a bar or club, while union representatives might be more useful contacts than management when seeking access to many workplaces.

Gaining access may require some sort of mediation with these individuals, and research bargains may necessarily be struck. Once a gatekeeper sees the research in a favorable light, he or she may be willing to go to bat for the researcher should obstacles arise during the course of study. Conversely, if the gatekeeper disapproves of the project or the researcher, or is somehow bypassed, he or she may become an unmovable obstacle: Angry gatekeepers may actively seek ways to block one's access or progress.

Guides and Informants   One way to handle initial relationships is to locate *guides* and *informants.* Guides are indigenous persons found among the group and in the setting to be studied (O'Leary, 2005). These persons must be convinced that the ethnographers are who they claim to be and that the study is worthwhile. The worth of the study must be understood and be meaningful to the guides and their group. Similarly, these guides must be convinced that no harm will befall them or other members of the group as a result of the ethnographers' presence. The reason for these assurances, of course, is so the guide can reassure others in the group that the ethnographers are safe to have around. In essence, the guide extends his or her credibility to cover the researcher as well.

Guides, or other key informants, are crucial participants in much of our fieldwork. Convincing a guide to take on this role is often more complicated than just getting past a gatekeeper. The researcher may need the ongoing and committed participation of the guide. In one notable case, Mitch Duneier came to recognize his guide, Hakim Hasan, as a collaborator in his study of sidewalk book dealers, and asked Hasan to write the afterword to the book that came from this work. In this chapter, Hasan tells his own story, relating how he came to be a sidewalk dealer and how he came to be Duneier's guide.

> In the first chapter Mitch recalls his difficulty in convincing me to become a subject—at that time the sole subject—of the book. Indeed, I found myself hearing the decree of my mother, whenever she had to leave my siblings and me at home alone: *Do not open the door for anyone while I'm gone.*
>
> If I defied the maternal decree and opened *this* door, on what basis would I weigh Mitch's intentions? How could I prevent him from appropriating me as mere data, from not giving me a voice in how the material in his book would be selected and depicted? How does a subject take part in an ethnographic study in which he has very little faith and survive as something more than a subject and less than an author?

It is worth recalling the point raised earlier about the perspective from which one enters a research site. Sometimes, persons who are willing to be guides or informants turn out to be restricted in their groups. Perhaps they are resented or disliked by others in the group. If you, as a researcher, strike a deal with such a guide, then your own subsequent access will be restricted. Consequently, ethnographers may recruit multiple guides and seek a snowballing of informants to assist their maneuverability while in the field. *Snowballing*, in the sense it is used here, refers to using people whom the original guide(s) introduces to the ethnographer as persons who can also vouch for the legitimacy and safety of the researcher. Other times researchers may limit their subjects only to those who are connected to the guide, providing an in-depth and thorough look at a research setting from a particular perspective. Elliot Liebow's *Tally's Corner* is a classic example of this approach, wherein the title of the book itself identifies the role of the guide in the study. With Tally's help, Liebow conducted an in-depth ethnography of a group of African American "streetcorner men" on and around the corner where Tally, his guide, hung out. Tally's involvement made this one corner uniquely available to Liebow, but probably closed off other corners and other groups around the same neighbourhood.

The larger the ethnographers' network of reliable guides and informants, the greater their access and ability to gain further cooperation. Eventually, the need for specific guides decreases as subject networks grow in size, and the ethnographers are able to begin casual acquaintanceships by virtue of their generally accepted presence on the scene. This will be further discussed in the next section of this chapter, "Becoming Invisible." The preceding guidelines and illustrations suggest some broad considerations and tactics ethnographers may use in order to gain entry to a specific setting. Similar accounts of entry may be found throughout the literature on ethnography and field research. However, some accounts also suggest that entry is determined by the innate abilities and personalities of the ethnographers. This attitude is comparable to the notion that only certain innately gifted people can conduct effective in-depth interviews—and it is likewise inaccurate (see Chapter 4 for a comprehensive examination of this argument regarding interviewing). A more accurate description of the effects of persona may be effects from the type of role and personality an ethnographer projects. In other words, just as the characterizations and social roles played out by the interviewer affect the quality of the interview performance, so too do these activities affect the ethnographer's performance. Sometimes a person's presentation of self works particularly well, or poorly, in some setting. But that is not the same as having an innate advantage in all research settings.

Naturally, indigenous ethnographers—persons who already are members of the group to be studied—possess certain strategic advantages, but as several nurses who conduct ethnography have suggested, neither their indigenous status nor special knowledge about the healthcare profession made conducting their research any easier (Denzin & Lincoln, 2005; Ostrander, 1993; Peterson, 1985).

Becoming Invisible

As mentioned previously, one obstacle to conducting ethnographic research is the very presence of the ethnographer in the field. Early in the history of field research, Fritz Roethlisberger and William Dickson (1939) identified a phenomenon now commonly called the *Hawthorne effect*. Briefly, the Hawthorne effect suggests that when subjects know they are subjects in a research study, they will alter their usual (routine) behavior. That is, they react to the presence of the researcher. Fortunately, this effect is often short-lived, and the behavior of subjects eventually returns to a more routine style. But the persistent presence of ethnographers in a social setting might certainly reactivate the Hawthorne effect in varying degrees every time someone new is introduced to the researchers. Ethnographic accounts, therefore, understandably offer readers explanations of how the ethnographers' presence was made relatively *invisible* to the subjects.

The status as an *invisible researcher*, as Stoddart (1986) described it, is the ability to be present in the setting, to see what's going on without being observed, and, consequently, to capture the essence of the setting and participants without influencing them. While few research settings allow one to be completely invisible, there are ways of reducing the researcher *reactivity*, to approach invisibility. Stoddart (1986, pp. 109–113) identified six possible variations on this theme of invisible status:

1. When the ethnographers have been present in a domain for a long time, the inhabitants tend not to be aware of them anymore. The notice inhabitants initially took of them has eroded or worn off. They cease to be a concern by just being there without interacting much.
2. Act like one belongs. Eventually, ethnographers just fit into the domain they are studying by downplaying the differences between themselves and their study population. This might involve dressing like a local, acting more like a member of the community, or demonstrating an insider's knowledge of jokes, expectations, and other people.
3. Participate with ordinary inhabitants in their everyday routines. By working shoulder to shoulder with inhabitants, the researchers' ethnographer status blends with their new roles in the group or community. Subjects will be aware of the researchers but tend to primarily recognize their nonresearch role.
4. Make friends. This is a strong case of establishing rapport. Subjects will still be conscious of the researcher's role, but they may develop the habit of helping anyway, because of the personal relationship.

5. Define yourself as a researcher, but distract the subjects with a false impression of your research topic. Subjects may be self-conscious about, for example, their job performance while at work, but relaxed about their social relations during break times. The researcher will therefore be as though invisible during the breaks.

6. In the final variation suggested by Stoddart (1986), ethnographers do not represent themselves to the normal inhabitants as ethnographers: In other words, they conduct covert ethnography. Since the normal inhabitants of the domain under examination are not aware of the ethnographers' real activities in the setting, the ethnographers eventually become socially invisible. For the most part, this is not a recommended strategy, as discussed in Chapter 3.

Dangers of Invisibility

From the ethnographers' perspective, it may seem ideal to obtain invisible status, but several ethical—and real—dangers exist. At least three types of dangers are inherent in conducting research invisibly. These include researcher-originated or intentional misidentification, accidental misidentification, and learning more than you want to know.

Intentional Misidentification   The first potential danger results when the ethnographers' intentional attempts to misrepresent their identity as researchers successfully isolate the subjects of a study. As Thomas's (Thomas & Swaine, 1928) frequently quoted statement expresses, "If men define situations as real, they are real to them in their consequences." In other words, when researchers misrepresent themselves and become invisible to normal inhabitants in a study domain, their assumed role as something else may be taken for real! In one classic case, Rosenhan (1973), in a study of psychiatric hospitals, described how he and several research associates became psychiatric patients (actually pseudopatients) by acting out various schizophrenic symptoms during intake assessments. By misrepresenting their role as researchers, Rosenhan and his associates managed to have themselves committed.

From the assumed identity of psychiatric patient, Rosenhan and his associates were able to observe and record the behavior of the hospital staff (nurses, aides, psychiatrists, etc.). After being admitted, all of the researchers discontinued their simulation of symptoms, but each had difficulty convincing doctors that they were not schizophrenic! The length of stay in the hospitals ranged from 5 to 52 days, with an average stay of 19 days. Eventually, each researcher was released with the discharge diagnosis of schizophrenia in remission.

Rosenhan's original purpose of demonstrating the effects of labeling in psychiatric facilities was accomplished, but this study illustrates the dangers for researchers misidentifying themselves as other than ethnographers.

Accidental Misidentification   In contrast to intentional misidentification as researchers, ethnographers who gain invisible status may be found guilty by association. Persons outside the immediate domain under investigation may not know who the ethnographers are and simply assume they belong to the group. Although this may allow accurate assessment of many social interactions among the various participants, it is also potentially dangerous.

Particularly when investigating certain so-called deviant groups (e.g., violent youth gangs, drug dealers or smugglers, car thieves), even if the ethnographers are socially invisible (as researchers) to members of this group, they may be taken as actual group members by others outside this group. As a result, the ethnographers' personal safety could be jeopardized in the event of a violent confrontation between gangs, for example. If the ethnographers are with one gang, they may be guilty of membership through association in the eyes of the rival gang.

Learning More Than You Want to Know   Another danger of researcher invisibility is learning more than you might want to know. During the course of an ethnographic study on adolescent involvement in alcohol, drugs, and crime (Berg et al., 1983), field ethnographers found that their presence was often invisible. It was common for the ethnographers to be present, for example, during criminal planning sessions. Often, the ethnographers had information concerning planned burglaries, drug deals, shoplifting sprees, car thefts, and fights several days before the event. In the case of this particular study, possession of this knowledge presented more of an ethical problem than a legal one, since the study group also possessed a Federal Certificate of Confidentiality.

Federal Certificates of Confidentiality ensure that all employees of a research study and all research documents are protected from subpoena in civil or criminal court actions. The certificate also specifies that the researchers cannot divulge confidential material. Thus, the field ethnographers could not divulge their knowledge of impending crimes without violating this agreement. Nonetheless, it was sometimes difficult for the field ethnographers to maintain their personal sense of integrity knowing in advance that certain crimes would occur and knowing also they could do nothing to stop them. One partial solution to the ethical/moral dilemma was an agreement among all of the study participants concerning special circumstances. Under certain special circumstances—that is, if information were obtained that convinced the ethnographers that someone's life or limb could be saved (e.g., if a contract were placed on someone's life or if plans were made to break someone's arm or leg)—appropriate authorities would be notified. Of course doing so would almost certainly terminate the research itself as well as putting the ethnographers in danger of reprisals.

Certificates of Confidentiality   Certificates of Confidentiality are issued by the National Institutes of Health (NIH) to protect the privacy of research subjects by ensuring that researchers and research institutes cannot be compelled to release information that could be used to identify subjects used in a given research study. Certificates of Confidentiality are issued on behalf of the researchers to their institutions or universities. Such certificates allow the researcher and others working on the project who have access to records and data to refuse to disclose identifying information in any civil, criminal, administrative, legislative, or other proceeding, whether at the federal, state, or local level. This translates quite literally into a protection for the interviewer from being compelled to bear witness against a subject whom the researcher may have heard or observed plan a crime.

Generally certificates are issued for a single research project and not for groups or classes of projects. In some instances, however, they can be issued to projects that may have multiple data-collection or analysis sites. The main or coordinating center (what may be called the lead institution) can apply on behalf of all the other research sites or institutions working on the project. It is the responsibility of the lead institution to ensure that all of the sites comply with the applications made on their behalf.

Application information for Certificates of Confidentiality can be found online at http://grants.nih.gov/grants/policy/coc/. The application must be written on the university or research institute's letterhead and meet a number of human subject criteria, including assurances of informed consent, privacy, confidentiality, and having already been approved by the researcher's local institutional review board (see Chapter 3). Application for a Certificate of Confidentiality is not an assurance of being granted one.

Many nonresearchers and novice researchers, and even experienced professionals who do not conduct fieldwork, have difficulty understanding why we need these certificates. As discussed earlier, it seems simple enough that a researcher who witnesses a crime should report it. But the real question is not whether to report or withhold. It is whether to conduct research among potential criminal groups at all. Frequently, such research could not take place without protections for our informants. This does not mean that researchers aid in the commission of crimes or help to cover them up. Those who engage in criminal acts are still taking the same risks, and inflicting the same harms that they would without a researcher present. By agreeing to act in all respects as though we were not present, we get to be present.

Other Dangers During Ethnographic Research

Most novice researchers do a fairly effective job of protecting the rights and safety of their subjects. Less common among inexperienced researchers, however, are serious concerns during the design stage of research about the investigator's own personal safety. Some research, especially ethnographic research, may be in dangerous places or among dangerous people (Williams, Dunlap, Johnson, & Hamid, 2001). Howell (1990), for example, discussed a number of crimes researchers are apt to encounter in the field (e.g., robbery, theft, rape, and assault). Field investigators have encountered illness, personal injury, and even death during the course of ethnographic research.

Interestingly, the potential for personal or emotional harm to subjects is extensively covered in virtually all research methods books. The problem of personal or emotional harm to *researchers*, however, is seldom discussed (Sluka, 1990; Williams et al., 2001). Some basic elements about caution when conducting research in general and ethnographic research in particular can be found—indirectly—in the broad methodological literature on ethnography (Adler, 1985; Adler & Adler, 1987; Broadhead & Fox, 1990; Ferrell, 2006; Fetterman, 1989; Johnson, 1990; Rose, 1990; Williams et al., 2001). On the other hand, when ethnographers tell their "war stories" about their work, there is a kind of romance and excitement about having deliberately put oneself in danger to bring back the story which, honestly, is not easy to find in academic life (Venkatesh, 2008). Such romanticism may encourage novice researchers to make poor decisions when planning their work.

Yet, contemporary ethnographers often work in settings made dangerous by violent conflict or with social groups among whom interpersonal violence is commonplace. As Lee (2001) suggests, in many cases, it is the violence itself or the social conditions and circumstances that produce this violence that actively compel attention from the social scientist. Understanding that there are potential dangers and risks to the ethnographer, therefore, is an important lesson. Knowing about these risks allows the novice researcher to determine how best to deal with them, what precautions to take, and perhaps how to avoid them. In addition to the general dangers that investigators may confront while undertaking field research, female investigators may face the additional risks of sexual harassment or even sexual assault (Lewis-Beck, Bryman, & Liao, 2004).

Speaking generally, it is possible to identify at least two distinct forms of danger that may arise during the course of ethnographic research. These include *ambient* and *situational risks.* Similar distinctions have been offered by Lee (2001), Brewer (1993), and Sluka (1990).

Ambient dangers arise when a researcher exposes himself or herself to otherwise avoidable dangers, simply by having to be in a dangerous setting or circumstance to carry out the research. Nurses who conduct research in infectious disease wards, for example, place themselves in ambient danger (Lewis-Beck et al., 2004). I recall the situation of one of my former colleagues who was conducting interviews among female drug users, many of whom were unable to maintain regular jobs or stable home situations due to the extent of their drug consumption and therefore had to rely on other kinds of income and support. Returning from a bathroom break during one interview, the researcher found her informant taking money from her purse. Yet when she expressed surprise at this breach of trust, the informant replied, "I *told you* I steal." The informant was correct; the researcher should not have been surprised.

Situational danger occurs when the researcher's presence or behaviors in the setting trigger conflict, violence, or hostility from others in the setting. For instance, an ethnographer researching tavern life, who engages in alcohol consumption as a means of gaining greater acceptance by regular participants, may also evoke trouble among the regular drinkers (Lee-Treweek & Linkogle, 2000).

Often the safety precautions you must take in research amount to little more than good common sense. For instance, you should never enter the field without telling someone where you will be and when you expect to leave the field. Carry a phone. Learn to be aware of your environment. What's going on around you? Is it nighttime and dark out? Is it nighttime but well lighted? Are there other people around? Being aware of your environment also means knowing your location and the locations where help can be obtained quickly (e.g., locations of police stations, personal friends, your car).

It is important for the researcher's safety to know insiders who are ready to vouch for him or her. Often a quick word from an established insider will reassure others in a group of the researcher's sincerity or purposes. This is particularly important if you are attempting anything covert among subjects who have reason to fear police or other infiltration.

Additionally, there are places one should avoid if possible. For example, often I send my classes out to public spaces to practice their observational skills. The single proviso I admonish students with is this: Do not conduct observations in the public bathrooms! I do this not merely because public bathrooms are designed as places for private activities. I do this because public bathrooms are potentially very dangerous places for researchers. Usually, they are unmonitored and secluded from the view of others. They are sometimes frequented by thieves trying to deal stolen property or drug dealers trying to sell their wares. In other words, public bathrooms may draw a variety of potentially dangerous people and activities. If you are conducting actual research on these activities in public bathrooms, of course, they cannot be avoided. However, in such a situation, you are likely to take proper safety precautions. For the casual practice of observational skills, however, bathrooms are simply too risky a setting.

It is also important to note that while potential risks to researchers clearly exist, only a very small proportion of researchers has ever actually been seriously injured or killed as a direct result of research (Williams et al., 2001). Perhaps one reason for this low injury rate is that experienced researchers do recognize the potential dangers and develop plans and procedures to reduce or avoid the risks involved. IRBs (Chapter 3) also filter out dangerous research plans before they start, forcing researchers to better plan their fieldwork.

TRYING IT OUT

Suggestion 1   Position yourself in a public location where many people congregate. Shopping malls, bus terminals, and airports are good examples of the sorts of places I mean. Next, simply sit and watch and listen. Construct field notes of the observations and what you heard (do not engage in any conversations or interviews). Repeat this activity for several days. Be certain that you write up notes about what you have observed soon after you have left the field each day. Bear in mind that the time you spend in the field geometrically increases when you write up your full notes. Initially, spend no more than 15 or 20 minutes at a time in the field.

Watching, Listening, and Learning

Much ethnographic research involves entering the setting of some group and simply watching and listening attentively. Because it would be virtually impossible to observe everything or hear all that is going on at one time, ethnographers must watch and listen only to certain portions of what happens. That is why proper planning is so important to research. Researchers must determine exactly what they want to learn about at various points in the research and focus their attention accordingly. If you enter a public space for the purpose of observing different public conversational styles among groups, pairs, and individuals (with phones, presumably), then your attention and your notes should be on conversations. There is no need to fill pages of notes with descriptions of people's clothing, approximate ages, or ethnic markers, much less details on who was walking in what direction or why you think they were there at all.

Once the ethnographers have determined their essential aims, it should be possible to partition off the setting. This may be accomplished by bracketing certain subgroups of inhabitants of the domain and observing them during specific times, in certain locations, and during the course of particular events and/or routines. Frequently, a given partitioning snowballs into other relevant locations, subgroups, and activities. For example, during an ethnographic study of adolescents' involvement in alcohol, drugs, and crime (Carpenter, Glassner, Johnson, & Loughlin, 1988), a central focus was how adolescents structured their leisure time. The ethnographers spatially began by spending time with adolescents during their free periods in local junior and senior high schools. Temporally, this meant during the time before classes in the morning (approximately one hour), during their lunch periods (approximately two hours), and after school was dismissed (approximately one hour).

In addition to learning how the observed youths structured their leisure time during these free-time periods on and around school campuses, the ethnographers began to learn where, when, and how youths spent their time outside of school. New spatial partitioning began to emerge and snowball. In addition to continuing their observations of the youths at and around school campuses, the ethnographers followed various subgroups of youths in other areas of the community and during various activities (both routine and special ones).

By the conclusion of 18 months of ethnography, the field workers had observed youths in parks, skating rinks, people's homes, school dances, video arcades, bars, movie theaters, local forests, and an assortment of other locales.

Verenne (1988) similarly wrote about how youths formed cliques and made use of various spaces throughout their high school and community. Describing the availability of spaces throughout the high school, Verenne (1988, p. 216) stated the following:

The adults gave the students a complex building which, surprisingly for a modern construction, offered various types of spaces that various groups could call their own. For example, there were many tables in the cafeteria, there were nearly a dozen small and only intermittently occupied offices in the library, there were the guidance office and the nurses' office. There were bathrooms, isolated stairway landings, the backstage area in the auditorium. There were hidden spots on the grounds—behind bushes, in a drainage ditch.

Regarding some of the times and ways students used various spaces, Verenne (1988, p. 216) explained:

During the times when they were not required to be in class, the students thus continually had to make decisions about where to go or where to sit. By ordinary right they could be in only three places: the "commons" [the cafeteria was so designated when not in use for lunch], the library, or a study hall. By extraordinary right, most often by virtue of membership in some special "club," students could be found in the private offices in the back of the library, in the coordinator's office, in the room where the audiovisual equipment was kept. . . . By self-proclaimed right, students might also be found in the bathrooms for very long periods of time not solely dedicated to the satisfaction of biological functions, or on the stairway landing from which the roof could be reached.

As indicated by the preceding illustrations, often subjects group themselves in meaningful ways, which allows the ethnographer to observe them more systematically.

In some instances, the researchers can partition or restrict certain places where they watch and listen and increase observational capabilities through filming or videotaping the area. This style of observation has grown increasingly popular in educational settings (when undertaken with the full cooperation of the institution and parents). For example, in a study by Hart and Sheehan (1986), social and cognitive development among children during preschool years was investigated in relationship to play activities. To accomplish their study, Hart and Sheehan (1986, p. 671) restricted the use of the playground to two groups of preschoolers and videotaped the children at play:

For seven weeks from the beginning of the preschool year in the fall before the observations began, children from each of the two groups had equal access to both sides of the playground during their 30-minute outdoor play period each day. During the observational period, barricades were placed in the access routes between the two playgrounds and children from each separate class . . . were asked to stay on an assigned side.

Videotaped observations then took place over a four-week period on fair weather days while preschool activities were conducted as usual. In general, the use and versatility of videotaping during research have increased enormously as the costs of doing so have continued to fall. Other uses of videotape in research are discussed in Chapter 8.

How to Learn: What to Watch and Listen For

When inexperienced ethnographers enter the field for the first time, they are impressed by the sheer number of activities and interactions going on in the setting. The initial activities of ethnographers frequently involve getting acclimated to the setting. This involves four general aspects:

1. Taking in the physical setting
2. Developing relationships with inhabitants (locating potential guides and informants)
3. Tracking, observing, eavesdropping, and asking questions
4. Locating subgroups and stars (central characters in various subgroups)

Taking in the Physical Setting   During the first few days, ethnographers usually wander around the general location they plan to use as the setting. As they walk around the area, they should begin to map the setting carefully. This may mean literally drawing an accurate facsimile of the various physical locales in the setting (the streets, the buildings, the specific rooms where inhabitants pass their time, etc.). It may mean writing detailed field notes (to be discussed later) that describe the setting. Or it may mean some combination of both mapping and detailing in field notes.

Several purposes are served by this initial task of taking in the physical setting. First, while mapping out the spatial elements of the setting, researchers can begin to think about how to cover these areas in the most efficient and effective manner (the number of hours required, which days or which hours during the day or night are best, etc.).

Second, wandering around the area allows the ethnographers to begin getting acquainted with inhabitants and vice versa. Frequently, a smile or greeting during this initial phase will pay back tenfold later during the research.

Third, often merely by walking around and watching and listening, important first impressions are drawn. The first impressions may not be entirely accurate, but they will become *points of reference* later as the researchers become more familiar and knowledgeable about the setting and its inhabitants (Guy et al., 1987).

Developing Relationships with Inhabitants   During the initial phase of research in the field, researchers typically rely heavily on *guides*. Guides may have been located before the research through friends, acquaintances, or colleagues who knew someone among the group the researchers planned on studying (McLean & Campbell, 2003; Somekh & Lewin, 2005). Alternatively, in the event that no guides can be identified before entering the field, one or more guides simply must be located during the early period following entry (Peshkin, 1986).

Concerning this latter form of locating guides, researchers may find that having smiled and greeted several inhabitants while taking in the setting actually becomes an essential means of beginning relationships. Although it is more difficult than simply walking up and introducing themselves, ethnographers are better advised to assume a more passive role until some relationships have been established.

Another important point to impress on locals is that all information collected during the research study will be held in strict confidence. Similarly, it is critical to impress on potential guides that the researchers are who they claim to be. This may be simply accomplished by carrying a letter of introduction and photo identification or it may require a more extensive process of having the potential guides check you out through either official channels (calling the sponsoring institution) or, in some situations, the guides' own channels!

Researchers should assure potential guides that their extensive knowledge of the people and domain will make them extremely valuable to the study. Certainly, researchers should be cautious not to become overtly insincere in their flattery. But, in truth, guides do possess certain expert knowledge and are virtually invaluable to the ethnographers for helping them gain access.

Having established a rapport with one or more guides, ethnographers can begin snowballing additional relationships with other inhabitants (McLean & Campbell, 2003). The most direct way to accomplish this is to gain permission from the guides to spend some time hanging around the setting with them. As others begin to pass time in proximity, the ethnographers can ask questions of their guides about these others and may possibly obtain an introduction—including having the guides reassure newcomers of the legitimacy of the ethnographers.

Tracking, Observing, Eavesdropping, and Asking Questions   Having established relationships with several guides and inhabitants, ethnographers are free to begin really learning what goes on among the inhabitants of their study domain. This is done by tracking, observing, eavesdropping, and asking questions.

Tracking literally means following the guides around during their usual daily routines and watching their activities and the other people they interact with. As researchers follow and observe, they can also eavesdrop on conversations. Although social norms typically prohibit eavesdropping, such a proscription is untenable when conducting certain types of ethnography. Bogdan (1972) has suggested that although eavesdropping is necessary, it is also sometimes difficult to accomplish for people who have been reared in a noneavesdropping society. As well, there are ethical issues about intruding on people's privacy. As a general rule, people engaged in conversation have a reasonable expectation that their talk is their own business, not ours. In contrast, people talking loudly in public spaces, whether in person or by phone, are making their talk public. As a researcher you should neither move surreptitiously into earshot of a private conversation nor sneak up on people in order to listen in. Nonetheless, researchers often learn a great deal about a phenomenon or an event simply by being present while people are discussing it.

Sometimes it takes a lot of physical presence to capture the essence of events, or to witness significant moments or conversations. Rueben May, for example, spent 18 months of "deep hanging out" at a Chicago bar in order to collect the conversational fragments, recurring themes, and descriptive language described in his (2001) book *Talking at Trena's*. Trena's is "an African American tavern," and May, through the process of becoming a regular there, used the site to study how individual and collective identities are formed and expressed over drinks in safe, segregated spaces among the black middle class. The talk was the data.

On some occasions, during the process of eavesdropping, researchers hear terms or learn about situations that may be important but that fall on deaf ears. In other words, the ethnographers do not understand the significance of what they hear. On these occasions, ethnographers must ask questions, but, again, they should consider taking a passive role during such informal questioning. Perhaps jotting a cryptic note to ask a guide at a later time would serve better than interrupting the ongoing action with a question. Or perhaps arranging another meeting with some participant in the conversation (other than the guide) would offer a more fruitful approach. Decisions about how to pursue information will vary from situation to situation. Again note that this situation assumes that the researcher is recognized as having been present at the conversation, and not hiding behind the shrubbery with a tape recorder.

Locating Subgroups and Stars   During the course of tracking and observing, ethnographers are able to identify certain inhabitants who tend to spend more time with one another than with others. These subgroupings may or may not represent formal groups but certainly suggest a kind of social networking. Among these social networks, researchers can sociometrically identify individuals who appear to be more or less the central figures in a given network of inhabitants. Such central figures may be referred to as opinion leaders or *stars*. Although ethnographers may not always need to establish a guide-type relationship with a star, it is sometimes necessary to obtain his or her goodwill.

In a manner similar to what Bogdan and Taylor (1975, pp. 30–33) described as accessing *gatekeepers*, developing a relationship with a star may be a critical element in an ethnographic project. Even when ethnographers locate a guide and gain access to the basic setting, a star may hold the key to deeper penetration into the lives and perceptions of inhabitants of that setting. Sometimes a single gesture or word from a star will open more doors than weeks and weeks of attempts to gain access to these portals. Conversely, that same single gesture can slam doors that took months for the ethnographer to get opened. Whenever possible, it is advisable to find and gain the confidence of a star as soon as possible after entering the field.

Field Notes

The central component of ethnographic research is the *ethnographic account*. Providing such narrative accounts of what goes on in the lives of study subjects derives from having maintained complete, accurate, and detailed field notes. From the approach endorsed here, field notes should be completed immediately following every excursion into the field, as well as following any chance meeting with inhabitants outside the boundaries of the study setting (e.g., at the supermarket, in a doctor's office, at a traffic light). Notes are rarely taken during the actual encounters or observations, but should be recorded frequently after short bursts of fieldwork. Memory fades quickly and details are easily lost if one does not note them right away.

Field notes can provide accounts of at least three categories of observable experiences (Goodall, 2000). These include the following:

1. Verbal exchanges (between others or the researcher and others);
2. Practices (various routines, actions, and interactions among and between participants); and
3. Connections between and among observed exchanges and practices.

Verbal Exchanges Verbal exchanges may include interviews with participants, overheard conversations (eavesdropped exchanges), messages and communications between various individuals, conversations, arguments, discussions, dialogues, complaints, critiques, and any similar types of communication-based interactions spoken to or overheard by the researcher.

Practices Observed practices refer to the ways individuals or groups say or do things routinely. In other words, the way actions, interactions, and activities participants of the setting are regularly engaged or involved.

Connections These connections refer to implied, inferred, or interpreted connections and associations between observed actions, interactions, and behaviors. Connections, then, operate along the dimension of meanings and understandings as apprehended by the researcher (etic meanings) and the participants (emic meanings).

There are many variations on how to take field notes. Some researchers wait until they have left the field and then immediately write complete records (Bogdan, 1972; Rossman & Rallis, 2003). Others take abbreviated notes covertly while in the field and later translate them into complete field notes (see Angrosino, 2007; Gibbs, 2007). Burgess (1991a, p. 192) has suggested that "Note-taking is a personal activity that depends upon the research context, the objectives of the research, and the relationship with informants." Burgess also offered some general rules for note-taking. Among these rules are recommendations for establishing a regular time and place for writing up one's notes (including the date, time, and location of the observations) and duplicating notes for safety reasons. Note-taking strategies must balance the desire for immediacy with the fear of reactivity. While there are many public and private locations where one can sit with books, notebooks, and/or computers, writing notes without attracting attention, it is generally difficult to make note of your observations without concern that others are observing you doing so.

Notes taken in the field need to be brief, but with enough information to be elaborated on later. Chiseri-Strater and Sunstein (2001) have devised a list of what they believe should go into all field notes. This list includes the date, time, and place of the observations; specific facts, numbers, and details of what happened at the site; sensory impressions such as sights, sounds, textures, smells, tastes; personal responses as recorded in the field notes; specific words, phrases, summaries of conversations, and insider language; questions about people or behaviors at the site for future consideration; and page numbers to keep the observations in order. Computer files don't need page numbering, of course, whereas pockets-full of cocktail napkins would be almost useless without them.

Text messages to oneself are conveniently time-stamped, and easily sent without attracting too much attention.

Carol Bailey (1996, 2006) suggests a three-step process moving from the field to the notes. Field notes initially consist of *mental notes*, collected while interacting in the research setting. These are then transformed into *jotted notes*, or brief reminder notes actually written down and used later to jog the researcher's memory when he or she writes more *complete* field notes.

There are various ways to take field notes. For example, some ethnographers carry tape recorders and periodically enter their own notes or record various conversations they witness. Other researchers carry slips of paper or index cards and simply tweet notes and verbatim quotes periodically throughout the field excursion. Once out of the field, the researchers can use these notes and sketches to write full accounts. My personal preference is simply to carry a laptop and look as though I'm working on something else. This wouldn't work at a bar or baseball game, but it seems to be effective within most organizational settings.

From my perspective, there are four distinct elements that go into creating full and detailed field notes: cryptic jottings, detailed descriptions, analytic notes, and subjective reflections.

Cryptic Jottings   Cryptic jottings are taken while still in the field. These may include brief statements (a sentence or less), sketches (line drawings), short notes (a paragraph or so), and odd or unusual terms or phrases heard while in the field that might serve as a memory trigger later when writing full field notes.

Detailed Descriptions   Detailed descriptions are undertaken once you have exited the field. Detailed descriptions are the heart of any narrative field notes. They should include as much texture, sensation, color, and minutia as your memory permits. Conversations should be replicated as near to verbatim as memory permits (the cryptic jotting can help a great deal with this). Details should include how people appeared, what they said, what they did, and even if they had any noticeable characteristics (speech impediments, scars, tattoos, concealed weapons, etc.).

Analytic Notes   Analytic notes, sometimes referred to as *observer comments*, are ideas that occur to you as you write up the full field notes. These may be linkages between people in the study, theories that might serve to explain something happening in the field, or simply a judgmental observation about a participant (e.g., "The guy looked like a thug"). To make sure these are kept separate from the actual narrative, it is important to encapsulate these in brackets clearly labeled *Observer Comments*, or simply O.C. (e.g., [O.C.: this guy looked like a thug to me.]).

Subjective Reflections   Subjective reflections are a self-reflexive opportunity for you as the researcher to make personal observations and comments about feelings that you might have developed as a result of having observed some scary or personally rewarding event in the field. These may include statements about how angry something made you or how surprised you were when you learned some piece of information. Like *observer comments*, these remarks should be encapsulated in brackets, labeled *Subjective Reflections*, or S.R. (e.g., [S.R.]).

Several additional elements to include in field notes are the time and duration of the field excursion and a consistent alteration of names and places. Concerning the former, in addition to indicating the time researchers enter and exit the field, it is important to make note of the time at which conversations, events, or activities occurred throughout the field session. These temporal sequencing marks allow ethnographers to recreate more systematically the field session. With regard to the latter issue of altering the names of people and places, the point is to protect the identities of inhabitants. Toward this end, it is advisable for ethnographers to maintain a continuous list of pseudonyms assigned to every person and location recorded in their field notes. This will assist both confidentiality and systematic retrieval of data during later analysis phases of the research.

Finally, even the opinions, preconceived notions, and general feelings about certain observed situations are also legitimate entries in field notes. However, these ethnographer-originated entries should always be bracketed and identified so that they are not mistaken as actual observations or perceptions the inhabitants themselves made.

Erosion of Memory   Individuals vary in the extent and degree of accuracy with which they can remember—in detail—events and conversations witnessed during a field excursion. Through repetition, concentration, and sincere effort, the researchers' ability to retain even minute elements, such as facial grimaces, tongue clicks, and even belt-buckle ornaments, begins to increase greatly. In addition, carefully concentrating on remembering elements of observed situations assists ethnographers in maintaining their role as researchers.

Clues and Strategies for Recalling Data   Precise reproduction of every nuance of behavior, conversation, and event during a field excursion would be nice, but is impossible; however, highly accurate, detailed field notes can be produced. Novice ethnographers are frequently quite amazed to learn just how much material they can recall (over a short period of time) even without any specific training. On the other hand, studies on eyewitness reliability have demonstrated how subjective and flexible our memories can be, particularly after our time and attention have been distracted by other things.

Some field researchers use various systems of mnemonics as memory aids. Mnemonics are devices—sometimes verbal, sometimes spatial, and sometimes physical—that aid in recall. Based on the idea that people more easily remember information if it is attached to a spatial, personal, or otherwise meaningful image, mnemonics relies on associations between the material to be memorized and a construct that makes it memorable.

Many people, for example, use some variation on the following common mnemonic device to remember how many days are in each month of the year:

Thirty days hath September,

April, June, and November;

All the rest have thirty-one

Excepting February alone:

Which hath but twenty-eight, in fine,

Till leap year gives it twenty-nine.

Mnemonics may also take the form of acronyms (words formed out of the initial letters of other words). For example, many of us recall from our elementary school days learning the name ROY G. BIV as a mnemonic device for remembering the color spectrum (red, orange, yellow, green, blue, indigo, and violet). For no good reason at all, I still remember the episode of *Monk* where the dying man's last words were "girls can't eat ten pizzas." (He had been run down by a car with license plate GCE 10P.) It's been years since I saw that episode.

Some ethnographic researchers develop various mnemonic devices in order to remember how people looked, the description of settings, and so forth. These various devices serve as memory triggers to help the researcher recall nuances of his or her observations when he or she sits down to draft full field notes. It is also important to note, as Stommel and Wills (2004) similarly state, that while field notes usually contain short accurate and characteristic remarks overheard by the investigator, field notes are not a verbatim transcription of long conversations, in the same way a written transcript of a formal interview will be.

Of course, as they gain experience, ethnographers tend to develop their own cryptic note-taking styles for use in the field. Nonetheless, several general suggestions can be offered to novice ethnographers to facilitate their recollection of events that occur during a field session. Some suggestions have been implied or mentioned previously in this chapter and are summarized here for the sake of convenience.

1. *Record key words and key phrases while in the field.* It would be ill advised to try to stop the participants in a conversation and attempt to write down their every word. It would also be distracting to pull out a tape recorder and place it between the participants in a natural conversation. On the other hand, it may be possible during the course of their conversation to abstract certain key terms or sentences and jot these down. Whether researchers write these phrases on a napkin, the back of one's hand, or a scrap of brown paper bag is unimportant. What is important is that these phrases are taken down. It is also advisable to indicate the time the conversation occurred. Interestingly, later, in the privacy of their offices, ethnographers can usually reconstruct almost the entire conversation simply by rereading these cryptic key terms and sentences. Researchers typically will have a certain amount of memory erosion, but because of the memory-triggering effects of the key words and phrases, this erosion should be lessened.

2. *Make notes about the sequence of events.* From one perspective, activities occurring during a field session are beyond the control of the ethnographers and are consequently unstructured. However, if ethnographers gain a certain perspective, it is possible to apply a kind of pseudostructure: identifying a sequence of events. As researchers jot brief, cryptic notes, they should indicate their observed sequence of events: what occurred before the noted action, what was observed, and what occurred following this noted event. Researchers frequently find it useful, when sorting through their scraps of in-field notes, to lay them out in sequence. By rethinking the field session, following the sequence in which it actually occurred, researchers are able to recall the details and substance of even very long conversations.

3. *Limit the time you remain in the setting.* Field-note writing operates at approximately a 4:1 ratio with the time in the field. If researchers spend two hours in the field, it may require as long as eight full hours to write comprehensive field notes. Particularly for novice ethnographers, whose skill at recall may not be fully developed, only very short (15–30 minute) intervals in the field should be attempted at first. Although it is sometimes tempting to remain in the field for hours and hours, researchers must remember that in doing so, they reduce the likelihood of producing high-quality, detailed field notes.

Four hours in the field followed by one hour of writing is likely to be much less useful than the other way around.

On occasion, of course, ethnographers may be willing to forgo comprehensive notes in order to gain entry to some special event or ceremony. On these occasions, researchers actually turn off their intentional field concentration until the special event occurs. This, too, should be mentioned in the notes in order to account for the two or three hours during which nothing has been annotated in the field notes.

4. *Write the full notes immediately after exiting the field.*   Although this may seem obvious, it still needs to be mentioned. As previously indicated, erosion of memory begins immediately and progresses rapidly. The longer researchers wait to translate their cryptic notes to full notes, the greater the likelihood of contamination from erosion. It is advisable to schedule field sessions in such a manner that full notes can be written immediately after exiting the field. Even the interruption for a meal could be sufficient to flaw the full notes.

5. *Get your notes written before sharing them with others.*   Ethnographic research is often very exciting. Ethnographers frequently observe some event or conversation that so excites them that they simply need to share it with someone (often a colleague). The basic rule of thumb here is to refrain from talking; write it up and talk about it later. Besides possibly forgetting important details from a time lag before writing up notes, researchers may also accidentally embellish events. Although this embellishment may be completely unintentional, it can still flaw and contaminate otherwise important data. As long as you can limit your information sources to just the fieldwork, you can know that whatever you recall came from there. By contrast, if you have ever read a book, seen the movie based on the book, read reviews of the movie, and discussed it with friends, you would probably have a very hard time identifying which memories only related to the book.

What Complete Notes Should Look Like   Both in order to increase the systematic structure of later data retrieval and in order to ensure comprehensive detail without loss of quality, field-note pages should be standardized as much as possible. This means that every sheet of field notes should contain certain consistent elements: the time the ethnographer entered and exited the field; the date of the field session; a brief, descriptive topic label that captures the essence of the field session; and a page number.

As an illustration, consider the following field-note excerpt, which represents approximately two or three minutes in the field setting:

June 15, 2002, Longlane Beach
Time In: 10:00 A.M.
Time Out: 11:00 A.M.

TIME: 10:00 A.M. [O.C.: I arrived at the beach and found parking. It was slightly overcast out and gray—June gloom—as many locals called it.] I exited my car and walked toward the pier. There were many empty stalls near the pier and only a few cars pulling in. I walked up a set of cement steps to the wooden pier. The pier stretched for about a quarter of a mile into the ocean and was about 20 feet wide. At the end of the pier was a fast-food restaurant called Jaspers. I could see several people standing at the end of the pier fishing.

There were no people standing along the railings toward my end of the pier, but a tall, very slim man in his early forties had just exited the public bathrooms located at the base of the pier, about 12 feet from where I stood. He walked swiftly toward and then past me. He was wearing a bright orange tank top and black narrow Speedo trunks. His hair was graying and thin; his face was long and narrow and was punctuated by a huge, gray mustache that flowed into double-turned handlebars at each end. Around his waist he wore a fanny-pack that bounced as he moved toward Jaspers at the end of the pier. On his feet the man wore water socks with a Nike swoosh on the side.

I walked toward Jaspers and was about a halfway there when I noticed a woman walking toward me (away from Jaspers). The woman, in her late twenties or early thirties, held the hand of a small boy who was screaming, "I want ice cream! I want ice cream!" Streams of tears were running down the little boy's cheeks. The boy was about three or four years old and wearing a pair of swim trunks with the Big Dog logo on it, no shirt and barefoot. The woman wore a blue cover-up (like a sarong). Her blonde hair was pulled back and held with a wooden clip. Her face was almost hidden by an oversized pair of black sunglasses. On her feet she wore black flip-flops.

As illustrated in the preceding field-note excerpt, considerable detail about the setting and the people moving around in this setting is included. As well, the notes begin with an example of how an observer comment might be included. After reading the ethnographer's full field notes, it should be possible for a person to visualize what the ethnographer saw and heard during the field session.

As an observer, you place yourself between two extremes of note-taking practices. On one side is the tendency to try to be a human video recorder, obsessively noting the color and size of everyone and everything that moves. Such a catalog of detail is unlikely to reveal much of the scene and may actually hide the important events. On the other extreme is the tendency to think like a novelist, filling in the spaces between observations with extensive personal reflections and suggestive description. You might have, at some moment, felt a chill wind like the cold hand of death, but the observable facts are simply that there was a breeze, possibly cold.

Having concluded their field sessions (the data-gathering phase of the project), ethnographers have often amassed hundreds or even thousands of pages of field notes. These field notes take up considerable space and an even longer time to read. Organizing large quantities of such notes is very time consuming and both physically and mentally exhausting. It is desirable, then, to amass these notes in some systematic fashion and perhaps even to reduce their bulk for analytic purposes.

To accomplish the dual task of keeping large quantities of field notes and reproducing them in reduced form, most researchers rely on computers. (Some people also like large pieces of paper taped to the wall.) There are several ways one can make use of computers when developing field notes. The most obvious is to use any commercial word-processing program. Word-processing programs are designed to handle, store, and retrieve textual material or, in this case, data. One can use just about any word processor to store notes, add annotations, search for phrases, highlight key phrases, and replace real names with pseudonyms. Alternately, one might choose one of the commercial programs designed for qualitative data storage and analysis (see, e.g., Dennis, 1984; Kikooma, 2010; Tallerico, 1991). These programs provide a structure into which novice researchers can pour their field notes, annotate, code, and edit. More importantly, data analysis software allows one to run reports highlighting associations between concepts, frequently used terms, and quantitative summaries of types of events. As well, all computer applications provide a method by which to efficiently create a duplicate set or a data-reduced set of field notes, to share the data among collaborators, to apply password protection to the data, and to archive the entire project when complete without the use of a file cabinet.

You must be cautious when reducing qualitative data such as field notes. If you reduce too much, details and nuance of the data may be lost, impairing if not ruining the analysis (Patton, 2002). As well, some studies will require greater amounts of detail than others. In these cases, field notes will need to be kept closer to their original form. In most cases, however, various aspects of field notes may be redundant. For example, descriptions of the same individuals, locations, and settings need not be reproduced in full every time they arise. Researchers may find it better to briefly summarize such material or cite it only once. Similarly, many researchers find it more effective for analytical purposes to create a set of summarized field notes that is keyed or cross-indexed to its original lengthier versions. Thus, two or three pages of notes may be reproduced to perhaps a half page of summary. Because the full notes are cross-indexed to this summary, the researcher can fairly easily retrieve these lengthier versions during analysis.

Computers and Ethnography

It seems safe to say that qualitative researchers have been slower than their quantitative counterparts to take advantage of the technological benefits afforded by computers and the Internet. As suggested here and in Chapter 4, qualitative researchers are now seemingly making up for lost time.

With new types of computing media provided by the Web, CD-ROMs, flashdrives, high-speed DSL, and public WiFi, a new world has opened to ethnographers. It may be, as Mason and Dicks (1996) once suggested, that *hypermedia ethnography* is the new frontier.

This new hypermedia ethnography can permit ethnographers to include the full gamut of what Spradley (1979) had called the *ethnographic record*: photographs, music, field notes, interview data, digital video, documents, and so forth. Computer technologies allow the ethnographer to bridge the gaps that exist between audio, visual, and written documentation of field events. Hypermedia potentially allows the ethnographer to produce more richly textured and at the same time more accessible (in the broadest sense of this term) narrative reports, complete with an assortment of links among data, analysis, and interpretative and supportive texts that might comment on the analysis (Gibbs, Friese, & Mangabeira, 2002).

Online Ethnography

Researchers also use computer systems to explore online social worlds, such as interactive multiplayer games, wikis, blogs and discussion boards, and other social media. The concept of online ethnography is quite interesting since one can view it as describing *places that are not places* (Rutter & Smith, 2005, p. 84). The fodder of online ethnographers is largely composed of locations occupied by disembodied persons, and *observations* are based on communication within networks. Certainly, for the ethnographer, there is no obvious place to *go* where he or she may carry out what we understand today as fieldwork (physically watching, listening, and recoding persons, places, and practices). There is no literal *getting your hands dirty with data* as many of the old anthropologists and street ethnographers used to talk about doing when conducting research out in the field. Instead, online ethnographers can conduct their field work from the privacy of their office or home (or even while sitting on a beach if they have broadband Internet connectivity and a laptop computer).

Online ethnography is similar in many respects to traditional ethnography and different in some crucial ways. Certainly, the act of looking over some people's posted comments offers far less data for an ethnographer than even such mundane events as meeting the people in question or looking at them while they speak. Yet, online social media offer numerous forms of social interactions and relations that only occur in cyberspace. So the intrepid social scientist must go where the interactions are.

The Internet is a technological innovation linked to social life and cultures—a variety of mainstream and subcultural groups. Access to these subcultures has clear implications for the study of practices and patterns of expression, ways of thinking, and even how people are likely to behave. Williams (2006), for example, undertook an online ethnography to examines the relative roles of music and the Internet for self-identifying members of the straightedge youth subculture. As Williams (2006) suggests, this youthful subculture (the straightedge) has been around for nearly 30 years, and has been conceptualized primarily by their music and styles of dress. However, because it is a fairly closely knit group of insiders, it had been difficult to undertake research on this subcultural group—until recently, with the advances in online communications, including the sale, use, and transfer of music over the Internet. Access to online sites frequented by members of the straightedge subculture has increased, providing a means for outsiders (online ethnographers) to participate with members that might not otherwise have been possible.

What is particularly interesting about using the orientation of an online ethnographer is that it uniquely allows one to study everyday experiences and forms of cultural life as they occur on a global level (Wilson, 2006). Distance, from the perspective of the Internet, is meaningless. Further, the cost for undertaking Internet-based ethnography is enormously less than were one to seek a similar data collection using traditional, on-the-scene type of a data collection. While cost is a real factor in research, and inexpensive access can be a boon, there is also the danger that many researchers will turn to online studies merely as a response to tight budgets, thereby masking the true cost of lost research opportunities and ethnographic studies that must be shelved.

Like more traditional ethnographic studies, online ethnographies may extend over a period of days, weeks, or even months and beyond. Information may be gleaned from a variety of sources, including blogs, diaries, digital photographs, explanations and stories about photographs, stories, poems, and even informal interviews—or prompts about specific actions. If you are sitting there reading this and thinking, "hey, those are pretty much the types of data one might collect in an on-the-site data collection," you are correct. If you are thinking, "wow, I could do fieldwork without having to go anywhere," you are also correct, but possibly missing the point of being in the field.

At one level, online ethnographic research is simply ethnographic research. Perhaps the largest differences between the two (traditional and online ethnography) is the means by which the research accesses the data and the *reach* of the investigator. With traditional ethnography, the investigator is pretty much limited to the on-site location where he or she gathers the data. With online ethnography, the researcher can reach diverse populations all involved in similar types of groups, in distant locations across the country or the globe. But in this case, one is limited to the types of data that someone has bothered to put online, which is a great deal less than what one can observe in a physical space.

Analyzing Ethnographic Data

Analysis of data is not an exact science. With some types of data (particularly survey questionnaire data), there are many different ways to make sense of the information once the data are collected, organized, and coded. However, when dealing with ethnographic data, researchers must make somewhat narrower choices. For example, even though it is certainly possible to test hypotheses using ethnographic data, the process differs somewhat from research that uses quantitative data. Ethnographic research can potentially demonstrate the plausibility of a hypothesis, but it cannot actually prove its validity. Using reductionistic procedures to cull numbers from the ethnographic data is not really in keeping with the ethnographic process. Nor is it the best way to generate numbers. Thus, two effective ways remain to analyze ethnographic research while preserving the rich textual detail of the data: inductive content analysis and ethnographic narrative accounts.

Systematic analysis of ethnographic data typically begins by reading the field notes—whether one wants to produce ethnographic accounts or a content analysis of the data. The purposes of this initial reading of the notes are to reinforce any hypotheses or themes developed during the data-collection phase and to generate new hypotheses and themes previously unrealized—in short, to ground themes and hypotheses to the data (Glaser & Strauss, 1967). During this initial coding, researchers undertake what is called *open coding* (explained comprehensively in Chapter 11). Briefly, open coding allows researchers to identify and even extract themes, topics, or issues in a systematic manner.

Next, ethnographers should begin to notice and systematically create records of patterns in the conversations and activities of people depicted in the notes. This *coding* process is also discussed more elaborately in Chapter 11.

At this juncture, the researchers must decide whether to undertake a comprehensive content analysis or to rely on lengthy textual accounts to document themes and patterns observed in the data. In the first instance, researchers may easily accomplish a comprehensive content analysis, but if the second, conceptual stance is taken, the researchers must demonstrate topics and patterns by presenting appropriate (and often lengthy) narrative textual accounts from the field notes.

As with all analytic strategies, strengths and weaknesses are associated with each approach. The most important problem commonly associated with qualitative data of any type is the question of confidence in the accuracy of suggested patterns. In the case of content analysis, researchers might manage to convince their audience by suggesting the consistency (frequency) of a given theme or pattern (see Chapter 11). In the case of ethnographic narratives, researchers must rely on the pattern being sufficiently clear in itself (as presented in the field notes) to convince an audience of its accuracy (Stoddart, 1986).

T. F. Burns (1980) illustrated how one effectively uses ethnographic narrative accounts in his "Getting Rowdy with the Boys." Burns offered a detailed examination of the drinking behavior of a single group of young working-class males. His procedure involved describing the sequence of events and interactions experienced by these young men during one evening in several different drinking environments. As Burns indicated, his analysis of the ethnographic narrative account offered may be termed *thick description* (Geertz, 1973). This type of analysis is directed toward drawing out a complete picture of the observed events, the actors involved, the rules associated with certain activities, and the social contexts in which these elements arise. Burns (1980) accomplished this by first presenting the narration (chiefly the detailed field notes of his ethnographic experience during the observed evening). Next, Burns stepped out of the field and, in his role as a social scientist, analyzed the narrative contents, highlighting apparent structural components of situations, meanings suggested by actors and events, and patterns that emerge during the course of the narrative.

Katherine Chen adopted a mixed methods approach to her "organizational ethnography" of the organization behind the Burning Man arts event. In addition to attending nine annual Burning man events as a participant observer, Chen immersed herself in the related events and discussions of the Burning Man community throughout the year. After describing her participant observation sites, interviews, and "concentrated observation" opportunities, she listed some of the other fieldwork activities (Chen, 2009, p. 157):

> In addition, I observed and participated in year-round formal and informal Burning Man-related events, such as town hall meetings, gallery openings, fund-raisers, performances, and parties for volunteers and participants in the San Francisco Bay area and in the Reno area of Nevada.... I also observed two meetings between Burning Man organizers and federal and local officials in Nevada.... I also monitored a constant stream of e-mails and electronic newsletters. I followed eight years of *Jack Rabbit Speaks*, the official e-mail newsletter that disseminates communication from the Burning Man organization to a large audience of subscribed readers. Departmental and theme camp e-mail lists, which often included exchanges among subscribers, recounted organizers' and volunteers' perspectives on issues, activities, and relevant information. I examined eight years of the Media Mecca list, six months of the Tech team list, four years of the Burning Man staff list, and one or two years of theme camps lists.

Other Analysis Strategies: Typologies, Sociograms, and Metaphors

Data analysis is an interesting and creative part of the research process. Ethnographic data lend themselves to several different methods of interpretation and analysis beyond strict content analysis techniques. Some of these techniques include *typologies*, *sociograms*, and *metaphors*. Each of these is briefly discussed next.

Typologies

A *typology* is a systematic method for classifying similar events, actions, objects, people, or places, into discrete groupings. For example, McSkimming and Berg (1996) did a study of gambling and gaming in rural American taverns. After more than six months of observations in the field, they found four major types of tavern patrons:

1. *Regular drinking patrons.* These individuals regularly sat at the bar and chatted among themselves as they consumed several alcoholic beverages. They were highly in-group oriented and would not speak with outsiders (transient patrons).

2. *Regular gaming patrons.*   These individuals sporadically consumed alcoholic beverages but primarily socialized with others involved mostly in playing darts or billiards.
3. *Regular gambling patrons.*   These individuals sporadically consumed alcoholic beverages and involved themselves in darts and/or billiards. A primary distinction between these and gaming patrons was that gambling patrons regularly placed wagers (of cash, drinks, or other valuable items) against the outcome of a dart or billiard game.
4. *Transient patrons.*   These individuals drifted into and out of the tavern scene, sometimes returning for a second or occasionally a third visit but not with any sort of regular pattern of attendance. Transient patrons were excluded from conversations among regular drinking patrons but were permitted to game and gamble occasionally with others.

McSkimming and Berg's typology permitted them to see various distinctions among the people who frequented the tavern. For example, regular drinkers were more interested in *maintaining friendships* with one another and discussing family activities than with establishing new friendships or light social banter. Such observations permitted McSkimming and Berg to better understand some of the social roles and interaction patterns they observed among people moving through the social world of the tavern.

Not all typologies are textually based. Again, owing to changes in technology and a growing emphasis in visual ethnography or photoethnography (Pink, 2001; Schwartz & Jacobs, 1997), some typologies are photographically based. For example, in a study by Kephart and Berg (2002) the researchers examined 452 photographs of graffiti created by gangs in a city in southern California. After carefully examining each photo for patterns of similarity or dissimilarity, they sorted the pictures into five groups: (1) Publicity Graffiti (spreading the gang's name); (2) Roll Call Graffiti (listing the names of the members of the gang); (3) Territorial Graffiti (the name of the gang in specific locations identifying turf); (4) Threatening Graffiti (specific threats toward other gangs or individuals); and (5) Sympathetic Graffiti (condolences to gang members and their families upon deaths).

Typically, researchers follow a basic three-step guideline for developing typologies. First, they assess the collected material and then seek out mutually exclusive categories. Second, researchers make sure that all of the elements being classified have been accounted for (an exhaustive grouping of elements). Third, researchers examine the categories and their contents and make theoretically meaningful appraisals. The use of mutually exclusive categories assures that every element being considered appears only in a single category. But, to be exhaustive, each element needs to be placed into one or another of these categories. Ideally, one can achieve both of these traits, though frequently the data do not divide so neatly. A theoretically meaningful appraisal does not necessarily mean that you link your observations to lofty theories such as Durkheim's theory of *anomie*. Rather, it simply means that there is an attempt to attach some social meaning to the way things fall into categories in your typology.

Although typologies may seem like oversimplification of social life, this is actually their beauty. They permit the researcher to present data in an organized and simple fashion, allowing the reader to better understand the explanations offered as interpretation and analysis of the typology scheme. A major goal of typologies, then, is to provide additional understanding of the material collected during the course of the research.

Sociograms

Sociograms are part of a larger group of techniques known as *sociometry*. These procedures allow the researcher to make assessments about the degree of affinity or disdain that members of a group have toward one another. Thus, they allow you to consider friendship patterns, social networks, work relationships, and social distance in general. Sociometry can be described as a means of assessing group relational structures such as hierarchies, friendship networks, and cliques. Sociograms, then, are graphic displays of how close people are to one another based on responses to a sociometric test. A sociometric test typically includes three basic characteristics:

1. Specific number of choices are used (varying with the size of the group).
2. Specific number of choices are allowed (varying according to the functions and/or activities of the groups tested).
3. Levels of preference are assigned to each choice.

Positive Peer Nominations   The early users of sociometric tests typically employed a *peer nomination* version of this test. In this procedure, the group members were asked to name three or more peers whom they liked the most, or whom they best liked working with, or who were their best friends (depending on the kind of group). A group member's score was then computed as the number of nominations he or she received from other members of the group. This version of the sociometric test is called *positive peer nominations*. As users of sociometric tests refined these procedures, adaptations naturally arose.

Negative Peer Nominations   One such adaptation to peer nominations initially was introduced by Dunnington (1957) and again by Moore and Updergraff (1964). This adaptation involved a request for negative nominations. In other words, in addition to asking for three especially liked peers, a second request was made that members identify the three peers least liked (or least desirable to work with). This strategy was used to identify two groups of peers—namely, a *popular group* (high frequency of positive nominations) and a disliked or *rejected group* (high frequency of negative nominations). Subsequent research in which juveniles are identified as members of these groups indicates that rejected children often are more aggressive and likely to engage in antisocial behavior (Dodge, Cole, & Brakke, 1982; Hartup, Glazer, & Charlesworth, 1967). This suggests significant utility for those interested in studying delinquents, youth movements, school cliques, and even gang structures.

Peer Rating Procedures   Another adaptation that has come into common use is the *peer rating procedure*, a sociometric test similar in many ways to the nomination procedure. Group members respond to the usual sociometric questions (Who do you like to work with? Be with? etc.) for every other member of the group. Each group member is given a list containing the names of all group members and asked to rate every other member using a five-point Likert-like scale. The scale for these five points is typically a graduated series of statements that moves from expressions of favor to expressions of disfavor for members of the group. An example of this sort of scale is shown in Figure 6.1. As in traditional Likert scales, you assess the mean rating score for each person. A mean rating in the low range indicates that the group member is not well liked by others in the group. A mean rating in the high range indicates that the group member is well liked. As Jennings (1948) warned, however, identification of this sociometric pattern *is not* the completion of the research but only the beginning. The use of mathematics to locate sociometric stars, then, should not be overemphasized. It is a convenient tool but not the substantive result of research.

Once you have identified the social relations and social structures that exist, you still must examine the incumbents of positions in this structure. Assisted by the sociometric information, you are better equipped to locate appropriate guides, informants, and gatekeepers of the group. Thus, you might begin an investigation with a sociometric survey and then pursue the research through other ethnographic field techniques, interviews, or even unobtrusive measures. Sociometric choice tests, then, provide yet another line of action you can use in a triangulated research design.

Figure 6.1 A Sample Sociometric Assessment

(Question/Choices)
Directions: On a separate sheet, write the name of everyone in your group or organization. Read the following paragraphs and place their corresponding numbers in front of every name for which they apply. You may use the number 1 only once, and please place only a single number by each name. By your own name, please place a zero.

My Very Best Friend
1. I would like to have this person as one of my very best friends. I would like to spend a great deal of time with this person. I think I could tell some of my problems and concerns to this person, and I would do everything I could to help this person with his or her problems and concerns. I will give a number 1 to my very best friend.

My Other Friend(s)
2. I would enjoy working and doing things with this person. I would invite this person to a party in my home, and I would enjoy going places with this person and our other friends. I would like to talk and do a variety of things with this person and to be with this person often. I want this person to be one of my friends. I will give a number 2 to every person who is my friend.

I Do Not Know This Person
3. I do not know this person very well. Maybe I would like this person if I got to know him or her; maybe I would not. I do not know whether I would like to spend time or work with this person. I will place a number 3 in front of the name of every person I do not know very well.

I Do Not Care for This Person
4. I will greet this person when I see him or her around school or in a store, but I do not enjoy being around this person. I might spend some time with this person–if I had nothing to do, or I had a social obligation to attend where this person also was in attendance. I do not care for this person very much. I will place a number 4 in front of the name of every person I do not care for very much.

I Dislike This Person
5. I speak to this person only when it is necessary. I do not like to work or spend time with this person. I avoid serving on the same groups or committees with this person. I will place a number 5 in front of the name of every person I do not like.

Mapping and the Creation of Sociograms Another way you can create sociograms is to do them in the field. In this case, you use direct observations of individuals and objects as they are arranged in the setting. Essentially, this involves the creation of social/environmental maps and, from these, sociograms.

This strategy of sociometric mapping depends on a fairly stable setting, and as such, it is not always applicable. Often, this type of sociometric mapping is used in social-psychological applications of organizational research. For example, how executives place themselves around a meeting table may be mapped and may delineate power and informal influence structures. By knowing this information, a researcher (or executive) can interrupt or weaken the amount of influence emanating from certain segments of the members. For instance, by placing himself or herself or a nonmember of some informal influence clique among several actual members, he or she can affect the ability of those members to wield influence and authority during a board meeting.

Similarly, knowledge about sociometric body language and even furniture placement can influence interactions. For example, when you enter someone's office, how is it arranged? Is there a chair near the desk, inviting you to sit near the desk's occupant? Or is the chair far from the desk, perhaps across the room, requiring a guest to physically move it to be near the desk's occupant? Usually, when you move furniture in another person's office, you must first ask permission. Thus, tacitly, you hold a subordinate role in the relationship. Alternately, you might choose to stand while the other party sits. This, of course, immediately shifts the power structure to the seated occupant of the office because he or she is able to leave you standing or suggest you pull up a chair. This situation is also somewhat reminiscent of school days, when one was called before the school's principal to stand, at the foot of the desk, being scolded.

The arrangement of people and objects in a setting may have an impact on interactions and relationships. This, in turn, can be a useful tool in research. This type of applied sociometric strategy frequently begins with a *mapping* of the setting. This sort of mapping is also useful in other types of institutional investigations. For example, it could prove useful in a study of how inmates use environmental space in a prison or a study of the effect of environmental design on inmates. Alternatively, it might prove fruitful in an examination of how children use and perhaps territorially divide playground space. It might even be useful in a study of a game arcade located in some mall or in similar studies of leisure-time activities in amusement parks. Again, sociometric strategies are extremely flexible. They are limited only by your imagination.

To describe how you might develop the sort of sociometric maps just discussed, let us assume an investigator wants to study some group of youths in a particular neighborhood. One way to begin this task is to create a drawing or *map* of the setting. All the stable physical elements observed in the setting (e.g., access ways, trees and shrubs, buildings, stores, street lamps) should be included in this map. The original version of the map should be saved and copied so that every time the researcher enters the field, he or she can work on a fresh map.

While in the field, the researcher can add symbols to represent individuals, dyads (groups of two), triads (groups of three), gender, leadership roles, and so forth. Over time, and by assessing the successive annotated maps and actual field notes, the researcher will be able to identify the stars and any satellite cliques that constitute the groups under study. Stars will become apparent *over time* when you use observation to create a sociogram. Typically, you find only one or two stars in a given group. Even when you locate several stars, typically one will demonstrate himself or herself to hold some degree of influence over the others.

Satellite cliques are sometimes mistaken as representing a star and his or her followers. In fact, satellite cliques usually contain several members influenced by what appears to be a single individual. However, this individual frequently is himself or herself influenced by a more centralized star.

Sociometric maps also can assist the investigator in understanding how a group uses its environmental space and maintains territorial control over areas, the locus of control in various power and influence arrangements, and the social space (proximity) between different members and nonmembers of the group(s).

Metaphors

Another analytic strategy is to use metaphors (Bailey, 1996, 2006; Becker, 1998). *Metaphors* are descriptions that reveal aspects of the subject through comparison with other subjects, such as Max Weber's famous term "the iron cage" for bureaucracy. Identifying a metaphor that fits some aspect of your setting or your study population can help you see things in a different way. Begin by asking, "What does this situation or circumstance seem to be?" "What else is it like?" "What does it remind me of?" Trying to come up with an appropriate metaphor is a good exercise for reflecting on the material and data you have already collected and begun to interpret and analyze. It also will require you to consider these data from different conceptual angles than you might otherwise have used.

For example, some critics suggest that police arrest suspects, only to have the courts let them go (on bail, for example) by using the phrase *revolving door* justice. Metaphors provide an avenue to see important elements of social support, interaction, networking, relationships, and a variety of other socially significant factors, and allow the researcher to represent action when theorizing about various explanations or relationships.

Disengaging: Getting Out

Although it is certainly possible to maintain complete professional distance when distributing questionnaires to anonymous subjects, it is not as easy during ethnography. Because relationships are virtually the stock and trade of a good ethnographer, care must be taken when leaving the field.

Exiting any field setting involves at least two separate operations: first, the physical removal of the researchers from the research setting and, second, emotional disengagement from the relationships developed during the field experience. In some situations *getting out* is described as a kind of mechanical operation, devoid of any (personal) emotional attachments on the part of the ethnographer. Concern is sometimes shown, and efforts made, to avoid distressing a research community. However, negative repercussions can occur in the forms of possible effects on the group(s) as a whole or with the possible reception future field investigators might expect (Morris, 2006; Shaffir, Stebbins, & Turowetz, 1980).

Even when the emotions of field relationships are mentioned, they are frequently described exclusively as concern over the perspective of the inhabitant of the natural setting. For example, Shaffir et al. (1980, p. 259) state the following:

> Personal commitments to those we study often accompany our research activity. Subjects often expect us to continue to live up to such commitments permanently. On completing the research, however, our commitment subsides and is often quickly overshadowed by other considerations shaping our day-to-day lives. When our subjects become aware of our diminished interest in their lives and situations, they may come to feel cheated—manipulated and duped.

The point is not to underplay the possible emotional harm a callous investigator might cause a research group, but it should be noted that relationships are two-way streets. Subjects make personal emotional commitments, and so, too, do many researchers—even without actually bonding (Nagy Hesse-Biber & Leavy, 2006). Often, when researchers leave the field, they have developed some deep feelings for their subjects. These feelings may not always be positive but are nonetheless psychologically affecting.

Ethnographers can certainly absent themselves from the field and simply dismiss the subjects from their minds, but it is likely that the ethnographers will continue to hold at least some proprietary interest in the welfare of the subjects. For example, during the course of conducting the research discussed in Carpenter and colleagues (1988), the ethnographers commonly spoke about "their" kids with almost parental concern or, on occasion, with almost parental pride in certain accomplishments.

A strong commitment and attachment developed between many of the youthful subjects and the ethnographers. When it came time to leave the field, the ethnographers informally continued to keep an eye on many of the subjects for over a year. This essentially amounted to asking about specific kids when they accidentally ran into mutual acquaintances or getting involved in the lives of these special kids when their paths crossed by chance (e.g., in a supermarket or shopping mall). Other field investigators have indicated similar prolonged interest in research subjects, even many years after physically leaving the setting. Letkemann (1980, p. 300), for instance, indicates that even 10 years after exiting the field, and more than 800 miles away from the site, he continued to stay informed about the welfare of his subjects.

Because of the uniqueness of every field situation, there are different nuances to exiting. Ethnographers, however, must always be mindful that the time will come to leave—at least physically. Toward this end, researchers must prepare both the community members and themselves for the exit. Perhaps a quick exit will work in some cases (Rains, 1971), whereas a more gradual drifting off may be required in other circumstances (Glaser & Strauss, 1967). Unfortunately, these research-related decisions are not easily made.

TRYING IT OUT

As with all research methods, researchers must practice, stumble, and even sometimes fail to accomplish the research project in order to appreciate how ethnographic strategies operate. Several suggestions for a brief microethnographic project follow. As with the practice of interviewing strategies (see Chapter 4), these suggestions are intended as exercises, not actual research projects in themselves.

Suggestion 2   Go to your school's library or cafeteria every day at the same time for about a week. Each day, sketch a simple map (a sociogram) of the room. Include any tables, chairs, devices, and people you see each day. At the end of the week, compare the drawings, to see if any changes can be detected.

REFERENCES

Adler, P. A. (1985). *Wheeling and Dealing*. New York: Columbia University Press.

Adler, P. A., & Adler, P. (1987). *Membership Roles in Field Research*. Newbury Park, CA: Sage.

Agar, M. H. (1973). *Ripping and Running: A Formal Ethnography of Urban Heroin Addicts*. New York: Seminar Press.

Agar, M. H. (1986). *Speaking of Ethnography*. Beverly Hills, CA: Sage.

Agar, M. H. (1996). *The Professional Stranger* (2nd ed.). San Diego, CA: Academic Press.

Allen, J. D. (1986). Classroom management: Students' perspectives, goals, and strategies. *American Educational Research Journal 23*(3), 437–459.

Angrosino, M. (2007). *Doing Ethnographic and Observational Research*. London, England: Sage.

Babbie, E. (2007). *The Practice of Social Research* (11th ed.). Belmont, CA: Wadsworth.

Bailey, C. A. (1996). *A Guide to Field Research*. Thousand Oaks, CA: Pine Forge Press.

Bailey, C. A. (2006). *A Guide to Field Research* (2nd ed.). Thousand Oaks, CA: Pine Forge Press.

Becker, H. S. (1963). *Outsiders: Studies in the Sociology of Deviance*. New York: Free Press.

Becker, H. S. (1998). *Tricks of the Trade: How to Think About Your Research While You're Doing It*. Chicago, IL: University of Chicago Press.

Berg, B. L., Ksander, M., Loughlin, J., & Johnson, B. (August 1983). Cliques and groups: Adolescents' affective ties and criminal activities. Paper presented at the annual meeting of the Society for the Study of Social Problems, Detroit.

Bogdan, R. (1972). *Participant Observation in Organizational Settings*. Syracuse, NY: Syracuse University Press.

Bogdan, R., & Knopp Bilken, S. (2003). *Qualitative Research for Education* (4th ed.). Boston, MA: Allyn & Bacon, Inc.

Bogdan, R., & Taylor, S. (1975). *Introduction to Qualitative Research Methods*. New York: John Wiley and Sons.

Boyle, J. S. (1994). Styles of ethnography. In Janice M. Morse (Ed.), *Critical Issues in Qualitative Research Methods* (pp. 159–185). Thousand Oaks, CA: Sage.

Brewer, J. D. (1993). Sensitivity as a problem in field research: A study of routine policing in Northern Ireland. In C. M. Renzetti & R. M. Lee (Eds.), *Researching Sensitive Topics* (pp. 125–145). Newbury Park, CA: Sage.

Broadhead, R. S., & Fox, K. J. (1990). Takin' it to the streets: AIDS outreach as ethnography. *Journal of Contemporary Ethnography 19*(3), 322–348.

Brown, P. (1996). Catskill culture: The rise and fall of a Jewish resort area seen through personal narrative and ethnography. *Journal of Contemporary Ethnography 25*(1), 83–119.

Burgess, R. G. (1991a). Keeping field notes. *Field Research: A Sourcebook and Field Manual*. New York: Routledge.

Burgess, R. G. (1991b). Sponsors, gatekeepers, members, and friends: Access in educational settings. In W. B. Shaffir & R. A. Stebbins (Eds.), *Experiencing Fieldwork: An Inside View of Qualitative Research* (pp. 43–52). Newbury Park, CA: Sage.

Burns, N., & Grove, S. K. (2000). *The Practice of Nursing Research: Conduct, Critique and Utilization* (2nd ed.). Philadelphia, PA: W. B. Saunders.

Burns, T. F. (1980). Getting rowdy with the boys. *Journal of Drug Issues 80*(1), 273–286.

Calhoun, T. C. (1992). Male street hustling: Introduction processes and stigma containment. *Sociological Spectrum 12*(1), 35–52.

Carpenter, C., Glassner, B., Johnson, B., & Loughlin, J. (1988). *Kids, Drugs, and Crime.* Lexington, MA: Lexington Books.

Carspecken, P. F. (1996). *Critical Ethnography in Educational Research: A Theoretical and Practical Guide.* New York: Routledge.

Chen, K. K. (2009). *Enabling Creative Chaos: The Organization Behind the Burning Man Event.* Chicago, IL: University of Chicago Press.

Chiseri-Strater, E., & Sunstein, B. S. (2001). *Fieldworking: Reading and Writing Research* (2nd ed.). New York: St. Martin's Press.

Clifford, J. (1980). Fieldwork, reciprocity and the making of ethnographic texts: The examples of Maurice Leenhardt. *Man 15*(3), 518–532.

Creswell, J. W. (1999). *Qualitative Inquiry and Research Design: Choosing Among Five Traditions.* Thousand Oaks, CA: Sage.

Creswell, J. W. (2007). *Qualitative Inquiry and Research Design: Choosing Among Five Traditions* (2nd ed.). Thousand Oaks, CA: Sage.

Cromwell, P., & Nielsen, A. L. (1999). *In Their Own Words: Criminals on Crime.* Los Angeles, CA: Roxbury Publishing.

Dennis, D. L. (1984). Word crunching: An annotated bibliography on computers and qualitative data analysis. *Qualitative Sociology 7*(1–2), 148–156.

Denzin, N. K. (1970). *Sociological Methods: A Sourcebook.* Chicago, IL: Aldine.

Denzin, N., & Lincoln, Y. S. (2005). *The Sage Handbook of Qualitative Research* (3rd ed.). Thousand Oaks, CA: Sage.

Dodge, K. A., Cole, J. D., & Brakke, N. P. (1982). Behavioral patterns of socially rejected and neglected adolescents: The roles of social approach and aggression. *Journal of Abnormal Child Psychology 10*, 389–410.

Dunnington, M. J. (1957). Behavioral differences of sociometric status groups in a nursery school. *Child Development 28*(1), 103–111.

Ellen, R. F. (1984). *Ethnographic Research.* New York: Academic Press.

Ellen, R. F. (1987). *Ethnographic Research* (2nd ed.). New York: Academic Press.

Ellis, C., & Bochner, A. P. (Eds.) (1996). *Composing Ethnography: Alternative Forms of Qualitative Writing.* Walnut Creek, CA: Alta Mira.

Feldman, M., Bell, J., & Berger, M. T. (2003). *Gaining Access: A Practical and Theoretical Guide for Qualitative Researchers.* Walnut Creek, CA: Altamira Press.

Fenwick, J., Barclay, L., & Schmied, V. (June 1999). Activities and interactions in level II nurseries: A report of an ethnographic study. *Journal of Perinatal & Neonatal Nursing 13*(1), 53.

Ferrell, J., (2006). Criminological verstehen: Inside the immediacy of crime. In J. M. Miller & R. Tewksbury (Eds.), *Research Methods: A Qualitative Reader.* Upper Saddle River, NJ: Pearson/Prentice Hall.

Ferrell, J., & Hamm, M. S. (1998). *Ethnography at the Edge: Crime, Deviance, and Field Research.* Boston, MA: Northeastern University Press.

Fetterman, D. M. (1989). *Ethnography: Step by Step.* Newbury Park, CA: Sage.

Geertz, C. (1973). Thick description: Toward an interpretive theory of culture. In C. Geertz (Ed.), *The Interpretation of Culture* (pp. 3–30). New York: Basic Books.

Gibbs, G. R. (2007). *Analyzing Qualitative Data.* Los Angeles, CA: Sage.

Gibbs, G. R., Friese, S., & Mangabeira, W. C. (May 2002). The use of technology in qualitative research. Introduction to issue 3(2) of Forum Qualitative Social Research. Available online at www.qualitative-research.net/fqs/fqs-eng.htm.

Glaser, B. G., & Strauss, A. (1967). *The Discovery of Grounded Theory: Strategies for Qualitative Research*. Chicago, IL: Aldine.

Goodall, H. L. (2000). *Writing the New Ethnography*. Lanham, MD: Alta Mira Press.

Guy, R. F., Edgley, C. E., Arafat, I., & Allen, D. E. (1987). *Social Research Methods*. Boston, MA: Allyn and Bacon.

Hagan, F. E. (2006). *Research Methods in Criminal Justice and Criminology* (7th ed.). Boston, MA: Allyn and Bacon.

Hammer, R. (2002). *Antifeminism and Family Terrorism: A Critical Feminist Perspective*. Lanham, MD: Rowman & Littlefield.

Hammersley, M., & Atkinson, P. (2007). *Ethnography: Principles in Practice* (3rd ed.). New York: Routledge.

Hart, C. H., & Sheehan, R. (1986). Preschoolers' play behavior in outdoor environments: Effects of traditional and contemporary playgrounds. *American Educational Research Journal 23*(4), 668–678.

Hartup, W. W., Glazer, J. A., & Charlesworth, R. (1967). Peer reinforcement and sociometric status. *Child Development 38*(4), 1017–1024.

Hertz, R. (1997). Introduction: Reflexivity and voice. *Reflexivity and Voice*. Thousand Oaks, CA: Sage.

Hertz, R., & Imber, J. B. (1993). Fieldwork in elite settings (Introduction). *Journal of Contemporary Ethnography 22*(1), 3–6.

Horowitz, R. (1983). *Honor and the American Dream: Culture and Identity in a Chicano Community*. New Brunswick, NJ: Rutgers University Press.

Howell, N. (1990). *Surviving Fieldwork: A Report of the Advisory Panel on Health and Safety in Fieldwork*. Washington, DC: American Anthropological Association.

Janesick, V. J. (1994). The dance of qualitative research design. In N. K. Denzin & Y. S. Lincoln (Eds.), *Handbook of Qualitative Research*. Thousand Oaks, CA: Sage.

Janesick, V. J. (2003). The choreography of qualitative research design. In N. K. Denzin & Y. S. Lincoln (Eds.), *Strategies of Qualitative Inquiry* (2nd ed., pp. 46–79). Thousand Oaks, CA: Sage.

Jennings, H. H. (1948). *Sociometry in Group Relations*. Washington, DC: American Council on Education.

Johnson, B., Goldstein, P. J., Preble, E., Schmeidler, J., Lipton, D. S., Spunt, B., & Miller, T. (1985). *Taking Care of Business*. Lexington, MA: Lexington Books.

Johnson, J. M. (1975). *Doing Field Research*. New York: Free Press.

Johnson, J. C. (1990). *Selecting Ethnographic Informants*. Newbury Park, CA: Sage.

Jones, R. (1995). Prison as a hidden social world. *Journal of Contemporary Criminal Justice 11*(2), 106–118.

Kephart, T., & Berg, B. L. (March 2002). Gang graffiti analysis: A methodological model for data collection. Paper presented at the annual meeting of the Academy of Criminal Justice Sciences, Anaheim, CA.

Lee, R. M. (2001). *Dangerous Fieldwork*. Thousand Oaks, CA: Sage.

Kikooma, J. (2010). Using qualitative data analysis software in a social constructionist study of entrepreneurship. *Qualitative Research Journal 10*(1), 40–51.

Leedy, P. D., & J. E. Ormrod. (2005). *Practical Research: Planning and Design*. Upper Saddle River, NJ: Pearson/Prentice Hall.

Lee-Treweek, G., & Linkogle, S. (2000). *Dangers in the Field: Ethics and Risks in Social Research*. New York: Routledge.

Leinen, S. (1993). *Gay Cops*. New Brunswick, NJ: Rutgers University Press.

Leininger, M. (Ed.). (1985). *Qualitative Research Methods in Nursing*. Orlando, FL: Grune & Straton.

Leininger, M., & McFarlane, M. (2002). *Transcultural Nursing: Concepts, Theories, Research and Practice* (3rd ed.). New York: McGraw-Hill.

Letkemann, P. (1980). Crime as work: Leaving the field. In W. Shaffir, R. Stebbins, & A. Turowetz (Eds.), *Field Work Experience*. New York: St. Martin's Press.

Lewis-Beck, M. S., Bryman, A., & Liao, T. F. (2004). *The Sage Encyclopedia of Social Science Research Methods*. Thousand Oaks, CA: Sage.

LoBiondo-Wood, G., & Haber, J. (2002). *Nursing Research: Methods, Critical Appraisal and Utilization* (5th ed.). St. Louis, MO: Mosby.

Lofland, J. (1996). Analytic ethnography: Features, failings, and futures. *Journal of Contemporary Ethnography 24*(1), 30–67.

Lofland, J., & Lofland, L. H. (1984). *Analyzing Social Settings: A Guide to Qualitative Observation and Analysis*. Belmont, CA: Wadsworth Publishing.

Lofland, J., Snow, S., Anderson, L., & Lofland, L. H. (2006). *Analyzing Social Settings: A Guide to Qualitative Observations and Analysis* (4th ed.). Belmont, CA: Wadsworth/Thomson.

Lune, H.(2007). *Urban Action Networks: HIV/AIDS and Community Organizing in New York City*. Boulder, CO: Rowman and Littlefield.

Madison, D. S. (2005). *Critical Ethnography: Method, Ethics, and Performance*. Thousand Oaks, CA: Sage.

Mason, B., & Dicks, B. (1996). The digital ethnographer. *Cybersociology 6*. Available online at www. socio.demon.co.uk/magazine/6/dicksmason.html.

Matza, D. (1969). *Becoming Deviant*. Englewood Cliffs, NJ: Prentice Hall.

May, R. A. B. (2001). *Talking at Trena's: Everyday Conversations at an African American Tavern*. New York: New York University Press.

McGettigan, T. (2001). Field research for boneheads: From naïveté to insight on the Green Tortoise. *Sociological Research Online 6*(2). Available online at www.socres online.org.uk/6/2/mcgettigan.html.

McLean, C., & Campbell, C. (2003). Locating research informants in a multi-ethnic community: Ethnic identities, social networks and recruitment methods. *Ethnicity & Health 8*(1) 41–61.

McSkimming, M. J., & Berg, B. L. (March 1996). Methodological strategies for a rural study of tavern gambling and gaming, presented at the annual meeting of the Academy of Criminal Justice Sciences, Las Vegas.

Mehan, H. (1978). Structuring school structure. *Harvard Educational Review 48*(1), 32–64.

Miller, J. M., & Tewksbury, R. (2006). *Research Methods: A Qualitative Reader*. Upper Saddle River, NJ: Pearson/Prentice Hall.

Moore, S. G., & Updergraff, R. (1964). Sociometric status of preschool children related to age, sex, nurturance giving, and dependence. *Child Development 35*, 519–524.

Morris, T. (2006). *Social Work Research Methods*. Thousand Oaks, CA: Sage.

Morse, M. M., & Field, P. A. (1995). *Qualitative Research Methods for Health Professionals*. Thousand Oaks, CA: Sage.

Munhall, P. L. (2006). *Nursing Research* (4th ed.). Boston, MA: Jones & Bartlett Publishers.

Nagy Hesse-Biber, S., & Leavy, P. (2006). *The Practice of Qualitative Research*. Thousand Oaks, CA: Sage.

Nagy Hesse-Biber, S., Leavy, P., & Yaiser, M. L. (2004). Feminist approaches to research as a process: Reconceptulatizing epistemology, methodology, and method. In S. Reinharz (Ed.), *Feminist Perspectives on Social Research* (pp. 3–26). New York: Oxford University Press.

O'Leary, Z. (2005). *Researching Real-World Problems: A Guide to Methods of Inquiry*. Thousand Oaks, CA: Sage.

Ostrander, S. A. (1993). Surely you're not in this just to be helpful: Access, rapport, and interviews in three studies of elites. *Journal of Contemporary Ethnography 22*(1), 7–27.

Ostrander, S. A. (2004). Moderating contradictions of feminist philanthropy: Women's community organizations and the Boston Women's Fund, 1995 to 2000. *Gender and Society 18*(1), 29–46.

Patton, M. Q. (2002). *Research and Evaluation Methods* (3rd ed.). Thousand Oaks, CA: Sage.

Peshkin, A. (1986). *God's Choice: The Total World of a Fundamentalist Christian School*. Chicago, IL: University of Chicago Press.

Peterson, B. H. (1985). A qualitative clinical account and analysis of a care situation. In M. M. Leininger (Ed.), *Qualitative Research Methods in Nursing*. Orlando, FL: Grune & Stratton.

Pink, S. (2001). *Doing Visual Ethnography*. Thousand Oaks, CA: Sage.

Polit, D. F., & Hungler, B. (1995). *Nursing Research: Principles and Methods*. Philadelphia, PA: Lippincott Williams & Wilkins.

Preble, E., & Casey, J. J. (1969). Taking care of business: The heroin user's life on the street. *International Journal of Addiction 4*(1), 1–24.

Punch, M. (1986). *The Politics and Ethics of Field Work*. Newbury Park, CA: Sage.

Rains, P. (1971). *Becoming an Unwed Mother*. Chicago, IL: Aldine.

Reinharz, S. (1992). *Feminist Methods in Social Research*. New York: Oxford University Press.

Ribbens, J., & Edwards, R. (1998). *Feminist Dilemmas in Qualitative Research*. Thousand Oaks, CA: Sage.

Roethlisberger, F. J., & Dickson, W. (1939). *Management and the Worker*. Cambridge, MA: Harvard University Press.

Roper, J., & Shapira, J. (2000). *Ethnography in Nursing Research*. Thousand Oaks, CA: Sage.

Rose, D. (1990). *Living the Ethnographic Life*. Newbury Park, CA: Sage.

Rosenhan, D. L. (1973). On being sane in insane places. *Science 179*(19), 250–258.

Rossman, G. B., & Rallis, S. F. (2003). *Learning in the Field: An Introduction to Qualitative Research*. Thousand, Oaks, CA: Sage.

Rubin, H. J., & Rubin, I. S. (1995). *Qualitative Interviewing: The Art of Hearing Data*. Thousand Oaks, CA: Sage.

Rutter, J., & Smith, G. W. H. (2005). Ethnographic presence in a nebulous setting. In C. Hines (Ed.), *Virtual Methods: Issues in Social Research on the Internet*. New York: Berg Publishing.

Saukko, P. (2003). *Doing Research in Cultural Studies: An Introduction to Classical and New methodological Approaches*. Thousand, Oaks, CA: Sage.

Schwartz, H., & Jacobs, J. (1979). *Qualitative Sociology: A Method to the Madness*. New York: Free Press.

Schwartz, H., & Jacobs, J. (1997). *Qualitative Sociology: A Method to the Madness* (2nd ed.). New York: Free Press.

Shaffir, W. B., Stebbins, R. A., & Turowetz, A. (1980). *Fieldwork Experience: Qualitative Approaches to Social Research*. New York: St. Martin's Press.

Shenton, A. K., & Hayter, S. (2004). Strategies for gaining access to organizations and informants in qualitative studies. *Education for Information 22*(3–4), 223–231.

Sluka, J. A. (1990). Participant observation in violent social contexts. *Human Organization 49*(2), 114–126.

Somekh, B., & Lewin, C. (2005). *Research Methods in the Social Sciences*. Thousand Oaks, CA: Sage.

Spindler, G. (1988). *Doing the Ethnography of Schooling*. Prospect Heights, IL: Waveland Press.

Spindler, G., & Spindler, L. (1988). Roger Harker and Schonhausen: From familiar to strange and back again. In G. Spindler (Ed.), *Doing the Ethnography of Schooling*. Prospect Heights, IL: Waveland Press.

Spradley, J. P. (1979). *The Ethnographic Interview*. New York: Holt, Rinehart & Winston.

Spradley, J. P. (1980). *Participant Observation*. New York: Holt, Rinehart & Winston.

Stommel, M., & Wills, C. E. (2004). *Clinical Research: Concepts and Principles, for Advances Practice Nurses*. Philadelphia, PA: Lippincott Williams & Wilkins.

Strauss, A. L. (1987). *Qualitative Analysis for Social Scientists*. New York: Cambridge University Press.

Stoddart, K. (1986). The presentation of everyday life. Some textual strategies for adequate ethnography. *Urban Life 15*(1), 103–121.

Styles, J. (1979). Outsider/insider: Researching gay baths. *Urban Life 8*(2), 135–152.

Tallerico, M. (1991). Application of qualitative analysis software: A view from the field. *Qualitative Sociology 14*(3), 275–285.

Tedlock, B. (2000). Ethnography and ethnographic representation. In N. K. Denzin & Y. S. Lincoln (Eds.), *Handbook of Qualitative Research* (2nd ed.). Thousand Oaks, CA: Sage.

Tedlock, B. (2003). Ethnography and ethnographic representation. In N. K. Denzin & Y. S. Lincoln (Eds.), *Strategies of Qualitative Inquiry* (2nd ed., pp. 165–213). Thousand Oaks, CA: Sage.

Tewksbury, R. (1995). Cruising for sex in public places: The structure and language of men's hidden, erotic worlds. *Deviant Behavior: An Interdisciplinary Journal 17*(1), 1–19.

Tewksbury, R. (1997). Assumed and presumed identities: Problems of self-presentation in field research. *Sociological Spectrum 17*(2), 127–155.

Tewksbury, R. (2001). Acting like an insider: Studying hidden environments as a potential participant. In J. M. Miller & R. Tewksbury (Eds.), *Extreme Methods: Innovative Approaches to Social Science Research* (pp. 4–12). Boston, MA: Allyn and Bacon, Inc.

Tewksbury, R. (2002). Bathhouse intercourse: Structural and behavioral aspects of an erotic oasis. *Deviant Behavior: An Interdisciplinary Journal 23*(1), 75–112.

Tewksbury, R. (2006). Acting like an insider: Studying hidden environments as a potential participant. In J. M. Miller & R. Tewksbury (Eds.), *Research Methods* (pp. 3–12). Upper Saddle River, NJ: Pearson/Prentice Hall.

Thomas, J. (1993). *Doing Critical Ethnography*. Newbury Park, CA: Sage.

Thomas, W. I., & Swaine, D. (1928). *The Child in America*. New York: Knopf.

Vallance, R. J. (2001). Gaining access: Introducing referred approval. *Issues in Educational Research 11*(2), 65–73.

Van Maanen, J. (1982). Fieldwork on the beat. In J. Van Maanen, J. Dabbs, Jr., & R. R. Faulkner (Eds.), *Varieties of Qualitative Research*. Beverly Hills, CA: Sage.

Van Maanen, J. (1988). *Tales of the Field: On Writing Ethnography*. Chicago, IL: University of Chicago Press.

Venkatesh, S. A. (2008). *Gang Leader For a Day: A Rogue Sociologist Takes to the Streets*. New York: Penguin Press.

Verenne, H. (1988). Jocks and freaks: The symbolic structure of the expression of social interaction among American senior high school students. In G. Spindler (Ed.), *Doing the Ethnography of Schooling*. Prospect Heights, IL: Waveland Press.

Warren, C. A. B., & Karner, T. X. (2005). *Discovering Qualitative Methods: Field Research, Interviews, and Analysis*. Los Angeles, CA: Roxbury.

Wax, R. H. (1971). *Doing Fieldwork: Warnings and Advice*. Chicago, IL: University of Chicago Press.

Weppner, R. S. (1977). *Street Ethnography*. Beverly Hills, CA: Sage.

Werner, O., & Schoepfle, G. M. (1987). *Systematic Fieldwork: Foundations of Ethnography and Interviewing* (Vol. 1). Newbury Park, CA: Sage.

Whyte, W. F. (1955). *Street Corner Society*. Chicago, IL: University of Chicago Press.

Wilcox, K. (1988). Ethnography as a methodology and its applications to the study of schooling: A review. In G. Spindler (Ed.), *Doing the Ethnography of Schooling*. Prospect Heights, IL: Waveland Press.

Williams, J. P. (2006). Authentic identities: Straightedge subculture, and the Internet. *Journal of Contemporary Ethnography 35*(2), 173–200.

Williams, T., Dunlap, E., Johnson, B. D., & Hamid, A. (2001). Personal safety in dangerous places. In J. M. Miller & R. Tewksbury (Eds.), *Extreme Methods: Innovative Approaches to Social Science Research* (pp. 216–238). Boston, MA: Allyn and Bacon.

Wilson, B. (2006). Ethnography, the Internet, and youth culture: Strategies for examining social resistance and "Online-Offline" relationships. *Canadian Journal of Education 29*(1), 307–328.

Wolcott, H. F. (1973). *The Man in the Principal's Office: An Ethnography* (Reprint, 1984). Prospect Heights, IL: Waveland Press.

Wolcott, H. F. (2008). *Ethnography: A Way of Seeing* (2nd ed.). Lanham, MD: AltaMira Press.

Zigarmi, D., & Zigarmi, P. (1980). The psychological stresses of ethnographic research. *Education and Urban Society 12*(3), 291–322.

Chapter 7

Action Research

L ET'S SAY YOU HAVE been called to assist a neighborhood walk-in clinic that is interested in conducting an evaluation of its service-delivery system. Or let us assume an office of juvenile probation is interested in assessing its effectiveness working with clients. The actual problems are not known, so careful initial assessment on your part will be necessary. You are aware that understanding the clients' situations, needs, and responsibilities will emerge slowly during the course of the project. Time, however, is limited, so identifying some time-efficient research methods is essential. As well, the healthcare professionals running the clinic or the director of probation services informs you that it is critical that you include client-based perspectives in your study.

About now, you are probably thinking back to your studies on research methods and perhaps to earlier chapters in this book. What type of a research design will permit you to examine a variety of yet undetermined situational and conditionally based issues? At this point, you really don't have much more than a general idea about the research. As Chapter 2 indicates, design is an excellent place to begin, but how do you proceed? A trip to the library to consult pertinent literature is helpful for general and background information, but the literature will not provide much insight about specific conditions and situations facing the clients at the walk-in clinic you have been asked to evaluate. There may be an answer, however, to this dilemma: *action research*.

The practice of *action research* has been a fairly common mode of investigation in educational research, especially among researchers interested in classroom teaching practices and teacher education (see, e.g., Bray, Lee, Smith, & Yorks, 2000; Brown & Dowling, 1998; Burnaford, Fischer, & Hobson, 2001; Calhoun, 1994; Hendericks, 2008; Kemmis & McTaggart, 1988; Stringer, 2004, 2007a). Many sources credit Kurt Lewin (1890–1947) with coining the term *action research* in about 1934 (Mills, 2000). According to Lewin, action research is a process that "gives credence to the development of powers of reflective thought, discussion, decision and action by ordinary people participating in collective research on 'private troubles' that they have in common" (Adelman, 1993, p. 8). Today action research represents a viable, practical strategy for social studies requiring systematic, organized, and reflective investigations (Stringer, 2004, 2007a). In its present use, action research is one of the few research approaches that embrace principles of participation, reflections, empowerment, and emancipation of people and groups interested in improving their social situation or condition.

Action research (AR), sometimes called *participatory action research* (PAR), is a research framework that evolved from a number of different intellectual traditions. It can be defined as a kind of collective self-reflective enquiry undertaken by participants in social relationship with one another in order to improve some condition or situation with which they are involved. These participants include both the researcher and those stakeholders normally referred to in nonaction research as the research "subjects." Thus, it is a highly collaborative, reflective, experiential, and participatory mode of research in which all individuals involved in the study, researcher and subjects alike, are deliberate and contributing actors in the research enterprise (Gabel, 1995; Stringer & Dwyer, 2005; Wadsworth, 1998).

The origins of action research are not entirely clear. Holter and Schwartz-Barcott (1993), and more recently, Greenwood and Levin (2007), suggest that action research originated in the field of psychology with Kurt Lewin (1946), a social psychologist who was particularly interested in the concept of social change. Yet, it has also been traced to anthropological- and sociological-based community research by investigators such as William Goodenough (1963), Elton Mayo (1933), William Foote Whyte (1943, 1991), and Valach, Young, and Lynam (2002). Action research can also be found in feminist literature (see, e.g., Burman, 2004; Reid, 2000, 2004; Reinharz, 1992) and in the literature on educational change and teaching practices (e.g., Anderson, 2007; Anderson, Herr, & Nihlen, 1994; Hendericks, 2008; Kemmis & McTaggart, 1988; Stringer & Dwyer, 2005, Stringer, 2007a). Action research also shares certain goals and characteristics with what Michael Burowoy calls public sociology, which has garnered many adherents. And participatory action research has become a more common methodological framework employed in nursing research studies (e.g., Holter & Schwartz-Barcott, 1993; Jenkins et al., 2005; Polit & Beck, 2007; Stringer & Genat, 2003).

Action research has a wide range of applications in classrooms, schools, hospitals, justice agencies, and community contexts. The commonalities that draw these disciplines together in the conducting of action research are the following:

- A highly rigorous, yet reflective or interpretive, approach to empirical research
- The active engagement of individuals traditionally known as subjects as participants and contributors in the research enterprise
- The integration of some practical outcomes related to the actual lives of participants in this research project
- A spiraling of steps, each of which is composed of some type of planning, action, and evaluation.

Stated slightly differently, action research can be understood as a means or a model for enacting local, action-oriented approaches of investigation and applying small-scale theorizing to specific problems in particular situations (Reason, 1994; Stringer, 2007b). In Akihiro Ogawa's (2009) study of civil society in Japan, for example, he conducted interviews, participatory observation, and archival research within and among Japanese nonprofit organizations (NPOs) in order to understand the goals, means, and limitations of these NPOs in relation to national governmental policies. His underlying interest, however, was in the idea of civil society in a contemporary democracy. Given this focus, Ogawa felt that it was necessary to collaborate with his research subjects, helping them to identify and solve the problems that he was studying. "By underlying my research with public interest anthropology, I become committed to the democratization of knowledge in research and practice. ... My ultimate objectives as an anthropologist in doing this type of research are to help empower ordinary people and to forward the democratization of society by practicing action-oriented social research" (Ogawa, 2009, p. 19).

Action research may be thought of as a method of research carried out with a team approach that includes a researcher and members of some organization, community, or network (those who may be thought of as a stakeholder in the research effort), who collectively are seeking to improve the organization or situation of participants—in effect, where the goal of the research is not simply research for the sake of research or theory, but is an effort at creating a positive social change is the lives of the stakeholders (Greenwood & Levin, 2007).

Drawing on various traditions from which action research originates, a number of assumptions or values can be outlined. These include the following:

- The democratization of knowledge production and use
- Ethical fairness in the benefits of the knowledge generation process

- An ecological stance toward society and nature
- Appreciation of the capacity of humans to reflect, learn, and change
- A commitment to positive social change.

Johnson (2008, pp. 29–30) offers 10 descriptors intended to allow the reader to better bring action research into methodological focus. The following is an abbreviated adaptation of Johnson's descriptors:

1. *Action research is systematic.* Data can be collected, analyzed, and presented in a variety of ways, but the researcher should create a systematic way of looking at data. Thus, action research should not be understood as an *anything goes* type of methodology. Nor is it simply a matter of describing what the researcher thinks about some issue or explaining a pedagogical method that works well in a classroom. Action research is a planned, methodical observation related to one's study focus.

2. *You do not start with an answer.* An assumption underlying any research is that you do not begin *a priori* knowing what you will find through the research before you start. You must begin as an unbiased observer. After all, if you already know the answers, why do the research?

3. *An action research study does not have to be complicated or elaborate to be rigorous or effective.* Many beginning action researchers make the mistake of creating overly thick descriptions of every detail of their study in an attempt to be rigorous. This may be equated with *attempting to shoot rabbits with a cannon!* If the researcher includes too much detail about the methods, it may become methodologically top-heavy, complex, and confused; this may detract from the reader understanding what was actually being sought in the research or what may have been learned. A well-organized, concise description of the study methods is preferable to a confusing complicated description.

4. *You must plan your study adequately before you begin to collect data.* As described in Chapter 2, having a clear plan for conducting your research provides a means for an effective systematic inquiry. The novice researcher should also recognize, however, that the best laid plans may need to change and should be flexible enough to accommodate the various changes that may occur during the course of the research.

5. *Action research projects vary in length.* The length of a data collection in an action research project, as in any study, is determined based on your questions, the nature of the inquiry, the research setting, and any formal parameters to your study and data collections (e.g., a master's thesis, where data will only be collected during a single semester's time-frame; or where costs may affect one's data collection time).

6. *Observations should be regular, but they do not necessarily have to be long.* As suggested in Chapter 6, in any type of field research endeavor, the less experienced a researcher is, the shorter the periods of time should be initially when undertaking observations in the field. Thus, five minutes at a time may be sufficient at first, until the researcher becomes more familiar and comfortable with entering the field to gather data. Gradually, more time may be added to the amount of time spent in the field. While observations need not be long, they do need to be undertaken on a consistent, intentionally planned schedule.

7. *Action research projects exist on a continuum from simple and informal to detailed and formal.* As with other methodological frameworks, some studies will be short, deliberate, and simple. Other studies will require lengthier, and perhaps more complicated, types of data-collection schemes. It is advisable for inexperienced researchers to begin with simple projects before attempting to undertake too large and complicated a study.

8. *Action research is sometimes grounded in theory.* Relating the research question, results, and conclusions to existing theory provides a context in which to understand your research and what you may have learned from your study. Linking your research to aspects of the extant literature on the subject is not really an option; it is a requirement of any good study.

9. *Action research is not necessarily quantitative.* Some beginning action researchers are under the mistaken belief that action research must be undertaken from a quantitative perspective. But many action research projects do not simply compare one thing to another or seek to prove anything in particular (they are not usually causal in nature). Action research projects do not require controls or experiments. The goal of most action research projects is to improve understandings about something, uncover problems, and identify possible solutions to problems.

10. *The results of quantitative action research projects are limited.* When quantitative techniques are used in action research projects, caution should be exercised in coming to conclusions and making generalized forecasts to other settings. Caution is necessary because, like case studies, most action research studies are tailored to a particular group or organization and any other stakeholders who may be affected by this group or organization. The changes that may be identified as necessary to improve the conditions of these stakeholders may or may not be applicable to other groups and organizations—regardless of how similar these other groups and settings may be.

Action research targets two primary tasks. First, it is intended to uncover or produce information and knowledge that will be directly useful to a group of people (through research, education, and sociopolitical action). Second, it is meant to enlighten and empower the average person in the group, motivating each individual to take up and use the information gathered in the research (Johnson, 2008; Reason, 1994).

The Basics of Action Research

Action research is a collaborative approach to research that provides people with the means to take systematic action in an effort to resolve specific problems. This approach endorses consensual, democratic, and participatory strategies to encourage people to examine reflectively their problems or particular issues affecting them or their community. Furthermore, it encourages people to formulate accounts and explanations of their situation and to develop plans that may resolve these problems.

Action research focuses on methods and techniques of investigation that take into account the study population's history, culture, interactive activities, and emotional lives. Although action research makes use of many traditional data-gathering strategies, its orientation and purpose are slightly different. It does not use, for instance, elaborate and complex routines originating exclusively from the perspective of the researcher; instead, action research collaborates with the very people it seeks to study. The language and content of action research also differ from other approaches—especially those that utilize complex, sophisticated, difficult-to-understand statistical techniques. Language and content with this approach are easy to understand by both professional researchers and laypeople alike. Simplistically, one can suggest that the action research process works through three basic phases, namely, looking, thinking, and action:

> **Looking**—The researcher assesses the situation and creates a picture about what is going on. This involves gathering information, considering who the stakeholders are, and what their interests may be. When evaluating, the researcher defines and describes the problem to be investigated and the context in which it is set. The researcher should also consider (nonjudgmentally) what all stakeholders have been doing.

> **Thinking**—Thinking involves making interpretations and offering some explanation about the case at hand. During evaluation, the researcher analyzes the information (data) collected while looking over the situation and interprets the situation as it currently exists. Next, the researcher reflects on what participants have been doing. The participants often share

in this process of reflection. This provides a means for further assessment of areas of success and any deficiencies, issues, or problems that may confront the organization or the stakeholders.

Action—The central purpose of action research is to come to some resolve and use it to take action toward improving the lives of the participants (stakeholders). In terms of evaluation, the researcher considers which actions might effect the best positive changes in the organization and lives of the participants. Judgments should fall along the lines of the worthiness of a change, its potential effectiveness and appropriateness, and the outcomes of any activities that may be made toward these changes. *Working with the stakeholders*, the researcher formulates plans for solutions to any problems that have been mutually identified. These plans are then brought back to the stakeholders for further discussion and elaboration. Ultimately, it is the stakeholders themselves who are responsible for choosing a new plan of action.

A slightly more sophisticated version of this basic action research procedural routine involves four stages: (1) identifying the research question(s), (2) gathering the information to answer the question(s), (3) analyzing and interpreting the information, and (4) sharing the results with the participants. Similar to the way we described the general research process in Chapter 2, action research follows a kind of spiraling progression rather than the more traditional linear one (see Figure 7.1).

Figure 7.1 The Action Research Spiral Process

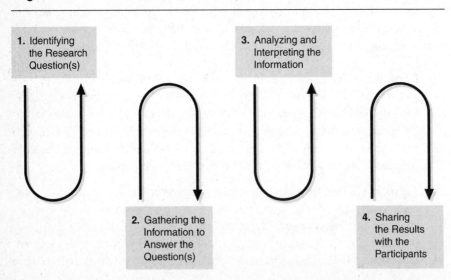

1. Identifying the Research Question(s)

3. Analyzing and Interpreting the Information

2. Gathering the Information to Answer the Question(s)

4. Sharing the Results with the Participants

One could reasonably argue that all research requires action. After all, research itself is a type of action, and most research produces some sort of consequence (even apathy). With many types of research, the consequence is some sort of change or modification with the way something is done or understood. If our approach is metaphysical, the very act of asking questions and actively seeking answers can be viewed as a kind of intervention into a situation or problem and will inevitably bring about changes in those individuals involved. Whether these individuals then choose to continue along the same paths as they had before the research was conducted or to change their course means the new situation will either be different from before or remain essentially the same. In either event, the decision to change or not to change constitutes action or, more precisely, action or inaction.

In action research, investigators are aware of the inevitable effect of intervention and the subsequent potential for change. The work is action-oriented. Most action research, then, consciously seeks to study something in order to change or improve it. This may be a situation uncovered by the researcher or brought to the attention of the investigator by some interested or involved party. Let's consider the four stages described in the current discussion of the action research process.

Identifying the Research Question(s)

The first stage of the action research process involves the researcher assisting the people in the research population—the stakeholders—to examine their situation and to recognize their problems. Alternatively, the researcher may identify a problem and bring it to the attention of the stakeholders. It is important for the action research investigator to recognize that the issues to be studied are considered important by the stakeholder and are not simply of interest to the researchers. This means that the task of the investigator is to assist individuals in the stakeholding group to jointly formulate research question(s), and as the research questions are created, to assist in formulating questions that are actually answerable. To some extent, this notion relates to the size of the problem at hand, but it also has to do with the type of information that may be available to the researcher. For example, the study may involve a community health workshop where many of the participants are drug addicts. Although considerable information may be available concerning drug addiction, treatment programs, and even direct information from participants, in this study it may not be possible to extend findings from gathered information beyond this particular community health workshop.

A good way to develop answerable relevant questions is to brainstorm or perhaps conduct focus groups with stakeholders (see Chapter 5). In these meetings, the investigator simply can ask, "What are the kinds of problems or issues you face?" With a little bit of digging, the investigator should be able to uncover relevant problems for study.

Gathering the Information to Answer the Question(s)

Any information the investigator gathers can potentially be used to answer the questions or solve the problems that have been identified. How one goes about gathering these data is essentially a matter of the investigator's choice and largely depends on limitations set by the stakeholders or the nature of the problem and setting. Thus, as in any standard methodological approach (see Chapter 2) the investigator is guided by the research question. Some problems will direct the investigator toward conducting interviews with relevant parties. Other problems may require various types of ethnographic or observational data. Still other studies may seem to be best addressed with archival data. Naturally, some investigators may choose to triangulate their studies in an effort to strengthen their findings and potentially enrich the eventual analysis and understandings.

Analyzing and Interpreting the Information

At this stage of the research process, participants need to focus on analyzing and interpreting the information that has been gathered. Data analysis, from the action research perspective, involves examination of the data in relation to potential resolutions to the questions or problems identified during the first stage of the research process.

The actual task of analysis will depend on the data-gathering method or methods used in stage 2 of this research process. The overall effort will be to create descriptive accounts based on the information captured by various data-collection technologies. Following are two alternative sets of general procedures investigators may consider to assist stakeholders in formulating descriptive accounts of the problems and issues that confront them. Readers should recognize similarities to processes for analyzing and understanding interviews, ethnography, and other forms of qualitative techniques described earlier in this text.

Procedures for Using Interview and Ethnographic Data

The process for recording responses in Chapter 4 outlines interviewing; Chapter 5, focus groups; and Chapter 6, ethnographic research. These same techniques may also be used in an action research framework. Hence, responses to questions (from interviews) and statements from field notes (ethnography) should be recorded, summarized, and analyzed. In most cases, analysis involves creating categories or themes and then sorting answers to questions or statements from the fieldwork into these categories. The data are sorted into piles that share some broader characteristic (the theme or category name). After accomplishing this, you can then write a summary that captures the essence of each broader categorical characteristic. This material will be used to create descriptive accounts of the stakeholders (discussed later).

Guiding Questions of Analysis: Why, What, How, Who, Where, When?

There are a number of questions one can pose to the data at a meeting with participants that will provide a guiding procedure for analyzing this material. The first question, *why*, establishes a general focus for the investigator and stakeholders, reminding everyone what the purpose of the study originally was. The remaining questions—*what, how, who, where*, and *when*—enable participants to identify associated influences (Stringer, 2007b). The intent is not merely to create categories or themes but rather to better understand the data in context of the setting or situation. *What* and *how* questions help to establish the problems and issues: What is going on that bothers people? How do these problems or issues intrude on the lives of the people or the group? *Who, where*, and *when* questions focus on specific actors, events, and activities that relate to the problems or issues at hand. The purpose here is not for participants to make quality judgments about these elements; rather, it is to assess the data and clarify information that has been gathered. This process is likely to draw out more than a mere explanation of already gathered information. It is likely to provide further history and context to the material (in a manner similar to a focus group interview). In addition, this process provides a means for participants to reflect on things that they themselves have discussed (captured in the data) or that other participants have mentioned.

Descriptive Accounts and Reports

There are two major concerns in developing descriptive accounts and creating reports of these accounts. First, it is critical that accounts reflect the perceptions of all stakeholders in the study population. If accounts exclude portions of the group, the resulting analysis may provide inadequate bases for viable action. Accounts, then, need to be created collaboratively (Stringer, 2007b). Second, except in situations in which the stakeholders amount to only a very few people, all of them usually cannot be included in all steps of the process all of the time. In such situations, the investigator needs to make every effort to regularly keep all stakeholders informed of various activities and provide opportunities for people to read various accounts as they develop (not simply after the project is complete). In this way, these individuals can also be afforded the opportunity to provide their own input by way of feedback to what they have read.

Sharing the Results with the Participants

One of the operative principles of action research is to inform and empower people to work collectively to produce some beneficial change. This necessarily includes both informal and formal meetings with the investigator at every stage of the research process. Stringer (2007b) suggests a number of activities that an investigator can use in order to maximize participation by many of the participants, especially when these participants may include large numbers of diverse stakeholders:

- *Focus groups* in which people with similar interests or agendas discuss particular issues
- *In-group forums* in which people from single-interest or stakeholder groups discuss particular issues
- *Informal meetings* that form spontaneously in response to particular circumstances or issues
- *Agency* institution or departmental meetings that provide personnel with opportunities to discuss common interests or agendas
- *Community group meetings* in which community members meet to explore interests or agendas

It is also important that when the study is over, the stakeholders still need to know what the results are. This can be accomplished in a wide variety of ways. Traditionalists are likely to think about providing some form of a report to each participant in the study. However, this may still make the information inaccessible to some participants. Traditional methods of presenting participants with paper copies of technical reports tend to include stiff or stilted scientific jargon that is meaningless to the average layperson. Meetings and presentations tend to be better suited, perhaps accompanied by the full report for those who want it.

Technology provides additional means for communicating with a large number of people in an interesting, engaging, and accessible manner. For example, information may be placed on a project Web site. Others may be more interested in seeing material presented via some form of live or recorded presentation. This may entail a recording of one's verbal presentation, or even a dramatic presentation or some type of role-played reenactment of situations uncovered in the research, and so on.

When to Use and When Not to Use Action Research

One should not use action research if you want to draw comparisons, simply describe or explore a group or organization, or plan to undertake some form of inferential evaluation of a situation, setting, set of events, or phenomenon (McNiff & Whitehead, 2006). If, for example, you want to see if male police officers are more or less effective on road patrols than female officers, you would be better served using some type of observational technique. If you desire to investigate what effect the gender of a student may have on a teacher's interaction style, again, some form of straightforward observational strategy should work well in a classroom setting. If you are interested in examining the leadership qualities among nurses practicing in some specialty unit or another (an ICU, CCU, Cardiac Step-Down unit, etc.), this might be accomplished using some type of sociometric survey of individuals in that unit, or even depth interviews. *All* of these social concerns involve researchers asking questions such as, "What exactly are people in these settings doing?" "What do people say about specific phenomena and events in question?" "How many people do things in a certain way, or think about things in a specific way, under the various circumstances?" and similar concerns. Action research, however, runs along a slightly different line of questions and concerns. For an investigator using an action research strategy, the questions might be more like, "What are the concerns and problems as perceived by the people in this setting?" "How do I, as an outsider (the researcher), understand what seems to be happening in these situations and settings?" "How can I, as an outsider (researcher), assist these participants' resolve or change the problems in order to improve the situations?" In short, the emphasis is not so much *What information the researcher can gather and then take away from the setting*, but, *What information can the researcher gather with the assistance of the stakeholders*, to be shared and used to actuate change in the setting or situation(s) for personal and social improvement. This tends to be a very different and more reflective approach from traditional research orientations and requires a slightly different researcher's role than one might expect in traditional research orientations.

The principles of action research may, however, be selectively applied to any research. That is to say, if you can identify people who have some stake in your findings, it is often a good idea to communicate the findings to those stakeholders. Just because your research questions are inherently academic, it does not have to mean that only academics can hear about it. Chances are good that any informant who has given time to an interview, or has provided a researcher with access to a field site, or even just filled out a survey, would be interested in knowing what came of that. Reporting back to the affected communities also helps you to fulfill the ethical mandate (Chapter 3) to respect the support given to your work by the subjects.

The Action Researcher's Role

The formally trained researcher stands with and alongside the community or group under study, not outside as an objective observer or external consultant. The researcher contributes expertise when needed as a participant in the process. The researcher collaborates with local practitioners as well as stakeholders in the group or community. Other participants contribute their physical and/or intellectual resources to the research process. The researcher is a partner with the study population; thus, this type of research is considerably more value laden than other more traditional research roles and endeavors.

The approach a researcher takes when conducting action research, therefore, must be more holistic, encompassing a broad combination of technological, social, economic, and political aspects of relationships and interactions between the researcher and the stakeholders in the project.

Types of Action Research

Several sources outline three distinct types of action research. For example, Grundy (1988, p. 353) discussed three modes of action research: technical, practical, and emancipating. Holter and Schwartz-Barcott (1993, p. 301) also presented three types of action research—that of a technical collaborative approach, a mutual collaborative approach, and an enhancement approach. McKernan (1991, pp. 16–27) listed three types of action research: the scientific-technical view of problem solving, the practical-deliberate action research mode, and a critical emancipating action research. Along similar lines, Greenwood and Levin (2007, pp. 186–192) describe three types of *participatory evaluation*: Constructive evaluation, utilization and participation, and empowerment evaluation.

If we collapse these generally similar categories, we derive something like a *technical/scientific/collaborative mode, a practical/mutual collaborative/ deliberate mode, and an emancipating/enhancing/critical mode.*

Technical/Scientific/Collaborative Mode

According to Janet Masters (1998), early advocates of action research advocated a fairly rigorous scientific method of problem solving. From this approach, the primary goal was to test a particular intervention based on a prespecified theoretical framework. The relationship in this mode of action research was between the research and a practitioner. For example, a relationship might arise between a researcher and a clinical psychologist working with a family support group of some type. The researcher would serve as a collaborator and a facilitator for the practitioner, whereas the practitioner could bring information from the researcher to his or her clients (Holter & Schwartz-Barcott, 1993, p. 301). In effect, the researcher works with the clinical psychologist, who in turn acts as a kind of liaison between the researcher and his or her clients throughout the research process. The communication flow within this type of research would primarily be between the facilitator (practitioner) and the group, so that the researcher's ideas may be communicated to the group (Grundy, 1988). In other words, the researcher is apart from the group; he or she identifies a problem after collaborating with the practitioner and then provides information to this practitioner who facilitates its implementation with the group.

A Practical/Mutual Collaborative/Deliberate Mode

In this mode of action research, the researcher and the practitioner come together and collaboratively identify potential problems and issues, their underlying causes, and possible interventions (Holter & Schwartz-Barcott, 1993, p. 301). The research problem is defined only after the researcher and practitioner have assessed the situation and reached a mutual understanding. This sort of "practical action research," as Grundy (1988, p. 357) described it, seeks to improve practice-and-service delivery of the practitioner through application of the "personal wisdom of the participants." The communication flow in this mode of action research starts with the researcher and facilitator working collaboratively and then flows from the practitioner (facilitator) to the group of stakeholders.

This design of action research creates a more flexible approach than the *technical/scientific/collaborative mode* in that it embraces a greater concern for empowering and emancipating stakeholders working with the practitioner. The gain in flexibility and effects of emancipating participants does, however, reduce some degree of measurement precision and control over interpretations, interactive communications, and detailed descriptions (McKernan, 1991). These are not seen, however, as the primary goals in this mode of action research. Rather, "the goal of practical action researchers is understanding practice and solving immediate problems" (McKernan, 1991, p. 20).

Practitioners involved in such mutual collaborative approaches to action research tend to reflect on their own practice styles, incorporate new information developed by the research, and implement interventions that may effect lasting changes in the groups with whom they participate. Unfortunately, the changes that result in such projects tend to be associated with the change agents (those facilitators working in the research); consequently, the interventions may cease to be used when these individuals leave the system.

Emancipating or Empowering/Enhancing/ Critical Science Mode

This third mode of action research "promotes emancipatory praxis in the participating practitioners; that is, it promotes a critical consciousness which exhibits itself in political as well as practical action to promote change" (Grundy, 1987, p. 154). There are actually two distinct goals in this approach to action research. The first goal is an attempt to increase the closeness between the day-to-day problems encountered by practitioners in specific settings and the theories used to explain and resolve the problem; in other words, an attempt to bring together theory and book knowledge with real-world situations, issues, and experiences.

The second goal is to assist practitioners in lifting their veil of clouded understandings and help them to better understand fundamental problems by raising their collective consciousness (Holter & Schwartz-Barcott, 1993). This is accomplished by developing a social critique, wherein the consideration of theory and practice comes together. Development of this sort of social criticism has three parts: theory, enlightenment, and action (see Grundy, 1988). The generation of action-oriented policy, then, may be seen as following from this mode of action research and this tri-part notion of theory, enlightenment, and action. It is actually the coming together of theory and enlightenment that provides the emancipation and empowerment to the participants, which then leads to action and change.

Photovoice and Action Research

During the past several decades, the use of photographs in ethnographic research has begun to move toward a greater action research orientation. That is to say that before the 1990s, qualitative investigators used photographs more or less traditionally to either serve as data in themselves (see, e.g., Dowdall & Golden, 1989; Jackson, 1977; Musello, 1980) or simply to illustrate and/or document the ethnographic record (see Spradley, 1979). The current trend among some action researchers is to use photographs as a means to enable the investigator to gain perceptual access to the world from the viewpoint of individuals who have not traditionally held control over the means of imaging the world. This technique is called *photovoice* (Clark & Zimmer, 2001; Dixon & Hadjialexiou, 2005; Wang, Cash, & Powers, 2000; Wang & Redwood-Jones, 2001).

Photovoice researchers literally give their subjects a camera and ask them to photograph certain aspects of their lives (Ulin, Robinson, & Tolley, 2004). Often this is undertaken in addition to more traditional elements of observation and field note-taking or photos taken by the investigator. For example, as part of a larger investigation, Clark and Zimmer (2001) gave disposable cameras to women in their study at three-month intervals and asked them to record events or situations these women felt were relevant to their children's health in general. This activity resulted in 1,018 mother-generated photographs. These were added to photographs taken by both researchers and their assistants during home visits to these women (an additional 943 photographs). In effect, the photovoice method puts cameras in the hands of folks in the community so that they can document what they see in their community from the ground up. In turn, these photos are discussed among participants and then brought to the attention of community leaders or appropriate policymakers.

In another study conducted by Caroline Wang and her associates (2000), 41 youths and adults (including a number of political leaders of the community) were given cameras and asked to photographically document their community's assets and concerns and then to critically discuss these images with policymakers of that community. The project provided these youths an opportunity to express their concerns about violence in their neighborhood and provided policymakers with an opportunity to hear concerns and consider ways to provide funding for local violence-prevention programs.

A comparable project was initiated by the Compassion Worcester Youth Capacity Project in Worcester, Massachusetts, in 2008 (Worcester Youth, 2009). "PhotoVoice pictures are not meant to be self-consciously 'artistic,' but rather are intended to tell what a local area literally looks like to the people who live there," the project report explains. Teams of young residents received cameras and training in photography, followed by months of photo documentation of their lives and city. The photographers then selected their favorite images, wrote the text to accompany them, and submitted their work for the final documentation. The final documentation of the project explains that photo-voice was perceived as a technique for "promoting positive community change" by revealing things that are visible to all, but only noticed by some.

The Goals in Photovoice

There are essentially three major goals when using photovoice as an action research strategy:

1. Empowering and enabling people to reflect their personal and community concerns.
2. To encourage a dialogue and to transfer knowledge and information about personal and community issues through discussions about photographs among participants.
3. To access the perception of those not in control of various issues and to share this information with those who are in control (policymakers, politicians, healthcare professionals, educators, etc.).

Central to action research is the notion of participation. Photovoice allows participants to define themselves, their families, their work, and anything else that can be focused through the viewfinder of a camera. Because these photographs are then discussed with others, they provide a means by which others can share the meanings participants attach to the people, scenes, objects, and situations captured in the photographs.

According to Wang (2000), study members themselves guide each step of the research process so that their voice can be fully expressed. After the photographs have been taken, the method has three stages: selecting photographs, contextualizing stories, and codifying issues.

Selecting Photographs   The participants will need to identify which of the photographs they believe most accurately reflect their concerns and issues or which photographs best depict their view about the world around them. As in other action research strategies, this can be accomplished in small or large groups.

Contextualizing Stories   In this stage, the participants share stories about their photographs. In more traditional research terms, they *offer accounts* about the photographs, why they were taken, what the image means to the individual, and what they intended the photograph to depict. Sharing stories is a key element in this technique because it quite literally offers the voice element to the photographs. In the absence of this stage, photographs do not provide the inner perceptions of their creators (the participants who took the photographs).

Codifying   Like any other coding stage, this one identifies the central issues, themes, or theories that emerge during the course of contextualizing and discussing the photographs in the various groups. During this stage, participants may earmark certain concerns that they want to target for action or prioritize issues for action.

Photovoice provides a means for involving people in both sharing and defining issues, problems, and concerns. As an action research technique, it allows the investigator to gain insights as well as to inform relevant policymakers or other change agents. It is a means by which participants can reflect, both individually and together, on their own concerns, made visible in photographs and given voice through discussions and accounts.

Action Research: A Reiteration

In an effort to better summarize the various activities, procedures, and data-collecting strategies available to researchers through use of an action research framework, I offer Figure 7.2, which is loosely adapted from John Creswell's (2004, 2007) *Taxonomy of Action Research Data Collection Techniques*.

Note that this figure continues to follow the overall structure suggested earlier in this chapter of *identifying a research question, gathering information to answer the question, analyzing and interpreting the information,* and *sharing the results with the participants*. Also note that the various modes of *enquiry* are not intended as absolutes nor intended to be read across the figure. Rather, they should be considered as similar to lines of action, as described in Chapter 2 in the discussion on *triangulation*. Hence, one can mix and match, so to speak, various elements shown in this figure in order to structure an action research framework for a study.

Figure 7.2 A Taxonomy of the Action Research Framework

Experience (through collaboration, observation, and sharing)	→	Enquiry (methods of asking questions by researchers and/or stakeholders)	→	Examining (reviewing and making use of collected information)
Meet with Shareholders (individually or town meeting)		Discuss issues		Review relevant literature (scholarly and specific document related to the stake holders)
Participant Observation (Actively involved participation)		Interviews (informal or arranged semistructured)		Analysis of interview transcripts
Collaborative Observation (actively involved participant with other stakeholders)		Focus groups		Assessment of focus group transcripts
		Photovoice		Discussion of Photographs (possible public display)
Accessed Observation (passive observer, working with stakeholders)		Archival (use of available records)		Review of Archived Documents Presentation of results to stakeholders

TRYING IT OUT

1. Divide the class into two separate groups. Designate one of the students in each group as *researcher*. Next, see if you can identify problems and issues facing each group of students. Remember, this may involve several meetings of the group (small town meetings) led by the *researcher* of each group. Once each group has devised a list of concerns and issues (the action focus), have the *researcher* report this to one large town meeting of the entire class. How similar were the concerns listed by each group?

2. Divide the class into three groups. Have each group identify a concern or interest of the entire group that exists on campus. Now have students take photographs that depict their group's concern or interest. The groups will need to meet separately to discuss their photographs and share their meanings. Finally, have the groups

exhibit their photographs. The exhibition may be accomplished by hanging the photographs in a hall, using the classroom walls, publishing them on the Web, and so on. Be sure some narratives have been included with the photographs.

REFERENCES

Adelman, C. (1993). Kurt Lewin and the origins of action research. *Educational Action Research 1*(1), 7–25.

Anderson, G. L., Herr, K., & Nihlen, A. S. (1994). *Studying Your Own School.* Thousand Oaks, CA: Corwin Press.

Anderson, J. P. (2007). *A Short Guide to Action Research* (3rd ed.). Boston, MA: Allyn and Bacon.

Bray, J., Lee, J., Smith, L., & Yorks, L. (2000). *Collaborative Inquiry in Practice: Action, Reflection, and Making Meaning.* Thousand Oaks, CA: Sage.

Brown, A., & Dowling, P. (1998). *Doing Research/Reading Research. A Mode of Interrogation for Education.* London: Falmer Press.

Burman, E. (2004). Organizing for change? Group-analytic perspectives on a feminist action research project. *Group Analysis 37*(1), 91–108.

Burnaford, G. E., Fischer, J., & Hobson, D. (2001). *Teachers Doing Research: The Power of Action Through Inquiry* (2nd ed.). Mahwah, NJ: Erlbaum.

Calhoun, E. (1994). *How to Use Action Research in the Self-Renewing School.* Alexandria, VA: Association for Supervision and Curriculum Development.

Clark, L., & Zimmer, L. (2001). What we learned from a photographic component in a study of Latino children's health. *Field Methods 13*(4), 303–328.

Creswell, J. W. (2004). *Educational Research* (2nd ed.). Upper Saddle River, NJ: Prentice Hall.

Creswell, J. W. (2007). *Educational Research* (3rd ed.). Upper Saddle River, NJ: Prentice Hall.

Dixon, M., & Hadjialexiou, M. (2005). Photo voice: Promising practice in engaging young people who are homeless in health promotion and planning. *Youth Studies Australia 24*(2), 52–63.

Dowdall, G. W., & Golden, J. (1989). Photographs as data: An analysis of images from a mental hospital. *Qualitative Sociology 12*(2), 183–213.

Ferrance, E. (2000). *Action Research.* Providence, RI: Northeastern and Island Regional Educational Laboratory at Brown University.

Gabel, D. (1995). Presidential address. National Association for Research in Science Teaching (NARST), San Francisco.

Goodenough, W. (1963). *Cooperation in Change: An Anthropological Approach to Community Development.* New York: Russell Sage.

Greenwood, D. J., & Levin, M. (2007). *Introduction to Action Research: Social Research for Social Change* (2nd ed.). Thousand Oaks, CA: Sage.

Grundy, S. (1987). *Curriculum: Product or Praxis.* London, England: Falmer Press.

Grundy, S. (1988). Three modes of action research. In S. Kemmis & R. McTaggert (Eds.), *The Action Research Reader* (3rd ed.). Geelong, Australia: Deakin University Press.

Hendericks, C. C. (2008). *Improving Schools Through Action Research: A Comprehensive Guide for Educators* (2nd ed.). Boston, MA: Allyn and Bacon.

Holter, I. M., & Schwartz-Barcott, D. (1993). Action research: What is it? How has it been used and how can it be used in nursing? *Journal of Advanced Nursing 128,* 298–304.

Jackson, B. (1977). *Killing Time: Life in the Arkansas Penitentiary*. Ithaca, NY: Cornell University Press.

Jenkins, E., Jones J., Keen, D., Kinsella, F., Owen, T., Pritchard, D., & Rees, S. (2005). Our story about making a difference in nursing practice through action research. *Educational Action Research 13*(1), 259–274.

Johnson, A. P. (2008). *A Short Guide to Action Research*. Boston, MA: Allyn and Bacon.

Kemmis, S., & McTaggart, R. (1988). *The Action Research Planner* (3rd ed.). Geelong, Australia: Deakin University Press.

Lewin, K. (1946). Action research and minority problems. *Journal of Social Issues 2*(4), 34–46.

Masters, J. (1998). The history of action research. In I. Hughes and B. Dicks (Eds.), *Action Research Electronic Reader*. Available online at www.scu.edu.au/schools/gcm/ar/arr/arow/default.html.

Mayo, E. (1933). *The Human Problems of an Industrial Civilization*. New York: Macmillan.

McKernan, J. (1991). *Curriculum Action Research. A Handbook of Methods and Resources for the Reflective Practitioner*. London: Kogan Publishers.

McNiff, J., & Whitehead, J. (2006). *All You Need to Know About Action Research*. Thousand Oaks, CA: Sage.

Mills, G. E. (2000). *Action Research: A Guide for the Teacher Researcher*. Upper Saddle River, NJ: Prentice Hall.

Musello, C. (1980). Studying the home mode: An exploration of family photography and visual communications. *Studies in Visual Communication 6*(1), 23–42.

Ogawa, A. (2009). *The Failure of Civil Society?: The Third Sector and the State in Contemporary Japan*. Albany, NY: SUNY Press.

Polit, D. F., & Beck, C. T. (2007). *Nursing Research: Generating and Assessing Evidence for Nursing Practice* (8th ed.). Philadelphia, PA: Lippincott Williams & Wilkins.

Reason, P. (1994). Three approaches to participative inquiry. In N. K. Denzin & Y. S. Lincoln (Eds.), *Handbook of Qualitative Research* (pp. 324–339). Thousand Oaks, CA: Sage.

Reid, C. (2000). Seduction and enlightenment in feminist action research. *Feminist Qualitative Research 28*(1–2), 169–189.

Reid, C. (2004). Advancing women's social justice agendas: A feminist action research framework. *International Journal of Qualitative Methods 3*(3). Available online at http://www.ualberta.ca/~iiqm/backissues/3_3/pdf/reid.pdf.

Reinharz, S. (1992). *Feminist Methods in Social Research*. New York: Oxford University Press.

Spradley, J. P. (1979). *The Ethnographic Interview*. New York: Holt, Rinehart & Winston.

Stringer, E. (2004). *Action Research in Education*. Upper Saddle River, NJ: Pearson/Merrill/Prentice Hall.

Stringer, E. (2007a). *Action Research in Education* (2nd ed.). Upper Saddle River, NJ: Pearson/Merrill/Prentice Hall.

Stringer, E. T. (2007b). *Action Research* (3rd ed.). Thousand Oaks, CA: Sage.

Stringer, E., & Genat, W. J. (2003). *Action Research in Health*. Upper Saddle River, NJ: Prentice Hall.

Stringer, E. T., & Dwyer, R. (2005). *Action Research in Human Services*. Upper Saddle River, NJ: Person/Merrill/Prentice Hall.

Ulin, P. R., Robinson, E. T., & Tolley, E. T. (2004). *Qualitative Methods in Public Health: A Field Guide for Applied Research*. San Francisco, CA: Jossey-Bass.

Valach, L., Young, R. A., & Lynam, M. J. (2002). *Action Theory: A Primer for Applied Research in the Social Sciences.* New York: Praeger Publishers.

Wadsworth, Y. (1998). What is participatory action research? Action Research International, Paper 2. Available online at www.scu.edu.au/schools/gcm/ar/ari/p-ywadsworth98.html.

Wang, C. (2000). *Strength to Be: Community Visions and Voices.* Ann Arbor, MI: University of Michigan Press.

Wang, C., & Redwood-Jones, Y. A. (2001). Photovoice ethics. *Health Education and Behavior 28*(5), 560–572.

Wang, C., Cash, J. L., & Powers, L. S. (2000). Who knows the streets as well as the homeless? Promoting personal and community action through photovoice. *Health Promotion Practice 1*(1), 81–89.

Whyte, W. F. (1943). *Street Corner Society.* Chicago, IL: University of Chicago Press.

Whyte, W. F. (Ed.). (1991). *Participatory Action Research.* Newbury Park, CA: Sage.

Worcester Youth (2009). *Seeing Ourselves Successful: The Worcester Youth Photovoice Project.* New England Network for Child, Youth, & Family Services. Retrieved [Feburary 23, 2011] from http://www.nenetwork.org/publications/WorcesterPhotoVoice.pdf.

Chapter 8

Unobtrusive Measures in Research

THE PRECEDING FOUR chapters have discussed research procedures that require an intrusion into the lives of subjects. Researcher reactivity—the response of subjects to the presence of an intruding investigator—has been considered as it applies to interviewers and ethnographers. In each case, we have offered suggestions concerning how to make positive use of the reactivity or to neutralize it. This chapter will examine unobtrusive (nonintruding) research strategies. For research to be completely unobtrusive, the fact that we are collecting data must be independent of the processes that produced it. In practice this means that we are examining social artifacts, traces, or other materials or events that were first created for some other reason prior to our examining them as data.

To some extent, all the unobtrusive strategies amount to examining and assessing human traces. What people do, how they behave and structure their daily lives, and even how humans are affected by certain ideological stances can all be observed in traces people either intentionally or inadvertently leave behind.

The more unusual types of unobtrusive studies are sometimes briefly highlighted in textbook descriptions of unobtrusive measures—just before dismissing these techniques in favor of measures regarded as more legitimate. For instance, it is still fairly common to hear how an investigator estimated the popularity of different radio stations in Chicago by having automobile mechanics record the position of the radio dial in all the cars they serviced (Z-Frank, 1962). (This was before digitally programmable car radios were used.) Sawyer (1961, cited in Webb, Campbell, Schwartz, Sechrest, & Grove, 1981) examined liquor sales in Wellesley, Massachusetts, a so-called dry town (i.e., no liquor stores were permitted). To obtain an estimate of liquor sales, Sawyer studied the trash from Wellesley homes—specifically, the number of discarded liquor bottles found at the Wellesley trash dump. Not very long following this study, *the science of garbology* began to arise with what has come to be known as the University of Arizona's Garbage Project, which originated in 1973 (Rathje & Murphy, 2001). This study, developed by anthropologists at the University of Arizona, and still ongoing today, sought to understand the relationship between mental, behavioral, and material realities that made up human consumption and disposal, including examination of diet and nutrition, recycling, waste disposal techniques, and food waste and food recovery. In short, garbology provides a kind of mirror on the society it investigates— especially if one follows the old adage *you are what you eat* (Lepisto, 2005).

Lee (2000) points out that what people leave as traces of themselves may speak more eloquently and truthfully about their lives than the account they themselves might offer. Shanks, Platt, and Rathje (2004), for example, undertook a study of the cultural experience of 9/11/2001 and its aftermath, and how this impacted American society. Thirty-three museums led by the Smithsonian and the New York City Museum were interested in documenting the event and determining what items might be collected and preserved for display and for representing this event historically. A year after the museums began their work, an exhibition opened at the Smithsonian entitled, *Bearing Witness to History.* The display included items found in the debris of the buildings after 9/11 including a wallet, a melted computer screen from the Pentagon, torn clothing, a structural joint from the World Trade Center, a window washer's squeegee handle, and a stairwell sign. While some might suggest that these items represented little more than *garbage* and debris to the garbologist, they represent pieces of historical artifacts with cultural meanings and important social content.

There is often a tongue-in-cheek aspect to descriptions of research on debris. In some instances, almost absurd situations have been ascribed to findings culled from unobtrusive data. For example, Jelenko (1980) describes a rock on the campus of Wright State University that was regularly painted by students. He determined the accretion of paint each time the rock was painted and calculated that in 7,778 years the rock would have grown (from the layers of paint) to a size that would encroach on the gymnasium located 182 meters away.

Unobtrusive studies of recent human activities have many pragmatic applications as well. During the past 40 years in law enforcement, an area commonly known as *crime analysis* has evolved. Crime analysis involves the study of criminal incidents, and identification of crime patterns, crime trends, and criminal problems. Crime analysis is accomplished by a variety of diverse and unobtrusive techniques. For instance, during the 1980s, the Florida Department of Law Enforcement (FDLE) officers regularly read local newspapers from across the state, looking for articles about fraudulent bank checks, car thefts, certain con-games, and other patterns of criminal behavior. As these patterns developed in the various cities' newspaper stories, they charted the cities and the crimes on a map of Florida. In this manner, they could see if there were any migrating patterns from one Florida city to the next and could predict the onslaught of certain crimes in particular areas in advance. When a pattern was identified, they contacted local law enforcement officials to warn them of the impending criminal activities. Today, these same kinds of activities are handled by inputting information to a computer program generically referred to as a geographic information system (GIS) or GIS mapping (Boba, 2008).

Regardless of whether this information is the consequence of hand-culled articles from newspapers or records of local crime incidents collected and entered into a GIS mapping program, the important fact is that these activities are actually an application of the utility of unobtrusive research strategies. Crime analysis, like the previous illustrations of unobtrusive data-collection strategies, demonstrates that information can be culled from various traces and records created or left by humans (whether intended or inadvertent).

Many types of unobtrusive data provide avenues for the study of subjects that might otherwise be very difficult or impossible to investigate. Helen Bramley (2002), for example, examined "Diana," Princess of Wales, as a contemporary goddess by undertaking a comparative content analysis of historical descriptions of goddesses of the past. Robert Pullen and his associates (2000) studied cheating by examining 100 discarded cheat sheets from a variety of disciplines discovered on and off campus. From the cheat sheets examined, the researchers assessed the location where the sheets had been discarded, the nature of their content, their physical size, and several other factors. Stan Weber (1999) used several literature sources to develop an assessment of the orientation and etiologies of citizen militia in the United States, an interesting contemporary phenomenon that might not otherwise have been successfully researched. And Brian Payne (1998) conducted a kind of meta-analysis of studies on healthcare crimes using existing literature and research studies on Medicare and Medicaid frauds as his data source.

In this chapter, several broad categories of unobtrusive strategies are examined in detail. This approach is not meant to suggest that the various unobtrusive techniques are necessarily ordered in this manner. It is intended, rather, to simplify presentation by simultaneously discussing similar techniques under like headings. The categories will be considered under the headings Archival Strategies and Physical Erosion and Accretion.

Archival Strategies

As Denzin (1978, p. 219) observed, archival records can be divided into public archival records and private archival records. In the case of the former, *records* are viewed as prepared for the express purpose of examination by others. Although access to public archives may be restricted to certain groups (certain law enforcement records, credit histories, school records, etc.), they are typically prepared for some audience. As a result, public archival records tend to be written in more or less standardized form and arranged in the archive systematically (e.g., alphabetically, chronologically, or numerically indexed).

In contrast to these public orientations and formal structures, private archival records typically are intended for personal (private) audiences. Except for published versions of a diary or personal memoirs (which in effect become parts of the public archival system), private archival records reach extremely small—if any—audiences.

Public Archives

Traditionally, the term *archive* brings to mind some form of library. Libraries are, indeed, archives; but so too are graveyard tombstones, hospital admittance records, police incident reports, computer-accessed bulletin boards, motor vehicle registries, newspaper morgues, movie rental stores, and even credit companies' billing records. As Webb and his colleagues (1981, 2000) suggest, virtually any *running record* provides a kind of archive.

In addition to providing large quantities of inexpensive data, archival material is virtually nonreactive to the presence of investigators. Many researchers find archival data attractive because public archives use more or less standard formats and filing systems, which makes locating pieces of data and creating research filing systems for analysis easier (see Lofland, Snow, Anderson, & Lofland, 2006).

Naturally, as in any research process, serious errors are possible when using archival data. If this possibility is recognized, however, and controlled through data triangulation, for example, errors may not seriously distort results (Webb, Cambell, Schwartz, & Sechrest, 2000).

Modifying and modernizing the four broad categories suggested by Webb and his colleagues (1966, 1981, 2000) result in a three-category scheme. This scheme identifies varieties of public archival data as commercial media accounts, actuarial records, and official documentary records.

Commercial Media Accounts   Commercial media accounts represent any written, drawn, or recorded (video or audio) materials produced for general or mass consumption. This may include such items as newspapers, books, magazines, television program transcripts, videotapes and DVDs, drawn comics, maps, blogs, and so forth. When we talk of information expressed in "the media," we are referring to these public, generally commercially produced sources.

One excellent illustration of the use of television program transcripts as a type of public archival record is Molotch and Boden's (1985) examination of the congressional Watergate hearings of 1973. In their effort to examine the way people invoke routine conversational procedures to gain power, Molotch and Boden created transcriptions from videotapes of the hearings. By examining the conversational exchanges between relevant parties during the hearings, Molotch and Boden (1985) manage to develop a blow-by-blow account of domination in the making.

In a similar vein, following the O. J. Simpson trial, Frank Schmalleger (1996) offered a commentary on the exchanges between the defense and prosecution based on court transcripts he downloaded from the Internet.

Molotch and Boden (1985) are primarily concerned with the audio portion of the videotapes. Schmalleger (1996) is similarly interested only in the written transcript of verbal exchanges. Other researchers, however, have concentrated on visual renderings, such as still photographs. Bruce Jackson (1977), for example, used photographs to depict the prison experience in his *Killing Time: Life in the Arkansas Penitentiary.* Another example of the use of still photographs is Erving Goffman's (1979) examination of gender in advertisements. Goffman's research suggests that gender displays, like other social rituals, reflect vital features of social structure—both negative and positive ones.

The realm of visual ethnography similarly explores and documents humans and human culture (Pink, 2006). Visual ethnography uses photography, motion pictures, hypermedia, the World Wide Web, interactive CDs, CD-ROMs, and virtual reality as ways of capturing and expressing perceptions and social realities of people. These varied forms of visual representation provide a means for recording, documenting, and explaining the social worlds and understandings of people. It is important, however, to emphasize that visual ethnography is not purely visual. Rather, the visual ethnographer simply pays particular attention to the visual aspects of culture as part of his or her ethnographic efforts (Berg, 2008a). As Berg (2008a) has outlined elsewhere:

> Beginning in around the mid to late 1970's visual anthropologists began to focus their attention on ethnographic film and video; they also began to question the idea of visual realism that had been the long-time anchor of visual aids in anthropological investigation. Visual sociologists who had also been developing their use of photography from the perspective of a realist paradigm began to react to feminist and postmodern critiques and shifted toward more reflexive and self-identifying orientations in their research, including the use of photography and film.

As another illustration, Simon Gottschalk (1995) used photographs as an intricate element in his ethnographic exploration of the "Strip" in Las Vegas. Gottschalk's use of photos evokes an emotional content about the Strip not actually possible in words alone. Their inclusion, then, significantly heightens the written account of his ethnography.

Actuarial Records   *Actuarial records* also tend to be produced for special or limited audiences but are typically available to the public under certain circumstances. These items include birth and death records; records of marriages and divorces; application information held by insurance and credit companies; title, land, and deed information; and similar demographic or residential types of records.

Private industry has long used actuarial information as data. Insurance companies, for example, establish their price structures according to life expectancy as mediated by such factors as whether the applicant smokes, drinks liquor, sky dives (or engages in other life-threatening activities), works in a dangerous occupation, and so forth. Similarly, social scientists may use certain actuarial data to assess various social phenomena and/or problems. Although each of these preceding categories of public archival data may certainly be separated conceptually, it should be obvious that considerable overlap may occur.

Although archival information is a rich source of primary data, albeit underused, such data frequently contain several innate flaws as well. For example, missing elements in an official government document may represent attempts to hide the very information of interest to the investigators, or missing portions of some official document may have merely resulted from the carelessness of the last person who looked at the document and lost a page.

It is sometimes difficult to determine possible effects from editorial bias and control over what gets published and what does not. Bradley, Boles, and Jones (1979) expressly mentioned this element as one of two weaknesses in their study of cartoons in men's magazines in relation to the changing nature of male sexual mores and prostitution. In addition, they indicate as a second weakness their inability to precisely measure audience reaction merely by examining cartoons that appeared in *Esquire* and *Playboy* over a 40-year period.

When dealing with aggregate statistical data, missing values or nonresponses to particular questions can be accounted for. In some instances, data sets can be purchased and cleaned of any such missing pieces of information. Unfortunately, when using archival data, it may sometimes be impossible to determine, let alone account for, what or why pieces of data are missing. This again suggests the need to incorporate multiple measures and techniques in order to reduce potential errors, but it should not prevent or discourage the use of archival data.

Formal actuarial records (e.g., birth, death, and marriage records) are used frequently as data in social science research. Aggregate data such as aptitude test scores, age, income, number of divorces, smoker or nonsmoker, gender, occupation, and the like are the lifeblood of many governmental agencies (as well as certain private companies). Sharon DeBartolo Carmack (2002) points out that there are a number of places one can locate interesting information about records of death. For example, death certificates, which can frequently be located in coroner's records or in local county courthouses (as public information) can provide fascinating information about the cause of death of an individual. Similarly, family Bibles can provide a host of information on births, marriages, and deaths and can serve as fodder for a number of interesting studies about families, genealogy, traits, and personality characteristics.

Among the more interesting variations on unobtrusive actuarial data are those described by Warner (1959). As part of his classic five-volume series on "Yankee City" (the other volumes include Warner & Low, 1947; Warner & Lunt, 1941, 1942; Warner & Srole, 1945), Warner offered *The Living and the Dead: A Study of the Symbolic Life of Americans.*

In his study, Warner (1959) used official cemetery documents to establish a history of the dead and added interviewing, observation, and examination of eroded traces as elements in his description of graveyards. From his data, Warner was able to suggest various apparent social structures present in grave-yards that resembled those present in the social composition of Yankee City (Newburyport, Massachusetts). For instance, the size of headstones typically was larger for men than for women, plots were laid out so that the father of a family would be placed in the center, and so forth.

Webb and his colleagues (1981, p. 93) pointed out that tombstones themselves can be interesting sources of data. They also mention the possible analysis of different cultures by, for example, considering the relative size of the headstones of men as compared to women.

In fact, tombstones often reveal several other interesting things. For example, most tombstones contain birth and death dates and many include social role information (e.g., "beloved son and father," "loving wife and sister"). In some cases, the cause of death may even be mentioned (e.g., "The plague took him, God rest his soul" or "Killed by Indians"). In consequence, tombstones cease to be merely grave markers and become viable actuarial records. Examination of information in a given cemetery can reveal waves of illness, natural catastrophes, relative social status and prestige, ethnic stratification, and many other potentially meaningful facts.

Dean Eastman, a history teacher at Beverly High School in Beverly, Massachusetts, used tombstone data in her class on "Primary History through the History of Beverly," and then on "Tiptoeing through the Tombstones."

These courses allow her students to analyze information on the tombstones as they evolved through Puritan New England. These gravestone symbols include death heads, cherubs, urns and willow branches, inscriptions, borders, and various styles popular in New England circa 1620–1820 (Eastman, 2002). Similarly, Szpek (2007) undertook a study of Jewish tombstones in Eastern Europe and examined the symbolic and literal depictions of epilates and engravings on these stones. Szpek suggests that the inscriptions on a stone, the material of the tombstones, the nature of the artisan's craft, and the ultimate fate of each tombstone all suggest that these Jewish tombstones can serve as material artifacts of Jewish heritage beyond their presentation of genealogical details.

Official Documentary Records Schools, social agencies, hospitals, retail establishments, and other organizations have reputations for creating an abundance of written records, files, and communications (Bogdan & Biklen, 1992). Many people regard this mountain of paper—or e-mails—as something other than official documents. In fact, *official documentary records* are originally produced for some special limited audiences, even if they eventually find their way into the public domain. These records may include official court transcripts, police reports, census information, financial records, crime statistics, political speech transcripts, internally generated government agency reports, school records, bills of lading, sales records, and similar documents. Official documents may also include less obvious, and sometimes less openly available, forms of communications such as interoffice memos, printed e-mail messages, minutes from meetings, organizational newsletters, and so forth. These materials often convey important and useful information that a researcher can effectively use as data.

Official documentary records may offer particularly interesting sources of data. Blee (1987), for example, bases her investigation of gender ideology and the role of women in the early Ku Klux Klan on a content analysis of official documentary records. As Blee (1987, p. 76) described it, "The analysis of the WKKK [Women's Ku Klux Klan] uses speeches and articles by the imperial commander of the women's klan, leaflets and recruiting material and internal organizational documents such as descriptions of ceremonies, rituals and robes and banners, membership application forms and the WKKK constitution and laws."

Naturally, not all research questions can be answered through the use of archival data, or at least not archival data alone. Some studies, however, are so well suited to archival data that attempts to examine phenomena in another manner might not prove as fruitful. For example, Poole and Regoli (1981) were interested in assessing professional prestige associated with criminology and criminal justice journals. In order to assess this, they counted the number of citations for various journals (in the *Index of Social Science Citations*) and ranked each cited journal from most to least citations. The operative assumption was that the journals with the greatest frequency of citation reflected the subjective preference of professionals working in the field. In consequence, those journals that enjoyed the most frequent reference in scholarly works possessed the greatest amount of prestige.

In a similar fashion, Thomas and Bronick (1984) examined the professional prestige of graduate criminology and criminal justice programs by ranking each on the basis of volume of publication citations per faculty member during a single year (1979–1980). Thomas and Bronick examined both the total number of citations of faculty in each department studied and the number of citations per each experience year of faculty members in each department. By assessing both the quantity of publications and publication weight (by considering proportions of publications in prestigious journals) Thomas and Bronick managed to rank the graduate programs.

Most archival data can be managed unobtrusively; however, researchers must sometimes be cautious regarding certain ethical concerns. For example, since some archives include certain identifiers such as names and addresses, their use requires that researchers take steps to ensure confidentiality. For instance, police complaint records typically are open to the public (with the exception of certain criminal complaints involving minors) and contain much identifying information. Similarly, during the recent past, a growing number of newspapers have begun publishing police blotter sections. These typically indicate the names, addresses, occupations, charges, and frequently the case dispositions of crimes committed during the day or evening preceding the published account. Certainly, these types of data could prove valuable in a variety of studies. But care is necessary if you are to avoid identifying the individuals depicted in these press accounts or crime reports.

A simple removal of certain particularly sensitive identifiers (e.g., names and addresses) and aggregation of the data according to some nonidentifying factor might be sufficient. For instance, in a study of crime in relation to geographic-environmental factors that was mapped by C. Ray Jefferys, particulars of identity were unnecessary. Using official criminal reports occurring in Atlanta during 1985 and 1986, Jefferys annotated a map of the city and identified high-risk locations for particular categories of crime.

Along similar lines, Freedman (1979) indicated that the self-admittance patient census in a New York state psychiatric facility located in Syracuse increased significantly following the first freeze (late November or early December). Conversely, Freedman suggested a like number of discharges occurred suddenly around late March and April (after which they tapered off) as the weather grew warmer. Freedman's explanation was that street people checked themselves into the facility to avoid the severely cold winter weather of Syracuse.

Social scientists have traditionally used a variety of official types of reports and records. Several governmental agencies exist literally in order to generate, assess, and disseminate research information. In many cases, in addition to straightforward statistical analysis, detailed reports and monographs are made available. Furthermore, because of the technological advances in audio- and videotaping devices, and the presence of C-SPAN in the United States, it is becoming increasingly possible to obtain verbatim accounts of governmental hearings, congressional sessions, and similar events.

Burstein and Freudenberg (1978), for example, were interested in how public opinion influenced legislative votes. Although legislators certainly possess the right to vote their consciences even against the general wishes of their constituents, they do not necessarily do so. Burstein and Freudenberg examined 91 bills and motions, concerning the issue of the Vietnam War, submitted both before and after the 1970 invasion of Cambodia. These bills were compared against public opinion poll information that had been conducted throughout the war years and ranged from opinions against the war from the beginning to those opinions that approved of and supported the ways the president handled the situation.

Stated simply, Burstein and Freudenberg (1978) found that before the 1970 invasion of Cambodia, public opinion had an influence on some of the dovish (antiwar) legislators but that hawkish (prowar) legislators were generally unaffected. Similarly, funding the Vietnam War, although not a particularly important dimension in affecting vote outcomes before 1970, did become relevant in votes after the 1970 invasion. The explanation offered by Burstein and Freudenberg suggests that while the financial costs of Vietnam were bearable before the invasion of Cambodia, these costs became insupportable after the invasion.

Today, in addition to voting records, the behavior of Congress and state legislatures can be unobtrusively assessed through other traces. Because of technological innovations and increased permissiveness on the part of state and federal legislators (perhaps in response to the secretiveness that surrounded Watergate) congressional and state legislature debates and votes are routinely televised.

Videotape can now capture the kind of joke-making at one another's expense that is rather common in state legislature committee meetings, as well as the various symbolic gestures and ceremonial rituals that typically occur but have gone unrecorded for years. Analysis of these types of interactions may reveal some interesting and telling things about how both politics and votes actually operate. (In some particularly egregious cases, these "legislative" moments also go viral on the Internet.)

For example, Masters and Sullivan, professors at Dartmouth College, have examined meanings encoded in the facial grimaces and symbolic gestures of politicians during speeches. In order to study the various clucks, furrowed brows, smiles, head tilts, hand motions, and so forth, Masters and Sullivan examined videotapes of speeches made by political leaders (Masters & Sullivan, 1988).

Videotape in a variety of settings is becoming one of the most useful and complete running records available to archival researchers. Many law enforcement agencies, for example, now routinely videotape persons as they are tested for driving while intoxicated or when conducting crime scene investigations, and maintain these taped records for prolonged periods of time (Berg, 2008b). Front-mounted cameras in police squad cars provide evidence that the police are following, or failing to follow, approved procedures during stops and arrests. Some of these videos also enjoy a second life as entertainment on the Web.

Educational researchers have long recognized the utility of videotaping in classroom- and playground-based studies; the videotapes frequently provide access for other investigators who may use these videotapes as a source of secondary data for analysis (Stigler, Gonzales, Kawanaka, Knoll, & Serrano, 1999).

As noted in Chapter 6, many ethnographies of schooling have been compiled by using videotaping strategies. For example, Erickson and Mohatt (1988) described their efforts to uncover cultural organizations of participation structure in classrooms. They videotaped both first-grade teachers and their students across a one-year period. In order to capture the students and their teachers in usual interaction routines, each hour-long tape cassette was photographed with a minimum of camera editing. In other words, the camera operator did not pan the room or zoom in and out for close-ups. Rather, wide-angle shots of the classroom and its participants were utilized. The result was an effective collection of data that gave a microethnographic look at how interactions between teachers and students differ when the two groups belong to different cultural groups (in this case, Native American and non–Native American).

Certainly videotapes should prove to be important and useful as audiovisual transcripts of official proceedings, capturing emergent and/or serendipitous acts in various social settings, and creating behavioral records. In fact, in 1987, the *American Behavioral Scientist* devoted an entire issue to the use of VCRs in research. The ubiquity of digital video cameras in phones greatly expands the potential uses of recording devices, as well as yielding a vast quantity of raw data for future analysis. But other video-related official documents may prove equally useful—in particular, the receipt records from sales and rentals of DVDs.

For example, the issue of whether watching violence on television is related to committing violence in society is a long-standing question. As early as 1969, the National Commission on the Causes and Prevention of Violence (Eisenhower, 1969, p. 5) concluded: "Violence on television encourages violent forms of behavior, and fosters moral and social values about violence in daily life which are unacceptable in civilized society."

Since 1969, a number of studies have similarly concluded that watching violent television programs encourages violent behavior (see Comstock, 1977; Eron, 1980; Phillips, 1983). Yet the debate over whether watching violence on television encourages violent behavior continues. Central issues in this debate include the question of whether people who became aggressive after viewing violent programs might already have been aggressive; whether the violence depicted on the program was or was not rewarded and/or justified (i.e., was it the good guys or the bad guys who were violent?), and whether the viewer was watching a real-life violent event (e.g., hockey, boxing, football) or a fictionalized one. More to the point, after decades of demonstrating that a relationship between viewing and acting exists, we still cannot demonstrate the exact mechanism by which it works.

Many researchers regard the link between media violence and violent behavior as well established. Other researchers claim that this link remains unsubstantiated. Jeffrey Johnson and his associates (2002) reported on a 17-year study of a community sample of 707 individuals. The researchers found that there was a significant association between the amount of time spent watching television during adolescence and early adulthood and the likelihood of subsequent aggressive acts against others. For example, the researchers found that 14-year-old boys who were allowed to watch three hours or more of television a day were about twice as likely as those who watched less than an hour of television a day to commit a crime by the time they reached early adulthood.

By identifying and tabulating the rental rate of certain movies that depict a range and variety of violence, researchers may be able to discover which dimensions of violence appear to be the most popular (e.g., vigilant behavior, retaliation, national reprisals, and sporting events). Rental records, TiVo queues, and media downloads identify both consumers and the products consumed. It is possible to gain demographic information on who rents what by checking membership application records (another official document record). Estimates of which films are rented how frequently and by whom may allow greater understanding of Eron's (1980) notion that watching violence may encourage desensitization, role-modeling, and approval of violence in others.

Webb and his colleagues (1981) may have been correct at the time when they suggested that videotaped records were disorganized and not widely accessible, but times have changed. In the past several years, there has been tremendous growth in the use of visual and auditory media and equipment by official agencies, researchers, and private citizens. In addition to an increased number of sales and rental suppliers, many libraries now offer fairly sizable collections of DVDs. Even children's books and games are produced in video formats of one type or another. Supermarkets and convenience stores carry huge selections of DVDs. Large movie rental chains have cropped up across the nation, and where you do not find one, you are likely to find a mom-and-pop movie rental store. The array of possible uses for and access to video and digital film data have simply grown too large to be overlooked or ignored by researchers.

As Chapter 9 more fully details, oral histories are often recorded or transcribed, creating excellent data for present or future unobtrusive researchers (Yow, 2005). This form of *history-telling* (Portelli, 1992), creating records of oral histories, also suggests some intrusion into the lives of subjects. However, oral historians and historiographers (discussed in Chapter 9) often create and archive documents that later researchers can use as unobtrusive data.

Private Archives: Solicited and Unsolicited Documents

Thus far, the discussion has centered on running records prepared primarily for mass public consumption. Other types of archival records, however, are created for smaller, more specific audiences than the public in general. These private archival records include autobiographies (memoirs), diaries and letters, home movies and videos, and artistic and creative artifacts (drawings, sketches). In some cases, these documents occur naturally and are discovered by the investigators (unsolicited documents); in other situations, documents may be requested by investigators (solicited documents). An example of an unsolicited private record might be an existing house log, for instance, of a delinquency group home, which could be used to investigate staff and client relationships in order to determine misbehavior patterns. An example of a solicited document, on the other hand, would be a daily work journal kept by nurses in an intensive care unit at the request of researchers for the purpose of assessing staff and task effectiveness.

Private records are particularly useful for creating case studies or life histories. Typically, owing to the personal nature of private documents, the subjects' own definitions of the situation emerge in their private records, along with the ways they make sense of their daily living routines. Precisely, these bits of self-disclosure allow researchers to draw out complete pictures of the subjects' perceptions of their life experiences.

Perhaps the most widely accepted form of personal document is the autobiography (Chamberlayne, Bornat, & Wengraf, 2007). In their discussions of autobiographies, Bogdan and Taylor (1975), Denzin (1978), Webb et al. (1981), and Taylor and Bogdan (1998), each draw extensively from Allport's classic (1942) monograph entitled *The Use of Personal Documents in Psychological Science*. Allport distinguishes among three types of autobiography: comprehensive autobiographies, topical autobiographies, and edited autobiographies.

Comprehensive Autobiography Inexperienced researchers are usually most familiar with the comprehensive autobiography. This category of autobiography spans the life of the individual from his or her earliest recall to the time of the writing of the work and includes descriptions of life experiences, personal insights, and anecdotal reminiscences (Goodley, 2004; Taylor & Bogdan, 1998).

Topical Autobiography In contrast to the rounded and complete description of experiences offered in comprehensive autobiographies, a *topical autobiography* offers a fragmented picture of life. Denzin (1978, p. 221) suggests that Sutherland's (1956) treatment of "Chic Conwell," who was a professional thief, illustrates this type of autobiographical style. In this and other cases, the story is presumably interesting to readers or researchers because of the nature of the topic rather than the identity of the author. Other examples of this sort of excision are Bogdan's (1974) examination of "Jane Fry," a prostitute, and Rettig, Torres, and Garrett's (1977) examination of "Manny," a criminal drug addict. Foster, McAllister, and O'Brien (2006) used this reflective method to consider their own therapeutic experiences as mental health nurses, whereas Johnstone (1999) recommends the use of topical autobiography in nursing research as a technique that gives prominence to the subjective understandings and systems of meaning of the research subjects, rather than the understandings of the researcher.

Edited Autobiography In the case of edited autobiographies, researchers serve as editors and commentators, eliminating any repetition in descriptions, making lengthy discourses short and crisp, and highlighting and amplifying selected segments of the material while deleting other segments. Regarding the issue of which segments should be edited and which retained as intended by the author, Allport (1942, p. 78) offered a broad guideline and suggested that all unique styles of speech (slang, colloquialism, street jargon, etc.) remain unedited. Researchers should only edit for the sake of clarity. An example of such an edited life history can be found in the writing of Jane Ribbens (1998) who describes the nature of motherhood from an autobiographical perspective.

The intimacy afforded by diaries and personal journals remains an under-utilized element in research. In diaries, individuals are free to fully express their feelings, opinions, and understandings (Alaszewski, 2006). In contrast, published autobiographies must maintain the readers' interest or perhaps distort reality in order to project the author's desired public image. Of course, diarists may claim to be writing for themselves while later readers might believe that the text was prepared with posterity in mind (Dawson, 2000).

Researchers may also assign research subjects the task of maintaining a daily diary. Kevin Courtright (1994) has suggested there are several important advantages to using the *diary method*. First, it provides a defense against memory decay as respondents are typically asked to record their events either as they happen or shortly thereafter. Second, respondents who are asked to keep diaries act both as *performers* and as *informants*. Thus, diaries are able to provide information about the writer (as performer) and of others who interact with the respondent/writer (as observer). As informant, the respondent is able to reflect on his or her own performance and that of those with whom he or she has interacted. The respondent can further articulate explanations of purpose, allocate praise or blame, and even act as a critic. Finally, the diary method provides an opportunity for the subject to reflectively recreate the events, since the diary is written and maintained by the subject himself or herself (Courtright, 1994).

The use of autobiography continues to meet resistance in some academic circles and has even been called "self-indulgent" (Mykhalovskiy, 1996). In defense of the strategy of autobiography, Mykhalovskiy (1996, p. 134) has written, "The abstract, disembodied voice of traditional academic discourse [is] a fiction, accomplished through writing and other practices which remove evidence of a text's author, as part of concealing the condition of its production." But, all in all, autobiography, whether offered as a full and lengthy unfolding of one's life or as snippets of disclosure in prefaces and appendices, can be extremely useful. This information offers more than simply a single individual's subjective view on matters. An autobiography can reflect the social contours of a given time, the prevailing or competing ideological orientations of a group, or the self-reflections about one's activities in various roles. In short, autobiographies offer a solid measure of data for the research process.

Increasingly, people of all ages and social circumstances are publishing their own daily journals online, as *blogs* (Berger, 2004; Taylor, 2002; Thottam, 2002). Blogs—the term is short for *weblog*—vary in their content from fairly traditional diary entries, such as the woes and joys of the writer, to descriptions and criticisms of books, movies, and life events. In addition, many link the reader to other bloggers, informational Web pages, photographs, search engines, and various other locations on the Web. Blogs are not just simple Web pages; rather, they are often sophisticated pages with multiple frames, links, audio elements, streaming video, and considerable interconnectivity. Yet, blogs are actually fairly simple to construct, and most end users begin with a template or shell that is frequently provided by the blog site. There are also blogs about blogging. Perhaps the most fascinating thing about blogs is their potential as research data. Like any unsolicited documents, they provide insights into their creators' perceptions on a wide assortment of subjects and interest areas (Branscum, 2001).

One could also employ blogs as a means for intentionally soliciting journal or diary data that could be easily accessed by the researcher from any computer with a Web connection. The logic of using such a solicited journal document is not uncommon in educational research and assessment research in which instructors may ask students to maintain journals during the course of the semester (see, e.g., Lockhart, 2002).

Another distinct form of intimate private record is the *letter*. In contrast to the autobiography or diary, the letter is not simply a chronicle of past experiences. Letters are designed to communicate something to some other person. As a result, they are geared toward a *dual audience*—namely, the writer and the recipient. The topic of the letter and the social roles and personal relationships of both the writer and receiver must, therefore, be considered.

The classic example of letters as a source of research data, of course, is Thomas and Znaniecki's (1927) *The Polish Peasant*. In their study, Thomas and Znaniecki learned of an extensive correspondence among recent Polish immigrants in America and their friends and relatives remaining in Poland. As part of their pool of data, Thomas and Znaniecki solicited copies of letters written to Poland as well as those received by Polish immigrants from their homeland. A small fee was offered for each letter submitted. Typically, however, they received only one side of a given letter exchange. In spite of limitations, Thomas and Zaniecki managed to uncover a variety of social values and cultural strains associated with the transition from Poland to America.

Suicide has been studied using letters as a viable data source (Garfinkel, 1967; Jacobs, 1967; Salib, Cawley, & Healy, 2002). In one study, Jacobs examined 112 suicide notes and found that the notes could be categorized into six groups, the largest of which was what Jacobs termed "first form notes." From the content of these suicide notes, Jacobs deduced that the authors were involved in long-standing and complex problems. Unable to solve these problems, they found no alternative other than taking their own lives. In order to justify this final act, the individuals begged indulgence and forgiveness from the survivors.

In another study, by Salib et al. (2002), the researchers investigated suicide notes in 125 older people whose deaths were ruled suicides by a coroner over a period of 10 years. The goal of the study was to see whether there was a difference between older victims of suicide who left notes and those who did not. The study found that many older people may be isolated and have no one with whom to communicate, while others may no longer have the ability to express themselves. Interestingly, the investigators could not identify consistent parameters to differentiate between those who left notes and those who did not; nonetheless, the lack of specific findings does not mean that absence of a suicide note necessarily indicates a less serious attempt (Salib et al., 2002).

A Last Remark about Archival Records

Throughout the preceding review of various archival studies, a variety of research topics were related to archival materials. The purpose of this was to suggest the versatility and range of knowledge that can be served by archival research.

An attempt was also made to indicate both the enormous quantity of information and the technological innovations available in connection to archival data. Collections of both privately and publicly held video materials are certainly among the most striking and exciting of recent additions to viable archival sources.

However, researchers should be cautious in the use of archival data. Although an extraordinarily useful source of data for some research questions, archives may be the wrong source of data for some other questions. It is particularly important to use multiple procedures (triangulation) when working with archival data in order to reduce possible sources of error (missing data, etc.).

Physical Erosion and Accretion: Human Traces as Data Sources

As implied in the section title, what follows is an examination of various physical traces. Quite literally, traces are physical items left behind by humans, often as the result of some unconscious or unintentional activity, that tell us something about these individuals. Because these traces have been left behind without the producers' knowledge of their potential usefulness to social scientists, these pieces of research information are *nonreactively produced*. Two distinct categories of traces are *erosion measures* (indicators of wearing down or away) and *accretion measures* (indicators of accumulation or buildup).

Erosion Measures

Physical evidence is often the key to solving criminal cases. Similarly, physical evidence is frequently the key to resolving social scientific questions in research. *Erosion measures* include several types of evidence indicating that varying degrees of selective wear or use have occurred on some object or material. In most cases, erosion measures are used with other techniques in order to corroborate one another.

An example of an erosion measure would be using replacement records in order to determine which of a series of high school French language tapes was most frequently used. The hypothesis would be that the tape that required the greatest amount of repair or replacement was the one most frequently used. Unfortunately, several other explanations exist for why a particular tape frequently needs repair. In other words, there can be alternative hypotheses to explain this erosion. Thus, caution is once again advised when using erosion measures alone.

In spite of their obvious limitations as data sources, erosion measures do contribute interestingly to social scientific research. Perhaps the most widely quoted illustration of how erosion measures operate involves a study at the Chicago Museum of Science and Industry cited by Webb and colleagues (1981, p. 7):

> A committee was formed to set up a psychological exhibit at Chicago's Museum of Science and Industry. The committee learned that the vinyl tiles around the exhibit containing live, hatching chicks had to be replaced every six weeks or so; tiles in other areas of the museum went for years without replacement. A comparative study of the rate of tile replacement around the various museum exhibits could give a rough ordering of the popularity of the exhibits.

Webb and his colleagues (1981) additionally note that beyond the erosion measure, unobtrusive observations (covert observers) indicated that people stood in front of the chick display longer than they stood near any other exhibit. Additional evidence may be necessary to determine whether the wear shown on tiles near the chick exhibit resulted from many different people walking by or smaller numbers of people standing and shuffling their feet over prolonged periods of time. Nonetheless, the illustration does indicate the particularly interesting kinds of information provided by augmenting data sources with erosion measures. This case further illustrates how multiple measures may be used to corroborate one another.

Another example of an erosion measure cited by Webb and colleagues (1981) involves the examination of wear on library books as an index of their popularity. A variation on this book-wear index might be the examination of textbooks being sold back to a bookstore in order to determine if any signs of use are apparent. For example, if the spine of the book has been broken, it might indicate that the student had actually opened and turned the pages. You might likewise consider whether page corners have been turned down or sections of text highlighted.

Accretion Measures

In contrast to the selective searching out of materials suggested in erosion measures, *accretion measures* represent deposits over time. These trace elements are laid down naturally, without intrusion from researchers (Gray, 2004). The early American sociologist Thorstein Veblen (1899) analyzed the possessions that people of wealth displayed conspicuously to explain the social identities of the "leisure class." In contrast, Monica Smith (2007) studied material items that people purchased and did not display to examine the nature of "reflexive identity," or that portion of our identity that is distinct from our public presentations of ourselves.

In a similar manner to the example of book wear, suggested earlier, the amount of dust accrued on library books might indicate the inactivity of these books—in other words, the lack of use of these books (Kimmel, 2007).

Although accretion measures may seem more immediately related to the example of paint deposits described in the beginning of this chapter, that is but one form of accretion. The deposit of almost any object or material by humans can be an accretion. In fact, as illustrated by the work of Rathje (1979), even garbage may contain important clues to social culture.

Another illustration of accretion is the examination by Kephart and Berg (2002a, 2002b) of gang graffiti collected from various locations throughout a single city in Southern California. Kephart and Berg were able to establish a typology of symbolic messages concealed in the various renderings of gang graffiti and to distinguish between certain categories of messages and mere graffiti *tags* (names and/or initials of individual artists left on walls, poles, and curbs). Interestingly, although accretion data are generally nonreactive, since the researcher enters the picture after the data were created, there are other forms of reactivity that can arise from the mining of recent historical data which are evidenced in this study. Because the researchers could actually link specific instances of graffiti with their artists, local law enforcement was able to identify these vandals and obtain reparations to cover the cost of the graffiti's removal. As the researchers entered the scene long after the graffiti had been produced, they had no obligation to hide this knowledge.

Some Final Remarks about Physical Traces

There are several advantages to erosion and accretion measures. Certainly, it should be clear that they are themselves rather inconspicuous and unaffected by researchers who locate and observe them. In consequence, the trace data are largely free of any reactive measurement effects. However, interpreting these physical traces and affixing meaning is problematic and may severely bias the results. Thus, researchers must always remember to obtain corroboration.

Similarly, any single trace of physical evidence may have strong *population restrictions* (Webb et al., 1981, p. 32). It is not likely, for example, that a complete description of some group can be accomplished on the merits of some worn spot on a tile or a smudge on some wall. Similarly, physical traces may be selectively found only at certain times and in only certain places.

In conclusion, physical traces, although terribly interesting and useful in many ways, are only one of several possible strategies that should be used in concert.

TRYING IT OUT

Researchers can practice using unobtrusive measures in a variety of ways. Some of the unobtrusive data more readily accessible for students/researchers are those offered in the headlines of daily newspapers, the covers of magazines, the commercials on television, the titles of movies they view, and so forth.

Suggestion 1   Locate an old cemetery in your community (the older the better). Now, using headstones and grave markers as your primary data, develop an assessment of the symbols used on the gravestones and markers. You might want to take photographs or draw facsimiles of various symbols illustrated on the gravestones and markers. These may include religious symbols (crosses, stars, etc.), decorative elements (urns, leaves, angels, etc.), epitaphs (e.g., "here lies John Brown, a good father, brother and husband"). Take note of the dates on the headstones and grave markers—in what year did they start being flat metal markers rather than standing stone gravestones? Is there any indication of military status? After compiling your data, write a brief report explaining what you found.

Suggestion 2   Locate blog membership lists from any blog community list. Systematically locate the profile or self-description of 50 blog members and record all demographic information (e.g., gender, age, marital status, educational level, or whatever other information they provide). Examine your results and assess whether there are certain categories of people, based on your sampling, that are involved in blogging on this site.

Suggestion 3   A final practice suggestion requires obtaining permission from a campus organization or group to review the minutes of meetings for the past several years. Using these data, identify possible patterns such as cliques of members who seem to make similar motions, voting records, who holds positions of leadership, and so forth. It may be best to use a group or organization that you belong to (a fraternity, sorority, or political group).

REFERENCES

Alaszewski, A. M. (2006). *Using Diaries for Social Research*. London: Sage.

Allport, G. (1942). *The Use of Personal Documents in Psychological Science*. New York: Social Science Council.

Berg, B. L. (2008a). Visual ethnography. In Lisa M. Given (Ed.), *The SAGE Encyclopedia of Qualitative Research Methods* (pp. 934–937). Thousand Oaks, CA: Sage.

Berg, B. L. (2008b). *Criminal Investigation*. New York: McGraw Hill.

Berger, P. (2004). Are you blogging yet? *Information Searcher 14*(2), 1–2.

Blee, K. (1987). Gender ideology and the role of women in the 1920s Klan movement. *Sociological Spectrum 7*(1), 73–97.

Boba, R. L. (2008). *Crime Analysis with Crime Mapping*. Thousand Oaks, CA: Sage.

Bogdan, R. (1974). *Being Different: The Autobiography of Jane Fry*. New York: John Wiley and Sons.

Bogdan, R., & Biklen, S. K. (1992). *Qualitative Research for Education* (2nd ed.). Boston, MA: Allyn and Bacon.

Bogdan, R., & Taylor, S. (1975). *Introduction to Qualitative Research Methods*. New York: John Wiley and Sons.

Bradley, D. S., Boles, J., & Jones, C. (1979). From mistress to hooker. *Qualitative Sociology 2*(2), 42–62.

Bramley, H. (2002). Diana, princess of Wales: The contemporary goddess. *Sociological Research Online 7*(1). Available online at www.socreasonline.org.uk/7/1/bramley.html.

Branscum, D. (March 5, 2001). Who's blogging now? More and more Internet users are sharing their lives in public online journals called Weblogs that can be strangely addictive. *Newsweek*, 62.

Burstein, P., & Freudenberg, W. R. (1978). Changing public policy: The impact of opinion, antiwar demonstrations, and war costs on Senate voting in Vietnam War motions. *American Journal of Sociology 84*, 99–122.

Chamberlayne, P., Bornat, J., & Wengraf, T. (2007). *The Turn to Biographical Methods in Social Sciences*. New York: Taylor & Francis.

Comstock, G. S. (1977). Types of portrayal and aggressive behavior. *Journal of Communication 27*(3), 189–198.

Courtright, K. E. (March 1994). An overview of the use and potential advantages of the diary method. Paper presented at the annual meeting of the Academy of Criminal Justice Sciences, Boston, MA.

Dawson, M. S. (2000). Histories and texts: Refiguring the diary of Samuel Pepys histories and texts: Refiguring the diary of Samuel Pepys. *The Historical Journal*, 43(2), 407–431.

DeBartolo Carmack, S. (2002). *Your Guide to Cemetery Research*. Cincinnati, OH: Betterway Books.

Denzin, N. K. (1978). *The Research Act*. New York: McGraw-Hill.

Eastman, D. (2002). Tiptoeing through the tombstones. Common-Place. *The Interactive Journal of Early American Life 2*(2). Available online at www.common-place.org/vol-02/no-02/school/.

Eisenhower, M. (1969). Commission statement on violence in television entertainment programs. National Commission on the Causes and Prevention of Violence. Washington, DC: U.S. Government Printing Office.

Erickson, F., & Mohatt, G. (1988). Cultural organization of participation structures in two classrooms of Indian students. In G. Spindler (Ed.), *Doing the Ethnography of Schooling*. Prospect Heights, IL: Waveland Press.

Eron, L. D. (1980). Prescriptions for reduction of aggression. *American Psychologist 35*(3), 244–252.

Foster, K., McAllister, M., & O'Brien, L. (2006). Extending the boundaries: Autoethnography as an emergent method in mental health nursing research. *International Journal of Mental Health Nursing 15*(1) 44–53.

Freedman, J. (1979). *Lecture Notes from a Course on Clinical Sociology*. Syracuse, NY: Syracuse University.

Garfinkel, H. (1967). *Studies in Ethnomethodology*. Englewood Cliffs, NJ: Prentice Hall.

Goffman, E. (1979). *Gender Advertisements*. New York: Harper and Row.

Goodley, D. (2004). *Researching Life Stories: Methods, Theory, and Analysis in a Biographical Age*. New York: Routledge Falmer.

Gottschalk, S. (1995). Ethnographic fragments in postmodern spaces. *Journal of Contemporary Ethnography 24*(2), 195–228.

Gray, D. E. (2004). *Doing Research in the Real World*. London: Sage.

Jackson, B. (1977). *Killing Time: Life in the Arkansas Penitentiary*. Ithaca, NY: Cornell University Press.

Jacobs, J. (1967). A phenomenological study of suicide notes. *Social Problems 15*, 60–72.

Jelenko, C., III (1980). The rock syndrome: A newly discovered environmental hazard. *Journal of Irreproducible Results 26*, 14.

Johnson, J. G., Cohen, P., Smailey, E. M., Kasen, S., & Brook, J. S. (2002). Television viewing and aggressive behavior during adolescence and adulthood. *Science 297*, 2468–2471.

Johnstone, M.-J. (1999). Reflective topical autobiography: An underutilised interpretive research method in nursing. *Collegian: Journal of the Royal College of Nursing Australia 6*(1), 24–29.

Kephart, T., & Berg, B. (March 2002a). The use of photographs as data in a study of gang graffiti: A research note. Presented at the annual meeting of the Academy of Criminal Justice Sciences, Anaheim, CA.

Kephart, T., & Berg, B. (February 2002b). Gang graffiti analysis: A methodological model for data collection. Presented at the annual meeting of the Western Criminal Justice Society, San Diego, CA.

Kimmel, A. J. (2007). *Ethical Issues in Behavioral Research: Basic and Applied Perspectives* (2nd ed.). Malden, MA: Blackwell Publishing.

Lee, R. M. (2000). *Unobtrusive Measures in Social Research*. Philadelphia, PA: Open University Press.

Lepisto, C. (April 24, 2005). The garbage project Treehugger. Available online at http://www.treehugger.com/files/2005/04/the_garbage_pro.php.

Lockhart, M. (2002). The use of student journals to increase faculty and learner inquiry and reflection. *Academic Exchange Quarterly 6*(1), 6–15.

Lofland, J., Snow, D. A., Anderson, L., & Lofland, L. H. (2006). *Analysing Social Settings: A Guide to Qualitative Observation and Analysis* (4th ed.). Belmont, CA: Wadsworth.

Masters, R., & Sullivan, D. (1988). Happy warriors: Leaders' facial displays, viewers' emotions and political support. *American Journal of Political Science 32*(2), 345–368.

Molotch, H., & Boden, D. (1985). Talking social structure: Discourse domination and the Watergate hearing. *American Sociological Review 50*(3), 273–287.

Mykhalovskiy, E. (1996). Reconsidering table talk: Critical thoughts on the relationship between sociology, autobiography, and self-indulgence. *Qualitative Sociology 19*(1), 131–151.

Payne, B. (1998). Conceptualizing the impact of health care crimes on the poor. *Free Inquiry in Creative Sociology 26*(2), 159–167.

Phillips, D. P. (August 1983). The impact of mass media violence on U.S. homicides. *American Sociological Review 48*, 560–568.

Pink, S. (2006). *Doing Visual Ethnography: Images, Media and Representation in Research* (2nd ed.). Thousand Oaks, CA: Sage.

Poole, E. D., & Regoli, R. M. (1981). Periodical prestige in criminology and criminal justice: A comment. *Criminology 19*, 470–498.

Portelli, A. (1992). History-telling and time: An example from Kentucky. *Oral History Review 20*(1/2), 51–66.

Pullen, R., Ortloff, V., Casey, S., & Payne, J. (2000). Analysis of academic misconduct using unobtrusive research: A study of discarded cheat sheets. *College Student Journal 34*(4), 616–625.

Rathje, R. H. (1979). Trace measures. In L. Sechrest (Ed.), *Unobtrusive Measurement Today*. San Francisco: Jossey-Bass.

Rathje, R. H., & Murphy, C. (2001). *Rubbish: The Archaeology of Garbage*. Tucson, AZ: University of Arizona Press.

Rettig, R. P., Torres, M. J., & Garrett, G. R. (1977). *Manny: A Criminal Addict's Story*. Boston, MA: Houghton Mifflin.

Ribbens, J. (1998). Hearing my feeling voice? An autobiographical discussion of mother-hood. In J. Ribbens & R. Edwards (Eds.), *Feminist Dilemmas in Qualitative Research*. Thousand Oaks, CA: Sage.

Salib, E., Cawley, S., & Healy, R. (2002). The significance of suicide notes in older adults. *Aging and Mental Health 6*(2), 186–190.

Sawyer, H. G. (1961). The meaning of numbers. Paper presented at the annual meeting of the American Association of Advertising Agencies. Cited in Eugene J. Webb, Donald T. Campbell, Richard D. Schwartz, Lee Sechrest, and Janet Belew Grove, Nonreactive Measures in the Social Sciences. Boston, MA: Houghton Mifflin, 1981.

Schmalleger, F. (1996). *The Trial of the Century: People of the State of California vs. Orenthal James Simpson*. Englewood Cliffs, NJ: Prentice Hall.

Shanks, M., Platt, D., & Rathje, W. L. (2004). The perfume of garbage: Modernity and the archaeological. *Journal of Modernism/Modernity 11*(1), 61–83.

Smith, M. L. (2007). Inconspicuous consumption: Non-display goods and identity formation. *Journal of Archaeological Method and Theory 14*(4), 412–438.

Stigler, J. W., Gonzales, P., Kawanaka, T., Knoll, S., & Serrano, A. (1999). *Third International Mathematics and Science Study*. Washington, DC: National Center for Education Statistics.

Sutherland, E. H. (1956). *The Professional Thief*. Phoenix, 1937. (Reprint). Chicago, IL: University of Chicago Press.

Szpek, H. M. (2007). And in their death they were not separated: Aesthetics of Jewish tombstones in Eastern Europe. *The International Journal of the Humanities 5*(4), 165–178.

Taylor, C. (February 11, 2002). Psst, wanna see my blog? Impromptu online journals are popping up all over the Web. If I can figure out how to build one, you can too. *Time 159*(6), 68.

Taylor, S. J., & Bogdan, R. (1998). *Introduction to Qualitative Research Methods* (3rd ed.). New York: John Wiley and Sons.

Thomas, C., & Bronick, M. J. (1984). The quality of doctoral programs in deviance criminology and criminal justice: An empirical assessment. *Journal of Criminal Justice 12*(1), 21–37.

Thomas, W. I., & Znaniecki, F. (1927). *The Polish Peasant.* New York: Knopf.

Thottam, J. (January–February 2002). Dotcom diaries: Online journals called blogs show you the lives—and links—of fascinating strangers. *On 7*(1), 24–33.

Veblen, T. (1899). *The Theory of the Leisure Class.* London: MacMillan.

Warner, L. W. (1959). *The Living and the Dead: A Study of the Symbolic Life of Americans.* New Haven, CT: Yale University Press.

Warner, L. W., & Low, J. O. (1947). *The Social System of the Modern Community. The Strike: A Social Analysis.* New Haven, CT: Yale University Press.

Warner, L. W., & Lunt, P. S. (1941). *The Social Life of a Modern Community.* New Haven, CT: Yale University Press.

Warner, L. W., & Lunt, P. S. (1942). *The Status System of a Modern Community.* New Haven, CT: Yale University Press.

Warner, L. W., & Srole, L. (1945). *The Social Systems of American Ethnic Groups.* New Haven, CT: Yale University Press.

Webb, E., Campbell, D. T., Schwartz, R. D., & Sechrest, L. (1966). *Unobtrusive Measures: Nonreactive Research in the Social Sciences.* Chicago, IL: Rand McNally.

Webb, E., Campbell, D. T., Schwartz, R. D., Sechrest, L., & Grove, J. B. (1981). *Nonreactive Measures in the Social Sciences.* Boston, MA: Houghton Mifflin.

Webb, E., Cambell, D. T., Schwartz, R. D., & Sechrest, L. (2000). *Unobtrusive Measures* (Rev. ed.). Thousand Oaks, CA: Sage.

Weber, S. C. (1999). Origins, orientations and etiologies of the U.S. citizen militia movement, 1982–1997. *Free Inquiry in Creative Sociology 27*(1), 57–66.

Yow, V. R. (2005). *Recording Oral History: A Guide for the Humanities and Social Sciences.* New York: Altamira Press.

Z-Frank stresses radio to build big Chevy dealership (1962). *Advertising Age 33*, 83.

Chapter 9

Social Historical Research and Oral Traditions

What is Historical Research?

What exactly is meant by historical research, or what some call *historical event research* (Bachman & Schutt, 2003; Lewenson & Herrmann, 2007)? The obvious answer to this question is that historical research, or *social historical research* to put it in the context of this book, is an examination of elements of history. Unfortunately, this answer begs the next question: What is history? Often, in common parlance, the term *history* is used synonymously with the word *past* and refers conceptually to events of long ago (McDowell, 2002). Also in conversational usage, we tend to view history as a collection of *facts* about the past. Neither of these captures our uses of the term. From a social science perspective, history is an *account* of some past event or series of events. Historical research, then, is a method for discovering, from records and other accounts, what happened during some past period. But it is not simply fact centered; rather, historical research seeks to offer theoretical explanations for various historical events (Johnson & Christensen, 2003, 2007). Social historical research is a perspective on historical research that attempts to understand and explain social life in historical settings. It can be distinguished, for example, from political histories which explain shifting political systems, distributions of power, and the impact of nations on other nations, but which do not provide much detail about what life was like for "ordinary" people under these political systems.

You can open textbooks from many disciplines and locate *time lines*, lists, or drawings of time-ordered events shown in chronological sequence. This chronology of historical events allows the presenter to describe interesting or important past events, people, developments, and the like. It is a classification system some might call *historical*. Furthermore, it provides the reader with a sense of which things or events came before others. It is not, however, social historical research. Historical time lines can be quite illuminating and do have their place. Often they represent a summary of vast amounts of historical research. They are, however, passive, and often somewhat lifeless. Social historical research, on the other hand, attempts to fashion a descriptive written account of the past. Such a narrative account, at its best, is flowing, revealing, vibrant, and alive!

Social history involves far more than the mere retelling of facts from the past. It is more than linking together pieces of information found in diaries, letters, or other documents, important as such an activity might be. Social historical research is at once descriptive, factual, and fluid (Matejski, 1986). Nor is historical research merely creative nostalgia. In fact, it is important to distinguish nostalgia from research. Various methods may be used when undertaking social history, but all are informed by a theory or theories that provide a set of parameters that focus on asking about history as it unfolds, particularly the relationship between people, events, phenomena, and the historical situations that create history. Social history also overlaps with *historiography*, which is the study of how history is studied and written. In effect, the process of social history does not occur in a theoretical vacuum but examines the social contours of history in a kind of *praxis* (action) analysis and narration (Tobin & Kincheloe, 2006).

Nostalgia, or the retelling of comfortable past pleasantries, events, or situations, lacks research rigor. In contrast to nostalgia, *historical research* attempts to systematically recapture the complex nuances, the people, meanings, events, and even ideas of the past that have influenced and shaped the present (Hamilton, 1993; Leedy & Ormrod, 2005; McDowell, 2002). In nursing research, as Burns and Grove (2004) note, historical research provides a means for history of a profession to be transmitted to those entering the profession. Historical analysis of social knowledge, traditions, and conditions can increase appreciation and understanding of contemporary issues of health, race relations, crime and corrections, education, business trends, and an infinite array of social, political, and spiritual realms. Lusk (1997a) summarized the importance of historical research for nurses when she studied nursing's claim to professional status by examining classifications of American nurses as professional and nonprofessional from 1919 to 1930 (see also LoBiondo-Wood & Haber, 2002; Lusk, 1997b).

Historical research is the study of the relationships among issues that have influenced the past, continue to influence the present, and will certainly affect the future (Glass, 1989). Ironically, it is only during recent history that standard social science research methods books have begun looking seriously at historical research. Many methods texts omitted any consideration of this methodology (e.g., Bogdan & Biklen, 1992; Fitzgerald & Cox, 2002; Gilgun, Daly, & Handel, 1992; Taylor & Bogdan, 1998). In some cases, history is mentioned only in terms of its possible threat to internal validity (Frankfort-Nachmias & Nachmias, 2007; Rosnow & Rosenthal, 2007; Shaughnessy, Zechmeister, & Zechmeister, 2008) or its effect on construct validity (Taylor, 1994). In other texts, the use of historical research is used synonymously with comparative analysis (see, e.g., Babbie, 2007; Schutt, 2006). Sarnecky (1990) and Tobin & Kincheloe (2006), however, suggest that an increased interest in social historical methods has been evident during recent years, which they attribute to the move away from a traditional focus on abject positivism and toward a broader perspective that is more generally supportive of knowledge offered by historical research.

Historical research, then, involves a process that examines events or combinations of events in order to uncover accounts of what happened in the past. Historical research allows contemporary researchers to "slip the bonds of their own time" (Hamilton, 1993, p. 43) and descend into the past. This provides access to a broader understanding of human behavior and thoughts than would be possible if we were trapped in the static isolation of our own time.

Such tragic isolation is illustrated in H. G. Wells' classic, *The Time Machine* (published in 1895). When the protagonist arrives in the distant future, a near utopia seems to exist. Yet the people of the future millennia have been actually raised as the slaves and food of a group of mutant creatures. When the protagonist tries to learn how such a situation could have developed, no one can tell him. They have no sense of their history. How things had come to be as they are and how things might be changed were concepts lost on these people. They were oblivious to their past, living in the isolation of a single time period—the present.

Apart from historians, most American students are never formally introduced to historical methods of research and analysis. Instead, there seems to be an assumption that one can become skilled at historical research through some tacit process, that merely by taking a history course or two, one can automatically gain the ability to perform historical research (Leedy & Ormrod, 2005; Salkind, 2008). This is, of course, not accurate. There is a simple reason why one cannot learn how to do historical research and analysis in typical history courses: Such courses present the end product of the research, not the process by which it was uncovered. Hence, many nonhistorians confuse the study of history—reading history books—with the methods of historical research. (This chapter won't make you an expert either, but it's a good start.)

Nonetheless, understanding the historical nature of phenomena, events, people, agencies, and even institutions is important. In many ways, it may be as important as understanding the items themselves. One cannot fully evaluate or appreciate advances made in knowledge, policy, science, or technology without some understanding of the circumstances within which these developments occurred (Salkind, 2008). Nor can one recognize mistakes or costs borne through social change without some sense of what has been lost. There is a parallel with dating. When you go out on a first date, there is usually considerable small talk between yourself and your date. Each person attempts to get to know the other. Small talk often centers on questions about your background and the other person's. Where were you born, raised, and educated? What do you like to do in your spare time? What are your favorite foods, books, and television shows? Do you or your date have brothers or sisters, and how well do you each get along with your parents? All of this information goes into the process of getting to know each other and into decisions about the near or farther future. Could you make the decision to continue a relationship and perhaps even to marry without knowing about the other person's background? It is unlikely, and so it is with historical research. Knowledge of the past provides necessary information to be used in the present in order to determine how things may be in the future.

What, then, does historical research involve?

The major impetus in historical research, as with other data-collection strategies, is the collection of information and the *interpretation* or analysis of the data, generally in order to answer a particular research question. Specifically, historical research is conducted for one or more reasons: to uncover the unknown; to answer questions; to seek implications or relationships of events from the past and their connections with the present; to assess past activities and accomplishments of individuals, agencies, or institutions; and to generally aid in our understanding of human culture.

As with the example of getting to know your date, a basic assumption underlying historical research is that you can learn about the present from the past. You must use care, however, and avoid imposition of modern thoughts or understanding when considering information about the past (Marshall & Rossman, 2006). Researchers must seek to understand both literal and latent meanings of documents and other historical sources within their historical time frames. Definitions and connotations for terms change over time. A hundred years ago, the word *nurse* conjured up images of handmaidens and subservient clinical helpers to physicians. Today, however, one envisions nurses as health-care professionals—members of a team that includes physicians. Yet, we also now use the term "male nurse," which seems to mean "a nurse, like any other nurse, but not a woman in case you were assuming that." It's a term that indicates that circumstances have changed faster than expectations. We will know that people in this society have stopped assuming that nurses are female, and doctors male, when we stop using terms such as "male nurse" and "female doctor."

This is likewise true regarding different cultures and cultural terms and meanings. You must be careful not to impose your own cultural judgments on other cultures' meanings. For example, in Israel, the common word for *nurse* in Hebrew actually translates to *sister*. It is likely this corresponds more to the connotation in early American history of the subservient handmaiden. Yet it would not be appropriate, as it would not be in other research strategies, to make judgmental statements about the term's connotation.

Passing judgment about the rightness or wrongness of earlier connotations or meanings within other cultures literally misses the point of historical research. What should be of interest and importance to the social historian is the progression from the older image to the newer one. In the case of different cultures, the historical research is interested in comparisons, not judgments. For example, the historical researcher might be interested in the impact of changed images on modern practices. You might consider how the meaning of *nurse* affects patient care, other healthcare professionals, and medical institutions in general.

Also, historical research today provides a window to understanding various symbols used in the past. Elman (1996), for example, examines the use of pink and black triangles by the Nazis to designate gay men and women, respectively. Elman's (1996, p. 3) discussion indicates that the "pink triangles symbolized the femaleness of this group of detainees whose masculinity was diminished within the context of Nazi heterosexism." Lesbians were classified as asocials who were made to wear black turned-down triangles. These asocials were especially despised because the color of their triangle was viewed as an insult to the black uniform of the elite black-uniformed SS (*Schutzstaffel*).

Life Histories and Social History

Like the confusion between the concepts of history and historiography, there is sometimes confusion between life histories and social history. Researchers taking life histories, as a variation on traditional depth interviewing strategies, are sometimes confronted with problems similar to those faced by social historians. This is because researchers involved in life histories often move beyond the limits of the depth interview and seek external corroborating pieces of evidence.

This may be called *construction of a life history* and involves depth interviewing as merely a single line of action. This may also cause confusion because in the construction of a life history, the researcher may find it necessary to assess the motives of authors of crucial documents. This action is quite similar to how historiographers attempt to make such assessments. For example, the comments made in a diary or a suicide note must be assessed in order to ensure who the author is or was and what his or her motive might have been. Some diaries are private, and some are written with future readers in mind. In any case, the written or recalled versions of events are seen as accounts; stories about the past, rather than catalogs of facts.

These concerns, however, are really issues that lie at the heart of any form of document analysis. As historical methods unfold throughout the remainder of this chapter, readers will also see similarities with previous descriptions of archival unobtrusive strategies.

From the perspective presented in this book, depth interview–based life histories or constructed documentary–based life histories are merely elements that are potentially useful as data in the larger historiographic analysis. Thus, any strategies that attempt to collect information from the past and to weave these pieces of information into a meaningful set of explanations fit my perspective of historical research. Let us further consider the types and sources of data used in historical work.

What are the Sources of Data for Historical Researchers?

The sources of data used by social historians parallel those of many other social scientists: confidential reports, public records, government documents, newspaper editorials and stories, essays, songs, poetry, folklore, films, photos, diaries, letters, artifacts, and even interviews or questionnaires. The historiographer classifies these various data as *primary, secondary,* or *tertiary sources.*

- *Primary Sources.* These sources involve the oral or written testimony of eyewitnesses. They are original artifacts, documents, and items related to the direct outcome of an event or an experience (Salkind, 2008). They may include documents, photographs, recordings, diaries, journals, life histories, drawings, mementos, or other relics.
- *Secondary Sources.* Secondary sources involve the oral or written testimony of people not immediately present at the time of a given event. They are documents written or objects created by others that relate to a specific research question or area of research interest (Rubin & Babbie, 2005).

These elements represent secondhand or hearsay accounts of someone, some event, or some development. Secondary sources may include textbooks, encyclopedias, oral histories of individuals or a group, journal articles, newspaper stories, and even obituary notices (Heaton, 2004; Leedy & Ormrod, 2005). They may also include information that refers not to a specific subject but to a class of people (Denzin, 1978). These may involve court records of juveniles, lab information about asthmatic patients, reading scores of an entire grade level at an elementary school, and other aggregated information about some group. The timelines mentioned earlier are secondary sources.

- *Tertiary Sources.* Tertiary sources involve primary and/or secondary information that has been distilled and presented in some sort of a collection or anthology format. Examples of these include almanacs (e.g., the *Farmer's Almanac*), bibliographies (which some may consider secondary sources), dictionaries and encyclopedias (again, considered by some as secondary sources; however, given their limited content, I place them in the tertiary category), books of facts and knowledge trivia, indexes, abstracts, annotated bibliographies, and similar items used to actually locate primary and/or secondary sources and manuals (Presnell, 2006).

Doing Historiography: Tracing Written History as Data

You begin historical research just as you begin any research project. This was described in detail in Chapter 2 but bears some reiteration here. You begin with an idea or a topic. This may be organized as a research problem, a question, a series of questions, or a hypothesis or series of hypotheses.

Next, you seek basic background information through a literature review. As you create this literature review, your topic and questions may be altered or refined and become clearer and better delineated. As you refine the research focus, you also begin to consider where and what you will use as sources of historical data. You might outline this procedure as follows:

1. Identify an idea, topic, or research question.
2. Conduct a background literature review.
3. Refine the research idea and questions.
4. Determine that historical methods will be the data-collection process.
5. Identify and locate primary and secondary data sources.

6. Evaluate the authenticity and accuracy of source materials.
7. Analyze the data and develop a narrative exposition of the findings.

As described in Chapter 2, you often begin with a broad idea or question for research. Initially, it may reflect an area of research more than it does a specific research statement: for instance, "women in law enforcement." You then need to begin seeking basic background information about this broad topic, just as you would with any other research problem. As you read the literature, you might begin to refine the topic and realize that how women are treated in police work has changed over time.

For example, you might notice that in 1845, when the first woman was hired by the New York City police department, she was hired as a *matron* (Berg, 1999; Feinman, 1994; Van Wormer & Bartollas, 2007). You might also notice that during the nineteenth century, matrons seemed to fit a social worker role more than they did a law enforcement one. That is, their primary responsibilities were to assist victims of crime, runaways, prostitutes, and children (Feinman, 1994; Hamilton, 1924). Moreover, this general social work orientation carried through until late into the 1960s (Berg, 1999; Berg & Budnick, 1986). You might now refine the original research focus to examine the changing role of policewomen. ("Policewoman": like a policeman, but a woman; different from "matron.") You might also begin to consider historiography as an appropriate way to examine this research problem. That is, in addition to collecting historical "facts" about your topic, you will need to develop a framework for evaluating the data in terms of the beliefs, assumptions, habits, practices, and politics of the times and places in which the historical record was recorded. Your reconstruction of the history of the participation of women in policing will have to be informed by your reconstruction of the processes by which data about women in policing were recorded and evaluated.

Next, you will need to locate sources of data regarding the topic. These will be sorted into primary and secondary classifications. Looking over the various books and journal articles you have already amassed during this preliminary literature review is a good first step. Certainly, many of these documents will fit into the secondary source classification. However, by examining the reference sections in these documents, you might also locate leads to actual primary data or leads to these sources. These may include references to autobiographies written by people during the period of interest or newspaper stories reporting interviews with people of the time. These may also include references to diaries, letters, notes, or personal journals. They may even include the court transcripts of some hearing or the minutes of some agency's meeting.

In other words, you begin to seek primary sources that contain the descriptions of a witness to the time or to the event that is now the focus of the research. You may be able to obtain these documents directly from a library or similar archive, or you may need to contact agencies or organizations. You may even need to contact individuals directly who are still alive and can bear witness to some situation or aspect of interest to the research.

For many, locating and gathering primary data is considered the actual data-collection component of historical research (Glass, 1989). Historical researchers must make serious efforts to locate as much source material related to the original event as possible. These may be memos, diary entries, witnesses' accounts—all of which serve to establish a cohesive understanding of the situation. This will eventually result in insights into the meaning of the event or situation. Metaphorically, this becomes a drawing together of the pieces of a puzzle to form a complete picture.

However, it is also important to recognize that secondary sources often provide both access to primary ones and details not always immediately apparent in the primary sources. Many different pieces of information—both primary and secondary—will be necessary before the researcher can adequately fit them all together into a cogent exposition.

For example, Victoria Time examined the exposition of criminological theory as elaborated through the characterizations of William Shakespeare. To demonstrate her argument, that Shakespeare was in fact reflecting various contemporary criminological positions, Time (1999) presents various noted criminological theorists of that time and their theories (primary data). Then she explores the various characters in Shakespeare's plays and demonstrates how these characters display or project these theoretical propositions (potentially a type of primary data—as Shakespeare's work—or secondary data as demonstrating the theoretical works of various theorists).

Primary source materials are subject to two kinds of evaluations or criticisms: First, you must determine whether a document or artifact is authentic, which is sometimes referred to as *external criticism* or *validity*. Second, you must determine the accuracy of meaning in the material, which is called *internal criticism* and is related to the document's reliability. Tertiary sources are very useful in assisting in the location of primary and/or secondary sources.

External Criticism

External criticism is primarily concerned with the question of veracity or genuineness of the source material. Was a document or artifact actually created by the author (Polit & Tatano Beck, 2008)? Wilson (1989, p. 137) suggests that "documents cannot be taken to reflect the truth unless they are really what they appear to be rather than forgeries or frauds." In short, is it authentic, and as such, a valid piece of primary data?

External criticism is a process seeking to determine the authenticity of a document or artifact. In effect, this level of criticism questions, "Is the author or source of the item in question who or what it is claimed?" Thus, the process establishes *why, where, when, how,* and *by whom* the document or artifact was created (Brickman, 2007). As well, external criticism should identify whether the item is an original or from a later production, printing, edition, or a reproduction. Further, the process should consider whether the item has been paraphrased, interpreted, translated, or is one of several versions. Poor translations, censored documents, and inaccurate memories all yield unreliable documents. External criticism may even go so far as to use forensic tests to assess a document or artifact's age, type of medium used (e.g., paper, canvas, clay, and ink or paint content), watermarks, glue in bindings, and even handwriting.

Counterfeit documents are not uncommon. Throughout history, there have been numerous hoaxes perpetrated on the literary, historical, scientific, and social science communities. For example, there have been many literary forgeries. Major George de Luna Byron claimed to be the natural son of Lord Byron, and a Spanish countess. He successfully produced and sold many forgeries of works alleged to have been written by Shelley, Keats, and others—including his alleged father, Byron (*Encyclopaedia Britannica*, 1987, p. 136).

More commonly known is the Thomas Chatterton–Rowley manuscripts incident. In this case, poems written by Thomas Chatterton (1752–1835) were passed off by the young writer as the works of a medieval cleric. Controversy over these poems caused a scholarly feud that lasted for many years. In fact, it has been said that this controversy actually led to the Gothic revival in literature (*Encyclopaedia Britannica*, 1987, p. 136).

An even more bizarre incident occurred in the early 1980s, when two men passed off 60 volumes alleged to be the diaries of Adolf Hitler. They sold them to the German magazine *Stern* for a sum amounting to nearly $3 million. Almost three years later, *Stern* discovered that these diaries were complete phonies, and the magazine sued the sellers. The forgers were forced to return their ill-gotten money and were sentenced to prison ("Hitler Diaries," 1985; "Two Charged," 1984).

In 1993, George Jammal appeared on national television claiming to have obtained a piece of the original Noah's Ark (Jaroff, 1993). Jammal claimed to have obtained the chunk of ark during a 1984 search for the ark on Mount Ararat in Turkey. He explained that he and a friend known only as Vladimir had "crawled through a hole in the ice into a wooden structure. [They] got very excited when [they] saw part of the room was made into pens, like places where you keep animals" (Jaroff, 1993, p. 51). Unfortunately, Vladimir was allegedly killed, and all photographic evidence was lost on the journey. But Jammal had managed to return safely with a piece of the ark.

The television network made no effort to verify Jammal's story. After the story was aired, however, network executives learned that Jammal was an actor who had been telling this and other versions of the ark story for years (Jaroff, 1993). There never was a Vladimir, and the piece of ark is nothing more than a piece of ordinary pine Jammal soaked in fruit juices and baked in his oven (Jaroff, 1993).

Several other literary hoaxes have come to light during recent years, including Margret B. Jones' (2008) and James Frey's (2005) alleged "memoirs." Jones' book claimed that she had been an abused half white, half native American girl raised by a black foster family on the dangerous streets of South Central Los Angeles. But it was discovered that, in fact, the author was a white woman named Margaret Seltzer who had been raised in a middle-class neighborhood in Sherman Oaks, California, by her biological parents and was actually educated in a private school. Author James Frey was exposed as a fraud on the *Oprah Winfrey Show*, after Oprah had selected to feature his book on her Oprah Winfrey best books list. Frey was actually found to be a fraud by the Smoking Gun Web site, who learned that Frey's claim of having been jailed for crashing his car while being drunk and high on crack cocaine and then hitting a police officer was pure fiction (Kakutani, 2006). Frey sidestepped the issue of truth or lie by describing his "memoire" as a "subjective story."

Frauds, hoaxes, and forgeries are not uncommon, and this can be particularly problematic for the naïve or novice researcher. It is very important, therefore, that researchers carefully evaluate their sources. You must ensure that the document or artifact is genuine. This is true for credibility of both the research and the historical researcher. Being duped can jeopardize your ability to be taken seriously during later research investigations. Authenticating documents and objects, of course, is a study in itself. Therefore, researchers should not hesitate to seek the assistance of others more proficient than themselves when attempting to authenticate source material. This may mean calling on handwriting experts, scientists for carbon dating, linguists knowledgeable in writing dialects or period styles, and other specialists.

When undertaking an external criticism of some document, the following questions should be asked:

- Who wrote the source (primary or secondary)?
- What is the authenticity, authority, bias/interest, and intelligibility of the source?
- What was the view of the event or phenomenon when the document was written?
- What or who was the intended audience?
- What sources were privileged or ignored in the narrative?

- Do other sources from the period refer to the source in any way?
- What evidence is offered or compiled?
- In what historical context was the document itself written?

Internal Criticism

The question, "Is this material genuine?" is separate from the question, "What does this document mean?" Important collateral questions include, What was the author trying to say? Why did the author write the document? and even, What inferences or impressions can be taken from the contents of the document? (Leedy & Ormrod, 2005; Polit & Tatano Beck, 2008). Internal criticism, then, seeks to assess the meaning of the statements in the document or the possible meanings and/or intentions of some artifacts, which have now (through external criticism) been established as genuine (Brickman, 2007). In this process, the accuracy and trustworthiness are considered. Internal criticism is essential. Just because a document has been established as genuine does not assure that it is not replete with errors, mistakes of fact, error in judgment, or even intentional statements of bias.

For example, what exactly did Mary Hamilton (1924, p. 183) mean when in reference to police matrons, she wrote, "The policewoman has been likened to the mother. Hers is the strong arm of the law as it is expressed in a woman's guiding hand"? Was she endorsing the role of matron as nurturing social worker? Or was she suggesting that because women possess the capacity to be nurturers, they can also provide strong abilities as law enforcers? This example is a bit unfair since the quote is taken somewhat out of the context of Hamilton's writings. However, it should serve to illustrate the sometimes difficult task faced by historical researchers when they attempt to consider the internal validity of documents.

Court documents and official government reports can be excellent sources of data, but they are not without their own biases and errors. To take one example, there are numerous official records compiled by the British government during the time of the United Irish uprising of 1798. Given that the Irish were rising against the British government, and that many of the rebellion's leaders who have gone down in Irish history as the equivalent of George Washington or Thomas Jefferson, the copious "evidence" compiled by the British condemning these same men as traitors, self-serving liars, or worse can be viewed with suspicion. Of course the British records on Washington and Jefferson from the period would presumably also be biased and self-serving. But then, the American official record on Washington and Jefferson would as well, but in a different direction. It takes more than an official seal to make something true.

Another example of this task of assessing internal meaning might be assessing the meaning of propaganda offered on various hate-mongering Web sites. Questioning the content's accuracy is certainly one level of internal criticism the researcher might undertake. But another example might involve questioning what the content of statements conveys in terms of intent. Is the material intended to simply spew racial or religious disgust and hate? Or is the material intended to attract supporters, gain notoriety, or do something else? If a Web site calls someone an "enemy," are they criticizing that person or provoking violence against them? Intent is elusive, but vitally important. When you are making these kinds of internal meaning criticisms, the task becomes questioning exactly what the words mean and why those words were chosen.

To assess this deeper level of meaning required in an internal criticism, the following sorts of questions are helpful:

- What was the author trying to say?
- What was the author's motive for making the statement or creating the document?
- What inferences are offered in the statement by the author?
- What references are included? Does the language invoke other works that would be known to readers of the time?
- Are the author's statements accurate?
- Was the sentiment of the author similar or contrary to one of the time period?
- Was the statement or document supposed to provide moral lessons?

These issues of external and internal criticism are very important for ascertaining the quality of the data and, in turn, the depth of the interpretation or analysis. Rigorous evaluations of the external and internal value of the data ensure valid and reliable information and viable historical analysis.

These external and internal evaluations also tend to separate historical research from most other forms of archival unobtrusive measures. Traditional archival methods also use secondary source material, such as medical history files, court records, or even arrest reports. However, these are treated as primary data sources and are seldom checked by external or internal evaluations. Instead, there is the tacit assumption of authenticity and accuracy and, therefore, validity and reliability of the data.

During the analysis phase of historical research, data are interpreted. The researcher will review the materials he or she has been so carefully collecting and evaluating. Data will be sorted and categorized into various topical themes (more fully described in Chapter 11). This *content analysis* strategy will allow the researcher to identify patterns within and between sources. Additional sources may be required in order to further explain these patterns as they arise. Any research questions that are proposed may be explained, supported, or refuted only insofar as the data can successfully argue such positions. If the data are faulty, so too will the analysis be weak and unconvincing.

The analysis and synthesis of the data allow the researcher to return to the original literature review and compare commentaries with the researcher's own observations. Thus, the analysis in historical research is deeply grounded in both the data and the background literature of the study. Exposition involves writing a narrative account of the resulting patterns, connections, and insights uncovered during the process of the research. These may extend well into the external and internal criticism you made of the data, as well as the patterns identified through content analysis.

Historians view history as a field of human action and action as the result of individual and collective reasoning (Roberts, 1996). Historiographers include the writing of history as one of those actions that humans choose to undertake, also as a result of reasoning. This reasoning is understood as mediated through various circumstances and impacted by a variety of social, political, economic, ideological, and cultural influences. The actual task of historical researchers, then, is to reconstruct the reasons for past actions. They accomplish this by identifying evidence of past human thinking, which are established as valid and meaningful data. These, in turn, are interpreted with regard to how and why decisions and actions have occurred.

What are Oral Histories?

From the historiographic approach offered in this chapter, historical documentary evidence is taken to include both written and oral sources. As suggested earlier, the term *written document* may include personal documents such as letters, journals, blog entries, diaries, poems, autobiographies, and even plays. However, novice researchers should be aware that historical researchers use a wide variety of data sources and combine numerous methodologies. Perhaps because of the varied historiographic lines of action one might use when undertaking oral histories, Bogdan and Kopp-Bilken (2003) categorize this strategy as a *case history* (discussed in Chapter 10).

The understandings about what oral histories are, as currently apprehended by most modern researchers, are relatively new and likely owe much to the innovation of the tape recorder and the Internet. But oral history is quite literally as old as history itself; in fact, as Thompson (2000) points out, oral histories were actually the *first* kind of history. The cultural history of many early groups was accomplished through an oral tradition where one oral historian passed the information to an apprentice oral historian, and so on. More recently, oral histories have referred to oral evidence that can be used to analyze people, situations, and events as history progresses, or when using documentary versions of oral histories, to bring to light the events and social contours of the past for contemporary consideration and analysis (Yow, 2005).

The written sources of documentary evidence can indeed be varied. Even when examining the history of some local event, person, or phenomenon, a researcher will likely encounter a wide range of written documents. Whether the study focuses on a local event, an individual, a community, or some larger phenomenon, the documents available to a researcher will influence his or her perspective. As Samuel (1975, p. xiii) commented, "It is remarkable how much history has been written from the vantage point of those who have had the charge of running—or attempting to run—other people's lives, and how little from the real life experience of people themselves." As a result, researchers often obtain only one perspective on the past—the perspective represented in official or residual documents of leaders, administrators, or other elites. To put that differently, official histories favor a political historical perspective, and frequently privilege the views of the ruling powers. Newer approaches, such as social historical perspectives, look for evidence of the day-to-day circumstances of "the people." Oral histories are a powerful tool for capturing such details before they are entirely lost to time.

Examples of selecting oral history as a strategy to overcome these deficiencies are found in the works of Studs Terkel (1997, 2000, 2004, 2005). Terkel, who may be regarded as America's leading proponent of oral histories with ordinary people, spent a lifetime interviewing a wide range of Americans, musing on fundamental questions about their lives, hopes, and dreams. In his various books, Terkel discussed life with hard-hat construction workers, rock singers, death row inmates, and even Paul Tibbets, the pilot of the plane that dropped the bomb on Hiroshima.

Many historiographers realize that oral histories allow researchers to escape the deficiencies of residual and official presentations in documentary records (Samuel, 1991). This is especially true when researchers construct original oral histories and are capable of reconstructing moderately recent histories—those that are part of a link to a given living memory. This provides access to the past for, perhaps, as long as 100 years.

But this research strategy required locating a population of individuals who possessed firsthand information on the subject area that the researcher desired to investigate. Thus, one of the major stumbling blocks for these researchers has been proximity. Even if the researcher could not always locate individuals with whom to create original oral histories, there were a number of archives that housed existing oral histories on a number of topics. However, a number of archives of oral histories across the country (and the globe) were not widely accessible; you had to travel to use these oral histories. In addition, in some cases, only copies (at the researcher's expense) of transcribed versions of certain oral histories were available.

Today, thanks to the Internet, there are literally hundreds of oral history archives that provide online audio versions of many of their oral histories, as well as written transcripts that are immediately available for downloading or printing. Contemporary oral history archives offer material on a wide assortment of subjects. You can find material online on everything from jazz musicians to women in American history. One can even find an interview with Studs Terkel, the man who has literally interviewed America (Albin, 1999). There are numerous culturally related archives and an assortment of political and religious ones. The potential reach of oral histories today has expanded far beyond the possibilities of even 10 years ago. It is important to note, however, that as with all online information, researchers must take special care with historical information to ensure that this information is accurate. One suggestion is to keep a core list of reliable sources identified and verified on the Internet, so these may be used in future projects and historiographic reports.

One particularly useful Internet tool is the *Internet Archive* (http://www.archive.org/index.php). The Internet Archive (IA) is run by a nonprofit company and seeks to identify and *archive* literally billions of Web pages, user postings, movies, and governmental documents. IA provides access to these Web links, which in turn can assist researchers seeking historical information on a wide variety of topics and areas. Particularly for the novice researcher, this is an excellent place to start looking for information when undertaking historical research and oral history collections.

Oral histories certainly can provide considerable background and social texture to research. However, given the growing number and accessibility of these documents, they also provide an increased understanding and *lifeline* between the present and the past. Oral histories are extremely dynamic.

Written documents sometimes may dictate the structure of a research project. In other words, the inherent limitations of the documents are imposed on the research. If these documents have filtered through official agencies or organizations, they may reflect only front-stage information. Facts critical for understanding research questions or hypotheses may have been combed out of the written documents (see Chapter 8 on archival data). However, the real-life experiences and memories of people cannot so easily or so thoroughly be omitted, edited, erased, shredded, or swept away.

Oral histories also offer access to the ordinary, unreported interests and tribulations of everyday life along with the better documented occurrence of floods, earthquakes, and other natural disasters (Burgess, 1991; Ritchie, 1995; Terkel,

2005; Tonkin, 1995; Yow, 2005). Oral histories allow researchers to investigate ordinary people as well as documents (e.g., Blythe, 1973; Harkell, 1978; Newby, 1977; Patai & Gluck, 1991; Terkel, 1997, 2000).

Single oral histories as well as series oral histories have been transcribed and published as both analyzed and unanalyzed documents (Reinharz, 1992). Collections of these published oral histories have been accumulated and stored in archives that are now easily accessible via the Internet. Often, these archived oral histories are biographical in nature or may share the autobiographical impressions of an individual regarding some segment of his or her life. For example, the Columbus (Ohio) Jewish Historical Society has a Web site (http://www.ajhs.org/) that contains audio recordings of interviews with an assortment of elderly people from Columbus, Ohio, who tell of their early life in the city.

Other sites offer narratives by people who had been born into slavery (*Born in Slavery: Slave Narratives from the Federal Writer's Project*, 1936–1938, located online at http://memory.loc.gov/ammem/snhtml/snhome.html) or the oral histories of women who served in the U.S. Army during World War II (*What Did You Do in the War, Grandma?*, http://www.stg.brown.edu/ projects/WWII_Women/tocCS.html). In addition, many archives have Web sites that provide access to abstracts of oral histories and permit investigators to use these audio and transcribed oral histories (e.g., the University of Kentucky, The Louie B. Nunn Center for Oral History, http://www.uky.edu/Libraries/ libpage.php?lweb_id=11&llib_id=13, and the Hogan Jazz Archive, housed at Tulane University in New Orleans, located at http://specialcollections.tulane .edu/Jazz/OralHistoryIntroduction.html).

Biography has always been an important aspect of social science research. This is because biographies draw people and groups out of obscurity; they repair damaged historical records, and they give powerless people a voice. The use of oral histories and biographical data has also been popular among women in feminist literature (Hertz, 1997; Patai & Gluck, 1991; Reinharz, 1992; Ribbens & Edwards, 1998). For example, Griffith (1984, p. xix) details the usefulness of biographical data in understanding the women's movement in the United States:

> Initial efforts to record the lives of eminent American women were made in the 1890s, as the first generation of college-educated women sought to identify women of achievement in an earlier era. [These women] established archives for research and wrote biographies of colonial and contemporary women, like Abigail Adams and Susan B. Anthony. Organizations like the Daughters of the American Revolution related their members to the past that provided proud models of accomplishment. The second surge of biographies came with the renaissance of women's history in the late 1960s.

As suggested by Griffith (1984), first-person accounts such as oral histories and biographies are necessary if a researcher is to understand the subjectivity of a social group that has been "muted, excised from history, [and] invisible in the official records of their culture" (Long, 1987, p. 5).

The historical method can be used to access information otherwise simply unavailable to researchers. It provides a means for answering questions and offering solutions that might otherwise go unmentioned and unnoticed. Using a historical method to answer questions or examine problems in one area also facilitates answers to questions and problems in other areas. For example, the historical examination of correctional officers will necessarily draw in consideration of social reforms, role development, institutional development, questions about education, and numerous other areas. The strength of historical research rests on its applicability to diverse areas and the enormity of information and knowledge it can uncover.

TRYING IT OUT

Suggestion 1   Locate the obituaries of 10 public figures (famous actors, political figures, etc.). Next, locate at least one newspaper story about their deaths from a different source.

Suggestion 2   Obtain an oral history from an elderly person in your family. Have him or her tell you about his or her life as a child, an adolescent, an adult, and now as an older adult. You might want to consult Chapter 4 before you begin. Record the oral history on audio tape or videotape.

Suggestion 3   Create a brief history of your major department, college, or university. You should include both achieved documents (old college catalogs are a good place to start and are likely to be found in the library) and oral histories (talk with some of the older school administrators or faculty).

REFERENCES

Albin, K. (1999). Studs Terkel: An interview with the man who interviews America. Available online at www.grandtime.com/studs.html.
Babbie, E. (2007). *The Practice of Social Research* (11th ed.). Belmont, CA: Wadsworth.
Bachman, R., & Schutt, R. K. (2003). *The Practice of Research in Criminology and Criminal Justice* (2nd ed.). Thousand Oaks, CA: Pine Forge Press.
Berg, B. L. (1999). *Policing Modern Society*. Boston, MA: Butterworth/Heinemann.

Berg, B. L., & Budnick, K. J. (1986). Defeminization of women in law enforcement: A new twist in the traditional police personality. *Journal of Police Science and Administration 14*(4), 314–319.

Blythe, R. (1973). *Akenfield: Portrait of an English Village.* New York: Dell.

Bogdan, R., & Biklen, S. K. (1992). *Qualitative Research for Education* (2nd ed.). Boston, MA: Allyn and Bacon.

Bogdan, R., & Kopp-Bilken, S. (2003). *Research for Education* (4th ed.). Boston, MA: Allyn and Bacon.

Brickman, W. W. (2007). *Guide to Research in Educational History.* New York: Brickman Press.

Burgess, R. G. (1991). Personal documents, oral sources and life histories. In R. G. Burgess (Ed.), *Field Research: A Sourcebook and Field Manual* (pp. 131–135). New York: Routledge.

Burns, N., & Grove, S. K. (2004). *The Practice of Nursing Research* (5th ed.). Philadelphia, PA: Elsevier.

Denzin, N. K. (1978). *The Research Act.* Chicago, IL: Aldine.

Elman, R. A. (1996). Triangles and tribulations: The politics of Nazi symbols. *Journal of Homosexuality 30*(3), 1–11.

Encyclopaedia Britannica (Vol. 14, pp. 135–138) (1987). Chicago, IL: University of Chicago Press.

Feinman, C. (1994). *Women in the Criminal Justice System* (3rd ed.). New York: Praeger.

Fitzgerald, J. D., & Cox, S. M. (2002). *Research Methods and Statistics in Criminal Justice* (3rd ed.). Belmont CA: Wadsworth.

Frankfort-Nachmias, C., & Nachmias, D. (2007). *Research Methods in the Social Sciences* (7th ed.). New York: Worth Publishing.

Frey, J. (2005). *A Million Little Pieces.* New York: Anchor.

Gilgun, J. F., Daly, K., & Handel, G. (Eds.). (1992). *Qualitative Methods in Family Research.* Newbury Park, CA: Sage.

Glass, L. (1989). Historical research. In P. J. Brink & M. J. Wood (Eds.), *Advanced Design in Nursing Research.* Newbury Park, CA: Sage.

Griffith, E. (1984). *In Her Own Right: The Life of Elizabeth Cady Stanton.* New York: Oxford University Press.

Hamilton, D. B. (1993). The idea of history and the history of ideas. *Image: Journal of Nursing Scholarship 25*(1), 45–48.

Hamilton, M. (1924). *The Policewoman: Her Service and Ideas* (Reprint 1971). New York: Arno Press and the New York Times.

Harkell, G. (1978). The migration of mining families to the Kent coalfield between the wars. *Oral History 6*, 98–113.

Heaton, J. (2004). *Reworking Qualitative Data.* Thousand Oaks, CA: Sage.

Hertz, R. (1997). *Reflexivity and Voice.* Thousand Oaks, CA: Sage.

Hitler diaries trial stirs judge to disbelief and ire. (January 6, 1985). *New York Times,* p. A14.

Jaroff, L. (July 5, 1993). Phony arkaeology: In a pseudo documentary, CBS falls victim to a hoaxer. *Time 142,* p. 51.

Johnson, B., & Christensen, L. B. (2003). *Educational Research: Quantitative, Qualitative, and Mixed Approaches* (2nd ed.). Boston, MA: Allyn and Bacon.

Johnson, B., & Christensen, L. B. (2007). *Educational Research: Quantitative, Qualitative, and Mixed Approaches* (3rd ed.). Thousand Oaks, CA: Sage.

Jones, M. B. (2008). *Love and Consequences: A Memoir of Hope and Survival*. New York: Riverhead.

Kakutani, M. (January 17, 2006). Bending the truth in a million little ways. *New York Times*, Section E; Column 1.

Leedy, P., & Ormrod, J. E. (2005). *Practical Research: Planning and Design* (8th ed.). Upper Saddle River, NJ: Prentice Hall.

Lewenson, S. B., & Herrmann, E. K. (2007). *Capturing Nursing History: A Guide to Historical Methods in Research*. New York: Springer Publishing Company.

LoBiondo-Wood, G., & Haber, J. (2002). *Nursing Research: Methods, Critical Appraisal and Utilization*. St. Louis, MO: Mosby.

Long, J. (1987). Telling women's lives: The new sociobiography. Paper presented at the annual meeting of the American Sociological Association, Chicago.

Lusk, B. (1997a). Professional classification of American nurses, 1910–1930. *Western Journal of Nursing Research 7*, 448–467.

Lusk, B. (1997b). Historical methodology for nursing research. *Image, Journal of Nursing Scholarship 29*(4), 355–359.

Marshall, C., & Rossman, G. B. (2006). *Designing Qualitative Research* (4th ed.). Thousand Oaks, CA: Sage.

Matejski, M. (1986). Historical research: The method. In P. Munhall & C. J. Oiler (Eds.), *Nursing Research: A Qualitative Perspective* (pp. 175–193). Norwalk, CT: Appleton-Century-Crofts.

McDowell, W. H. (2002). *Historical Research: A Guide for Writers of Dissertations, Theses, Articles, and Books*. Boston: Longman.

Newby, H. (1977). *The Deferential Worker*. London: Allen Lane.

Patai, D., & Gluck, S. B. (1991). *Women's Worlds: The Feminist Practice of Oral History*. New York: Routledge.

Polit, D. F., & Tatano Beck, C. (2008). *Nursing Research: Generating and Assessing Evidence for Nursing Practice*. Philadelphia, PA: Lippincott Williams & Walkins.

Presnell, J. L. (2006). *The Information-Literate Historian: A Guide to Research for History Students*. New York: Oxford University Press USA.

Reinharz, S. (1992). *Feminist Methods in Social Research*. New York: Oxford University Press.

Ribbens, J., & Edwards, R. (1998). *Feminist Dilemmas in Qualitative Research*. Thousand Oaks, CA: Sage.

Ritchie, D. A. (1995). *Doing Oral History* (Twayne's Oral History, No. 15). Toronto, Canada: Twayne Publishing.

Roberts, G. (1996). Narrative history as a way of life. *Journal of Contemporary History 31*, 221–228.

Rosnow, R. L., & Rosenthal, R. (2007). *Beginning Behavioral Research* (6th ed.). Upper Saddle River, NJ: Prentice Hall.

Rubin, A., & Babbie, E. (2005). *Research Methods for Social Work*. Belmont, CA: Thomson/Brooks/Cole.

Salkind, N. J. (2008). *Exploring Research* (7th ed.). Upper Saddle River, NJ: Prentice Hall.

Samuel, R. (1975). *Village Life and Labour*. London: Routledge and Kegan Paul.

Samuel, R. (1991). Local history and oral history. In R. G. Burgess (Ed.), *Field Research: A Sourcebook and Field Manual* (pp. 136–145). New York: Routledge.

Sarnecky, M. T. (1990). Historiography: A legitimate research methodology for nursing. *Advances in Nursing Science 12*(4), 1–10.

Schutt, R. (2006). *Investigating the Social World: The Process & Practice of Research* (5th ed.). Thousand Oaks, CA: Sage.

Shaughnessy, J. J., Zechmeister, E. B., & Zechmeister, J. S. (2008). *Research Methods in Psychology* (8th ed.). New York: McGraw-Hill.

Taylor, R. B. (1994). *Research Methods in Criminal Justice.* New York: McGraw-Hill.

Taylor, S. J., & Bogdan, R. (1998). *Introduction to Qualitative Research Methods* (3rd ed.). New York: John Wiley and Sons.

Terkel, S. (1997). *Working.* New York: The New Press.

Terkel, S. (2000). *Hard Times.* New York: The New Press.

Terkel, S. (2004). *Hope Dies Last.* New York: The New Press.

Terkel, S. (2005). *American Dreams: Lost and Found.* New York: The New Press.

Thompson, P. (2000). *The Voice of the Past: Oral History* (3rd ed.). New York: Oxford University Press.

Time, V. M. (1999). *Shakespeare's Criminals: Criminology, Fiction, and Drama.* Westport, CT: Greenwood.

Tobin, K., & Kincheloe, J. L. (2006). *Doing Educational Research.* The Netherlands: Sense Publications.

Tonkin, E. (1995). *Narrating Our Pasts: The Social Construction of Oral History.* Cambridge, England: Cambridge University Press.

Two charged in Hamburg in "Hitler diary" fraud. (March 23, 1984). *New York Times,* p. A4.

Van Wormer, K., & Bartollas, C. (2007). *Women in the Criminal Justice System* (2nd ed.). Boston, MA: Allyn & Bacon.

Wells, H. G. (1895). *The Time Machine* (Rev. ed., 1977). In F. D. McConnell (Ed.), New York: Oxford University Press.

Wilson, H. S. (1989). *Nursing Research* (2nd ed.). Reading, MA: Addison-Wesley.

Yow, V. R. (2005). *Recording Oral History: A Guide for the Humanities and Social Sciences* (2nd ed.). New York: Rowman & Littlefield.

Chapter 1 0

Case Studies

The Nature of Case Studies

The case study method is defined and understood in various ways. Some sources define the case study method as an attempt to systematically investigate an event or a set of related events with the specific aim of describing and explaining these phenomena (see, e.g., Bromley, 1990). Bogdan and Biklen (2003, p. 54) define case study as "a detailed examination of one setting, or a single subject, a single depository of documents, or one particular event" (see also Gomm, Hammersley, & Foster, 2000; Yin, 2003a). Hagan (2006, p. 240) simply defines the case study method as "in-depth, qualitative studies of one or a few illustrative cases." Previous editions of this book (see Berg, 2004, 2007) defined case study as a method involving systematically gathering enough information about a particular person, social setting, event, or group to permit the researcher to effectively understand how the subject operates or functions. Interestingly, Creswell (2007) points out that Stake (2005a) actually suggests that case study research is not really a methodology at all; rather, Stake (2005a) claims that it involves a choice in what is to be studied. Taken together, these various definitions and explanations suggest that case study is an approach capable of examining simple or complex phenomenon, with units of analysis varying from single individuals to large corporations and businesses to world-changing events; it entails using a variety of lines of action in its data-gathering segments and can meaningfully make use of and contribute to the application of theory (Creswell, 2007; Yin, 2003a).

Discussions concerning the use and meaning of case study approaches reveal two essential elements with which we will begin. First, case studies require multiple methods and/or sources of data through which we create a full and deep examination of the case. Exactly which methods we use and exactly how we combine them will depend on the case itself. Second, to call certain research a case study means that there is some broader category of events (or settings, groups, subjects, etc.) of which the present study is one case. The question we ask is, "What is this a case of?"

Case studies are often adopted for post-facto (after the event) studies, rather than ongoing issues or questions. This contributes to the perception that they are atheoretical. But consider some classic examples. In 1972, a massive flood ripped through a mining community called Buffalo Creek in West Virginia leaving behind a scene of destruction and death of inestimable proportions. Shortly after the event, sociologist Kai Erikson was hired by the survivors' law firm to help give an estimate of the extent of that destruction, to make a quick "assessment" of the situation. Overwhelmed by what he saw, Erikson spent five years on his study prior to publishing his groundbreaking work *Everything in Its Path*. In a typical sociological study, he wrote "the particular case is selected in the hope that it will inform and give support to a larger generalization. My assignment on Buffalo Creek, however, was to sift through the store of available sociological knowledge to see what light it might shed on a single human event, and this, clearly, reverses the normal order of social science research" (Erikson, 1976, p. 12). After considerable immersion in the case, Erikson came to conceptualize it as a case of human disaster comparable to earthquakes, air raids, and other catastrophes, in the general sense, and as a specific case of a coherent but threatened culture shocked by a massive disruption in its way of life struggling to regain a sense of meaning.

Erikson's work later proved to be a crucial touchstone to New Yorkers' (and other sociologists') efforts to recover from the shock to their worldviews after the September 2001 attacks on the World Trade Center (Foner, 2005). The post-9/11 case studies found both unique patterns (New York City is not often compared to Appalachia) and great consistency when compared with Erikson's model (Abrams, Albright, & Panofsky, 2004).

Given the scope of the method, case studies either can be rather pointed in their focus or approach a broad view of life and society. For example, an investigator may confine his or her examination to a single aspect of an individual's life such as studying a medical student's actions and behaviors in a medical school. The actions of that single student provide one case of the general category defined by the actions of all the students. Or the investigator might attempt to assess the social life of an individual and his or her entire background, experiences, roles, and motivations that affect his or her behavior in society. The general category here might be thought of as socialization processes, or institutionalization, or human adaptability, or the interaction of life history and value formation. Extremely rich, detailed, and in-depth information characterize the type of information gathered in a case study. In contrast, the often extensive, large-scale survey research data may seem somewhat superficial in nature (Champion, 2006).

Many qualitative investigators use the case study approach as a guide to their research. By concentrating on a single phenomenon, individual, community, or institution, the researcher aims to uncover the manifest interactions of significant factors characteristic of this phenomenon, individual, community, or institution. In addition, the researcher is able to capture various nuances, patterns, and more latent elements that other research approaches might overlook. The case study method tends to focus on holistic description and explanation; and, as a general statement, any phenomenon can be studied by case study methods (Gall, Borg, & Gall, 1995, 1998). Others suggest a type of *embedded case study* approach (Hancock & Algozzine, 2006; Scholz & Tietje, 2002). Embedded case studies involve looking at one case study but including several levels or units of analysis. In other words, this case study approach includes examination of a subunit, or several subunits, of the overall focus of the research. For instance, let's say a given case study seeks to explore a single organization such as a community hospital; the analysis might additionally include focus and outcomes about clinical services, staff in specialty nursing units (e.g., ICU and CCU), or other staff employed by the hospital. In a study examining post-prison community reintegration, several programs involved in the overall effort of some agency might be evaluated, and this too would represent a kind of embedded case study (Yin, 2003a). Similarly, one may examine the process of community mobilization by looking at numerous organizations and planned actions all emanating from a single community in response to a single shared concern (Chambré, 1997). The case is composed of many actions and goals which together define the mobilization of the community.

The case study method is not a new style of data gathering and analytic technique. The fields of medicine and psychology, for example, by their very nature, require physicians and psychologists to examine patients case by case. Case studies are commonly used in business, information systems, and law curricula to help students bridge the gap between foundational studies and practice. The use of diaries and biographies, a popular method among some feminist and other social scientists, approaches the case study method, as does ethnobiography (Hesse-Biber & Yaiser, 2004; Reinharz, 1992). In education, case studies abound and include studies of unique people and programs, as well as special programming (Herreid, 2006; McLeod, 1994; Stake, 1995). In fact, case studies by certain social scientists represent classical research efforts in sociology and criminology. Consider, for example, Edward Sutherland's (1937) *The Professional Thief* or Clifford R. Shaw's (1930) *The Jack Roller*.

Theory and Case Studies

Yin (2003a) indicates that there has been a revived interest in the role of theory and case studies. Interestingly, a cursory review of the literature suggests that a vigorous renewal of this interest appears to occur in the areas of business, marketing, and information systems, as well as in the social sciences (see, e.g., Alexander & Bennett, 2005; Fernandez, 2005; Woodside & Wilson, 2004). Typically, although not exclusively, case study methods are found in the literature associated with theory building rather than theory testing (Woodside & Wilson, 2004), but some sources suggest the utility of case study strategies in theory testing or in combining both theory development and testing (Alexander & Bennett, 2005; Woodside & Wilson, 2004).

How does the case study method inform theory? Case studies can provide a kind of deep understanding of phenomenon, events, people, or organizations, similar to Geertz's (1973) notion of "thick description." In essence, case studies open the door to the processes created and used by individuals involved in the phenomenon, event, group, or organization under study (Weick, 1995). Sensemaking is the manner by which people, groups, and organizations make sense of stimuli with which they are confronted, how they frame what they see and hear, how they perceive and interpret this information, and how they interpret their own actions and go about solving problems and interacting with others. A case study approach to this problem-solving process can reveal both the shared and the unique sensemaking decisions.

Yin (2003a, pp. 4–5) tends to endorse a theory-before-research model (see Chapter 2) and indicates that theory development prior to the collection of case study data can be important for the following reasons:

- It can assist selecting the cases to be studied and whether to use a single-case or multiple-case design.
- It helps the researcher specify what is being explored when undertaking exploratory case studies.
- It aids in defining a complete and appropriate description when undertaking descriptive case studies.
- It can stimulate rival theories when undertaking explanatory cases studies.
- It can support generalizations the researcher may seek to make to other cases.

Others, however, argue that case studies can be used to generate theory (grounded theory) and follow a pattern similar to theory after research (see Chapter 2). Fernandez (2005, p. 47) cites Eisenhardt (1989, pp. 546–547), for instance, arguing that using case data to build grounded theory has three major strengths:

1. Theory building from case studies is likely to produce theory. Researchers who overemphasize existing theory when building new models may become too attached to the perspectives or assumptions that they bring to the work, and therefore fail to give attention to contradictory cases. But in the field, one is directly confronted by surprises and contradictions, and may be more open to creative insights in response to these.
2. Emergent theory, from case studies, generate new questions and propositions that can – and should – be tested in other cases and settings. Further work can lead to elaborations and improvements in one's initial explanation.
3. Theory that comes from cases is known to be basically valid in at least these cases. It remains to be seen how well this will generalize, but it cannot be a bad thing to begin with a strong empirical grounding.

In other words, theory can be uncovered and informed as a consequence of the data collection and interpretations of this data made throughout the development of the case study—hence, a grounded theory case study. What might this process look like? The researcher would start with some sort of research idea, then develop a plan—including whether to use a single- or multiple-case approach—identify the location of the study (in what group or organization), determine how access is to be obtained, and consider what data-collection strategies to use. Once access is obtained, data must be collected; as the data are collected, the researcher constantly considers what is being unearthed, making comparisons between information (data) collected and assessments with other researchers (to assure unbiased interpretations and analysis) and the literature. The investigator then must reflect on the information collected and the problem(s) initially addressed to deliberate over what the findings mean and what their implications may be. Finally, the researcher can offer some theoretical implications for whatever problems or issues were being explored, described, or explained in the study. Figure 10.1 offers a visualization of this model of developing grounded theory through the case study method.

Figure 10.1   Developing Grounded Theory Through the Case Study
Method

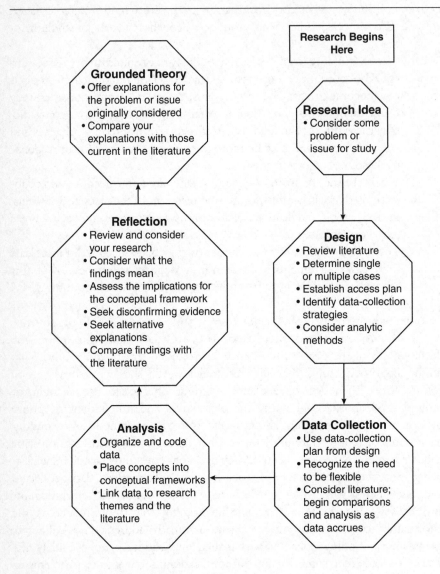

The Individual Case Study

As in any other research situation, one must determine how broad an area of
social life will be covered. In most research, this decision is largely dictated by the
research question and the nature of the research problem under investigation.

When examining an individual case study, a similar type of assessment must be undertaken. In some instances, a single lengthy interview may yield sufficient information to produce answers to the research question(s). In other circumstances, several interviews may be necessary, and these may require supplementation by field notes during direct observation, copies of journal or diary entries from the subject, or other forms of documentation.

Several reasons may make it necessary for a broader, more sweeping investigation. First, the research may itself focus on a broad area such as the subject's relationships in a particular group, necessitating that the group also be examined. It would be unwise, for example, to examine various aspects of changes in the quality of life of hemodialysis patients without also examining how family members perceive changes occurring in the family group itself.

A second reason for broadening a case study is the realization that all the aspects of an individual's social life are interconnected and often one of them cannot be adequately understood without consideration of the others. A third reason is triangulation. A single person's report of the events and relations that make up some portion of his or her life only gives you access to his or her own perceptions, through his or her filters. Other data are needed to gain additional perspectives on the same materials. As with other self-reported data, of course, our goal is to form a full picture of the perceptions offered to us; not to make a judgment about who is right or who is telling the truth.

The Use of Interview Data

One of the most effective ways to learn about the circumstances of people's lives is to ask them. (See Chapter 4.) Interview data collection in case study research is much like any other research interview, and typically less like an oral history. The nature of the case determines the topics that the interview must cover. Within those boundaries, the data are whatever the subjects have to say on the topic.

In one recent example, Susan Sullivan and Vivian Shulman set out to examine a period of significant managed change in a New York City school district. The changes were planned in response to new school mandates, and the researchers initially collected data from all of the different schools in the district as well as the central office. "When it became clear that the leadership of the superintendent drove all district practices, we shifted our focus to describing his particular style and its efficacy in promoting systemic change" (Sullivan & Shulman, 2005, p. 124). The study was still about the school district changes, but the focus shifted from studying a case of negotiation among offices to a case of leadership under constraint in a time of transition. The principal data collection method was one-on-one interviews with the superintendent, his staff, teachers, and principals in the affected schools.

The advantage of the case study over the individual interview is demonstrated in this example. Sullivan and Shulman spoke at length with the superintendent about his education and leadership philosophies. But they were able to triangulate their data by interviewing others about the ways in which the superintendent attempted to implement his philosophies. The additional data from the district schools provided a real-life measure of the impact of the district leadership on those who were responsible for running the individual schools.

In the previous example, the topic was leadership and its impact. Many individual case studies look at the multiple social roles occupied by the study subject, and therefore, require data from multiple sources connected to the key subject. Unless an individual is exceptionally isolated, he or she is likely to have some role in the neighborhood community. Some people enjoy an elevated position of respect and position in their business, social, or political life. Others may hold no particularly high level of respect but function as participants in various activities. Still others may actually be social outcasts. This type of information could be very useful for understanding how individuals fulfill their professional or other roles. Visits to neighbors, various social organizations to which the subject may be a member, conversations with local tradespersons, and even the subject's clergy person may all supply useful information.

Yin (1998) identified five researcher skills associated with conducting good case studies. To a large extent, these are similar to, but more extensive than, the three skills offered by Merriam (2001), and clearly these skills are useful for virtually all forms of research. The first is an *inquiring mind* and the willingness to ask questions before, during, and after data are collected, as well as to constantly challenge oneself about why something appears to have happened or be happening. The second is the ability of the investigator to *listen*, to include *observation* and *sensing* in general, and to assimilate large amounts of new information without bias. Third is *adaptability* and *flexibility* to handle unanticipated events and to change data-collection strategies if they do not seem to be functioning effectively and to use alternative sources of data that may be more fruitful. Fourth is a thorough *understanding of the issues* being studied in order not merely to record data but to interpret and react to these data once collected. The researcher must be able to determine, for example, if different sources of data are adequate or if additional sources are required. The fifth quality is *unbiased interpretation of the data*. Yin suggests that a good test for bias is the degree to which the researcher is open to contradictory findings. He recommends reporting preliminary findings to colleagues, who may offer alternative explanations that would require further investigation. This notion is similar to a researcher taking an intellectual risk by providing sufficient information for others to replicate the research and potentially to find contradictory results.

Throughout the preceding paragraphs, the chief suggestions for information (data) gathering have been the use of interviews and observation. As implied earlier, however, it is often also useful to supplement this information with various documentary sources. You should, therefore, be familiar with the possible use of records concerning the life course of the subject. These may include birth, marriage, divorce, property ownership, and educational records of the subject. They may additionally include an assortment of other more or less official documents such as police actions, court records, evaluations of work records, and so forth. All of these official documents are potentially valuable sources of information in a case study. As well, the subject might have written personal documents, letters, diaries, blogs, or a trove of e-mails that can be included in the study.

The Use of Personal Documents

The general use of personal documents is discussed in Chapter 8. As suggested there, personal documents involve any written record created by the subject that concerned his or her experiences. The common types of documents classified under this label include autobiographies, diaries and journals, letters, and memos written by a subject in a research investigation. In addition, and given the extent to which people use photographic and video equipment today, these items may also serve as categories of personal documents.

Autobiographical documents include a considerable variety of written material. They may be published or unpublished documents, cover an entire life span, or focus on only a specific period in a subject's life or even a single event. Even a written confession to a crime may be seen by some researchers as a type of autobiographical document. Certain manifestos may serve as both personal statements and confessions, though this is uncommon.

Diaries and journals also may arise in a number of varieties. A diary may be kept with no purpose in mind beyond the writer's personal desire to maintain a record of daily events. It may be maintained in order to provide some therapeutic release or as a kind of log and chronological listing of daily events during new experiences, such as an internship. Or a diary or journal may be created at the specific request of a researcher as a contribution to some study. In the latter case, one may consider the material in a solicited document (see Chapter 8).

Letters provide an intriguing view into the life of the author. Typically, letters are not created by the writer with the intention of having them used by a researcher. As a result, they frequently reflect the inner worlds of the writer.

They may record the writer's views, values, attitudes, and beliefs about a wide variety of subjects. Or they may describe the writer's deepest thoughts about some specific event or situation about which they report. Historians have long seen the value of letters to document events during the past. Letters written by military figures and politicians, for example, may allow researchers to better understand how and why certain battles have been fought. Letters written by criminals such as serial killers and bombers provide insight into how the culprit thinks and potential explanations for their actions. Letters are simply replete with potentially useful information.

For example, Elizabeth Roberson (1998) explored the letters of Eli Landers, a young Confederate soldier (see also Wasta & Lott, 2002). Landers wrote letters from the battlefield to his mother and sister that express his emotional views of the war, his personal losses, as well as specific details about the Civil War.

The use of memoranda, including e-mails, has become commonplace in virtually all work settings. Memos may contain strictly work-related information or casual insider jokes and communications. They may reflect the tone and atmosphere of a work setting as well as the potential level of anxiety, stress, and morale of the writer. Moreover, they may even show the research aspects of the workplace culture or work folkways. Also, they may contain information relevant to understanding the general organizational communications network used in the setting, the leadership hierarchy, various roles present in the setting, and other structural elements. Thus, a memorandum can provide an interesting self-disclosing aspect of its creator, or various aspects of a group or organization, when used as data in a case study.

Photographic and video equipment has become so inexpensive that many people now regularly record their lives and the lives of their family members in this manner. It becomes important, therefore, for researchers to consider how these items may illustrate various aspects of the subject's life and relationships. This may involve stepping back and examining the entire photograph in terms of what it shows in general; it may include an examination of the expressions of people shown in the picture; it could involve consideration of where the picture or video was taken or recorded such as on a vacation, in the home, or at a party; or it may involve determination of the reason the photograph or video was created—as a simple family record to commemorate some situation, to have as a keepsake, to document some event or situation, and so forth.

The literal value of personal documents as research data is frequently underestimated in contemporary research texts and courses. Although such documents are certainly extremely subjective in their nature, these data should not be viewed as a negative or, in this case, even as some sort of limitation or shortcoming. It is the very fact that these documents do reflect the subjective views and perceptions of their creators that makes them useful as data in a case study. It is precisely through this subjectivity that these documents provide information and insight about the subject that might not be captured through some other more pedestrian data-collection technique.

Intrinsic, Instrumental, and Collective Case Studies

Stake (1994, 1995) suggests that researchers have different purposes for studying cases. He suggests that case studies can be classified into three different types: *intrinsic, instrumental,* and *collective.*

Intrinsic case studies are undertaken when a researcher wants to better understand a particular case. It is not undertaken primarily because it represents other cases or because it illustrates some particular trait, characteristic, or problem. Rather, it is because of its uniqueness or ordinariness that a case becomes interesting (Creswell, 1998, 2007; Stake, 1994, 2000). The role of the researcher is not to understand or test abstract theory or to develop new or grounded theoretical explanations; instead, the intention is to better understand intrinsic aspects of the particular child, patient, criminal, group, organization, or whatever the case may be (Munhall, 2007). The case may generate findings or stimulate ideas that will be applicable to other cases, but the intrinsic case study is not performed for those reasons. Erikson's case study of the Buffalo Creek flood is an example. That study needed to be done because something important had happened there.

Instrumental case studies provide insights into an issue or refine a theoretical explanation, making it more generalizable (Creswell, 2002; Stake, 1994). In an instrumental case study, the researcher focuses on a single issue or concern and identifies a single case to illustrate this item of focus or concern (Creswell, 2007). In these situations, the case actually becomes of secondary importance, playing a supportive role (Denzin & Lincoln, 2005). The details of the case provide a background against which the larger research interests will play out. Instrumental case studies are often investigated in depth, and all aspects and activities are detailed but not simply to elaborate the case per se. Instead, the intention is to help the researcher better understand some external theoretical question, issue, or problem. Instrumental case studies may or may not be viewed as typical of other cases. However, the choice of a particular case for study is made because the investigator believes that his or her understanding about some other research interest will be advanced.

Stake (1994, 2000) also points out that because researchers often have multiple interests, there is no solid line drawn between intrinsic and instrumental studies. In fact, a kind of "zone of combined purpose separates them" (Stake, 1994, p. 237). My study of the origins and development of the field of organized collective action in response to HIV/AIDS in New York City (Lune, 2007) began in that combined zone. I viewed the AIDS example as an important case of collective action, but it took a while to define what factors defined this case or made it comparable to other cases.

Collective case studies (Stake, 1994, 2000, 2005b) are also known as multiple-case studies, cross-case studies, comparative case studies, and contrasting case studies (Gerring, 2006; Merriam, 2001). Thus, collective case studies involve extensive study of several instrumental cases, intended to allow better understanding, insight, or perhaps improved ability to theorize about a broader context. Yin (2003a) argues that multiple cases may be selected in order to try replicating insights found in individual cases or to represent contrasting situations. Regardless of one's purpose, Yin (2003a, p. 46) indicates that multiple-case studies are frequently "considered more compelling, and the overall study is therefore regarded as more robust."

In each of these three approaches, the validity of the research hinges on how we address the question, "What is this a case of?" Researchers interested in important but uncommon events might well choose a comparative case study approach in order to gather relatively large amounts of related data on their topic despite its lack of frequency. Revolutions, for example, do not occur very often. A single revolution can be rooted in a long and complex local history, and supported by myriad factors that can only be found through a deep understanding of the global economy and political alignments. Yet, by comparing the French Revolution of 1789 with the American Revolution of 1776 and the Cuban Revolution of 1959, researchers can identify crucial similarities and patterns that greatly help us to understand revolutionary events. But, not so fast. Are these cases best understood as cases of "revolution," or would it be more useful to call them cases of "successful revolutions"? After all, there have been many failed revolutions as well, which share many of the same precursors as the successful ones. Does it make sense to include revolutions across generations, or should we focus on cases of twentieth-century revolutions distinct from eighteenth- or nineteenth-century ones? Researchers also need to decide on other defining characteristics for their cases. Are revolutions that overthrow autocracies and install democracies significantly different from revolutions that go in the other direction? Are those that overthrow democracies better characterized as coups? All of these challenges point to the importance of the conceptualization stage of research design, as discussed in Chapter 2.

Case Study Design Types

According to Yin (1994, 2003a) and Winston (1997), there are several appropriate designs for case studies: exploratory, explanatory, and descriptive. These three approaches consist of either single- or multiple-case studies in which the cases studied are actual replications, not sampled cases. Each approach is discussed next.

Exploratory Case Studies

When conducting exploratory case studies, fieldwork and data collection may be undertaken before defining a research question. This type of study may be seen as a prelude to a large social scientific study—which may or may not in itself involve case studies. From our perspective, the study must have some type of organizational framework that has been designed prior to beginning the research. Others, however, such as Yin (2003b, p. 6), suggest that these exploratory case studies may follow "intuitive paths often perceived by others as sloppy." But, as Yin (2003b) also points out, the goal in these studies may be justified when they seek to discover theory through directly observing some social phenomenon in its natural and raw form. The sort of exploratory study may be useful as a pilot study, for example, when planning a larger, more comprehensive investigation (Swanson & Holton, 2005).

Explanatory Case Studies

Explanatory case studies are useful when conducting causal studies. Particularly in complex studies of organizations or communities, one might desire to employ multivariate cases to examine a plurality of influences. This might be accomplished using a pattern-matching technique suggested by Yin and Moore (1988). *Pattern-matching* is a situation in which several pieces of information from the same case may be related to some theoretical proposition; each piece has its place in the overall pattern. The explanatory case study, then, attempts to discover and analyze the many factors and conditions that can help us to build a causal explanation for the case. This is useful when something new or unexpected has occurred, and we can only begin to build a theoretical model to explain it by comparison to other cases that might be said to resemble our case. We know that some of these other cases can help explain the new case, but we don't yet understand the uniqueness of the present case.

Descriptive Case Studies

With descriptive case explorations, the investigator presents a descriptive theory that establishes the overall framework for the investigator to follow throughout the study. What is implied by this approach is the formation and identification of a viable theoretical orientation before enunciating research questions (Hancock & Algozzine, 2006; Munhall, 2007). The investigator must also determine before beginning the research what exactly the unit of analysis in the study will be. For example, if I define a particular disaster as an "industrial" disaster and not a "natural" disaster or an accident, then I am claiming that the kinds of factors that tend to cause industrial disasters are better explanations for the current case than the factors usually associated with other types of failures or related problems. My case study would be designed to measure the factors that I believe are most relevant, and also to measure the factors that I think are less relevant. I can then compare the influence of the different measures to see how well my interpretation holds against the other possibilities.

Designing Case Studies

Designing a case study is merely a special case of the problem of designing any study, as discussed in Chapter 2. Yet each methodological approach has its own strengths and uses, and therefore a unique set of terms, priorities, and considerations. In creating formal designs for case-study investigations, Yin (1994, p. 20) recommends five component elements:

- Study questions
- Study propositions (if any are being used) or theoretical framework
- Identification of the unit(s) of analysis
- The logical linking of the data to the propositions (or theory)
- The criteria for interpreting the findings

A study's *questions* are generally directed toward *how* and *why* considerations, and their articulation and definition are the first task of the researcher. Sometimes, the study's *propositions* derive from these how and why questions and assist in developing a theoretical focus. Not all studies will have propositions. An exploratory study, rather than having propositions, may have a stated purpose or criteria that will provide guidance and a kind of operating framework for the case study to follow. The *unit of analysis* defines what the case study is focusing on (what the case is), such as an individual, a group, an organization, a city, and so forth. *Linkages between the data and the propositions* (or theory) *and the criteria for interpreting the findings,* according to Yin (1994), typically are the least developed aspects of case studies.

Jason Jensen and Robert Rodgers (2001, pp. 237–239) offer a typology of types of case studies:

1. *Snapshot case studies.* Detailed, objective studies of one research entity at one point in time. Hypothesis testing by comparing patterns across subentities (e.g., comparing departments within the case study agency).
2. *Longitudinal case studies.* Quantitative and/or qualitative studies of one research entity at multiple time points.
3. *Pre–post case studies.* Studies of one research entity at two time points separated by a critical event. A critical event is one that on the basis of a theory under study would be expected to impact case observations significantly.
4. *Patchwork case studies.* A set of multiple case studies of the same research entity, using snapshot, longitudinal, and/or pre–post designs. This multidesign approach is intended to provide a more holistic view of the dynamics of the research subject.
5. *Comparative case studies.* A set of multiple case studies of multiple research entities for the purpose of cross-unit comparison. Both qualitative and quantitative comparisons are generally made.

Unfortunately, researchers do not always have good theories to work with, in a given situation, particularly when exploring cutting-edge issues. In these situations, a logic model, or what Patton (2001) calls a "theory of action," may be developed. This *theory of action* will define how the researcher expects an intervention, event, or process to take a case from one situation to the next. In effect, this theory of action will define the issues to be examined during the analysis, thereby providing linkages among the research question(s), propositions, and analytic criteria.

The Scientific Benefit of Case Studies

The scientific benefit of the case study method lies in its ability to open the way for discoveries (Shaughnessy, Zechmeister, & Zechmeister, 2008). It can easily serve as the breeding ground for insights and even hypotheses that may be pursued in subsequent studies. However, whenever one considers the scientific value of case studies, two points should be addressed. First, does this procedure involve too many subjective decisions made by the investigator to offer genuinely objective results? Second, does this method offer information that can be seen as useful beyond the individual case? In other words, can findings be generalized? Let us consider each of these questions separately.

Objectivity and the Case Method

Objectivity is a somewhat elusive term. For some researchers, it involves the creation of analytic strategies in an almost sterile environment. Often, qualitative research of any type is viewed as suspect when questions of objectivity are asked. However, objectivity is actually closely linked with reproducibility (replication). The question is not simply whether or not an individual researcher has made some subjective decision regarding how the researcher should progress or how the study is designed. These types of considerations are regularly undertaken by all who undertake social scientific research—whether quantitatively or qualitatively oriented.

When a quantitative methodologist identifies which level of statistical acceptability he or she will use for some statistical measure, it is often a subjective decision. For example, let's say the researcher sets the level at .01. Does that alter the findings when it is statistically significant at the .05 level but not at the .01 level? Thus, objectivity apparently lies someplace other than in the kinds of decisions made by a researcher regarding various aspects of the research strategy. In general, quantitative research requires interpretive decisions up front, in the design of data collection instruments, sampling strategies, and the conceptualization of variables. The analysis of the data occurs separately, and may be mostly done by computer. Thus, it appears objective, but only as long as we don't ask questions about where and how the data were produced. Qualitative research requires interpretations to occur during analysis, and so the hazards of subjectivity are on full display. In either case, pure objectivity is not a meaningful concept if the goal is to measure intangibles such as meanings, reasons, and understandings. These concepts only exist because we can interpret them.

For many researchers, objectivity rests on the ability of an investigator to articulate what the procedures are so that others can repeat the research if they so choose. Social researchers often prefer the term *intersubjectivity*, implying that if we all agree that the assumptions and definitions of the situation are valid, then it follows that the conclusions are also valid. Explaining one's assumptions and definitions also has the effect of placing the researcher's professional ego on the line. It is akin to saying, "Here is how I did my research, and here are my results. If any reader has questions or challenges, go out and repeat the study to see what you find." From this perspective, case studies, like any other research procedure, require that the investigator clearly articulate what areas have been investigated and through what means. If someone has doubts about the findings, he or she is free to replicate the research with a similar case subject. As well, since the decision processes and coding schemes are visible, any researcher who considers one or more of the decisions to be in error may attempt to replicate the study with a "corrected" design, for comparison.

If the investigator's findings and analysis were valid, subsequent research will corroborate this. If the research produced from a case study is faulty, in error, inaccurate, or anomalous is some way, this too will be shown by subsequent research. As in any scientific research, findings from a single study are seldom accepted immediately without question and additional research investigations. In this light, case methods are as objective as any other data-collection and analysis strategies used by social scientists.

Generalizability

The second concern addresses the question of generalizability. For many, the question is not even necessary to ask. This is because there is clearly a scientific value to gain from investigating some single category of individual, group, or event simply to gain an understanding of that individual, group, or event. For those who have concerns about generalizing to similar types of individuals, groups, or events, case methods are still useful and, to some extent, generalizable.

When case studies are properly undertaken, they should not only fit the specific individual, group, or event studied but also generally provide understanding about similar individuals, groups, and events. This is not to say that an explanation for why one gang member is involved in drug dealing immediately informs us about why *all* drug-dealing gang members are also involved in this activity. It does, however, suggest an explanation for why *some* other gang members are likely to be involved in these behaviors. The logic behind this has to do with the fact that few human behaviors are entirely unique, idiosyncratic, and spontaneous. In fact, if this were the case, the attempt to undertake any type of survey research on an aggregate group would be useless. In short, if we accept the notion that human behavior is fairly consistent—a necessary assumption for all behavior science research—then it is a simple jump to accept that case studies have scientific value.

Even so, there are limits to how far we can generalize our findings from case studies. In the earlier example with the gang members, we might follow a number of gang members on their criminal careers from small bands organized for self-protection, to gangs that sometimes break the law, to organized drug gangs. From this, we might conclude that the first steps taken by our subjects are the *stepping stones* to drug dealing. There might be some validity to this assertion. But note that if we had selected drug-dealing gang members as our subjects—because that is our topic—then we have no comparative data on all of the former gang members who took those same early steps before leaving the gang life and becoming something very different. Both those in our study and those not selected for the study share similar backgrounds. But our subjects were chosen because of where they ended up. From this work, we could discuss *how* one gets from small bands to drug dealing, but we cannot assert the expectation that this is a typical outcome.

Case Studies of Organizations

Case studies of organizations may be defined as the systematic gathering of enough information about a particular organization to allow the investigator insight into the life of that organization. This type of study might be fairly general in its scope, offering approximately equal weight to every aspect of the organization. For instance, you might conduct an organizational case study on a police department. During this investigation, you may examine subunits such as the juvenile division, traffic division, criminal investigations, homicide, and so forth. The results will be a thorough understanding about how the agency operates and how each subunit fits together and serves the overall objectives of the organization. For instance, Barbara French and Jerry Stewart (2001) examined how contemporary law enforcement agencies engage in new organizational practices that focus on empowering line officers, encouraging teamwork, and creating an atmosphere conducive for participative management.

On the other hand, you may specialize, during an organizational case study, by placing particular emphasis on a specific area or situation occurring in the organization. For example, Susan Slick (2002) explored how a learning community operated among a cohort of graduate students in education attending a special pilot master's degree program at the University of Wisconsin-Stevens Point campus. This learning community fostered group goals and values for working and learning collaboratively.

There are a number of reasons that a particular organization may be selected for a case study. For example, a researcher may undertake a case study of an organization to illustrate the way certain administrative systems operate in certain types of organizations. Or the researcher may be interested in accessing how decisions are made in certain types of organizations or even how communications networks operate. In fact, the case method is an extremely useful technique for researching relationships, behaviors, attitudes, motivations, and stressors in organizational settings. In addition to volumes of written material generated by most formal organization, each of the individual participants in the organization can provide a somewhat unique point of view on the subject organization.

Case Studies of Communities

A *community* can be defined as some geographically delineated unit within a larger society. There are also virtual communities and other variants in which a group that shares some interest or collective identity can act as a community without being delineated in space. Such communities are small enough to permit considerable cultural (or subcultural) homogeneity, to diffuse interactions and relationships between members, and to produce a social identification by its members. The literal application of the term *community* is somewhat fluid. However, it does not include an entire nation, a state, or even a large city. It would, however, include a particular neighborhood within a city such as a Chinatown, a Little Italy, or the Jewish section, or even an enclave of Amish farmers all residing within a four- or five-mile radius.

A case study of a community may, however, address a larger entity by placing its focus on a smaller unit of analysis, perhaps a group or social institution such as the Catholic church. Linkogle (1998), for example, undertook a study of the role of popular religion in social transformation in Nicaragua from 1979 to 1998. He examined some general issues around popular religion in Latin America and its relationship to the practice and pronouncements of the Catholic church. Linkogle's primary focus was how popular religious practices may impact and shape gender and political and religious identities.

Case studies of communities can be defined as the systematic gathering of enough information about a particular community to provide the investigator with understanding and awareness of what things go on in that community; why and how these things occur; who among the community members take part in these activities and behaviors, and what social forces may bind together members of this community. As with other variations of case studies, community case studies may be very general in their focus, offering approximately equal weight in all of the various aspects of community life. Or community case studies may specifically focus on some particular aspect of the community or even some phenomenon that occurs within that community. For example, you may consider a community in general, such as examining an Amish farming community. In such an investigation, you may be interested in the various daily routines of members as well as their social interactions. You might consider any political ideologies that predominate among members of the community and how these affect behaviors among both insiders and outsiders, and so forth. On the other hand, you may be interested in a particular phenomenon occurring within the Amish community. For instance, you may be interested in how social control mechanisms operate in the community. Will the community handle an errant youth who may have shoplifted some petty item such as a magazine, or will the outside, non-Amish community's laws apply? Of course, if you investigate the latter phenomenon, to remain a community case study, this exploration would have to be undertaken against the backdrop of the life of the community. Although there are other styles of research that might explore a particular question in isolation from the background of the community, these would not be accurately called case studies.

Robert and Helen Lynd's study of Middletown, first published in 1929, stands as a classic example of how community case studies operate. This research was among the earliest systematic studies of an American community where the purpose was primarily to develop a scientific understanding of community life.

Data Collection for Community Case Studies

The various data-collection strategies used in community case studies are, for the most part, those already discussed in this chapter, particularly those involving fieldwork (see Chapter 6). However, in addition, community case studies frequently make use of maps. These may include existing maps used for various human ecological purposes, as well as maps created by the researcher in order to indicate physical and social proximity of items and events occurring in the community.

Human ecological concerns have long been important foci in community case studies. Human ecology is concerned with the interrelationships among people in their spatial setting and physical environment. An ecological focus might consider how various physical environmental elements shape the lives of people in a community or the life of the community itself. Do rivers block a community's expansion? Are railroad tracks or major highways located close enough to encourage industry in a community? Has a coal mine played out and closed down, sending hundreds of community members to unemployment, and so forth? Maps are frequently the basic tool necessary for a consideration of such ecological concerns in a community case study.

Community Groups and Interests

In a manner similar to how one might break down a community into its constituent physical parts, its human members too can be divided into groups. These groups may be classified in a number of different ways. For example, there may be different ethnic groups all residing in the same community. Although some ethnic groups are sufficiently large and homogeneously located to constitute a community in themselves, this is not always the case. In many communities several distinct ethnic groups reside in both physical and social proximity but manage to retain their own individual ethnic identity. In some cases, the ethnic groups may retain certain of their distinctive ethnic features but merge or assimilate into their surrounding social life. In such a case, one would need to consider this ethnic group both as a thing apart from the community as well as an element of the larger community.

The study of any group in a community begins much as you would begin any research study, namely, in the library (see Chapter 2). The logical place to begin considering community groups is in published sources. In addition, community case studies may include an examination of census data, local histories, newspaper accounts of group activities and events, any official records of various organizations related to the group or community, and so on. As with other variations of case studies, interviews may provide useful information or even historical explanations for various groups or the presence of certain conditions in the community. Researchers even use fairly traditional strategies of observation to learn about groups in a community. Observations may include consideration of the types of homes and housing in the community, places used for leisure or amusement, schools and religious institutions in the community, and so forth.

Interest groups are another way you might divide up the inhabitants of a community. In this case, you may include street gangs, various social clubs or organizations in the community (Boy and Girl Scouts, YMCAs, Little Leagues, Bowling Leagues, etc.), lodges and fraternal organizations, political clubs, business associations, and the like. Membership in many of these interest groups is rather ephemeral and transient. Even the more stable of interest groups are likely to lack the continuity of ethnic or religious groups. Direct observation of these interest groups, along with interviews with members, is probably the best general method for studying these kinds of groups.

Social classes may also be viewed as a type of grouping that allows the researcher to divide up a community. Although you might argue about what division labels to actually use as categories of class, some categorical labeling schema can be conceived. In keeping with the community case study mode, you could consider how members of each social class operate in the community and how these categories fit together to form the entire community.

In essence, there are numerous ways of grouping together people of a community for the purpose of systematically exploring life in that community. Community case studies are large-scale undertakings. They may be time-consuming and expensive if they are to be comprehensive. The community is a sufficiently large segment of society that it permits a wide and diverse array of social phenomena to occur and to be observed. Although not as popular in recent years as they were during the 1930s and 1960s, especially in areas of urban sociology and urban ecology, community case studies continue to offer an important and valuable means to understanding communities and community members.

TRYING IT OUT

Suggestion 1   Using available archival information located in your school's library and various administrative offices, conduct an organizational case study of your college or university. This will involve using at least some historical tracings (see Chapter 9).

Suggestion 2   Select an adult relative and conduct a modified case study. For this project, examine only the roles and behaviors of the individual during some aspect of his or her life. This may be during school activities, work life, home life, and so forth. Limit the time on this project to one week of data collection. Remember, this is simply practice, not actual research.

REFERENCES

Abrams, C. B., Albright, K., & Panofsky, A. (2004). Contesting the New York community: From liminality to the "new normal" in the wake of September 11. *City and Community 3*(3), 189–220.

Alexander, G. L., & Bennett, A. (2005). *Case Studies and Theory Development in the Social Sciences.* Cambridge, MA: MIT Press.

Berg, B. (2004). *Qualitative Research Methods for the Social Sciences* (5th ed.). Boston, MA: Allyn and Bacon.

Berg, B. (2007). *Qualitative Research Methods for the Social Sciences* (6th ed.). Boston, MA: Allyn and Bacon.

Bogdan, R. C., & Biklen, S. K. (2003). *Qualitative Research for Education* (4th ed.). Boston, MA: Allyn and Bacon.

Bromley, D. B. (1990). Academic contributions to psychological counseling: A philosophy of science for the study of individual cases. *Counseling Psychology Quarterly 3*(3), 299–307.

Chambré, S. (1997). "Civil Society, Differential Resources, and Organizational Development: HIV/AIDS Organizations in New York City, 1982–1992." *Nonprofit and Voluntary Sector Quarterly 26*(4), 466–488.

Champion, D. J. (2006). *Research Methods for Criminal Justice and Criminology* (3rd ed.). Upper Saddle River, NJ: Pearson/Prentice Hall.

Creswell, J. W. (1998). *Qualitative Inquiry and Research Design: Choosing Among Five Traditions.* Thousands Oaks, CA: Sage.

Creswell, J. W. (2002). *Educational Research: Planning, Conducting, and Evaluating Quantitative and Qualitative Research.* Upper Saddle River, NJ: Merrill Prentice Hall.

Creswell, J. W. (2007). *Qualitative Inquiry and Research Design: Choosing Among Five Traditions* (2nd ed.). Thousands Oaks, CA: Sage.

Denzin, N. K., & Lincoln, Y. S. (2005). *The Sage Handbook of Qualitative Research* (3rd ed.). Thousand Oaks, CA: Sage.

Eisenhardt, K. (1989). Building theories from case study research. *Academy of Management Review 14*(4), 532–550.

Erikson, K. T. (1976). *Everything In Its Path: Destruction of Community in the Buffalo Creek Flood.* New York: Simon & Schuster.

Fernandez, W. (2005). The grounded theory method and case study data in IS research: Issues and design. In D. N. Hart & S. D. Gregor (Eds.), *Information Systems Foundations: Constructing and Criticising.* Canberra, Australia: Australian National University E-Press, pp. 43–60.

Foner, N. (2005). *Wounded City: The Social Impact of 9/11.* New York: Russel Sage Foundation.

French, B., & Stewart, J. (2001). Organizational development in a law enforcement environment. *The FBI Law Enforcement Bulletin 70*(9), 14.

Gall, M. G., Borg, W. R., & Gall, J. P. (1995). *Educational Research and Introduction.* New York: Longman Publishing Group.

Gall, M. G., Borg, W. R., & Gall, J. P. (1998). *Applying Educational Research.* New York: Longman Publishing Group.

Geertz, C. (1973). *The Interpretation of Culture.* New York: Basic Books.

Gerring, J. (2006). *Case Study Research: Principles and Practices.* New York: Cambridge University Press.

Gomm, R., Hammersley, M., & Foster, P. (Eds.). (2000). *Case Study Method.* Thousand Oaks, CA: Sage.

Hagan, F. E. (2006). *Research Methods in Criminal Justice and Criminology* (7th ed.). Boston, MA: Allyn and Bacon.

Hancock, D. R., & Algozzine, R. (2006). *Doing Case Study Research: A Practical Guide for Beginning Researchers.* New York: Teachers College Press.

Herreid, C. F. (2006). *Start With a Story: The Case Method of Teaching College Science.* Arlington, VA: National Science Teachers Association.

Hesse-Biber, S. N., & Yaiser, M. L. (2004). *Feminist Perspectives on Social Research.* New York: Oxford University Press.

Jensen, J. L., & Rodgers, R. (2001). Cumulating the intellectual gold of case study research. *Public Administration Review 61*(2), 236–246.

Linkogle, S. (1998). The revolution and the Virgin Mary: Popular religion and social change in Nicaragua. *Sociological Research Online 3*(2). Available online at www.socresonline.org.uk/socresonline/3/2/8.html.

Lynd, R. S., & Lynd, H. M. (1929). *Middletown.* New York: Harcourt, Brace.

Lune, H. (2007). *Urban Action Networks: HIV/AIDS and Community Organizing in New York City.* Boulder, CO: Rowman and Littlefield.

McLeod, B. (1994). *Language and Learning: Educating Linguistically Diverse Students.* Albany, NY: SUNY Press.

Merriam, S. B. (2001). *Qualitative Research and Case Study Applications in Education.* San Francisco: Jossey-Bass.

Munhall, P. L. (2007). *Nursing Research: A Qualitative Perspective* (4th ed.). Boston, MA: Jones & Bartlett Publications.

Patton, M. Q. (2001). *Utilization-Focused Evaluation: The New Century Text* (4th ed.). Thousand Oaks, CA: Sage.

Reinharz, S. (1992). *Feminist Methods in Social Research.* New York: Oxford University Press.

Roberson, E. W. (1998). *Weep Not for Me Dear Mother: The Letters of Eli Landers.* New York: Pelican.

Scholz, R. W., & Tietje, O. (2002). *Embedded Case Study Methods: Integrating Quantitative and Qualitative Knowledge.* Thousand Oaks, CA: Sage.

Shaughnessy, J. J., Zechmeister, E. B., & Zechmeister, J. S. (2008). *Research Methods in Psychology* (8th ed.). New York: McGraw-Hill.

Shaw, C. R. (1930). *The Jack Roller.* Chicago, IL: University of Chicago Press.

Slick, S. (2002). Teachers are enthusiastic participants in a learning community. *The Clearing House* 75(4), 198–202.

Stake, R. E. (1994). Case studies. In N. K. Denzin & Y. S. Lincoln (Eds.), *Handbook of Qualitative Research* (pp. 236–247). Thousand Oaks, CA: Sage.

Stake, R. E. (1995). *The Art of Case Study Research.* Thousand Oaks, CA: Sage.

Stake, R. E. (2000). Case studies. In N. K. Denzin & Y. S. Lincoln (Eds.), *Handbook of Qualitative Research* (2nd ed., pp. 435–454). Thousand Oaks, CA: Sage.

Stake, R. E. (2005a). Qualitative case studies. In N. K. Denzin & Y. S. Lincoln (Eds.), *Handbook of Qualitative Research* (2nd ed., pp. 443–466). Thousand Oaks, CA: Sage.

Stake, R. E. (2005b). *Multiple Case Study Analysis.* New York: Gilford Publications Incorporated.

Sullivan, S., & Shulman, V. (2005). Managing change: The superintendent as Line Director of instruction. *International Journal of Leadership in Education* 8(2), 123–143.

Sutherland, E. H. (1937). *The Professional Thief.* Chicago, IL: University of Chicago Press.

Swanson, R. A., & Holton III, E. F. (2005). *Research in Organizations: Foundations and Methods of Inquiry.* San Francisco, CA: Berrett-Koehler Publishers, Inc.

Wasta, S., & Lott, C. (2002). Eli Landers: Letters of a confederate soldier. *Social Education* 66(2), 122–130.

Weick, K. E. (1995). *Sensemaking in Organizations.* Thousand Oaks, CA: Sage.

Winston, T. (July 1997). An introduction to case study. *The Qualitative Report* 3(2). Available online at www.nova.edu/ssss/QR/QR3-2/tellis1.html.

Woodside, A. G., & Wilson, E. J. (2004). Case study research methods for theory building. *Journal of Business & Industrial Marketing* 18(6/7), 493–508.

Yin, R. K. (1994). *Case Study Research: Design and Methods* (2nd ed.). Beverly Hills, CA: Sage.

Yin, R. K. (1998). The abridged version of case study research: Design and method. In L. Bickman & D. J. Rog (Eds.), *Handbook of Applied Social Research Methods* (pp. 229–259). Thousand Oaks, CA: Sage.

Yin, R. K. (2003a). *Case Study Research* (3rd ed.). Thousand Oaks, CA: Sage.

Yin, R. K. (2003b). *Applications of Case Study Research* (2nd ed.). Thousand Oaks, CA: Sage.

Yin, R., & Moore, G. (1988). The use of advanced technologies in special education. *Journal of Learning Disabilities* 20(1), 60.

Chapter 11

An Introduction to Content Analysis

THROUGHOUT THE PRECEDING CHAPTERS, techniques and strategies for collecting and organizing data have been discussed. With a partial exception for Chapters 4, 6, and perhaps 7, in which limited analytic procedures are mentioned, analysis of data has not yet been extensively discussed. In this chapter, the task of qualitative data analysis is considered at length.

The instructions in this chapter are intended to assist novice researchers in their attempt to learn the methodological technique(s) for standard content analysis. The chapter begins with a brief explanation of what content analysis is in an effort to orient the discussion. Next, we offer a brief discussion of analysis approaches in qualitative research. Following this, some general discussion on concerns and debates regarding content analysis are presented. Then a number of procedures for analyzing content are examined. These include consideration of what to count and what to analyze, the nature of *levels and units of analysis*, and how to effectively employ *coding frames*. In the next section, the strengths and weaknesses of content analysis as an analytic technique are discussed, and *analytic induction* is examined in relation to content analysis procedures. Finally, this chapter addresses *word crunching*, the use of software in qualitative research.

What is Content Analysis?

Content analysis is a careful, detailed, systematic examination and interpretation of a particular body of material in an effort to identify patterns, themes, biases, and meanings (Berg & Latin, 2008; Leedy & Ormrod, 2005; Neuendorf, 2002).

Typically, content analysis is performed on various forms of human communications; this may include various permutations of written documents, photographs, motion pictures or videotape, and audiotapes. The analysis is designed to "code" the content as data in a form that can be used to address research questions. For example, Amy Binder analyzed the content of news articles and opinion pieces published in newsmagazines and major national newspapers between 1985 and 1990 concerning "dangerous" popular music. Binder found that while both heavy metal music and rap music were frequently "framed" as dangerous, the nature of the threat in each case was presented differently. Arguments against heavy metal raised concerns that the music would corrupt its listeners' moral sensibilities by glorifying drugs, alcohol, violence, promiscuity, and antiauthority sentiments. Rap music, on the other hand, was more often described as "a danger to society." The author notes that while the corruption frame raised the specter of harm to the listeners, who were presumed to be mostly white, the danger frame emphasized the supposed harm to the rest of us—that all of those presumably black listeners would inflict under rap's influence. Through this analysis she was able to identify a racialized pattern of reactions against changes in pop culture.

Content analysis has been used by a wide variety of disciplines, including sociology, criminology, psychology, education, business, journalism, art, and political science. Regardless of where it is used, content analysis is chiefly *a coding operation and data interpreting process* (Bogdan & Biklen, 2006; Maxfield & Babbie, 2006; Morse & Richards, 2002).

Analysis of Qualitative Data

There are a number of procedures used by qualitative researchers to analyze their data. Miles and Huberman (1994) identified three major approaches to qualitative data analysis: interpretative approaches, social anthropological approaches, and collaborative social research approaches.

Interpretative Approaches

This orientation allows researchers to treat social action and human activity as text. In other words, human action can be seen as a collection of symbols expressing layers of meaning. Interviews and observational data, then, can be transcribed into written text for analysis. How one interprets such a text depends in part on the theoretical orientation taken by the researcher. Thus, a researcher with a phenomenological bent will resist condensing data or framing data by various sorting or coding operations. A phenomenologically oriented researcher might, instead, attempt to uncover or capture the telos (essence) of an account. This approach provides a means for discovering the practical understandings of meanings and actions. Researchers with a more general interpretative orientation (dramaturgists, symbolic interactionists, etc.) are likely to organize or reduce data in order to uncover patterns of human activity, action, and meaning.

Social Anthropological Approaches

Researchers following this orientation often have conducted various sorts of field or case study activities to gather data. In order to accomplish data collection, they have necessarily spent considerable time in a given community, or with a given assortment of individuals in the field. They have participated, indirectly or directly, with many of the individuals residing in or interacting with the study population. This provides the researcher with a special perspective on the material collected during the research, as well as a special understanding of the participants and how these individuals interpret their social worlds.

Analysis of this sort of data can be accomplished by setting information down in field notes and then applying the interpretative style of treating this information as text. However, frequently this analytic process requires the analysis of multiple sources of data such as diaries, observations, interviews, photographs, and artifacts. Determining what material to include or exclude, how to order the presentation of substantiating materials, and what to report first or last are analytic choices the researcher must make.

Researchers employing the social anthropological approach usually are interested in the behavioral regularities of everyday life, language and language use, rituals and ceremonies, and relationships. The analytic task, then, is to identify and explain the ways people use or operate in a particular setting and how they come to understand things, account for, take action, and generally manage their day-to-day life. Many researchers using this approach begin with a conceptual or theoretical frame and then move into the field in order to test or refine this conceptualization.

Collaborative Social Research Approaches

Researchers operating in this research mode work with their subjects in a given setting in order to accomplish some sort of change or action (see Chapter 7 on action research). The analysis of data gathered in such collaborative studies is accomplished with the participation of the subjects who are seen by the researcher as *stakeholders* in the situation in need of change or action. Data are collected and then reflexively considered both as feedback to craft action and as information to understand a situation, resolve a problem, or satisfy some sort of field experiment. The actual analytic strategies applied in this effort may be similar to the interpretative and social anthropology approaches.

Hsieh and Shannon (2005) discuss three different approaches to the conduct of qualitative content analysis, namely, *conventional, directed,* and *summative content analysis.* From Hsieh and Shannon's perspective, the approaches differ based on the degree of involvement of inductive reasoning.

Conventional content analysis involves coding categories that have been derived directly and *inductively* from the raw data itself, what some methodologists might refer to as a grounded or grounded theoretical approach. The purpose of this orientation is the generation of theories or theoretically connected explanations of the content of the document under analysis.

Directed content analysis involves the use of more analytic codes and categories derived from existing theories and explanations relevant to the research focus. In this case the investigator will immerse himself or herself in the raw data, using these themes and those that may emerge from the data itself.

Summative content analysis begins from existing words or phrases in the text itself (the raw data), and counts these; then the researcher extends his or her exploration to include *latent meanings* and themes that are apparent in the data (latent meanings will be discussed later in this chapter).

Given these diverse yet overlapping approaches, you can see certain facets of research that recur during any style of qualitative analysis. Following is a fairly standard set of analytic activities arranged in a general order of sequence:

a. Data are collected and made into text or otherwise organized to be "read" (e.g., field notes, transcripts, image sequences).
b. Codes are analytically developed and/or inductively identified in the data and affixed to sets of notes or transcript pages.
c. Codes are transformed into categorical labels or themes.
d. Materials are sorted by these categories, identifying similar phrases, patterns, relationships, and commonalties or disparities.
e. Sorted materials are examined to isolate meaningful patterns and processes.
f. Identified patterns are considered in light of previous research and theories, and a small set of generalizations is established.

During the remainder of this chapter, these features will be discussed and considered in relationship to content analysis. The next section will consider the nature of content analysis as a research technique.

Content Analysis as a Technique

In content analysis, researchers examine artifacts of social communication. Typically, these are written documents or transcriptions of recorded verbal communications. Broadly defined, however, content analysis is "a research technique for making replicable and valid inferences from texts (or other meaningful matter) to the contexts of their use" (Krippendorff, 2004, p. 18). From this perspective, photographs, videotape, or any items that can be "read"—that is, virtually any qualitative data—are amenable to content analysis. In this chapter, objective analysis of messages conveyed in the data being analyzed is accomplished by means of explicit rules called *criteria of selection*, which must be formally established before the actual analysis of data.

The criteria of selection used in any given content analysis must be sufficiently exhaustive to account for each variation of message content and must be rigidly and consistently applied so that other researchers or readers, looking at the same messages, would obtain the same or comparable results. This may be considered a kind of reliability of the measures and a validation of eventual findings (Berg & Latin, 2008; Lune, Pumar & Koppel, 2009). The categories that emerge in the course of developing these criteria should reflect all relevant aspects of the messages and retain, as much as possible, the exact wording used in the statements. This, of course, is merely a restatement of proper sampling techniques. The researcher must define the appropriate criteria for inclusion first and apply them to the data after, without fear or favor.

Consider, by way of contrast, the more popular, less scientific discussions of media content that one might come across in cable news programs. There, a pundit might selectively isolate particular phrases, images, or claims that supposedly reveal a bias on the part of the writer or other content creator. Words or phrases that offend or challenge the pundit are pulled out of context and described as representative of the overall work. But are they? Were we to undertake a thorough content analysis of the materials, we would need to define systematic criteria by which any reader could identify the leanings present in different portions of the text. If, for example, our question was whether certain news stories accepted or denied scientific explanations for global climate change, we would have to first rigorously define (1) what that explanation is; (2) what kinds of claims, assumptions, or explanations represent support for this perspective; and (3) what claims, assumptions, and so on represent denial or doubt. Then, using this code system, we would identify all such events throughout the text. It would then be up to the researcher to decide whether to count the cases of each and see if one pre-dominates over the other, or to interpret the context and qualities of each coded incident. That is, the researcher has to decide whether to perform a quantitative analysis or a qualitative one.

Content Analysis: Quantitative or Qualitative?

Content analysis is not inherently either quantitative or qualitative, and may be both at the same time. Nonetheless, different researchers writing at different times have tended to see the technique exclusively from one or the other perspective. Berelson (1952), for example, suggested that content analysis is "objective, systematic, and quantitative." In contrast, Selltiz, Jahoda, Deutsch, and Cook (1959) argued that heavy quantitative content analysis results in a somewhat arbitrary limitation in the field by excluding all accounts of communications that are not in the form of numbers as well as those that may lose meaning if reduced to a numeric form (definitions, symbols, detailed explanations, photographs, and etc.). More recently, Burns and Grove (2005) suggested that because content analysis frequently involves *counting*, it is not considered a qualitative analysis technique by many qualitative researchers. Increasingly, however, this debate is becoming moot as researchers comfortably blend both quantitative and qualitative content analysis (e.g., Booth, 2000).

Some authors of methods books distinguish the procedure of *narrative analysis* from the procedure of content analysis (see, e.g., Manning & Cullum-Swan, 1994; Silverman, 2006). In narrative analysis, the investigator typically begins with a set of principles and seeks to exhaust the meaning of the text using specified rules and principles but maintains a qualitative textual approach (Boje, 1991; Heise, 1992; Manning & Cullum-Swan, 1994; Silverman, 2006). In contrast to this allegedly more textual approach, nonnarrative content analysis may be limited to counts of textual elements. Thus, the implication is that content analysis is more reductionistic and ostensibly a more positivistic approach. These two approaches may be seen as differences in degree (of analysis) rather than differences in technique. "Counts" of textual elements merely provide a means for identifying, organizing, indexing, and retrieving data. This may be a snapshot description of the data, or a first step toward an interpretive analysis. Interpretive analysis of the data, once organized according to certain content elements, should involve consideration of the literal words in the text being analyzed, including the manner in which these words are offered. In effect, the researcher develops ideas about the information found in the various categories, patterns that are emerging, and meanings that seem to be conveyed. In turn, this analysis should be related to the literature and broader concerns and to the original research questions. In this manner, the analysis provides the researcher a means by which to learn about how subjects or the authors of textual materials view their social worlds and how these views fit into the larger frame of how the social sciences view these issues and interpretations.

From this perspective, content analysis is not a reductionistic, positivistic approach. Rather, it is a passport to listening to the words of the text and understanding better the perspective(s) of the producer of these words.

This chapter strives for a blend of qualitative and quantitative analysis; the descriptions of quantitative analysis show how researchers can create a series of tally sheets to determine specific frequencies of relevant categories. The references to qualitative analysis show how researchers can examine ideological mind-sets, themes, topics, symbols, and similar phenomena, while grounding such examinations in the data.

Manifest versus Latent Content Analysis

Another long-standing debate concerning the use of content analysis is whether the analysis should be limited to *manifest content* (those elements that are physically present and countable) or extended to more *latent content*. In the latter case, the analysis is extended to an interpretive reading of the symbolism underlying the physical data. That is, manifest analysis describes the content while latent analysis seeks to discern its meaning. For example, an entire speech may be assessed for how radical it was, or a novel could be considered in terms of how violent the entire text was. Stated in different words, manifest content is comparable to the *surface structure* present in the message, and latent content is the *deep structural* meaning conveyed by the message.

By reporting the frequency with which a given concept appears in text, researchers suggest the magnitude of this observation. It is more convincing for their arguments when researchers demonstrate the appearance of a claimed observation in some large proportion of the material under study.

Researchers must bear in mind, however, that these descriptive statistics—namely, proportions and frequency distributions—do not necessarily reflect the nature of the data or variables. If the theme "positive attitude toward shoplifting" appears 50 times in one subject's interview transcript and 25 times in another subject's, this would not be justification for the researchers to claim that the first subject is twice as likely to shoplift as the second subject. In short, researchers must be cautious not to take or claim magnitudes as findings in themselves. The magnitude for certain observations is presented to demonstrate more fully the overall analysis. The meanings underlying these cases, however, are a matter of latent, context-sensitive coding and analysis.

Consider the problem of determining whether a book should be considered literature, and therefore appropriate for teaching, or pornography, and therefore maybe not. Pornography depicts sexual encounters and states of arousal. D. H. Lawrence's classic *Lady Chatterley's Lover* and Vladimir Nobokov's *Lolita* do so as well, and both were banned in countries throughout the world for much of the twentieth century. Somehow, authors, teachers, and critics have made the case that whereas porn depicts sexual accounts in order to create a sexual experience for the reader, these books depict them because they are important elements to the lives of the characters. Further, the merits of these two works, and so many others, are observable throughout the books, not just in the parts about sex. No one has ever succeeded in creating a rule structure that allows us to count or define scenes or acts in ways that can distinguish favorable literature from unfavorable literature, or even good or bad writing. But we tend to believe that there are differences, and one can create a valid schema with which to interpret these differences with reasonable and meaningful consistency.

To accomplish this sort of "deciphering" of latent symbolic meaning, researchers must first incorporate independent corroborative techniques. For example, researchers may include agreement between independent coders concerning latent content or some noncontent analytic source (Krippendorff, 2004; Neuendorf, 2002). Finally, and especially when latent symbolism may be discussed, researchers should offer detailed excerpts from relevant statements (messages) that document the researchers' interpretations.

Furthermore, it helps to include some amount of three-dimensionality when describing the creator or speaker of the text used as excerpts or patterns being illustrated. In other words, if the text being analyzed is from an interview, rather than simply stating, "Respondent Jones states ..." or, "One respondent indicates ...," the researcher should indicate some features or characteristics (often, but not necessarily, demographic elements) of the speaker; for instance, "Respondent Jones, a 28-year-old African American man who works as a bookkeeper, states...." By including these elements, the reader gets a better sense of who is saying what. As well, it provides a subtle sort of assurance that each of the illustrative excerpts has come from different respondents, rather than different locations of the same interview. To use a different language, such descriptives *situate* the data in relation to the source's perspective.

Communication Components

Communications may be analyzed in terms of three major components: the message, the sender, and the audience (Littlejohn & Foss, 2004). The message should be analyzed in terms of explicit themes, relative emphasis on various topics, amount of space or time devoted to certain topics, and numerous other dimensions. Occasionally, messages are analyzed for information about the sender of the communication.

Strauss (1990) similarly differentiated between what he calls *in vivo codes* and *sociological constructs*. In vivo codes are the literal terms used by individuals under investigation, in effect, the terms used by the various actors themselves. These in vivo codes then represent the behavioral processes, which will explain to the researcher how the basic problem of the actors is resolved or processed. For example, an interview subject may define some challenges as opportunities and others as threats. These descriptions, offered by the speaker, reveal the speaker's orientations and situational definitions. In contrast, sociological constructs are formulated by the analyst (analytic constructions). Terms and categories, such as *professional attitude*, *family oriented*, *workaholic*, and *educationally minded*, might represent examples of sociological constructs. These categories may be "revealed" in the coding of the text, but do not necessarily reflect the conscious perspective of the speaker. These constructs, of course, need not derive exclusively from sociology and may come from the fields of education, nursing, psychology, and the like. Strauss (1990) observed that these constructs tend to be based on a combination of things, including the researcher's scholarly knowledge of the substantive field under study. The result of using constructs is the addition of certain social scientific meanings that might otherwise be missed in the analysis. Thus, sociological constructs add breadth and depth to observations by reaching beyond local meanings and understandings to broader social scientific ones.

What to Count: Levels and Units of Analysis

When using a content analysis strategy to assess written documents, researchers must first decide at what level they plan to sample and what units of analysis will be counted. Sampling may occur at any or all of the following levels: words, phrases, sentences, paragraphs, sections, chapters, books, writers, ideological stance, subject topic, or similar elements relevant to the context. When examining other forms of messages, researchers may use any of the preceding levels or may sample at other conceptual levels more appropriate to the specific message. For example, when examining television programs for violent content, researchers might use segments between commercials as the level of analysis, or they might choose to use the entire television program (excluding commercials) as the level (see, e.g., Fields, 1988).

Category Development: Building Grounded Theory

The categories researchers use in a content analysis can be determined inductively, deductively, or by some combination of both (Mayring, 2000, 2004; Strauss, 1987). Abrahamson (1983, p. 286) described the inductive approach as beginning with the researchers "immersing" themselves in the documents (i.e., the various messages) in order to identify the dimensions or *themes* that seem meaningful to the producers of each message. The analysis starts with the patterns discernable in the text, which are subsequently explained by the application or development of a theoretical framework. In a deductive approach, researchers start with some categorical scheme suggested by a theoretical perspective. The framework is designed to explain cases, such as the one under investigation, and may be used to generate specific hypotheses about the case. The data itself, the documents or other texts, provide a means for assessing the hypothesis.

In many circumstances, the relationship between a theoretical perspective and certain messages involves both inductive and deductive approaches. However, in order to present the perceptions of others (the producers of messages) in the most forthright manner, a greater reliance on induction is necessary. Nevertheless, as will be shown, induction need not be undertaken to the exclusion of deduction.

The development of inductive categories allows researchers to link or *ground* these categories to the data from which they derive. Certainly, it is reasonable to suggest that insights and general questions about research derive from previous experience with the study phenomena. This may represent personal experience, scholarly experience (having read about it), or previous research undertaken to examine the matter. Researchers, similarly, draw on these experiences in order to propose tentative comparisons that assist in creating various deductions. Experience, thus, underpins both inductive and deductive reasoning.

From this interplay of experience, induction, and deduction, Glaser and Strauss formulated their description of grounded theory. According to Glaser and Strauss (1967, pp. 2–3), grounded theory blends the strengths of both inductive and deductive reasoning:

> To generate theory ... we suggest as the best approach an initial, systematic discovery of the theory from the data of social research. Then one can be relatively sure that the theory will fit the work. And since categories are discovered by examination of the data, laymen involved in the area to which the theory applies will usually be able to understand it, while sociologists who work in other areas will recognize an understandable theory linked with the data of a given area.

What to Count

Seven major elements in written messages can be counted in textual content analysis: words or terms, themes, characters, paragraphs, items, concepts, and semantics (Berg, 1983; Merton, 1968). Most of these elements have corresponding versions for visual content analysis, such as visual themes, items, or concepts, or variations such as recurring color patterns or paired images. Looking at the patterns of symbolic associations in images, or "reading" an image from top to bottom or center out, one can discern a visual "syntax" as well. With these building blocks, working as the basic syntax of a textual or visual content, a researcher may define more specialized and complex "grammars" of coded elements. Here we will briefly discuss the basic elements.

Words   The *word* is the smallest element or unit used in content analysis. Its use generally results in a frequency distribution of specified words or terms. One might, for example, count the use of gendered pronouns (*he* or *she*), the use of military terms for nonmilitary situations (*rout*, *blitz*), or the distributions of certain qualifiers (*great*, *superior*, *inferior*).

Themes   The *theme* is a more useful unit to count. In its simplest form, a theme is a simple sentence, a string of words with a subject and a predicate. Because themes may be located in a variety of places in most written documents, it becomes necessary to specify (in advance) which places will be searched. For example, researchers might use only the primary theme in a given paragraph location or alternatively might count every theme in a given text under analysis. How often does Hamlet invoke divine judgment? How frequently is a person's ethnicity referenced as part of an explanation for his or her behaviors?

Characters   In some studies, *characters* (persons) are significant to the analysis. In such cases, you count the number of times a specific person or persons are mentioned rather than the number of words or themes.

Paragraphs   The *paragraph* is infrequently used as the basic unit in content analysis chiefly because of the difficulties that have resulted in attempting to code and classify the various and often numerous thoughts stated and implied in a single paragraph. Yet, to the extent that each paragraph "covers" a unique idea or claim, it provides a straightforward way to divide and code the text.

Items   An *item* represents the whole unit of the sender's message—that is, an item may be an entire book, a letter, speech, diary, newspaper, or even an in-depth interview.

Concepts The use of *concepts* as units to count is a more sophisticated type of word counting than previously mentioned. Concepts involve words grouped together into conceptual clusters (ideas) that constitute, in some instances, variables in a typical research hypothesis. For instance, a conceptual cluster may form around the idea of deviance. Words such as *crime, delinquency, kiting,* and *fraud* might cluster around the conceptual idea of deviance (Babbie, 2007). To some extent, the use of a concept as the unit of analysis leads toward more latent than manifest content.

Semantics In the type of content analysis known as *semantics*, researchers are interested not only in the number and type of words used but also in how affected the word(s) may be—in other words, how strong or weak a word (or words) may be in relation to the overall sentiment of the sentence (Sanders & Pinhey, 1959).

Combinations of Elements

In many instances, research requires the use of a combination of several content analytic elements. For example, in Berg's (1983) study to identify subjective definitions for Jewish affiliational categories (Orthodox, Conservative, Reform, and Nonpracticing), he used a combination of both item and paragraph elements as a content unit. In order to accomplish a content analysis of these definitions (as items), Berg lifted every respondent's definitions of each affiliational category verbatim from an interview transcript. Each set of definitions was additionally annotated with the transcript number from which it had been taken. Next, each definition (as items) was separated into its component definitional paragraph for each affiliational category. An example of this definitional paragraphing follows (Berg, 1983, p. 76):

Interview #60: Orthodox

Well, I guess, Orthodox keep kosher in [the] home and away from home. Observe the Sabbath, and, you know …, actually if somebody did [those] and considered themselves an Orthodox Jew, to me that would be enough. I would say that they were Orthodox.

Interview #60: Conservative

Conservative, I guess, is the fellow who doesn't want to say he's Reform because it's objectionable to him. But he's a long way from being Orthodox.

Interview #60: Reform

Reform is just somebody that, they say they are Jewish because they don't want to lose their identity. But actually I want to be considered a Reform, 'cause I say I'm Jewish, but I wouldn't want to be associated as a Jew if I didn't actually observe any of the laws.'

Interview #60: Nonpracticing

Well, a Nonpracticing is the guy who would have no temple affiliation, no affiliation with being Jewish at all, except that he considers himself a Jew. I guess he practices in no way, except to himself.

The items under analysis are definitions of one's affiliational category. The definitions mostly require multiple sentences, and hence, a paragraph.

Units and Categories

Content analysis involves the interaction of two processes: specification of the content characteristics (basic content elements) being examined and application of explicit rules for identifying and recording these characteristics. The *categories* into which you code content items vary according to the nature of the research and the particularities of the data (i.e., whether they are detailed responses to open-ended questions, newspaper columns, letters, television transcripts).

As with all research methods, conceptualization and operationalization necessarily involve an interaction between theoretical concerns and empirical observations. For instance, if researchers wanted to examine newspaper orientations toward changes in a state's seat-belt law (as a potential barometer of public opinion), they might read newspaper articles and editorials. As they read each article, the researchers could ask themselves which ones were in favor of and which ones were opposed to changes in the law. Were the articles' positions more clearly indicated by their manifest content or by some undertone? Was the decision to label one article pro or con based on the use of certain terms, on presentation of specific study findings, or because of statements offered by particular characters (e.g., celebrities, political figures)? The answers to these questions allow the researchers to develop inductive categories in which to slot various units of content.

As previously mentioned, researchers need not limit their procedures to induction alone in order to ground their research in the cases. Both inductive and deductive reasoning may provide fruitful findings. If, for example, investigators are attempting to test hypothetical propositions, their theoretical orientation should suggest empirical indicators of concepts (deductive reasoning). If they have begun with specific empirical observations, they should attempt to develop explanations grounded in the data (grounded theory) and apply these theories to other empirical observations (inductive reasoning).

There are no easy ways to describe specific tactics for developing categories or to suggest how to go about defining (operationalizing) these tactics. To paraphrase Schatzman and Strauss's (1973, p. 12) remark about methodological choices in general, the categorizing tactics worked out—some in advance, some developed later—should be consistent not only with the questions asked and the methodological requirements of science but also with a relation to the properties of the phenomena under investigation. Stated succinctly, categories must be grounded in the data from which they emerge (Denzin, 1978; Glaser & Strauss, 1967). The development of categories in any content analysis must derive from inductive reference (to be discussed in detail later) concerning patterns that emerge from the data.

For example, in a study evaluating the effectiveness of a Florida-based delinquency diversion program, Berg (1986) identified several thematic categories from information provided on intake sheets. By setting up a tally sheet, he managed to use the criminal offenses declared by arresting officers in their general statements to identify two distinct classes of crime, in spite of arresting officers' use of similar-sounding terms. In one class of crime, several similar terms were used to describe what amounted to the same type of crime. In a second class of crime, officers more consistently referred to the same type of crime by a consistent term. Specifically, Berg found that the words *shoplifting*, *petty theft*, and *retail theft* each referred to essentially the same category of crime involving the stealing of some type of store *merchandise*, usually not exceeding $3.50 in value. Somewhat surprisingly, the semantically similar term *petty larceny* was used to describe the taking of cash whether it was from a retail establishment, a domicile, or an auto. Thus, the data indicated a subtle perceptual distinction made by the officers reporting juvenile crimes.

Dabney (1993) examined how practicing nurses perceived other nurses who worked while impaired by alcohol or drugs. He developed several thematic categories based on previous studies found in the literature. He was also able to inductively identify several classes of drug diversion described by subjects during the course of interviews. For instance, many subjects referred to *stockpiled drugs* that nurses commonly used for themselves. These drugs included an assortment of painkillers and mild sedatives stored in a box, a drawer, or some similar container on the unit or floor. These stockpiled drugs accumulated when patients died or were transferred to another hospital unit, and this information did not immediately reach the hospital pharmacy.

Classes and Categories

Three major procedures are used to identify and develop classes and categories in a standard content analysis and to discuss findings in research that use content analysis: common classes, special classes, and theoretical classes.

Common Classes The first are the *common classes* of a culture in general. These classes are used by virtually anyone in society to distinguish between and among persons, things, and events (e.g., age, gender, social roles). These common classes, as categories, provide for laypeople a means of designation in the course of everyday thinking and communicating and to engender meaning in their social interactions. These common classes are essential in assessing whether certain demographic characteristics are related to patterns that may arise during a given data analysis.

Special Classes   *Special classes* are those labels used by members of certain areas (communities) to distinguish among the things, persons, and events within their limited province (Schatzman & Strauss, 1973). These special classes can be likened to jargonized terms used commonly in certain professions but not by laypeople. Alternatively, these special classes may be described as *out-group* versus *in-group* classifications. In the case of the out-group, the reference is to labels conventionally used by the greater (host) community or society; as for the in-group, the reference is to conventional terms and labels used among some specified group or that may emerge as theoretical classes.

Theoretical Classes   The *theoretical classes* are those that emerge in the course of analyzing the data (Schatzman & Strauss, 1973). In most content analysis, these theoretical classes provide an overarching pattern (a key linkage) that occurs throughout the analysis. Nomenclature that identifies these theoretical classes generally borrows from that used in special classes and, together with analytically constructed labels, accounts for novelty and innovations.

According to Schatzman and Strauss (1973), these theoretical classes are special sources of classification because their specific substance is grounded in the data. Because these theoretical classes are not immediately knowable or available to observers until they spend considerable time going over the ways respondents (or messages) in a sample identify themselves and others, it is necessary to retain the special classes throughout much of the analysis.

The next problem to address is how to identify various classes and categories in the data set, which leads to a discussion of open coding.

Discourse Analysis and Content Analysis

The use of various *counting* schema, as suggested earlier, may seem to be less than qualitative and in some ways is different from some orientations more aligned with aspects of traditional *linguistic discourse analysis*. According to Johnstone (2003), discourse analysis may be understood as the study of language in the everyday sense of the term *language*. In other words, what most people generally mean when they use the term *language* is talk—words used to communicate and conduct a conversation or create a discourse (Phillips & Hardy, 2002). By extension, this would include written versions of this communication, or even transcribed *signs* of talking, such as might be used in exchanges between people using American Sign Language. To the social scientist, however, the interesting aspect of this discourse in not merely what is said, or which words are used, but the social construction and apprehension of meanings thus created through this discourse. Using the various analytic schema suggested earlier—including counts of terms, words, and themes—provides one avenue for the social scientist to better understand these meanings as produced and understood by parties involved in a communication exchange.

Content analysis, then, examines a discourse by looking at patterns of the language used in this communications exchange, as well as the social and cultural contexts in which these communications occur. The relationship between a given communication exchange and its social context, then, requires an appreciation of culturally specific ways of speaking and writing and ways of organizing thoughts. This includes how, where, and when the discourse arises in a given social and cultural situation (Paltridge, 2006; Wodak & Krzyzanowski, 2008). Further, this sort of content analysis should include examining what a given communication exchange may be intended to do or mean in a given social cultural setting. In effect, the ways in which one says whatever one is saying are also important in terms of constructing certain views of the social world. Counting terms, words, themes, and so on allows the researcher to ascertain some of the variations and nuances of these *ways* in which parties in an exchange create their social worlds.

Open Coding

Inexperienced researchers, although they may intellectually understand the process described so far, usually become lost at about this point in the actual process of coding. Some of the major obstacles that cause anguish include the so-called true or intended meaning of the sentence and a desire to know the real motivation behind a subject's clearly identifiable lie. If the researchers can get beyond such concerns, the coding can continue. For the most part, these concerns are actually irrelevant to the coding process, particularly with regard to *open coding*, the central purpose of which is to open inquiry widely. Although interpretations, questions, and even possible answers may seem to emerge as researchers code, it is important to hold these as tentative at best. Contradictions to such early conclusions may emerge during the coding of the very next document. The most thorough analysis of the various concepts and categories will best be accomplished after all the material has been coded. The solution to the novice investigators' anguish, then, as suggested by Strauss (1987, p. 28) is to "believe everything and believe nothing" while undertaking open coding. More to the point, our task is to find meanings that are present in the text or supported by it. This is not the same as discovering anyone's true motive or intent.

Strauss (1987, p. 30) suggests four basic guidelines when conducting open coding: (1) ask the data a specific and consistent set of questions, (2) analyze the data minutely, (3) frequently interrupt the coding to write a theoretical note, and (4) never assume the analytic relevance of any traditional variable such as age, sex, social class, and so forth until the data show it to be relevant. A detailed discussion of each of these guidelines follows.

1. *Ask the data a specific and consistent set of questions.* The most general question researchers must keep in mind is, What study are these data pertinent to? In other words, what was the original objective of the research study? This is not to suggest that the data must be molded to that study. Rather, the original purpose of a study may not be accomplished and an alternative or unanticipated goal may be identified in the data. If, for example, your research question concerns the nature of moral advice to be found within Harlequin romances, then you would begin your coding by coding statements of principles, expectations, or general notions of human nature within the text. As well, it would be important to look at the moral career of the main characters or the lessons implicit in the stories of side characters. You don't need to make extensive note of sexist language, political assumptions, descriptions of locales, or other factors that are unrelated to your question. Along the way, however, you may find that locations are associated with notions of deserved and undeserved outcomes, in which case it would become necessary to understand the symbolic use of place descriptions.

2. *Analyze the data minutely.* Strauss (1987, 1990) cautions that researchers should remember that they are conducting an initial coding procedure. As such, it is important to analyze data minutely. Students in qualitative research should remind themselves that in the beginning, more is better. Coding is much like the traditional funnel used by many educators to demonstrate how to write papers. You begin with a wide opening, a broad statement; narrow the statement throughout the body by offering substantial backing; and finally, at the small end of the funnel, present a refined, tightly stated conclusion. In the case of coding, the wide end represents inclusion of many categories, incidents, interactions, and the like. These are coded minutely

during open coding. Later, this effort ensures extensive theoretical coverage that will be thoroughly grounded. At a later time, more systematic coding can be accomplished, building from the numerous elements that emerge during this phase of open coding.

The question that arises, of course, is when to stop this open-coding process and move on to the speedier, more systematic coding phase. Typically, as researchers minutely code, they eventually saturate the document with repetitious codes. As this occurs and as the repetition allows the researchers to move more rapidly through the documents, it is usually safe to conclude that the time has come to move on.

3. *Frequently interrupt the coding to write a theoretical note.* This third guideline suggested by Strauss (1987) directs researchers closer to grounded theory. Often, in the course of coding, a comment in the document triggers ideas. Researchers should take a moment to jot down a note about these ideas, which may well prove useful later. If they fail to do so, they are very likely to forget the idea. In many instances, researchers find it useful to keep a record of where in each document similar comments, concepts, or categories seem to convey the same elements that originally triggered the theory or hypothesis. For example, during the coding process of a study on adolescents' involvement with alcohol, crime, and drugs, interview transcripts revealed youths speaking about drugs and criminal activities as if they were almost partitioned categories (Carpenter Glassner, Johnson, & Loughlin, 1988). Notes scribbled during coding later led to theories on drug-crime event sequences and the nexus of drug-crime events.

4. *Never assume the analytic relevance of any traditional variable such as age, sex, social class, and so on until the data show it to be relevant.* As Strauss (1987, p. 32) indicated, even these more mundane variables must "earn their way into the grounded theory." This assumes that these variables are necessarily contributing to some condition, but it does not mean you are prohibited from intentionally using certain variables deductively. The first guideline—What study are these data pertinent to?—is germane to the coding process. Consequently, if researchers are interested in gender differences, naturally, they begin by assuming that gender might be analytically relevant, but if the data fail to support this assumption, the researchers must accept this result. By the same token, if the study is not about gender-related issues, then there is probably no reason to measure gender differences.

It is also important to bear in mind that there is no single best way to code data. Morse and Richards (2002) point out that there are actually many ways of coding, and coding is undertaken in qualitative research for a variety of purposes. Morse and Richards (2002, p. 112) distinguish between three types of coding, each of which contributes differently to the overall process of analysis. The first type of coding they discuss involves the storage of information and is called *descriptive coding*. The second type is coding used to gather material by *topic*. The third is coding used when the goal is the development of concepts, which Morse and Richards (2002, p. 112) call *analytic coding*.

Bogdan and Biklen (2003, pp. 161–168) offer a virtual typology of code terms, including *setting/context codes, definition of the situation codes, process codes, activity codes, event codes, strategy codes, relationship and social structural codes, narrative codes, and methods codes*. Regardless of what terms are used to classify coding categories or how many are included in the analysis process, coding is a necessary aspect to organizing data and interpreting what the data say. Furthermore, the more organized and systematic the coding schemes, the easier it is to allow the data to *talk to you* and inform you about various research-related questions you might have. It is also important to note that qualitative analysis is not something that you begin after you completely finish collecting all the data (Warren & Karner, 2005). Rather, analysis starts as the data begin to indicate the necessary categories and codes to use and as these elements begin to form patterns and conceptual realities each time the researcher reads and rereads a transcript, undertakes another day of fieldwork, or reviews some document.

Coding Frames

Content analysis is accomplished through the use of *coding frames*. The coding frames are used to organize the data and identify findings after open coding has been completed (David & Sutton, 2004). The first coding frame is often a multileveled process that requires several successive sortings of all cases under examination. Investigators begin with a general sorting of cases into some specified special class. In many ways, this first frame is similar to what Strauss (1987, p. 32) describes as axial coding. According to Strauss (1987), *axial coding* occurs after open coding is completed and consists of intensive coding around one category. The first sorting approximates Strauss's description of axial coding. An example may better illustrate this process.

I (Berg, 1983) began my first sorting by separating all cases into Jewish affiliational categories declared by respondents during an initial telephone contact. Subjects' responses came after being asked the screening question, "With which of the following do you most closely associate yourself: Reform,

Orthodox, Conservative, or Nonpracticing?" (Subjects were consistently asked this question using the preceding affiliational ordering in an attempt to guard against certain acquiescent response sets.)

This procedure separated my sample (cases) into four groupings bearing the conventional affiliational titles listed previously. After completing this sorting, I carefully read the responses to the identical question asked in the course of each respondent's in-depth interview. Subsequently, each affiliational grouping was subdivided into three groups using the following criteria of selection:

1. The first subdivision in each category consisted of all cases in which respondents' answers to the interview version of the question, "With which of the following..." (1) were consistent with the response given during the telephone screening and (2) were offered with no qualification or exception.
2. The second subdivision in each category consisted of cases in which respondents qualified their responses with a simple modifier (usually a single adjective), but were otherwise consistent with the response offered on the telephone screening question (e.g., "I am a *modern* Orthodox Jew.").
3. The third subdivision consisted of all cases in which the respondents offered detailed explanations for their affiliational declarations that were also consistent with their telephone screening response. For example, one male respondent explained that just as his father had switched from being an Orthodox to a Conservative affiliate, so too did he make a switch from being a Conservative to a Reform affiliate. His declaration of *Reform,* however, was consistent with what he had originally declared during the telephone screening.
4. The fourth subdivision consisted of all cases in which the respondents contradicted their original telephone screening question response or indicated that they simply could not determine where they fit in terms of the four conventional affiliational categories.

Using the preceding criteria, I sorted my cases into the indicated subdivisions. Following this, and using a sorting process similar to the preceding one, I again subdivided each newly created subgroup to produce a typological scheme containing 16 distinct categories, the overarching or key linkage in every case being the subjective declaration of each respondent (at two distinct iterations of the same question).

Having sorted and organized my data, I was ready to interpret the patterns apparent from both the organizational scheme and the details offered in response to interview questions. At this juncture in my analysis, relevant theoretical perspectives were introduced in order to tie the analysis both to established theory and to my own emerging grounded theory. These theoretical considerations and sociological constructs led me to analyze several other detailed responses to interview questions. These other questions concerned respondents' involvement in and knowledge of religious symbols and ceremonies. In order to preserve the key linkages throughout the entire analysis process, each subsequent analysis of responses was performed against the newly created typological scheme of subjective identification labels (the 16-category scheme mentioned previously).

Strauss (1990) similarly outlines the coding process. According to Strauss (1990), the analyst begins with a procedure he calls *open coding*. This procedure is described as an unrestricted coding of the data. With open coding, you carefully and minutely read the document line by line and word by word to determine the concepts and categories that fit the data. These concepts, once uncovered, are entirely tentative. As you continue working with and thinking about the data, questions and even some plausible answers also begin to emerge. These questions should lead you to other issues and further questions concerning various conditions, strategies, interactions, and consequences of the data.

A Few More Words on Analytic Induction

Inductive reasoning is frequently used as a form of theory development in which the analyst seeks to discover the crucial patterns that can best explain the data. In this sense, deductive reasoning is considered to be a form of theory testing, in which one's conceptual framework guides the researcher to seek out and test anticipated patterns and relationships. The use of analytic induction, however, also has involved a number of refinements—including several variations on its style and purpose. For example, Sutherland and Cressey (1966) refined the method and suggested that it be used in the study of causes of crime. Even before Sutherland (1950), Lindesmith (1947) had discovered the usefulness of an analytic inductive strategy in a study of opiate users. Lindesmith (1952, p. 492) described analytic induction as follows:

> The principle which governs the selection of cases to test a theory is that the chances of discovering a decisive negative case should be maximized. The investigator who has a working hypothesis concerning the data becomes aware of certain areas of critical importance. If his theory is false or inadequate, he knows that its weakness will be more clearly and quickly exposed if he proceeds to the investigation of those critical areas. This involves going out of one's way to look for negative evidence.

Hypothesis testing cannot simply involve the examination of supportive evidence. A valid hypothesis must also be falsifiable, or "nullifiable." Inverting the statistical notion of the null hypothesis, Lindesmith accepted the validity of his hypothesis if he was unable to falsify it.

Adding further refinements to the method, Glaser and Strauss suggested that analytic induction should combine analysis of data after the coding process with analysis of data while integrating theory. In short, analysis of data is grounded to established theory and is also capable of developing theory. Glaser and Strauss (1967, p. 102) describe their refinements as the constant comparative method. In this approach, coding categories are not merely derived from theory, but refined on the fly as the data is examined. The authors suggested that such a joint coding and analysis of data is a more honest way to present findings and analysis. Similarly, Merton (1968, pp. 147–148) discussed the "logical fallacy underlying post factum explanations" and hypothesis testing. Merton stated the following:

> It is often the case in empirical social research that data are collected and only then subjected to interpretative comment.... Such post factum explanations designed to "explain" observations, differ in logical function from speciously similar procedures where the observational materials are utilized in order to derive fresh hypotheses to be confirmed by new observations.
>
> A disarming characteristic of the procedure is that the explanations are indeed consistent with the given set of observations. This is scarcely surprising, in as much as only those post factum hypotheses are selected which do accord with these observations.... The method of post factum explanation does not lend itself to nullifiability.

Throughout the analysis, researchers should incorporate all appropriate modes of inquiry. Thus, both logically derived hypotheses and those that have "serendipitously" (Merton, 1968) arisen from the data may find their way into the research.

Interrogative Hypothesis Testing

The process of negative case testing, as described by Lindesmith and others, involves the investigator intentionally seeking negative or unique cases until the data are saturated and built into an emerging pattern. At that point, the investigator looks for confirmation of a developing theory or a specific hypothesis. This testing process involves the following steps:

1. Make a rough hypothesis based on an observation from the data.
2. Conduct a thorough search of all cases to locate negative cases (i.e., cases that do not fit the hypothesized relationship).

3. If a negative case is located, either discard or reformulate the hypothesis to account for the negative case or exclude the negative case.
4. Examine all relevant cases from the sample before determining whether "practical certainty" (Denzin, 1978) in this recommended analysis style is attained.

For example, based on a reading of responses to the open-ended question, "With which of the following do you most closely associate yourself: Conservative, Orthodox, Reform, or Nonpracticing?" I (Berg, 1983) hypothesized that certain groups of persons offered instrumentally oriented answers (i.e., oriented to achievement and goals) while other groups offered expressively oriented answers (i.e., sentimental, feeling oriented, and symbolic). I further hypothesized that these styles of responses could be linked to particular categories relevant to the analysis of differential involvement with religious activities and subjective affiliational identification. However, after carefully reexamining each case, with these hypotheses in mind, I found many negative cases. At each negative juncture, I attempted to reformulate the hypotheses to account for the cases that did not fit. Unfortunately, I soon realized that my hypotheses had become artificial and meaningless. Consequently, I soon abandoned them. None of the successive formulations were constructed *de novo* but were based on some aspect of the preceding hypothetical relationship.

Howard S. Becker (1998) has offered a similar approach, which he calls the *null hypothesis trick*. Becker suggests that the researcher should initially assume that the data reveal no patterns or relationships. Then the researcher should tease out various conditions under which the observed pattern might develop. Esterberg (2002, p. 175) also offers an explanation of this null hypothesis trick, suggesting that you state a relationship in your research as not existing and then seek "clear evidence, based on examples from the data, that there is one." Again, effectively this so-called null hypothesis trick is paramount to interrogative hypothesis testing.

It may be argued that the search for negative cases sometimes neglects contradictory evidence (i.e., when a case both affirms and, in some way, denies a hypothetical relationship) or distorts the original hypothetical relationship (i.e., when the observers read into the data whatever relationship they have hypothesized—a variation on post-factum hypothesizing). To accomplish content analysis in the style recommended here, researchers must use several safeguards against these potential flaws in analysis. First, whenever numbers of cases allow, examples that illustrate a point may be lifted at random from among the relevant grouped cases. Second, every assertion made in the analysis should be documented with no fewer than three examples. Third, analytic interpretations should be examined carefully by an independent reader (someone other than the actual researchers) to ensure that their claims and assertions are not derived from a misreading of the data and that they have been documented adequately. Finally, whenever inconsistencies in patterns do emerge, these too should be discussed in order to explain whether they have invalidated overall patterns. Failure to mention these inconsistencies in pattern is a less than forthright presentation of the data and analysis.

In effect, the use of the foregoing safeguards avoids what Glaser and Strauss (1967, p. 5) describe as *exampling*. According to Glaser and Strauss, exampling is finding examples for "dreamed-up, speculative, or logically deducted theory after the idea occurred," rather than allowing the patterns to emerge from the data. For instance, in the course of analyzing responses to the question, "How do you celebrate Chanukkah, if at all?" during an early analysis of the data, I (Berg, 1983) suggested that gift giving was emphasized to a greater extent by some affiliational groups than by others. However, when this section was read by an independent reader, the reader noticed that several negative cases had been presented in evidence of this assertion. What I had originally missed was that the more traditional affiliational group members had described their style of gift giving in the midst of a number of traditional (religious) rituals. On the other hand, many of the nonpracticing affiliational group members had described gift giving as being in competition with an observance of Christmas and, thus, actually fused their observance of Chanukkah with an observance of Christmas.

Many nonresearchers write about the content of various texts, performances, or other products and artifacts. We hear that certain films are anti-[name of your group here] or that advertisements insult [other group]. These assertions may be valid, or not. But nonscientific discussions of content rarely attempt a scientific content analysis. Instead, most that I have seen use exampling. Identifying representative examples of an idea or phenomenon is a reasonable first step in an analysis, but it cannot be the last. We need systematic and reliable procedures to discover and explain patterns in the content.

A final warning on this topic, based on my experiences as a writer and an instructor: Anyone, anytime, can dismiss your findings when you use content analysis by claiming that you are just "cherry-picking" the cases that support your ideas and ignoring the rest. This places the burden on you, the researcher, to demonstrate that the things that you haven't discovered really weren't there. It's a difficult situation. For the most part, we just have to explain our methods clearly, follow them precisely, and trust that peer review will give us the credibility we need to make our arguments.

Stages in the Content Analysis Process

As a means of recapitulation of what has been described in this chapter as the content analysis process, consider the model offered in Figure 11.1. In the first stage of content analysis, you begin with the research question. Specifically, what are you interested in finding an explanation for? Next, many researchers move to developing a number of sociological constructs or analytic categories by sorting the themes or category labels of the various chunks of data (generally segments of text from field notes, interview transcripts, or whatever textual data are being analyzed). These analytic categories arise from reading

Figure 11.1 Stage Model of Qualitative Content Analysis

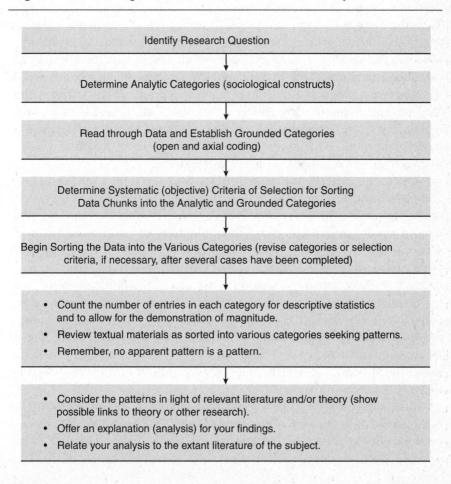

Identify Research Question

↓

Determine Analytic Categories (sociological constructs)

↓

Read through Data and Establish Grounded Categories
(open and axial coding)

↓

Determine Systematic (objective) Criteria of Selection for Sorting
Data Chunks into the Analytic and Grounded Categories

↓

Begin Sorting the Data into the Various Categories (revise categories or selection
criteria, if necessary, after several cases have been completed)

↓

- Count the number of entries in each category for descriptive statistics
  and to allow for the demonstration of magnitude.
- Review textual materials as sorted into various categories seeking patterns.
- Remember, no apparent pattern is a pattern.

↓

- Consider the patterns in light of relevant literature and/or theory (show
  possible links to theory or other research).
- Offer an explanation (analysis) for your findings.
- Relate your analysis to the extant literature of the subject.

the lite-rature, links to the research question, or even directly from interview questions (in the case of depth interviews).

After establishing the analytic categories, the next step is to read through the data. Although you need not read through all transcripts or every page of field notes, you should read through a fairly hefty amount of the data. As you do, you can begin to jot down what seem to be on the surface relevant themes and category labels for sorting the data. You are also likely to notice that some of the analytic categories you have already identified (or similar versions of them) emerge. As you conduct this segment of the analysis, it is important to keep in mind that the categories should have some relationship with the research question and should not simply be random words that seem to occur with some regular frequency.

After establishing the analytic and grounded categories, you need to establish objective criteria for selection. The idea here is to offer some explicit definition or coding rules for each category (either analytic or grounded). This criterion might simply be the specific statement of a particular phrase or word, or it might include several inferential levels. For example, you might sort data chunks into a category, provided the subject (or field notes) has described a particular event, such as a holiday, or a type of event or activity. In the Berg and colleagues (2004) study, for example, one analytic category they used was labeled *sexual risks*. Anytime the subject mentioned behaviors that represented a sexual risk, that information was sorted into this category. This included descriptions of unprotected sex or having sex with a partner who was a stranger, as well as having multiple sexual partners.

Once the criteria for selection for various categories have been accomplished, the next stage is to sort the data accordingly. This can be accomplished in a number of ways. Researchers who like to hold their data in hand may use color-coded highlighters or sticky notes to mark sections of text that are comparable. Software programs, including both word processors and specialized content analysis programs, have versions of both of these techniques. Specialized programs, however, also allow the researcher to assign multiple codes to different sections of text, to run comparative analysis of the occurrence patterns of different codes, and to produce summary reports relating all of the code categories. But whatever means we use, sorting is an important early step. By looking primarily at the assigned codes, we pull the relevant sections out of context and group them as instances of that category.

After sorting or locating data chunks, I recommend taking a surface look at the data by counting the number of items of data chunks that have been cast into each category. Although not really a finding in itself, having a larger number of chunks of data from many cases in a particular category does suggest to the researcher where to look for patterns. As well, if many of these items say similar things that establish a pattern, then you are able to offer the reader some idea of how strong the pattern is by describing its magnitude (the proportion of the sample that made similar comments or statements). A common rule of thumb is that a minimum of three occurrences of something can be considered a pattern. The rationale for this is as follows: Once may be an accident, twice is a coincidence, and three times moves beyond mere chance to a pattern.

Once thematic (categorical) patterns have been identified, they still need to be explained. Inexperienced researchers often see this segment of the analysis process as the most challenging. Once again you must consult the literature and consider your pattern findings in light of previous research and existing theory. Do your findings confirm previous similar research? Do they contradict previous studies? How can you explain these differences or similarities? As you begin to consider answers to these sorts of questions, you should also begin to see that you are conducting analysis.

Strengths and Weaknesses of the Content Analysis Process

Perhaps the most important advantage of content analysis is that it can be virtually unobtrusive (Webb, Campbell, Schwartz, & Sechrest, 2004). Content analysis, although useful when analyzing depth interview data, may also be used nonreactively: No one needs to be interviewed, no one needs to fill out lengthy questionnaires, no one must enter a laboratory. Rather, newspaper accounts, public addresses, libraries, archives, television shows, movies, and similar sources allow researchers to conduct analytic studies.

An additional advantage is that content analysis is cost effective (Babbie, 2007). Generally, the materials necessary for conducting content analysis are easily and inexpensively accessible. One college student working alone can effectively undertake a content analysis study, whereas undertaking a national survey, for instance, might require enormous staff, time, and expense.

A further advantage to content analysis is that it provides a means by which to study a process that occurs over long periods of time that may reflect trends in a society (Babbie, 2007). As examples, you might study the portrayal of women in the media from 1800 to 1993 or you might focus on changing images of women in the media from 1982 to 1992. For instance, McBroom (1992) examined women in the clergy as depicted in the *Christian Century* between 1984 and 1987. McBroom (1992, p. 208) found that while the Chrisitian media initially featured a number of positive references to the question of the ordination of women, by 1985 the pattern was less consistent, turning towards mostly negative representations by 1986–87. This pattern of coverage matched the brief rise and then fall of overall support for women in the clergy ending in a state of retrenchment in which there were fewer opportunities for women than there had been at the start. Thus, using content analysis, McBroom was able to examine data during individual years as well as over the span of all years under study.

The single serious weakness of content analysis may be in locating appropriate unobtrusive content relevant to the particular research questions. In other words, content analysis is limited to examining already recorded messages. The unobtrusive nature of the work means that we rely on existing content rather than generating our own. Although these messages may be oral, written, graphic, or videotaped, they must be recorded in some manner in order to be analyzed. We are therefore often limited to the examination of records that others have decided were worth preserving.

Of course, when you undertake content analysis as an analysis tool rather than as a complete research strategy, such a weakness is minimal. For example, if researchers use content analysis to analyze interview data or responses to open-ended questions (on written questionnaires), this weakness is virtually nonexistent.

Another limitation (although some might call it a weakness) of content analysis is that it is ineffective for testing causal relationships between variables. Researchers and their audiences must resist the temptation to infer such relationships. This issue reiterates the point made previously about motivations: We can use content analysis to say what is present, but not why. This is particularly true when researchers forthrightly present the proportion or frequency with which a theme or pattern is observed. This kind of information is appropriate to indicate the magnitude of certain responses; however, it is not appropriate to attach cause to these presentations. Causality may be suspected or suggested by the patterns of association among measured phenomena, but other means must be used to test that idea.

Computers and Qualitative Analysis

It has now been over 50 years since General Inquirer, the first software program designed to assist in the analysis of textual data, became public (Stone, Dunphy, Smith, & Ogilvie, 1966; Tesch, 1991). Of course, when General Inquirer came out, affordable personal computers did not exist. To use the original form of General Inquirer, one needed access to a large mainframe computer and sufficient time to read and digest its book-length instructions.

This program largely operated on the basis of counting and numerous calculations. Yet, it did work exclusively with textual data (Tesch, 1991). A version of General Inquirer is still available today for the modern personal computer and qualitative researcher via an online server and weblog (http://www.wjh.harvard.edu/~inquirer/).

Most experienced (and even many novice) qualitative researchers are aware that today a number of computer programs for qualitative data exist—even if they do not use them. An entire area of research and discussion known as *Computer Assisted Qualitative Data Analysis* (CAQDA) has evolved during the past two decades (Alpi, 2004; Dohan & Sanchez-Jankowski, 1998; LaPelle, 2004; Lewins & Silver, 2005, 2007). Throughout the 1980s, many academic journals published articles directing considerable attention toward commercially available software designed specifically for qualitative analysis (Conrad & Reinharz, 1984; Drass, 1980; Gerson, 1984; Heise, 1981; Jacobs, 1987; Seidel, 1984).

It would be impossible to estimate how many qualitative researchers today use either such dedicated software packages or word-processing programs in their analysis.

To be sure, the potential for using computers in qualitative research for analytic purposes is enormous. Some researchers have adapted commercial software packages to their personal qualitative sorting or data management needs. For example, Excel, Lotus 1–2–3, and similar spreadsheets can be applied to a wide assortment of tasks common in content analysis. You can, for instance, create fields to contain shorthand versions of themes, classes, or categories and corresponding fields to indicate tallies of these categorical containers. After you sort textual data into these fields, calculations of the magnitude (how many times a theme has been placed in a given thematic category) can be automatically determined. LaPelle (2004) argues that it is possible to use various components of word-processing programs to simulate many of the functions of dedicated qualitative data analysis software packages (see also Dabney, 1993; Norman, 1989).

If a researcher is new to spreadsheets or not very comfortable using them, it is probably better to begin with a simple word-processing program. If, on the other hand, the researcher is fairly well acquainted with software systems, he or she might want to explore one or another of a number of more dynamic database management programs.

Nagy Hesse-Biber and Crofts (2008) similarly point that the researcher should consider his or her level of computer literacy, along with a series of other reflective questions. Other reflective concerns for the researcher include consideration of what type of computer system one prefers to work on and feels most comfortable working on or does one need to gain newer programs, upgrade the system, or perhaps secure a new computer. Further, one should consider the overall look and feel of the program to determine if it will fit well with the investigator's style of research; this begs the question, of course, what is your particular style of research and analysis? How do you think a computer may assist your research and analysis? Nagy Hesse-Biber and Crofts (2008) suggest that the researcher should consider these, along with several other concerns, before actually selecting a qualitative data analysis program to use in their research.

Morse and Richards (2002, p. 80) point out that software intended for qualitative research allows researchers the versatility of not only storing materials but also storing "ideas, concepts, issues, questions, models, and theories. Researchers can relate the various materials by coding relevant sections of text, by linking them, or by writing about them."

Weitzman and Miles (1995) as well as Gibbs, Friese, and Mangabeira (2002) outline approximately six general types of functions available in software programs used in CAQDA. In many cases, multiple functions are available in a given program. These functions include word processing, text retrievers, textbase managers, code-and-retrieve programs, code-based theory builders, and conceptual network builders.

Word Processors

Word processors allow you to create text-based files and to effectively find, move, reproduce, and retrieve sections of the text in each file. These provide a means for transcribing interviews or audio portions of video, writing up or editing field notes, coding text for indexing and retrieval purposes, and even writing up findings in reports.

Text Retrievers

Software packages such as MetaMorph, Sonar, Professional, The Text Collector, WordCruncher, or ZYIndex are dedicated text search programs (Weitzman & Miles, 1995). These programs specialize in locating every instance of a specified word, phrase, or character string. As well, these programs are able to locate combinations of these items in one of several files.

Textbase Managers

Although similar in basic function to text retrievers, textbase managers provide a greater capacity for organizing, sorting, and making subsets of the textual data. Several examples of these programs include askSam, Folio Views,

DataCollector, and MAX. Some of these programs are intended to manage fairly structured text organized into records or specific case files and fields or specified areas in a given case. Other programs are capable of dealing with more free-flowing forms of text and, in some cases, even certain quantitative information.

Code-and-Retrieve Programs

Code-and-retrieve programs, according to Weitzman and Miles (1995), are often developed by qualitative researchers rather than commercial software developers. These programs are intended to assist the researcher in dividing text into segments or chunks, attach codes, and find and display these coded sections. These programs tend to fill in for the kind of cutting, pasting, and sorting of hard copy data qualitative researchers once used. HyperQual2, Kwalitan, QUALPRO, and The Ethnograph are all examples of code-and-retrieve types of programs.

Code-Based Theory Builders

These types of programs are also frequently developed by researchers. Usually, these programs include the capacity to code and retrieve and also offer special features that assist you in developing theoretical connections between coded concepts. As a result, higher-order classifications and connections can be formulated. Weitzman and Miles (1995) list AQUAD, ATLAS.ti, Hyper-RESEARCH, NVIVO, and QCA as examples.

Conceptual Network Builders

Programs designed for conceptual network building are intended to assist the researcher in building and testing theory. These programs provide the capacity to create graphic networks. Variables are displayed as nodes (usually rectangles or ellipses) linked to other nodes by lines or arrows representing relationships. These networks represent various types of semantic networks that evolve from the data set and the concepts used by the researcher. Examples of these programs include ATLAS.ti (which is also a code-based theory builder), and SemNet.

Although new computer packages and applications for qualitative research are introduced nearly daily, computer use in qualitative research remains in its infancy. For some researchers, it makes no difference whether they use a dedicated qualitative analysis program or apply some utility or word-processing program to the task. In part, this may be because none of the tasks currently accomplished by computers and used in qualitative research really move beyond data organization and management. Any computer program or adaptation still requires that the researcher think through the analytic and theoretical relationships between original conceptualizations and eventual empirical evidence. Quantitative application of computers, which is enormously fast, largely makes hand calculation obsolete. Computers make it easy for researchers to take hundreds of thousands of cases and quickly determine a vast number of statistical aspects of the data set. Yet, even quantitative computer programs cannot by themselves (at least not yet) extrapolate on or beyond the statistical manipulations made on the data.

In the case of qualitative analysis, this problem of extrapolation is made even more difficult. Analysis of data is often intertwined in the presentation of findings and the explanation of results. Creating an apparatus that can simultaneously present the findings and describe their analytic importance would require artificial computer intelligence. For the most part, the intelligence part of the analysis still rests with the researcher. The software, however, can greatly assist in the data organizing.

As a result, the use of computers by qualitative researchers remains, for now, an attempt to locate "chunks of technology" (Gerson, 1984) that are available, affordable, and seem to work for the present. It is important, however, to remember that computers are intended to reduce the amount of overall time a researcher spends in the data organization and analysis phase of research. If you spend enormous amounts of time trying to locate, learn how to use, and enter data into a computer program, this process may defeat the original time-saving purpose of computers. Nonetheless, the use of computers in qualitative research can significantly assist novice researchers. This is because programs such as Ethnograph provide clear directions on how to begin organizing data into a usable structure. As you become more experienced and adept at both data analysis and computer operations, you may feel more confident and try other computer applications or adaptations.

Qualitative Research at the Speed of Light

Many areas in quantitative research have been able to quickly adapt to the advances made in computer technology by creating faster and more advanced statistical analytic packages. Qualitative research, however, may seem to have lagged behind. In part, this may be because the natures of textual, visual, and auditor analyses simply have not lent themselves neatly to any computer program. Partly, however, this may only be the outward appearance of matters, because qualitative research can actually embrace a wider element of the contemporary computer age because of its interest in textual, visual, and auditor analyses. Specifically, I refer to the huge amount of information that is available to explore through the Internet.

Following is a list of just a few Internet sites that might allow interested readers to begin their journey into the vast space that is the Internet to locate the qualitative research areas of the Web.

1. Qualpage, a resource listing for qualitative researchers: http://www. qualitativeresearch.uga.edu/QualPage/
2. Qualitative Report, an online journal that also provides an alphabetized listing of helpful qualitative research Web sites on a variety of interesting topics: www.nova.edu/ssss/QR/
3. ATLAS.ti, a software site designed for qualitative text, audio and video data: http://www.atlasti.com/
4. CAQDAS Network, a general listing of computer-assisted qualitative analysis Web sites: http://caqdas.soc.surrey.ac.uk/

TRYING IT OUT

Suggestion 1 Select a topic of interest to you, such as crime, medical advances, ecology, technology, or another broad concern. Next, using your school library's collection of the *New York Times*, locate 10 consecutive weeks of the Sunday Week in Review section. Now see if you can locate articles with headlines that relate to your topic of interest. If you accomplish these tasks, you have actually conducted a rudimentary form of thematic content analysis. Your topic served as the theme and the newspaper story headlines as your units of analysis.

Suggestion 2 Without writing their names on the paper, have everyone in your class write a response to the following question: If you could change one thing in the world today, what would it be?

Ask each classmate to write his or her gender and age at the bottom of the response, but remind them not to write their names. Have each person make enough photocopies to distribute one copy to every person in the class. Now everyone has a set of data to work with.

Next, go through the responses and see if you can locate any patterns of similarity or difference. Sort the responses into groups according to the patterns or themes that emerge as you read through the responses. Try to make the following assessments:

1. How many times have students identified the same (or very similar) things they would change if they could?
2. What proportion of the class used identical words to describe what they would change?
3. Are patterns any different if you first sort them according to gender?
4. Are patterns any different if you first sort them into the following age groupings: *young* (under 20 years old), *older* (21–25 years old), *oldest* (over 25 years old)?

REFERENCES

Abrahamson, M. (1983). *Social Research Methods*. Englewood Cliffs, NJ: Prentice Hall.

Alpi, K. M. (2004). An introduction to computer assisted qualitative data analysis software. *Hypothesis 18*(1), 9–10.

Babbie, E. (2007). *The Practice of Social Research* (11th ed.). Belmont, CA: Wadsworth.

Becker, H. S. (1998). *Tricks of the Trade: How to Think About Your Research While You're Doing It*. Chicago, IL: University of Chicago Press.

Berelson, B. (1952). *Content Analysis in Communications Research*. Glencoe, IL: Free Press.

Berg, B. L. (1983). Jewish identity: Subjective declarations or objective life styles. Doctoral dissertation, Syracuse University, Syracuse, NY.

Berg, B. L. (1986). Arbitrary arbitration: Diverting juveniles into the justice system. *Juvenile and Family Court Journal 37*(5), 31–42.

Berg, B., Sanudo, F., Hovell, M., Sipan, C., Kelley, N., & Blumberg, E. (2004). The use of indigenous interviewers in a study of Latino men who have sex with men: A research note. *Sexuality and Culture 8*(1), 87–103.

Berg, K. E., & Latin, R. W. (2008). *Essentials of Research Methods in Health, Physical Education, Exercise Science and Recreation* (3rd ed.). Philadelphia, PA: Lippincott, Williams & Wilkins.

Bogdan, R. C., & Biklen, S. K. (2003). *Qualitative Research for Education* (4th ed.). Boston, MA: Allyn and Bacon.

Bogdan, R. C., & Biklen, S. K. (2006). *Qualitative Research for Education* (5th ed.). Boston, MA: Allyn and Bacon.

Boje, D. (1991). The story telling organization: A study of story performance in an office supply firm. *Administrative Science Quarterly 36*, 106–126.

Booth, K. M. (2000). Just testing: Race, sex and the media in New York's "Baby AIDS" Debate. *Gender and Society 14*(5), 644–661.

Burns, N., & Grove, N. K. (2005). *Nursing Research*. Philadelphia, PA: Elsevier/ Saunders.

Carpenter, C., Glassner, B., Johnson, B., & Loughlin, J. (1988). *Kids, Drugs, and Crime*. Lexington, MA: Lexington Books.

Conrad, P., & Reinharz, S. (Eds.). (1984). Computers and qualitative data. *Qualitative Sociology 7*(1–2).

Dabney, D. A. (1993). Impaired nursing: Nurses' attitudes and perceptions about drug use and drug theft. Master's thesis, Indiana University of Pennsylvania, Indiana, PA.

David, M., & Sutton C. D. (2004). *Social Research: The Basics.* Thousand Oaks, CA: Sage.

Denzin, N. K. (1978). *The Research Act.* New York: McGraw-Hill.

Drass, K. A. (1980). The analysis of qualitative data: A computer program. *Urban Life 9*(3), 322–353.

Dohan, D., & Sanchez-Jankowski, M. (1998). Using computers to analyze ethnographic field data: Theoretical and practical considerations. *Annual Review of Sociology 24,* 477–491.

Esterberg, K. G. (2002). *Qualitative Methods in Social Research.* Boston, MA: McGraw Hill.

Fields, E. E. (1988). Qualitative content analysis of television news: Systematic techniques. *Qualitative Sociology 11*(3), 183–193.

Gerson, E. M. (1984). Qualitative research and the computer. *Qualitative Sociology 17*(1–2), 61–74.

Gibbs, G. R., Friese, S., & Mangabeira, W. C. (2002). The use of technology in qualitative research. Introduction to Issue 3(2) of FQS. *Forum Qualitative Sozialforschung/Forum: Qualitative Social Research 3*(2). Available online at www.qualitative-research.net/fqs/fqs-eng.htm.

Glaser, B., & Strauss, A. (1967). *The Discovery of Grounded Theory: Strategies for Qualitative Research.* Chicago, IL: Aldine.

Heise, D. R. (Ed.). (1981). Microcomputers and social research. *Special Issue of Sociological Methods and Research 9*(4), 395–396.

Heise, D. (1992). *Ethnography* (2nd ed.). Chapel Hill, NC: University of North Carolina Press.

Hsieh, H.-F., & Shannon, S. E. (2005). Three approaches to qualitative content analysis. *Qualitative Health Research 15*(9), 1277–1288.

Jacobs, E. (1987). Qualitative research traditions: A review. *Review of Educational Research 57*(1), 1–50.

Johnstone, B. (2003). *Discourse Analysis.* Malden, MA: Blackwell Publishing Ltd.

Krippendorff, K. (2004). *Content Analysis: An Introduction to Its Methodology* (2nd ed.). Thousand Oaks, CA: Sage.

LaPelle, N. (2004). Simplifying qualitative data analysis using general purpose software tools. *Field Methods 16*(1), 85–108.

Leedy, P. D., & Ormrod, J. E. (2005). *Practical Research: Planning and Design* (8th ed.). Upper Saddle River, NJ: Pearson/Merrill/Prentice Hall.

Lewins, A., & Silver, C. (2005). Choosing a CAQDAS package. Available online at http://cagdas.soc.surrey.ac.uk/ChoosingCAQDASV2Lewins&SilverJun05.pdf.

Lewins, A., & Silver, C. (2007). *Using Software in Qualitative Research: A Step-by-Step Guide.* Thousand Oaks, CA: Sage.

Lindesmith, A. R. (1947). *Opiate Addiction.* Bloomington, IN: Indiana University Press.

Lindesmith, A. R. (1952). Comment on W. S. Robinson's the logical structure of analytic induction. *American Sociological Review 17,* 492–493.

Littlejohn, S. W., & Foss, K. A. (2004). *Theories of Human Communication.* Belmont, CA: Wadsworth.

Lune, H., Pumar, E. S., & Koppel, R. (Eds.) (2009). *Perspectives in Social Research Methods and Analysis. A Reader for Sociology.* Thousand Oaks, CA: Sage

Publications.Manning, P. K., & Cullum-Swan, B. (1994). Narrative, content, and semiotic analysis. In N. K. Denzin & Y. S. Lincoln (Eds.), *Handbook of Qualitative Research* (pp. 463–477). Thousand Oaks, CA: Sage.

Maxfield, M. G., & Babbie, E. (2006). *Basics of Research Methods for Criminal Justice and Criminology.* Belmont, CA: Thompson/Wadsworth.

Mayring, P. (2000). Qualitative Content Analysis. *Forum Qualitative Sozial-forsc-hung/Forum: Qualitative Social Research 1*(2). [On-line Journal]. Retrieved [July 9, 2011] from http://www.qualitative-research.net/index.php/fqs/article/view/1089/2386.

Mayring, P. (2004). Qualitative content analysis. In Flick, U., von Kardorff, E., & Steinke, I (Eds.), [Trans. Jenner, B.]. *A Companion to Qualitative Research* (2nd ed.). London: Sage.

McBroom, J. R. (1992). Women in the clergy: A content analysis of the Christian Century, 1984–1987. *Free Inquiry in Creative Sociology 20*(2), 205–209.

Merton, R. K. (1968). *Social Theory and Social Structure.* New York: Free Press.

Miles, M. B., & Huberman, M. A. (1994). *Qualitative Analysis: An Expanded Sourcebook* (2nd ed.). Thousand Oaks, CA: Sage.

Morse, J. M., & Richards, L. (2002). *Read Me First: For a User's Guide to Qualitative Methods.* Thousand Oaks, CA: Sage.

Nagy Hesse-Biber, S. & Crofts, C. (2008). User-Centered Perspectives on qualitative data analysis software: Emergent technologies and future trends. In S. Nagy Hesse-Biber & P. Leavy (Eds.), *Handbook of Emergent Methods* (pp. 655–673). New York: The Guilford Press.

Neuendorf, K. A. (2002). *The Content Analysis Guidebook.* Thousand Oaks, CA: Sage.

Norman, E. (1989). How to use word processing software to conduct content analysis. *Computers in Nursing 7*(3), 127–128.

Paltridge, B. (2006). *Discourse Analysis: An Introduction.* London: Continuum.

Phillips, N., & Hardy, C. (2002). *Discourse Analysis: Investigating Processes of Social Construction.* Thousand Oaks, CA: Sage.

Sanders, W., & Pinhey, T. K. (1959). *The Conduct of Social Research.* New York: Holt, Rinehart & Winston.

Schatzman, L., & Strauss, A. (1973). *Field Research: Strategies for a Natural Sociology.* Englewood Cliffs, NJ: Prentice Hall.

Seidel, J. (1984). The Ethnograph. *Qualitative Sociology 7*(1–2), 110–125.

Selltiz, C., Jahoda, M., Deutsch, M., & Cook, S. W. (1959). *Research Methods in Social Relations.* New York: Holt, Rinehart & Winston.

Silverman, D. (2006). *Interpreting Qualitative Data* (3rd ed.). Thousand Oaks, CA: Sage.

Stone, P. J., Dunphy, D. C., Smith, M. S., & Ogilvie, D. M. (1966). *The General Inquirer: A Computer Approach to Content Analysis.* Cambridge, MA: MIT Press.

Strauss, A. L. (1987). *Qualitative Analysis for Social Scientists.* New York: Cambridge University Press.

Strauss, A. L. (1990). *Qualitative Analysis for Social Scientists* (2nd ed.). New York: Cambridge University Press.

Sutherland, E. H. (1950). *Principles of Criminology* (2nd ed.). Philadelphia, PA: J. B. Lippincott.

Sutherland, E. H., & Cressey, D. (1966). *Principles of Criminology* (7th ed.). New York: J. B. Lippincott.

Tesch, R. (1991). Introduction. *Qualitative Sociology 14*(3), 225–243.

Warren, C., & Karner, T. (2005). *Discovering Qualitative Methods.* Los Angeles, CA: Roxbury.

Webb, E. J., Campbell, D. T., Schwartz, R. D., & Sechrest, L. (2004). *Unobtrusive Measures* (Rev. ed.). Thousand Oaks. CA: Sage.

Weitzman, E. A., & Miles, M. B. (1995). *Computer Programs for Qualitative Data Analysis.* Thousand Oaks, CA: Sage.

Wodak, R., & Krzyzanowski, M. (2008). *Qualitative Discourse Analysis in the Social Sciences.* Hampshire, England: Palgrave Macmillan.

Chapter 12

Writing Research Papers: Sorting the Noodles from the Soup

SOME YEARS AGO, BRUCE BERG'S children Alex and Kate, who were then nearly four and nearly six, respectively, sat around the kitchen table eating alphabet soup for lunch. Kate was stirring her soup with great care and deliberation. She managed to capture several letters on her spoon, carefully spilled off the liquid, and spelled out her name. "Look, Daddy, I wrote my name with my noodles! K-A-T-I-E." Alex, seeing the attention his sister received, pulled his dripping spoon from the soup and, spilling much of it onto the floor, proudly held it up and exclaimed, "Me too!" Unfortunately, his letters spelled out "XCYU," a unique spelling of Alex, or simply a failure to sort the noodles from the soup in a fashion that made his noodles mean something to others.

Qualitative research similarly can result either in improved social scientific understanding or in meaningless gibberish. This chapter is designed to enable inexperienced researchers to offer up their noodles for inspection by others in an understandable and meaningful fashion—in other words, to tell the world what you have found. But writing about research involves far more than just posting your data somewhere. The goal of this chapter is to enable you to write up the research so that it can be disseminated in an understandable form to appropriate audiences. Before actually getting to the mechanics of writing up research papers, I believe it is important to write a few lines on the perils of plagiarism.

Plagiarism: What it is, Why it's Bad, and How to Avoid it

Ironically, depending upon the source, you are likely to find a range of meanings and definitions for the term *plagiarism*. Regardless of these variations, at their root these definitions share the notion that plagiarism involves passing off the ideas and words of others as your own without clearly acknowledging the actual source of those ideas and words. Importantly, in academe as in the real world of the social sciences, journalism, the arts, the natural sciences, and virtually everywhere else, plagiarism is considered very bad regardless of whether it is done intentionally or unintentionally.

The label of plagiarism can describe any of the following actions:

- Turning in someone else's written work as your own (regardless of whether you have their permission to do so).
- Purchasing a written work from a professional *paper mill*, your sorority or fraternity, the smart kid in class, or any other source, and passing it off as your own work.
- Copying sentences, paragraphs, or whole pages from a textbook, Web site, or other written source without indicating the actual source of this material.
- Copying sentences, paragraphs, or whole pages from a textbook, Web site, or other written source without including proper quotation marks, page references, or indentation (in the case of longer excerpts)—even when proper citation of the actual source is offered.
- Paraphrasing sentences, paragraphs, or whole pages but failing to provide proper citation of the original source.
- False paraphrasing (changing one or two words) in sentences, paragraphs, or whole pages and failing to provide proper citation of the original source.

Why Plagiarism Occurs

It is likely that much of the plagiarism that occurs in colleges and universities, and perhaps even among some novice researchers, is what we classify as innocent or just *stupid* plagiarism; still, some is intentional and undertaken for a variety of reasons. Some of the more common intentional reasons for plagiarism include, "I was running out of time, and the source said exactly what I wanted to say."

"The source said it so much better than I possibly could have." "It was a stupid assignment, and I have more important things to do with my time." "Everybody else was doing it."

From time to time we also hear about professional researchers, writers, or journalists who are also found to have plagiarized other works. Among the most common explanations given by these authors is that they were writing from their notes, not the original sources, and could not clearly distinguish between the words they had come up with on their own while writing these notes and the phrases they had simply copied over more or less unchanged. This sort of plagiarism is understandable, but just as stupid. Surely, after a writer has struggled once or twice with the inconvenience of having to return to the original source just to find one sentence, you would hope they would have developed more careful note-taking practices.

Innocent or plain stupid plagiarism involves errors in citation because the students simply do not understand that their actions constitute plagiarism. By the way, authorities are typically no less sympathetic to stupid plagiaristic mistakes than they are to intentional ones. However, stupid mistakes are easier to correct because once you learn the errors of your ways, you can consciously avoid making stupid mistakes of plagiarism.

How to Avoid Plagiarism

"So now that you know how it's done, don't do it!"[1]

Avoiding the first two items in the previous list seems like a no-brainer. Obviously, if you go out and borrow or buy someone else's work, you have intentionally plagiarized these works, and there is no lenience for you—a minimum of 30 years' hard labor. Well, maybe that's a little drastic, but you should understand that the action of intentional plagiarism is seldom taken lightly, and in some schools, it can result in suspension or expulsion. In the real world, getting caught in such an act could result in the loss of a job or career, or at the very least the loss of trust in your work, probably forever.

Let us therefore concern ourselves with the remaining four items on the list, which do frequently occur among students and inexperienced writers as stupid mistakes. The first of these four items states: *Copying sentences, paragraphs, or whole pages from a textbook, Web site, or other written source without indicating the actual source of this material.* In truth, this one walks a thin line between a stupid mistake and an intentional one and may from time to time fall into either of these camps. However, in our combined 40 years of teaching in colleges and universities, we have heard some very sincere students claim they were unaware that lifting a few sentences or a paragraph here and there and dropping them into their own writing was plagiarism. Some of the blame for this rests with certain elementary school teachers who insist that their students look up the definition of words and write out the full definition without citing the dictionary as the source, or who encourage students to write topical papers using an encyclopedia as a source. Students who dutifully copy and paste the passages verbatim receive an A for their efforts but, again, do not bother to cite their source.

But regardless of why many students believe this sort of plagiarism is acceptable, it simply is not. It is plagiarism—but with a simple fix. Never use someone else's written work without giving credit to that original author or authors. Now, how the material is cited does, in fact, change slightly when you are directly quoting an author's or authors' work. This brings us to the next item on our list: *Copying sentences, paragraphs, or whole pages from a textbook, Web site, or other written source without including proper quotation marks, page references, or indentation (in the case of longer excerpts)—even when proper citation of the actual source is offered.*

The usual rule of thumb is when a quoted section is five lines or less, you encapsulate it between quotation marks ("quoted passage"). Following this quoted section, you cite, in text, the name of the author, the date of the publication, and the page reference where the original work appears. If you are quoting more than five lines of text, you should indent the passage on both sides—but without quotation marks; it's one or the other, *not both*—either indent or use quotation mark. Following the indented passage (typically on the next line and right justified), the citation is enclosed in brackets ([citation material]). Again, this citation should include the name of the author or authors, the date of the publication, and the page reference where the original passage appears.

The next item on our list is, *Paraphrasing sentences, paragraphs, or whole pages but failing to provide proper citation of the original source.* Apparently, many students believe that if they steal someone's ideas, but do not use every word in the same order as the original author or authors set the material down, it is not plagiarism; this is a very wrong assessment. This one, however, is at least a bit more understandable as a simple stupid mistake. The fact of the matter is, if you take another author's idea(s), you need to reference that author. In fact, in research citing someone else properly is more about giving them credit for their ideas than for their particular choice of words. This is often done with what are hopefully familiar phrases, such as, "According to Joe Jones (2006) ..." or "In a similar fashion, Marshal and Cates (2006) found...." The material following these sorts of statements can be heavily paraphrased, almost unidentifiable with the original, but if the main points have actually been lifted from the original version, it is proper to cite these original authors. It is also a solid way to document your writing.

Here it is worth noting the relationship between credit and credibility. If you wish to take credit for ideas that are not your own, you obviously risk losing credibility if you are found out. The reverse is also true. When you give credit to others for the work that you are using, you gain credibility. It shows that you are both honest and well read. Researchers are supposed to be familiar with the work of others. Building your work on a solid foundation of past research is more respectable than trying to build your whole project out of nothing. As well, it saves you from having to justify some of your claims, since others have already done that. This is particularly important when what you are saying, using the other author or author(s)' ideas, is at all controversial.

The last entry on our list describes a very sloppy strategy that results in plagiarism. This element states: *False paraphrasing (changing one or two words) in sentences, paragraphs, or whole pages and failing to provide proper citation of the original source.* In this case, you take a statement such as the one offered by Maxfield and Babbie (2006, p. 217), which follows, "Field research encompasses two different methods of obtaining data: (1) making direct observation and (2) asking questions." In your paper, you decide to falsely paraphrase the statement as follows: "Field research involves two different ways to collect data: (1) making direct observation and (2) asking questions." While you certainly have changed a few words, possibly even enough to fool some plagiarism detection software, it remains essentially what Maxfield and Babbie (2006) said in their original version. So, how do you avoid plagiarism? Simple—add the original authors as a citation as follows: According to Maxfield and Babbie (2006), field research involves two different ways to collect data: (1) making direct observation and (2) asking questions. Note that because it is not an exact quote—albeit a rather close paraphrasing—you are not required to place quotation marks around the statement. Failure to have cited Maxfield and Babbie, either as shown or with the citation enclosed in parentheses after the statement, would constitute plagiarism.

Now that you know what plagiarism is and some ways to avoid it, let us turn to some general issues regarding how to begin to write your research papers.

Identifying the Purpose of the Writing: Arranging the Noodles

When preparing to present one's research, investigators begin by considering the purpose of the study. If you want, as some sociological researchers do, to advance theory and conceptualization about certain patterns of behaviors, this is the goal you must aim for (see Chen, 2009; Eikenberry, 2009; Glassner & Berg, 1980). A slightly different goal may be necessary if the purpose is to improve some particular component of the practice of a particular discipline, such as nursing (see Flores, 2008; Gordon, Buchanan, & Bretherton, 2008; Peterson, 1985; Schenk, 2008). Similarly, as seen in much of the literature in criminology, corrections, the justice community, and other political spheres, researchers may seek to inform ongoing debates and discussions on policy issues (see Ireland & Berg, 2007; Michalowski, 1996; Skibinski & Koszuth, 1986; Tontodonato & Hagan, 1998).

In part, identification of the purpose goes hand in hand with understanding the audience. For effective written dissemination of research information, the character of the audience is as important to the writer as the character of the listening audience is to the speaker when presenting an oral presentation (Frankfort-Nachmias & Nachmias, 2007; Leedy & Ormrod, 2005). If researchers are interested in reaching a selected audience, their reports must speak to issues and concerns relevant to that particular community. This includes giving attention to "local knowledge" such as technical terms, controversial claims, and professional jargon. If, on the other hand, they want to reach a broader, more general audience, researchers must take care to address larger, more general concerns without assuming any particular background on the part of readers. A common mistake made by inexperienced researchers is coining terms to accommodate a given audience. One may "sociologize," for example, nursing issues, believing this will make them more understandable, or more impressive, to sociologists. Conversely, one may "nursiologize"—to coin a phrase—sociological terms in order to make them more comprehensible to nurse researchers by using terms like *ethnonursing, transcultural nursing, participatory nursing action research,* and so forth. Or one may simply toss in a lot of technical terms in order to demonstrate one's mastery of them. Such efforts are mistakes. Writing clearly and concisely and avoiding all unnecessary jargon are the best tactics.

It is also important to keep in mind that a research paper is about your topic, not about you. Even when your goal in writing it is to get a good grade, the paper is not about your adventures in research, or all of the hours that you spent reading and preparing. The paper reports the findings and conclusions of your research on a topic and should be of interest to anyone who is concerned with that topic. You write because you have something to say.

In the remainder of this chapter, major components of standard social scientific reports are described.

Delineating a Supportive Structure: Visual Signals for the Reader

Generally speaking, research papers can be conceptually divided into several different segments, each of which contributes some element necessary for the reader to understand fully what the researchers have to say. In essence, these

Figure 12.1 The Basic Scheme of the Traditional Research Report

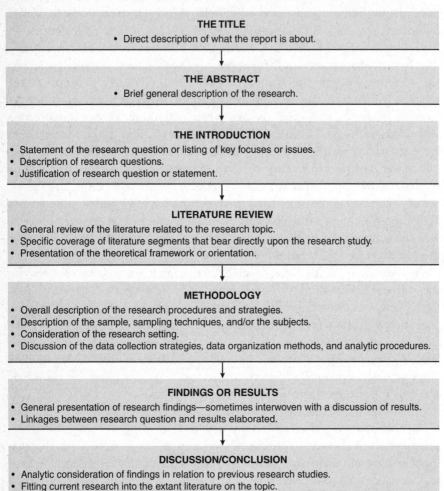

THE TITLE
- Direct description of what the report is about.

THE ABSTRACT
- Brief general description of the research.

THE INTRODUCTION
- Statement of the research question or listing of key focuses or issues.
- Description of research questions.
- Justification of research question or statement.

LITERATURE REVIEW
- General review of the literature related to the research topic.
- Specific coverage of literature segments that bear directly upon the research study.
- Presentation of the theoretical framework or orientation.

METHODOLOGY
- Overall description of the research procedures and strategies.
- Description of the sample, sampling techniques, and/or the subjects.
- Consideration of the research setting.
- Discussion of the data collection strategies, data organization methods, and analytic procedures.

FINDINGS OR RESULTS
- General presentation of research findings—sometimes interwoven with a discussion of results.
- Linkages between research question and results elaborated.

DISCUSSION/CONCLUSION
- Analytic consideration of findings in relation to previous research studies.
- Fitting current research into the extant literature on the topic.
- General discussion on the extent of research and its ramification or policy implications.
- Suggested directions for future research endeavors.

elements form the skeleton or supportive structure of the paper. Supportive structure, as it is used here, refers to a number of major headings that give order to the research report. See Figure 12.1. The headings in a research paper form a kind of outline of visual signals for the reader to follow. Headings can be classified as occurring at different levels reflecting the general level of importance. These levels or heads are sometimes listed alphabetically (A, B, C, and D). When writing, you can format your headings "by hand" in order to control the look of your document. More often, however, you can use predefined word-processing formats to identify certain text as a level 1 heading, a level 2 heading, a subhead, and so forth. Identifying headings to your software in this manner also allows you to automatically generate and update tables of contents for your documents, and to maintain a consistent style throughout the document.

Section headings are like road signs. They keep the reader oriented. An A head generally appears entirely in capital letters. Frequently, this heading will be centered or flushed left on the page and in bold type. In scholarly writing, the A head is reserved for announcing the major divisions of thought that appear in the written work or to designate major sections of the work. When readers encounter an A head, they receive a signal that the text is about to shift gears or introduce a new topic.

Example:

This Is an Example of an A Head

The B head is centered on the page with the first letter of each word capitalized (articles and prepositions are lowercase). This too is typically written in bold type. The B head signifies subdivisions of material related to the topic of the A head. It is important information, but not a major sectional division.

Example:

This Is an Example of a B Head

The C head is usually written flush left, and again, has the first letter of each word capitalized (articles and prepositions are lowercase), and is followed by a period. The C head is used to delineate subinformational categories of the B head. These are important for categorizing or explaining information relevant to the major topical area indicated by the B head.

Example:

This Is an Example of a C Head.

The D-level head is written indented from the left, with only the first letter of the first word capitalized. The heading is underlined and ends with a period (or occasionally with a colon). The D head is run into the paragraph, indented to line up with the other paragraph indentations on the page. Two spaces are generally left before the beginning of the first word of the paragraph. The D-level head is used to label a specific definitional point or to enumerate a categorical listing with explanations. Again, this information is related to the broader information mentioned or described in a C-level head.

Example:

> This Is an Example of a D Head.(:) The paragraph would begin here.

Many of the sections are requisites of all reports regardless of what specific label is used. A research paper typically consists of a series of A heads or sections that include the following:

1. *Title:*   usually appears on a *title page* (along with author information) as well as on the top of the *abstract page* (see later).
2. *Abstract:*   a brief description of the entire paper and its main findings.
3. *Introduction:*   basic research questions, key terms, and research focus.
4. *Literature review:*   a detailed examination of the extant research literature relevant to the paper's topic.
5. *Methodology:*   a comprehensive description of how the researchers gathered data and analyzed these data.
6. *Findings or results:*   the presentation of information uncovered during the research process.
7. *Discussion and/or conclusions:*   an examination of these findings and consideration of how they may impinge on relevant groups, communities, or agencies.
8. *References, notes, and/or appendices:*   a section that contains the evidence that supports the research.

Figure 12.1 illustrates the general scheme of a traditional research report. This arrangement of parts provides much more than a convenient way to divide your writing. It organizes your ideas. The structure of your paper should reflect the manner in which you have chosen to explain your work to your readers. Let's consider each section in detail.

The Title

The title initially appears on the *title page*. It should be an A head placed at approximately the middle of the page and centered. Below the title should be the author's name and affiliation, also centered:

Example:

DRINKING AMONG COLLEGE STUDENTS
ON AMERICAN CAMPUSES

By Dr. Bruce L. Berg
Department of Criminal Justice
California State University, Long Beach
Long Beach, CA 90840
(562) 985–1895

The title should give the reader a fairly good idea what the report is about. It should not be too cute or whimsical. Cute or comical titles may be encouraged in some creative writing situations, but it does not tend to bode well for social science venues and audiences. Simple puns are popular in titles, but the more clever the pun, the less likely that people will know what you're talking about. The important goal is to communicate.

The report title should also appear centered and at the top of the abstract page.

The Abstract

An abstract is a brief summary (50–200 words) of the most important (and interesting) research findings of a study. In addition, abstracts usually contain some mention of key methodological features of the study and relevant implications of the major findings. One does not include references in an abstract.

Abstracts are always found in the beginning of a research report, but given their content, they cannot be created until after the report has been written. The major function of an abstract is to provide potential readers with sufficient information both to interest them and to help them determine whether to read the complete article. I am aware of the fact that some writing instructors, and even some less informed social scientists, encourage students to write their abstracts first; this seems to fly in the face of simple logic. If an abstract is intended to summarize one's findings and highlight important areas of the research, how is it possible to accomplish this before the report is written? Obviously, it is not, and I reiterate, the abstract should be written last. Often, researchers scan collections of abstracts (e.g., search results from journal databases) in order to identify potentially useful elements for their own literature reviews (to be considered presently). It is therefore critical that an abstract be both concise and precise.

As a broad guide to writing an abstract, regardless of the researchers' particular substantive interests, the following four key facets should be included:

1. A statement identifying the key focus or issue considered in the study.

   Example: This is the first study of drug trafficking in the United States to penetrate the echelons of the marijuana and cocaine business—[it concerns] the smugglers and their primary dealers.

2. The nature of the data analyzed in the study.

   Example: We spent six years observing and interviewing these traffickers and their associates in southwestern California and examining their typical career paths.

3. The major finding or result examined in the report.

   Example: We show how drug traffickers enter the business and rise to the top, how they become disenchanted because of the rising social and legal costs of upper-level drug trafficking, how and why they either voluntarily or involuntarily leave the business, and why so many end up returning to their deviant careers, or to other careers within the drug world.[2]

   In some instances, you may want to include a fourth element that suggests the relevance of the research to a given agency, policy, or discipline:

4. Potential use or implication of the reported finding.

   Example: The findings of the current study outline the multiple conflicting forces that lure drug dealers and smugglers into and out of drug trafficking.[3]

These four elements should more or less suit virtually any research enterprise and may adequately produce an abstract consisting of as few as four sentences. On the other hand, if you find that you have written an entire research paper but you cannot state what it is about, that may signal a problem with the paper.

TRYING IT OUT

Suggestion 1   Go to the database access page of your institution's library Web site, assuming you have one. Choose a database for your field of study, such as SocIndex, Social Work Abstracts, or Medline. If given the options to limit your search, select journal articles only, not books, book reviews, or letters. Enter the search term "drug use." Read the abstracts of the first few pages of results. Depending on the database and your default settings, you may need to click on the titles to see the abstracts. Marvel at the variety of work and diversity of approaches to a single topic. When you are done marveling, sort them into articles you would like to read and ones you would not. What distinguishes the two? How much can you tell from the abstracts alone?

The Introduction

An introduction orients the reader to the study and the paper. It should acquaint the reader with the basic research question or problem (Leedy & Ormrod, 2005). Introductions should be written in statement sentences that are clear and concise, and describe the type of writing that will follow (e.g., a descriptive report, an ethnographic narrative, a research proposal). Sometimes, introductions are referred to as *maps for the report*. Ideally, in addition to stating the research problem and placing it into theoretical and/or historical context, an introduction offers a sequential plan of presentation for the paper. The reader is thus informed about what headings will be included and what each identified section will address.

It is additionally important to recognize that introductions can entice readers to continue reading, or turn them off so that they don't bother. The main attention-getting device, beyond the report title, is the opening sentence to an introduction (Harvey, 2003; Meyer, 1991). A number of strategies are available to the writer. You might use a startling finding from the research, suggest some interesting problem from literature, or relate some relevant recent news event. Whatever you choose, it should be as interesting as possible. The introduction may be a distinct section complete with heading(s), or it may be combined with a literature review.

Literature Review

The basic intention of the aptly named literature review is to give a comprehensive review of previous works on the general and specific topics considered in the study. As Merriam (2001, p. 53) suggests, "The scope of the search is determined by how well defined the research problem is, as well as the researcher's prior familiarity with the topic." At least to some extent, the literature review foreshadows the researcher's own study. Chapter 2 has already elaborated on the procedures usually surrounding the development of a literature review. During the writing stage of research, it is necessary to report on the state of the literature: its limitations and research directions. In some disciplines, a literature review may remain a simple summary of relevant materials, but more frequently, there is an organized pattern combined with both summary and synthesis of the materials. Thus, literature reviews may provide a kind of tracing of the intellectual progression of some field, subject, or topic, including major debates; or descriptions of the current state of technologies related to some focus in the research; or even, examination and discussion on what previous researchers have uncovered about some topic and how (methodologically) they may have accomplished this (Alred, Brusaw, & Oliu, 2006). It is also your best opportunity as a writer to ensure that your readers know the things that you want them to know in order to understand and appreciate your own research.

For example, researchers sometimes want to challenge previously accepted ideas or findings. It is important, therefore, that these competing conceptualizations be presented and errors or fallacies identified. If you have found some new and improved way of studying something, then you must first explain, fully and fairly, the old ways. Only then can you explain what is new in your work. In some situations, researchers might be attempting to replicate previous studies and improve on their use of theory or methods. In such cases, it is necessary to illustrate how these previous studies examined their subject matter, since your work is based on theirs.

To a large measure, the literature review may also serve as a kind of bibliographic index and guide for the reader, not only by listing other studies about a given subject but also by demonstrating where the current study fits into the scheme of things. As I mentioned in the discussion on plagiarism, you establish credibility for your work when you build on a solid foundation of existing knowledge. The literature review makes this connection explicit, using past research to raise the questions that you are answering. By the end of your literature review section, your readers should be excited to read more about your study.

Literature reviews should certainly include reference to classic works related to the investigation and should also include any recent studies. Omission of some relevant recent study may leave researchers open to criticism for carelessness—particularly if omitted studies have more exhaustively examined the literature, identified or conducted research in similar areas, or pointed out theoretical and methodological issues the current study overlooks. The more thorough the literature review, the more solid the research paper's foundation becomes. It is also very important that new researchers remember that if they want to make a contemporary argument, they *must* use recent contemporary documentation. It does not work to argue that "[n]ursing practice *today* involves more technology than ever before" and then show references from 1979 or 1984. It does not even make sense if you step back and think about it. You will need references that are no more than three or four years old. On the other hand, if you are doing an historical tracing on some subject, say, for example, the development of corrections in America, using a reference from 1924 to describe prisons during the late eighteenth century is perfectly appropriate and may make absolute historical sense. Likewise, if you are discussing the development of important ideas, then you need to acknowledge their earliest as well as their most current incarnations.

It is important to remember that not all sources of information are considered equal or can be legitimately used in writing literature reviews. There is a generally accepted hierarchy of informational sources. As I see this hierarchy, certain pieces of information are better accepted by the scientific community than others. This hierarchy is not a completely static or rigid rank ordering but follows something along the lines of what is listed hereafter:

1. Scholarly empirical articles, dissertations, monographs, and the like (including electronic articles from referred online journals on the Internet)
2. Scholarly, nonempirical articles and essays (both refereed and nonjuried articles and essays)
3. Textbooks, and similar secondary sources (e.g., encyclopedias and dictionaries, not necessarily including wikis.)
4. Trade journal articles
5. Certain nationally and internationally recognized newsmagazines (e.g., *Time*, *Newsweek*, *The Atlantic Monthly*)
6. Papers, reports, or other documents posted by individuals on various Internet Web sites, possibly including wikis.
7. Certain nationally and internationally recognized newspapers (e.g., *The New York Times*, *The LA Times*, *The Washington Post*, *The Times* [of London])
8. Acceptable, lower-order newspapers (e.g., *The Boston Globe*, *USA Today*)
9. Only when all other sources are unavailable, or when you want to add texture or detail, you should (sparingly) use a local newspaper
10. Written personal communications (letters, solicited comments)
11. Oral personal communications (face-to-face talks, telephone calls)
12. Blogs or other random Web sites.

It is your responsibility to know the source of your background materials. Advocacy and special interest groups, for example, have Web sites where they distribute reports of their own research, with the goal of convincing you to support their perspective. This isn't necessarily a bad thing, though it is clearly not as reliable as a peer-reviewed scientific article. On the other hand, hate groups and other extremists also operate their own Web sites where they may publish supposed research reports with claims that support their positions. Much of this work is fabricated or simply distorted. When you download a report, you need to know whether it comes from a legitimate source or not. Other people's lies and misinformation become your own lies and misinformation when you quote them.

The elements listed in 1–3 offer the strongest documentary support in scholarly writing. Items listed as 4–7 offer moderately strong support to a document, and items 8–12 offer useful, perhaps colorful documentary sources of information. As one moves down the list, one should realize there is considerable loss of scientific confidence in the information obtained from these sources. These lower-order sources should be used only when noting some event or highlighting some already well-documented piece of information. Moreover, using a lower-order source such as an encyclopedia or a random Web site when there are easily identifiable higher-order sources available actually undermines the integrity of the rest of your work. At the very least, it suggests a certain laziness on the part of the writer, though it may also reflect the writer's efforts to only reference sources that they agree with.

Like everything else, of course, too much of a good thing ruins the experience. Although certain types of research reports, such as a thesis or dissertation, expect lengthy (10–20 pages) literature reviews, reports and articles do not. Just as omitting a recent relevant article creates problems for a report, so too can an overdone literature review. An overly long review also distracts from the argument that you wish to make in the paper. The more material you include that diverges from your proper path, the less likely it is that the readers will find their way through it. Often, however, it is sufficient to flag the existence of key references without giving each its own discussion. For example, Victoria Johnson (2007, p98) concisely establishes the usefulness of her topic with one sentence: "Building on this idea, researchers have shown the lasting impact of founding context on a variety of phenomena, such as managerial structure (e.g., Baron, Hannan, and Burton 1999), the structure of interorganizational networks (Marquis, 2003), and survival rates (e.g., Romanelli, 1989)." The basic rule of thumb in writing literature reviews is to keep them long enough to cover the area but short enough to remain interesting.

Methodology

Inexperienced researchers often think the methodology section is the most difficult section to write. It need not be so. Since methodology sections typically report what you did during the course of a research project, it may well be one of the easiest sections to produce. In fact, if you had written out a research plan in advance, as we have recommended, then this section would almost already be done before you begin your paper.

The central purpose of a methodological section is to explain to readers how the research was accomplished—in other words, what the data consist of and how data were collected, organized, and analyzed. It is actually quite interesting; yet, people who have little trouble describing intricate instructions for operating complicated medical equipment or repairing cars and electrical appliances pale at the thought of describing research methods.

The simplest, most straightforward way to write up the methodology section is to imagine explaining the process to a friend who needs to do something similar. Explaining the details about how the research was conducted is reasonably similar to telling a story. The points of detail most important to the researchers may vary from study to study, just as certain details in classic tales vary from storyteller to storyteller. Nonetheless, certain salient features of research methods tend to be present in most, if not all, methods sections. These features include considerations of subjects, data, setting, and analysis techniques.

Subjects   Methodology sections should explain who the subjects are, how they have been identified (selected), what they have been told about their participation, and what steps have been taken to protect them from harm (issues of confidentiality and anonymity). As well, the researcher should be sure to indicate the appropriateness of the subjects used in the study. Many studies, for example, make use of college students simply because they are easy to include in the research (see Chapter 2 on *Sampling Strategies*); but college students may not be the appropriate subjects to use in a study on, say, prisoners' reentry into a community or even common adult activities such as job-search strategies. Ancillary concerns connected to discussions about the subjects may include how many were selected, what determined their numbers, and how many refused to take part in the research and why (if it is known). Other elements included in discussions on the subjects may involve various demographic characteristics and how these may relate to a given research focus.

Data   In addition to identifying the nature of the data (e.g., interviews, focus groups, ethnographies, videotapes), researchers should explain to readers how data were collected. Details about data collection have several important purposes. First, they allow readers to decide how much credence to attach to the results. Second, they provide a means for readers to replicate a research study, should they desire to do so. This notion of *replication* is very important to establishing that your research endeavor is objective. If someone else can replicate your study, then the original premises and findings can be tested in the future.

Finally, data-collection sections frequently are among the most interesting aspects of a research report—particularly when the researchers include details about problems and how they were resolved. Some self-reflection and disclosure may be necessary to offer what the literature sometimes calls *subjective views of the researcher*. In addition to offering interesting and vivid experiences, these subjective offerings may allow future researchers a way around problems in their own research studies.

Setting   Descriptions of the setting can be important in reporting an ethnographic study or a door-to-door interviewing project. The reliability of the research data, for example, may depend on demonstrating that an appropriate setting for the study has been selected. In some instances, settings are intricately related to the data and the analytic strategies and may possibly contaminate the research. Other researchers who find your work important may want to test the applicability of your results to other populations in other settings. A failure on the part of researchers to consider these elements during the study may weaken or destroy their otherwise credible arguments.

Analysis Techniques   Even when data are to be analyzed through generally accepted conventional means, a discussion and justification of the analytic strategy should be offered. Researchers should never assume that the readers will immediately understand what is meant by such vague terms as *standard content analysis techniques*. As suggested in Chapter 11, even so-called standard content analysis may have many possible analytic alternatives depending on which unit of analysis is selected and whether the approach is inductive or deductive. It is far better to explain yourself clearly than to be vague and allow others to fill in the blanks with their own assumptions.

Findings or Results

In quantitative research, the findings or results section commonly presents percentages and proportions of the data in the form of charts, tables, and graphs. Quantitative methodologists often use the two terms synonymously, although in fact, there is a slight distinction between them. *Findings* quite literally refer to what the data say, whereas *results* offer interpretations of the meaning of the data. In short, results offer an *analysis* of the data.

In the case of qualitative research reports, however, the findings and/or results section is not as easily explained. For example, in qualitative research reports, the analysis section often follows the methods section. Sometimes, however, the researchers forthrightly explain that data will be presented throughout their analysis in order to demonstrate and document various patterns and observations (see Berg, 1983; Bing, 1987; Dabney, 1993; Ireland & Berg, 2007). It is often difficult to distinguish what the data *are* from what the data *mean*. Sections of qualitative reports are also often organized according to conceptual subheadings (often arising from the terms and vocabularies of the subjects).

When ethnographic research is reported, the findings are more accurately represented and labeled an *ethnographic narrative* followed by a separate *analysis* (Berg & Berg, 1988; Burns, 1980; Creswell, 2007). Of course, there may be occasions when weaving the ethnographic observations throughout the analysis seems an effective presentation strategy, creating a type of *content and narrative analysis* (Cabral, 1980; Manning & Cullum-Swan, 1994; Potter & Wetherell, 1992).

Reporting observations from a content analysis of interview data or other written documents may similarly be accomplished either by separately presenting the findings or by interweaving findings and analysis. What should be clear from the preceding presentation is that with regard to qualitative research reports, several options are available for writing about the findings (data) and results (interpretation of the data).

Discussion/Conclusion

The basic content of the discussion section will vary depending on whether the researchers have presented an analysis or a findings section. In the former case, when an analysis section is included in a report, the discussion section frequently amounts to conceptual reiteration and elaboration of key points and suggestions about how the findings fit into the extant literature on the topical study area.

In the case of a separate findings section, the discussion section provides researchers with an opportunity to elaborate on presented observations. Frequently, in either case, after completing a research project, the social scientists realize they have gained both greater knowledge and insight into the phenomenon investigated. The discussion section provides a canvas on which the researchers may paint their insights. Occasionally, researchers gain Socratic wisdom; that is, they begin to realize what they—and the scientific community—still do not know about some substantive area. The discussion section allows the researchers to outline the areas requiring further research. It is not, however, sufficient justification for your research to conclude only that more research is needed.

The discussion section also provides an opportunity to reflexively consider the research study and the research results. More and more these days, researchers are being acknowledged as active participants in the research process and not passive observers or mere scribes (Hertz, 1996; Lune, 2007, afterword). It becomes essential, therefore, to indicate the researcher's location of self within the constellations of gender, race, social class, and so forth (DeVault, 1995; Edwards, 1990; Williams & Heikes, 1993). Through reflexive personal accounts researchers should become more aware of how their own positions and interests affected their research. In turn, this should produce less distorted accounts of the social worlds about which they report.

The discussion section interprets what the data mean in the context of the study. The conclusions, on the other hand, allow the author to consider what the research means beyond this context. This reiteration may appear repetitive, and allow humorists to describe research papers as "say what you will say, say why it needs to be said, then say that you have said it." But there are real differences between a discussion of a finding (e.g., students admit to cheating when they are afraid of failing) and a conclusion based on these results (e.g., people will sometimes compromise their values when they are afraid).

References, Notes, and Appendices

Throughout the sections of a research report, references should document claims, statements, and allegations. Although a number of style texts recommend various ways of referencing material, there are chiefly two broad options: *notes* or *source references*. Footnotes and endnotes are indicated with superscript numerals. They typically direct the reader to some amount of descriptive text along with the source, multiple sources, or URLs, located either at the bottom of the page on which they appear (footnotes) or at the conclusion of the paper (endnotes). The second broad option is source or in-text references, which appear immediately following the point in the text where a quote, paraphrase, or statement in need of documentation is made (the style used in this text). Source references are identified by the last name of a referenced author, the date of publication, and in the case of a direct quotation or claim, the page(s) from which the quote has been taken.

In the social sciences, source references are more often used for documenting statements made in the text, and notes generally give further explanation to the text rather than cite source references. Other disciplines have their own reference styles. The following points concerning source references should be observed:

1. If the author's name appears in the text, only the date of the publication appears in parentheses.

   Example: According to Naples (2008) ...

2. If the author's name is not used in the text, both the last name and the date of publication appear in parentheses.

    Example: The use of ethnographic narratives offers details on reflexive voice and anxiety (Silverman, 2006).

3. When a reference has two or three authors, the last name of each author is included in text. For reference material with more than three authors, the first author is shown in text followed by "et al.," (Latin for "and others").

    Examples: McSkimming and Berg (2008), Tewkbury (2007), and Swinford *et al.* (2000) have examined various aspects of deviant behavior.

4. For institutional authorship, the agency that produced the document is considered to be the author.

    Example: Information on index crimes suggests an increase (FBI, 2008).

5. When several sources are offered to document one claim or statement, each complete citation is separated by a semicolon and presented in chronological order. Some sources may suggest alphabetical order by authors' name; as long as you consistently do one or the other, you will usually be on solid ground.

    Example (chronological order): This has been suggested throughout the literature, especially by Glassner and Berg (1980); Cullen (1982); Johnson et al. (1985); and Beschner (1986).

    Example (Alphabetical order): This has been suggested throughout the literature, especially by Beschner (1986); Cullen (1982); Glassner and Berg (1980); and Johnson et al. (1985).

6. Source references tell readers where to find the information you are using, with as much detail as is needed for the particular reference. When quoting directly, it is important to offer the page reference as well as the author's name and publication date in one of two forms.

    Example: Doerner (1983, p. 22) states, "..." or Doerner (1983: 22) states, "..."

If you hang around with social or other scientists, you will find that we actually do refer to each other by last name and date in this way, even in conversation. We say, "I used that story about Berg's kids in my class today," or "I have been thinking about rereading Hegel this summer." "Goffman, 1959" is recognized as *The Presentation of Self in Everyday Life*, whereas "Goffman, 1979" refers to *Gender Advertisements*. These shorthand references to familiar works and authors reflect our writing style, but also indicate the importance scientists place on identifying findings with the researchers who came up with them. Students, on the other hand, are often unfamiliar with specific researchers and tend to identify papers by their titles, leading to unwieldy and incorrect in-text citations such as "recent work on the subject suggests otherwise ('Not All Students Cheat, Much,' 2010)." Identifying research by its authors is quicker, simpler, and actually more informative once you get to know the work in your field.

Source references to online items can be handled essentially as you would any other item. If there is an author, then the author's name is cited in the same manner as in the foregoing illustrations. If there is no specific author, but there is a sponsoring organization, then the organization is cited. For example, an article without an author found on the American Civil Liberties Union's Web site could cite ACLU, and any date indicated on the item. If no date is provided, then the convention should be to indicate *no date in* parentheses. *Example*: The use of such laws has been suggested to be both unjust and illegal (ACLU, no date). Where dates are available for online materials, they refer to publication dates. However, since online sources are dynamic, it is also important to indicate the download date in the full citation in the reference list at the end of the paper or chapter. Between the time when you have linked to your source and the time when someone reads your paper, the source might have been moved or deleted.

References are listed alphabetically by the first author's last name, in a separate section entitled "References." A reference section must include all source references included in the report. As a matter of practice, the abbreviation "et al.," which is appropriate for citations in text, is unacceptable in a reference section. The first names of authors may be either indicated in full or by initial, unless you are writing for some particular publication that specifies a preference.

The better academic journals of each discipline differ somewhat in the format for writing up full citations in the reference section. Nonetheless, these differences are matters of style, not content. Complete citations tell you what you need to know to identify a publication, and no more. I allow my students to use any identifiable style they like (ASA, APA, MLA, etc.), as long as they use it consistently and correctly. Journal specifications are generally given in the first few pages of each issue and may change slightly from time to time. A complete set of requirements for style, format, length, and so forth is generally available in an "Information for Authors" document on each journal's Web page. It is, thus, advisable to consult the particular journals associated with your discipline to ascertain the proper form for the reference citations. To get inexperienced researchers going, however, what follows is the format recommended for most social science journals and texts.

1. *Books:*   Ribbens, J., & Edwards, R. (1998). *Feminist Dilemmas in Qualitative Research.* Thousand Oaks, CA: Sage.

    The author and publication date are given first, which corresponds to the in-text citation, as in "the issue of the authority relations between researchers and subjects also presents challenges for fieldwork (Ribbens and Edwards, 1998)." The publisher information, including the publisher's home city, is enough to uniquely identify the work even with commonly used titles.

2. *Periodicals:*   Berg, B. L., & Berg, J. P. (1988). AIDS in prison: The social construction of a reality. *International Journal of Offender Therapy and Comparative Criminology 32*(1), 17–28.

    The article, "AIDS in prison," appears on pages 17–28 of issue 1 in volume 32 of the *International Journal of Offender Therapy and Comparative Criminology.*

3. *Collections:*   Peterson, B. H. (1985). A qualitative clinical account and analysis of a care situation. In M. M. Leininger (Ed.), *Qualitative Research Methods in Nursing,* 267–281. Orlando, FL: Grune & Stratton.

    The book, *Qualitative Research Methods in Nursing,* was edited by Leininger and contains chapters by different authors. Peterson's chapter, the one actually begin referenced, appears on pages 267–281.

When writing up an online documentary item in the reference section, the format is again similar to that of standard references. References are fitted into the alphabetical listing by author's last name, or the initials of the organization. Even the layout of the reference listing of the online item parallels, in most respects, the layout of any standard reference listing. The major difference is that at the end of the reference entry, you include the Web site address. You can accomplish this by writing *Available online at* and then the Web address.

Example: Brasted, Monica. (2010). Care Bears vs. Transformers: Gender Stereotypes in Advertisements. *The Socjournal,* available online at http://www.sociology.org/media-studies/care-bears-vs-transformers-gender-stereotypes-in-advertisements/, retrieved June 22, 2010.

The previous example refers to an article published in an online journal. In this case, the journal does not sort articles according to volume and issue numbers, using only a unique URL for the article. This is not uncommon for Web materials. Had there been a volume or issue, those would appear in the citation just as they would for any paper publication. Most importantly here, however, is the date on which I downloaded the work. This is the last known date on which the URL actually referred to this article. As long as *The Socjournal* keeps publishing, I expect the link to work. But unlike paper references, which refer to a physical object that has already been printed, the URL depends on the continuity of the host Web site. If the ownership of this journal moves to a sociology department somewhere, for example, then the entire Web site will probably relocate to a new host, and my link would be broken.

Terms and Conditions

I have been using the common terms and language for things related to publications, but I have not given you any formal definitions of them. In my experience, this can cause some confusion for students who have not yet worked with reference lists and in-text citations. So a few clarifications might help.

Researchers write papers. Some of these papers appear as reports, which typically present findings in a fairly descriptive manner. If you measure the frequency of difficulty in understanding changes in credit card policies, for example, you can publish these findings in a short report. If, however, you were seeking to analyze and explain these changes, the manner in which they are explained, and the implications of consumers' ability to fully understand them, then your paper would be more than a report, most likely a scholarly article.

A wide assortment of agencies and organizations conduct research and issue reports. Frequently these reports are sponsored by the agency that is distributing them, and the only editorial review that takes place is within that agency. Academic research papers, on the other hand, are submitted to academic journals for a process known as "peer review." The journal editors solicit outside reviewers with expertise in the paper's topic. The reviewers read and assess the article, identifying problems and making recommendations for improvements. Officially, neither the reviewers nor the authors know who each other are, in order to minimize the chance of a biased review. Only after the expert reviewers agree that the work is valid can the paper be published. This is the main reason that scholarly articles are at the top of the hierarchy of sources used in a literature review.

Journals generally publish one or more issues each year. For an annual journal, there is only one issue in each volume, where each year is a new volume. Articles published in the 2011 edition of the *Annual Review of Sociology* are identified as occurring in volume 37. *Sociological Forum*, on the other hand, is a quarterly journal. References to articles published there in 2011, volume 26, must also specify which issue, 1–4, the work appeared in.

Articles, therefore, are collected in issues of a journal, which are available in bound editions of a single volume covering the entire year. For some reason which I have never understood, students often refer to the articles in their literature review as "journals," as in "I have 12 journals in my bibliography," when they clearly mean 12 articles. Don't do this.

One other point will complete this section. I receive my *Sociological Forum* articles through an online subscription. When I cite them, however, the citation only needs to refer to the usual source information: author, title, date, journal, volume, issue, and page numbers. The fact that I have gotten my copy from some Web site does not have any impact on the article's publication information. I have no more need to specify when and where I downloaded the work than I would have to identify the library where I photocopied the paper version. Readers only need to know where to find their own copy.

Presenting Research Material

The purpose of social research is to find answers to social problems or questions. However, this is not enough: Once a possible solution is identified, it remains worthless until it has been presented to others who can use the findings, as I had indicated at the start of this chapter. Social scientists have a professional responsibility to share with the scientific community (and the community at large) the information they uncover, even though it may be impossible for researchers to predict in advance what impact (if any) their research will have on society. To a large measure, how the research is used is a different ethical concern from whether it is used at all. How research is implemented is discussed in Chapter 2. This section concerns the dissemination of information obtained in research.

Disseminating the Research: Professional Meetings and Publications

There are at least two major outlets for social scientific research: professional association meetings and professional journals. Although the social science disciplines have other formal situations for verbally sharing research (e.g., staff meetings, colloquia, training sessions), these gatherings are often very small and for limited audiences, perhaps as few as four or five people. Following the precepts of action research (Chapter 7), researchers may also bring their findings back to the communities in which the research occurred. Professional meetings, however, have the potential of reaching far greater numbers of persons from many different facets of the same discipline (Byrne, 2001; Oermann, Floyd, Galvin, & Roop, 2006).

It is common, for example, for the American Sociological Association to have 2,000 or more people attend a conference. The American Society of Criminology has, at each of the past several years' meetings, recorded more than 1,000 people in attendance. Although nursing conferences are not quite as well attended, several hundred people do attend the annual gatherings of the American Association of Nursing. Professional meetings provide opportunities for researchers to present their own work, as well as to hear about the work of colleagues. They keep you up to date on work in your area of study. Scholars often bring preliminary versions of their research to conferences up to several years before the finished piece is published. Particularly for inexperienced researchers, such meetings can be very edifying—not only with regard to the content of the papers but also for building confidence and a sense of competence. Graduate students attending professional meetings and listening to established scholars present papers can often be heard to mumble, "I could have written that," which is often true. Most professional association meetings now regularly include student sessions designed to allow student researchers to present their work in a less frightening and less intimidating forum than the main sessions but to present their work nevertheless.

The saying that academics need to publish or perish is still true today—only more so! The academic standards, for example, in nursing have risen to a level such that it is no longer sufficient for a person who wants to teach to hold a graduate degree in nursing. More and more nursing programs are requiring of potential teachers doctorates in nursing—and *publications*. Publishing articles both strengthens the social science disciplines and improves the chances of being hired in a vastly competitive academic market. In sociology, applicants to a good research university now need to have a record of professional work before they even get their first professional jobs.

Getting published is partly a political matter, partly a matter of skill and scholarship, and partly a matter of timing and luck. Mostly, however, it's still about the quality of your work. Good connections will get other people to read your papers, but ultimately the work will stand or fall on its own. I do not recommend that you worry too much about the politics. For most researchers, and especially for students and novice professionals, there is no benefit to trying to game the system. With the time and energy some people put into trying to anticipate the biases of particular editors or the preferences of unknown peer reviewers, you could write another paper. Good research is simply that. It does not matter in terms of publishability whether the approach is quantitative or qualitative (Berg, 1989).

Nonetheless, new researchers should be aware that a kind of bias does exist in the world of publishing. This bias tends to favor quantitative research for publication. Thus, in some journals, you may find no qualitative empirical research published at all. But this preference for numbers does not tell us anything about the quality standards of the journal. There are journals of both the highest and least quality publishing both qualitative and quantitative research. In general, good work will find a good outlet. It is not, as some quantitative purists might have you think, a matter of having large aggregate data sets and sophisticated multivariate analysis. While some people do seem to imagine that computer-generated numbers are somehow more truthful than the words that people put around them, the excessive dedication to a single approach to data analysis does a disservice to the field. Often, such orientations move so far from reality that the findings offer little of practical value and, even in statistical terms, have little practical validity.

The process of getting published is further complicated by the *blind referee system*, mentioned earlier. This system involves having a manuscript reviewed by two to four scholars who have expertise in the subject of the paper and who do not know the author's identity. Based on their recommendations, the journal will either publish or reject the manuscript. This process may intimidate new authors, but it actually protects them. It means that your first ever journal submission will be reviewed with the same seriousness as someone else's 30th paper, without the reviewers having preconceived ideas about the worth of your work. Blind review from your peers cuts through much of the politics, though it does not help with the luck, timing, or skill parts.

Routinely, much of the work submitted to each journal will be rejected. This can be very disheartening to inexperienced researchers, who probably have invested considerable effort in their research. (I don't care much for the experience either.) It is important not to take personally a rejection of a manuscript by a journal. There are countless war stories about attempts to have some piece of research published. Many excellent scholars have experienced split decisions when two reviewers have disagreed, one indicating that the manuscript is the finest piece of work since Weber's *Economy and Society* and the other describing the manuscript as garbage. It happens.

Particularly when attempting to have qualitative research published, researchers can anticipate certain problems. It is fairly common, for example, to receive a letter of rejection for an ethnographic account or life history case study, and be told, in the letter, that the manuscript was not accepted because it failed to provide *quantified* results, or because the sample size was too small to represent the population at large. In some cases this may have resulted because the journal sent your manuscript to a reviewer who does not understand qualitative research. In other cases, however, this may occur because the reviewer honestly felt your manuscript was not ready for publication. It is important not to always assume that the former explanation applies. You can't anticipate all of the possible politics and other problems that could limit your opportunities. But you can make sensible decisions about where to present and submit your work.

A quick keyword search through a couple of databases will sometimes reveal to inexperienced researchers several possible publication outlets. Researchers should carefully note which journals appear to publish which types of studies. It is also worthwhile to visit the library's stacks and page through recent volumes of the journals on the shelves, skimming the tables of contents, and examining the tone and language found in them. Often, a declaration of a journal's purpose is included on the inside of the front cover or on the first few pages. Once you have a possible venue in mind, you should identify what particular writing style and format the journal requires. This information is typically listed under the headings, "Notice to Contributors" or "Submission and Preparation of Manuscripts." Before submitting anything to any journal, make sure that you have downloaded or copied their requirements, and check those against your paper. Writing up a manuscript in the correct form the first time around often saves considerable time and lamentation later. There is simply no benefit to submitting a 30-page paper to a journal with a 25-page limit.

Once the manuscript has been written, it is time to make a final assessment. Perhaps the hardest decision to make honestly is how good the manuscript really is. It takes a lot of courage, but if you can face it I recommend reading your paper aloud to a select group of friends. If you find yourself cringing or apologizing for some unclear passages, then those need to be fixed. The important lesson here is not merely to have others read your drafts. It is important to *hear* what they have to say and to use this advice to improve the eventual final draft.

This critical self-review is necessary for several reasons. First, it is always wise to send a manuscript to the best journal in which the researchers realistically believe they can be published. Underestimating the quality of the work may result in publication in a less prestigious journal than might have been afforded in a better journal. On the other hand, sending a manuscript of lesser weight to a high-powered journal simply increases the time it may take to get the article in print; there will be enough time lags as it is without such misjudgments. Although many journals indicate that manuscript review time varies from five to twelve weeks, researchers often wait for six to eight months merely to hear that their manuscript has been rejected.

A second reason for carefully choosing a journal to which to send your manuscript is the academic restriction against multiple submissions. Because it is considered unethical to submit article manuscripts to more than one journal at a time, these time lags can be a considerable problem. Choosing the wrong journal may literally mean missing an opportunity to have a timely study published.

Inexperienced researchers are often hesitant to ask about the status of a manuscript, but they should not be. After patiently waiting a reasonable time (perhaps 10 weeks), it is not only acceptable but recommended to e-mail the journal's editor to check on the status of your manuscript. Journals are busy enterprises and like any other enterprise can make mistakes. Sometimes when researchers inquire they are informed that some error has been made and the manuscript has not been sent out for review. On other occasions, editors explain that they have been chasing after reviewers to make a decision. In yet other situations, editors may simply have no news about the manuscript. It is not likely, although inexperienced researchers may fear this, that a journal will suddenly reject a paper simply because the author has been asking for a decision. In short, authors have nothing to lose and everything to gain by checking.

As the library research may indicate, and as Zurcher (1983, p. 204) explicitly states, "Some journals are more likely than others to publish papers reporting qualitative studies." Some of the journals that have traditionally published qualitative research and have continued to do so during recent years include *Journal of Contemporary Ethnography, Symbolic Interaction, Qualitative Sociology, Human Organization, Human Relations, Journal of Creative Inquiry, Heart and Lung, Western Journal of Nursing, American Educational Research Journal, Journal of Popular Culture, Sociological Perspectives, Journal of Applied Behavioral Science, Signs, International Review for the Sociology of Sport, Nonprofit and Voluntary Sector Quarterly, American Behavioral Scientist, Journal of Criminal Law & Criminology, Policing: An International Journal of Police Strategies & Management, International Journal of Offender Therapy and Comparative Criminology, Journal of Marriage and the Family, Teaching Sociology, Criminal Justice Review, Nursing Research, Holistic Nursing Practice, Sociological Quarterly, Sociological Spectrum,* and to a slightly lesser extent during recent years, *Social Problems* and *Social Forces.*

There are a number of viable online electronic journals as well, and journals available online. While there are numerous sites on the Internet, I'll offer just a few here to get the inexperienced writer started: *The Qualitative Report* (http://www.nova.edu/ssss/QR/), *Sociological Research Online* (http://www.socresonline.org.uk/home.html), *Educational Insights* (http://www.ccfi.educ.ubc.ca/publication/insights/index.html), *Nursing Standard Online* (http://www.nursing-standard.co.uk/), *Journal of Contemporary Criminal Justice* (http://intl-ccj.sagepub.com/), *The New Social Worker Online* (http://www.socialworker.com/home/index.php). As even these short and incomplete listings suggest, there are numerous outlets for publishing qualitative research.

A Word About the Content
of Papers and Articles

Although it may go without saying that researchers must include in their reports accurate, truthful, and documented information, it may not be as obvious that it should be interesting as well. As Leedy (1985, p. 246) stated, "There is no reason why a report should be dull—any more than there is a reason why a textbook should be dull. Both of them deal with the excitement of human thinking prompted by the fascination of facts in the world around us." I cannot count the number of times I have attended a professional conference and listened to a boring presentation. I can only assume that the pained expressions on the faces of others in the audience reflected opinions similar to my own.

When you listen to a quantitative, statistical, and perhaps convoluted report or wade through an article full of regression equations and path diagrams, you may reasonably expect a certain amount of dullness. The significance of the findings may be hidden behind the density of abstract data with all of the interesting parts at the end. But when you hear or read dull qualitative research reports, there is no reasonable excuse. Qualitative research reflects the real world. In its purest form, it reveals elements previously unknown or unnoticed by others. It can be as creative a contribution to human knowledge as the *Mona Lisa* is a contribution to art. There are no dull facts about social life, only dull ways of presenting them!

Write it, Rewrite it, Then Write
it Again!

Experienced researchers realize that writing a research report is a multiple-level process. During those carefree high school days, many students could stay up late the night before a paper was due, writing the whole paper, and still receive a good grade. Unfortunately, in the so-called real world (which incidentally should include college) the submission of such a first draft is not likely to get the same results. Very few of my published papers bear more than a passing resemblance to their first drafts, or even their second or third versions.

Becker (1986) has asserted that one possible explanation for "one-draft writing" is that teachers do not tell the students how the books they read are actually written. Most students never have an opportunity to see either their teachers or professional writers or researchers at work and, thus, do not realize that more than one draft is necessary. Most textbooks on writing have chapters on revising and recomposing (Lester, 2006; Winkler & McCuen-Metherell, 2007), but students often think these chapters recommend merely editing for typographical and spelling errors. The notion of rewriting substantive portions of the report or adding interesting information learned after the first draft is complete may never occur to inexperienced researchers/writers.

Certainly, there is no single all-purpose way to compose a research report. In fact, in the social sciences, researchers may want to write for several distinct audiences. In such cases, it may be necessary to write both multiple drafts and multiple drafts of different versions. For example, researchers may write at one level when the audience is their academic colleagues, for example, attending a conference. But this academic level of writing may be unacceptable if the audience is more diverse, as in the case of a report to a governmental funding agency that would be reviewed by professionals from several different backgrounds.

Agar (1986, p. 15) similarly suggests that ethnographies may be written up differently for different audiences, "In my own work the presentation of the same chunk of ethnographic material takes different forms depending on whether I write for clinicians, drug policymakers, survey sociologists, or cognitive anthropologists." When researchers write for their own disciplines, they write for a limited audience that is thoroughly familiar with the particular field of study and shares similar educational backgrounds. In contrast, when the audience consists of different kinds of readers, special limitations must be set on the form the written report should take.

Beyond the realities of different audiences requiring different types or levels of language, there is no single right way to say something. Often one way of saying something may be correct but uninteresting. Another way may be interesting but inexact. After three, or four, or more attempts, the authors may finally find an acceptable way to express themselves, but even that is not necessarily the only good way to phrase their ideas.

A fairly common problem all writers have occasionally is trouble getting started (Becker, 1986). Often, after having written a rather weak beginning, researchers suddenly find the words begin to flow with ease. When the writers reread the weak opening section, they will likely notice that they must rewrite it, but if they do not bother to reread and rewrite the opening material, readers will probably not read beyond the poor beginning and get to those wonderful later sections.

Similarly, distance from their own writing frequently allows authors to see their presentations from a different perspective. Many researchers have experienced the phenomenon of reading a research paper they wrote several days or weeks earlier and then wondering, How on earth could I have written such drivel? On other occasions, many authors have reread something written a few days earlier and thought, I can hardly believe I actually said that—it's great! These self-reflective examinations of your own writing require some time between the actual penning of the words and the revisions. Usually several days is sufficient, although the actual time required may vary for different pieces of work. Sometimes a few months off will turn an insurmountable flaw into a minor inconvenience.

A Few Writing Hints

As instructors, we have noted a number of common mistakes that students appear to make on a fairly consistent basis when writing research reports, theses, and dissertations. We have listed hereafter 10 of what might be the most common ones. By reviewing these, hopefully, you can avoid the pitfalls of these writing errors.

1. *Date stamping.*   Avoid time- or date-stamping your work with comments such as "Recently," or "In recent studies." These limit your comments to very current observations and documentation. If you do make these kinds of comments, be certain you intend to address very current issues. Similarly, references to less current issues should be even more specific. Phrases like "in the past, people thought …" or, worse, "in the old days …" only serve to suggest that the writer has no idea what place or time they are discussing. Specific references such as "up until the potato famine of 1847 …" provide real points of comparison or moments of change.

2. *Vague referrals.*   You should avoid vague comments such as "Many studies …," "During the years that followed …," "Some research …," "Some researchers …," "There have been studies …," "Others argue …," and similar sort of statements. These sorts of vague references to things simply do not provide sufficient information for the reader and can weaken an argument. This is also a popular technique among bloggers and pundits when they don't actually have any data to back up their claims, which is not the sort of thing you want to invoke when discussing your research. If there is "some research," speak about it specifically; if there are "researchers," cite them. In other words, if you can document your claims, do so; do not simply vaguely allude to them offhandedly.

3. *Passive voice.*   Technically, passive voice is writing such that the voice of a sentence does not make clear what or who the subject is that is the recipient of the action in that sentence. In other words, if you write

the sentence, "Bill threw the red ball to Jim," you have written in *active voice*; as readers we know who threw what to whom. However, if the sentence said, "The red ball was thrown to him," we do not know who threw the ball to whom. Passive voice sentences can be very effective when intentionally used with a little poetic license—but most scientific writing frown on the use of passive voice at all. Stick to short, direct, active voice sentences.

4. *Long and run-on sentences.*   The rule of thumb I recommend to my students is, "If a sentence runs for five or more lines, it is a pretty safe bet that it is a run-on sentence." Run-on sentences typically involve two or more sentence fragments spliced together with no or improper grammatical connections. They often are confusing and may force the writer into creating passive voice sentences. Fixing run-on sentences is easy—rewrite the run-on as two or more short active voice sentences.

5. *Avoid lazy word beginnings.*   Avoid use of words such as "Although," "Since," "Because" and especially "However" as the first word in a sentence. They tend to weaken a sentence and are often entirely unnecessary. Such "subordinate conjunctions" can establish the connection between two thoughts, but many writers use them to create the false impression that one sentence has something to do with the other. Try removing the word and beginning with the next one as the first word of the sentence. You might also try moving (embedding) the word *however* between commas later in the sentence. For instance, "He was tired. However, he did not believe a nap would help the situation." could be better written as "He was tired. He did not, however, believe a nap would help the situation."

6. *Similar word confusions.*   Be mindful when you use words that connote possession, such as "have" and "has," and "there" and "their." Note that "affect" is a verb while "effect" is a noun. "A part" of something is connected to it; "apart" from something is the opposite. Choose your words carefully.

7. *Do not use rhetorical questions.*   Many creative writers employ the device of asking a series of rhetorical questions. Good scientific writers, however, do not use this device. So, unless you actually plan on immediately addressing these questions about some aspect of the research, do not ask them! For example, let's say you are writing about police officers, do not ask a question such as, "Why would a police officer accept a bribe?" as an interest hook unless you plan on using this as a literal research question. Do not simply ask rhetorical questions to focus the research or create an interesting series of foci—again, unless these are actually about to be substantively addressed in the writing.

8. *Write out small numbers.* The numerals one through ten should always be written out. Numbers higher than 10 may be shown as numerals, except when they begin a sentence. In the cases where a numeral begins the sentence, it should always be written out and not shown as a numeral.

9. *Do not CAPITALIZE for emphasis.* This works in e-mails and tweets, but not papers. If you want to emphasize a word or phrase, it should be *italicized*.

10. *Do not "quote" single words for emphasis.* If a single word is shown encapsulated in quotation marks, there had better be a reference immediately following it, because that is what quotation marks demark. There are no air-quotes in research papers. If this single word is not being quoted, the author has incorrectly sought to use quotation marks to emphasize the word. Again, one emphasizes a word for effect by italicizing the word.

A Final Note

Throughout this book, we have focused on qualitative techniques and analytic strategies, rather than quantitative ones. Although questionnaires and quantification procedures are probably the most extensively used techniques in the social sciences, they have tended to become inhuman and reductionist. This criticism is not so much against the procedures, which certainly could enhance understanding in the social sciences, as it is against their indiscriminate application. As Coser (1975, p. 691) warned almost 40 years ago, "The fallacy of misplaced precision consists in believing that one can compensate for theoretical weakness by methodological strength." Application of sophisticated statistical procedures frequently seems akin to hunting rabbits with a cannon.

As suggested throughout this book, no single measurement class—quantitative or qualitative—is perfect. But neither is any data-collection procedure scientifically useless (Webb, Campbell, Schwartz, & Sechrest, 2004; Webb, Campbell, Schwartz, Sechrest, & Grove, 1981;). Some readers may have been amused by Jelenko's (1980) description of the Wayne State rock (see Chapter 8) and others may have caught themselves smiling at the thought of Sawyer (1961, cited by Webb et al., 1981) sifting through the garbage of Wellesley, Massachusetts (see Chapter 8). Yet each of these studies suggests ways of accessing relevant and useful information. As a group, many of the nonreactive techniques described in this text are not as adequate in themselves as a well-constructed interview or ethnographic field study, but each strategy can be improved significantly through triangulation of methods.

The flexibility of the qualitative research approach permits exactly this combined use of innovative data-collection and data-analysis strategies. Conversely, many of the highly sophisticated quantitative data-manipulation strategies can become stilted because they require information in a limited specialized form and format. For better or worse, however, quantitative techniques are more quickly accomplished than qualitative ones, produce what is presumed by many social scientists to be more reliable conclusions, and offer what many public agencies consider truly reportable findings (percentages of variable occurrences).

That quantitative procedures remain predominant in the social sciences is not in itself a problem or a question. What must be questioned, however, is the preoccupation of so many quantitative social scientists with methods, often at the expense of both theory and substance. Qualitative strategies, on the other hand, are intricately intertwined with both the substance of the issues they explore and theories grounded in these substantive issues. If social science is to sort the noodles from the soup, it must do so in a substantively meaningful manner.

NOTES

1. This sentence is in quotes because it's actually a quote from *The Simpsons*, but it's also plagiarized because I don't have the episode number or broadcast date to cite it properly.

2. The abstract shown is reprinted from *Social Problems 31*(2), December 1983, p. 195.

3. This last statement is my own creation and does not appear in the original abstract. It is included, of course, in order to demonstrate the use of an implications statement.

REFERENCES

Agar, M. H. (1986). *Speaking of Ethnography*. Beverly Hills, CA: Sage.

Alred, G. J., Brusaw, C. T., & Oliu, W. E. (2006). *Handbook of Technical Writing*. New York: St Martin's Press.

Becker, H. S. (1986). *Writing for Social Scientists*. Chicago, IL: University of Chicago Press.

Berg, B. L. (1983). Jewish identity: Subjective declarations or objective life styles. Doctoral dissertation, Syracuse University.

Berg, B. L. (1989). A response to Frank Cullen's "Having trouble getting published?" essay. *The Criminologist 14*(6), 7–9.

Berg, B. L., & Berg, J. P. (1988). AIDS in prison: The social construction of a reality. *International Journal of Offender Therapy and Comparative Criminology 32*(1), 17–28.

Bing, R. L., III. (1987). Plea bargaining: An analysis of the empirical evidence. Doctoral dissertation, Florida State University, Tallahassee.

.urns, T. F. (1980). Getting rowdy with the boys. *Journal of Drug Issues 80*(1), 273–286.

Byrne, M. (2001). Disseminating and presenting qualitative research findings. *AORN Journal 74*(5), 731–733.

Cabral, S. L. (1980). Time-out: The recreational use of drugs by Portuguese-American immigrants in southeastern New England. *Journal of Drug Issues 80*(1), 287–300.

Chen, K. K. (2009). *Enabling Creative Chaos: The Organization Behind the Burning Man Event*. Chicago, IL: University of Chicago.

Coser, L. (1975). Presidential address: Two methods in search of a substance. *American Sociological Review 40*(6), 691–700.

Creswell, J. W. (2007). *Educational Research: Planning, Conducting, and Evaluating Quantitative and Qualitative Research* (3rd ed.). Upper Saddle River, NJ: Prentice Hall.

Dabney, D. A. (1993). Impaired nursing: Nurses' attitudes and perceptions about drug use and drug theft. Master's thesis, Indiana University of Pennsylvania, Indiana, PA.

DeVault, M. (1995). Ethnicity and expertise: Racial-ethnic knowledge in sociological research. *Gender and Society 9*(5), 612–631.

Edwards, R. (1990). Connecting method and epistemology: A white woman interviewing black women. *Women's Studies International Forum 13*(5), 477–490.

Eikenberry, A. (2009). *Giving Circles: Philanthropy, Voluntary Association, and Democracy*. Bloomington, IN: Indiana University Press.

Flores, N. (2008). Dealing with an angry patient. *Nursing 38*(5), 30–31.

Frankfort-Nachmias, C. & Nachmias, D. (2007). *Research Methods in the Social Sciences* (7th ed.). New York: Worth Publishing.

Glassner, B., & Berg, B. L. (1980). How Jews avoid alcohol problems. *American Sociological Review 45*(1), 647–664.

Gordon, S., Buchanan, J., & Bretherton, T. (2008). *Safety in Numbers: Nurse-To-Patient Ratios and the Future of Health Care*. Ithaca, NY: ILR Press/Cornell University Press.

Harvey, M. (2003). *The Nuts and Bolts of College Writing*. Indianapolis, IN: Hackett Publishing Company, Inc.

Hertz, R. (1996). Introduction: Ethics, reflexivity and voice. *Qualitative Sociology 19*(1), 3–9.

Ireland, C., & Berg, B. L. (2007). Women in parole: Respect and rapport. *International Journal of Offender Therapy and Comparative Criminology 20*(10), 1–18.

Jelenko, C., III. (1980). The rock syndrome: A newly discovered environmental hazard. *Journal of Irreproducible Results 26*, 14.

Johnson, V. (2007). What is organizational imprinting? Cultural entrepreneurship in the founding of the Paris opera. *American Journal of Sociology 113*(1), 97–127.

Leedy, P. D. (1985). *Practical Research*. New York: Macmillan.

Leedy, P., & Ormrod, J. E. (2005). *Practical Research: Planning and Design* (8th ed.). Upper Saddle River, NJ: Prentice Hall.

Lester, J. D. (2006). *Writing Research Papers* (12th ed.). Upper Saddle River, NJ: Longman/Person.

Lune, H. (2007). *Urban Action Networks: HIV/AIDS and Community Organizing in New York City*. Boulder, CO: Rowman and Littlefield.

Manning, P., & Cullum-Swan, B. (1994). Narrative, content, and semiotic analysis. In N. K. Denzin & Y. S. Lincoln (Eds.), *Handbook of Qualitative Research*. Thousand Oaks, CA: Sage.

Maxfield, M. G., & Babbie, E. (2006). *Basics of Research Methods for Criminal Justice and Criminology*. Belmont, CA: Thompson/Wadsworth.

Merriam, S. B. (2001). *Qualitative Research and Case Study Applications in Education.* San Francisco, CA: Jossey-Bass.

Meyer, M. (1991). *The Little, Brown Guide to Writing Research Papers.* New York: HarperCollins.

Michalowski, R. (1996). Ethnography and anxiety: Fieldwork and reflexivity in the vortex of U.S.—Cuban relations. *Qualitative Sociology 19*(1), 59–82.

Oermann, M. H., Floyd, J. A., Galvin, E. A., & Roop, J. C. (2006). Brief reports for disseminating systematic reviews to nurses. *Clinical Nurse Specialist: The Journal for Advanced Nursing Practice 20*(5), 233–238.

Peterson, B. H. (1985). A qualitative clinical account and analysis of a care situation. In M. Leininger (Ed.), *Qualitative Research Methods in Nursing* (pp. 33–72). Orlando, FL: Grune & Stratton.

Potter, J., & Wetherell, M. (1992). *Discourse and Social Psychology.* Thousand Oaks, CA: Sage.

Schenk, P. W. (2008). Just breathe normally: Six language traps and how to avoid them. *American Journal of Nursing 108*(3), 52–57.

Skibinski, G. J., & Koszuth, A. M. (1986). Getting tough with juvenile offenders: Ignoring the best interests of the child. *Juvenile and Family Court Journal 37*(5), 45–50.

Tontodanato, P. & Hagen, F. E. (1998). *The Language of Research in Criminal Justice: A Reader.* Boston, MA: Allyn & Bacon.

Webb, E. J., Campbell, D. T., Schwartz, R. D., & Sechrest, L. (2004). *Unobtrusive Measures* (Rev. ed.). Thousand Oaks, CA: Sage.

Webb, E. J., Campbell, D. T., Schwartz, R. D., Sechrest, L., & Grove, J. B. (1981). *Nonreactive Measures in the Social Sciences.* Boston, MA: Houghton Mifflin.

Williams, C., & Heikes, E. (1993). The importance of researcher's gender in the in-depth interview: Evidence from two studies of male nurses. *Gender and Society 7*(2), 280–291.

Winkler, A. C., & McCuen-Metherell, J. R. (2007). *Writing the Research Paper: A Handbook* (7th ed.). Belmont, CA: Wadsworth Publishing.

Zurcher, L. A. (1983). *Social Roles.* Beverly Hills, CA: Sage.

Name Index

Subject Index

Abstracting, of research material, 392
Abstracts, in research papers, 395–396
Accidental samples, 50
Accretion measures, 298
Action research, 258–277
  analyzing and interpreting information in, 266–268
  basics of, 263–265
  defined, 258
  gathering information to answer questions in, 264
  identifying questions in, 265–266
  origins of, 259
  photovoice and, 273–274
  role of researcher in, 270
  sharing results with participants in, 268–269
  spiral process, 264
  taxonomy of, 276
  triangulation in, 7
  types of, 270–273
Active consent, 76–79
Active interviews, 108
Actuarial records, 285–287
Adult check system, 88
Agency meetings, 311
Ambient risks, 222
American Medical Association (AMA), 63–64
American Nurses Association, 80
American Psychological Association, 67, 80
American Society of Criminology, 80, 410
American Sociological Association, 67, 80, 410
Analysis
  in action research, 266–268
  of interview data, 154–156
  presenting, in research papers, 402
Analytic coding, 367
Analytic ethnography, 197
Analytic induction, 369–370
Analytic notes, 231–232

Annual Review of Sociology, 408
Anonymity, 93–94, 130, 132
Anthropological methods, 198
AQUAD (software), 379
Archival strategies human traces as data sources, 283–296
  private archives, 292–296
  public archives, 283–292
Argot, 213
ARTICHOKE program, 66
Artificial intelligence, 380
askSam (software), 378
Asynchronous environments, for Web-based interviews, 133–134
ATLAS.ti (software), 379, 381
Attitude of ethnographer, 207–208
Audience, 152–153
  dual, 295
  knowing your, 152–153
  writing for, 391
Audio-CASI (Audio Computer Assisted Self-Interview), 132
Autobiography, 293–296. *See also* Biography
  comprehensive, 293
  documents in, 295–296
  edited, 293–296
  topical, 293
Autoethnographies, 208
Availability samples, 50
Aware hearing techniques, 151
Aware listening, 158
Axial coding, 367–369, 373

Behavioral research, ethical concerns in, 80–90
Biasing effects, 136
Biography, 209, 320–321. *See also* Autobiography
Biomedical research, ethics of, 68–69
Blind referee system, 411
Blogs, 294–295
Brooklyn Jewish Chronic Disease Hospital, 63
Buckley Amendments, 69

Case histories, 317
Case studies, 325–346
  broadening scope of, 331
  collective, 335–336
  individual, 330–335
  interview data in, 331–333
  nature of, 325–327
  personal documents in, 333–335
  theory and, 328–330
Categories
  classes and, 362–363
  units and, 361–362
Category development in content analysis, 358–363
CATI. *See* Computer Assisted Telephone Interviews (CATI)
Census samples, 185
Certificates of confidentiality, 220–221
Chain referral sampling. *See* Snowball sampling
Characters, 359
Chicago school, 10, 12–13, 199
Children
  informed consent and, 88–89, 98–99
  protection of, and Web-based research, 88–89
CIA, 66–67
Citations, 288, 408
Civil society, 260
Classes
  common, 362–363
  special, 363
  theoretical, 363
Clinton, Bill, 64
Cliques, 248
Code-based theory builders, 379
Code of Federal Regulations (CFR), 74
Code-and-retrieve programs, 379
Codes of ethics, 68, 80
Codifying data, 275
Coding frames, 367–369
Coding, open, 364–367
Cognitive reality, 37

427